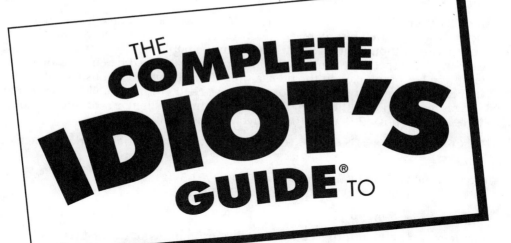

THE COMPLETE IDIOT'S GUIDE® TO

Being Psychic

by Lynn A. Robinson, M.Ed., and LaVonne Carlson-Finnerty

alpha books

Macmillan USA, Inc.
201 West 103rd Street
Indianapolis, IN 46290

A Pearson Education Company

Alpha Development Team

Publisher
Kathy Nebenhaus

Editorial Director
Gary M. Krebs

Managing Editor
Bob Shuman

Marketing Brand Manager
Felice Primeau

Development Editors
Phil Kitchel
Amy Zavatto

Production Team

Book Producer
Amaranth

Development Editor
Lynn Northrup

Production Editor
Robyn Burnett

Copy Editor
Susan Aufheimer

Cover Designer
Mike Freeland

Photo Editor
Richard H. Fox

Illustrator
Jody P. Schaeffer

Designer
Nathan Clement

Indexer
Chris Wilcox

Layout/Proofreading
Juli Cook
Mary Hunt
Pete Lippincott
Julie Trippetti

Contents at a Glance

Contents

Foreword

This engaging road map to all things psychic, intuitive, and paranormal is here to tell you that if you're having little inner pops of sixth-sense knowing, you're not weird. That's the good news. The bad news is, you're not special either.

Everyone is psychic, and it's no big deal. We were all born with a built-in ability to know things in ways other than logic. Our intuition is simple, standard-issue equipment, along with our eyes, ears, tongues, noses, and skin, and only as magical and ordinary as they are—which is plenty magical enough—but no more and no less.

No doubt this is how, eons ago, our ancestors avoided becoming a tasty hors d'oeuvre for some nasty sabertooth tiger. They certainly couldn't have outrun or out-brawned those powerful suckers. It had to be intuition that kept adrenalized encounters between us and them down to a blessed minimum.

Unfortunately, our left-brain–dominant culture tends to view psychic ability as anything but normal. It's been mystified, glorified, obfuscated, eroticized, demonized, and reviled. And that's probably why, up until recently, so many books about this much-maligned subject were so sadly out of balance: either so serious and weighty that they managed to take a really interesting subject and turn it into a big yawn, or so insubstantial and fluffy that they took awesome, transcendent mystery and gave it all the heft and staying power of cotton candy.

And that's too bad, too, because intuition is such a darned handy skill to have at our beck and call, so easy to integrate into our other ways of thinking, knowing, and doing, if we're not bent on ignoring it and keeping it separate from life as we know it.

That's one of the things I appreciate about *The Complete Idiot's Guide to Being Psychic*. Refreshingly light-hearted, but knowledgeable and practical all the same, this book is the perfect antidote for those who take psychic matters—and themselves, for that matter—either too seriously or too lightly.

I know you'll enjoy the considerable information, background history, practical tips, cautions, and encouragement waiting for you in these generous, wide-ranging pages. When you get done with this book, you'll be better able to recognize the functioning of this fabulous psychic equipment of yours, and better able to develop it and use it wisely and well.

Have fun, and enjoy the ordinary magic of your sixth sense!

—Belleruth Naparstek

Belleruth Naparstek, A.M., L.I.S.W., is the author of *Your Sixth Sense: Unlocking the Power of Your Intuition*. A clinical social worker and psychotherapist who has practiced for 33 years, she is a nationally recognized pioneer in the applications of guided imagery for healing and nutrition, and the creator of the popular, 24-title Time Warner audiotape series *Health Journeys*. Ms. Naparstek lives in Cleveland where she writes, lectures, consults, and runs Image Paths, Inc., her audiotape production company.

Introduction

It's easy to imagine why you picked up this book. After all, who hasn't heard of, or doesn't actually know, someone who's had a psychic (or what we prefer to call intuitive) experience? In all likelihood, you yourself have had such an experience, but don't know what to call it or feel afraid to assume it was truly psychic. But who isn't familiar with the feeling that they've sensed something unusual—something beyond the reach of their ordinary senses, and yet just as real?

Whether you know what to call your own experience or just want to check out what you've heard about from others, you're probably still wondering if it was "real." Maybe the experience was just a hyperactive imagination or a hypersensitive mind at work?

We're here to tell you: Trust your intuition on that one. It was real. And after you've read through this book, you'll have a much better sense of what to call these experiences and a greater understanding of why they occurred. We're here to offer insight into the various types of psychic abilities and how to put them to use in your own life.

First, let us explain who "we" are. Lynn is an intuitive consultant and seminar leader, with a masterful psychic ability that is sought by a wide range of clients. LaVonne is an editorial consultant and writer, with a strong religious upbringing that she often resists in favor of her rational side. Through the experience of working on this book, she has learned much about intuition—and has no doubt about its awesome power.

We worked together, culling the best from our different backgrounds, to show you how easy it can be to tap into your intuition. Throughout, we use the word "we" to refer to co-written sections. In special parts of the book where Lynn provides additional insight into the inner world of a working intuitive, she uses the word "I" to share her personal experiences. Here she offers deeper insight on the realm you're about to enter...

When I was a young girl, I was just as curious as you are now, but books like this one weren't very available. I haunted libraries (so to speak) and started reading the few materials I could find. The more I discovered about the psychic world, the more I wanted to know. I developed and practiced my own methods for strengthening my intuition. Eventually, of course, that led to my wanting to try doing readings myself.

Readings seemed to come naturally: I didn't have to work too hard to receive information. My friends who agreed to be subjects for my early experiments were often shocked by what I seemed to know about their private lives. And I'm sure that a few of my friendships cooled because certain friends became convinced I could read their minds.

Well, it wasn't so then, and it isn't so now (though you'd have a hard time convincing my husband of that). I can't read your mind, but I can tell you a lot about what's going on in your world, what could occur in your future, and how you could shape your life into something much closer to what you'd like it to be.

Not long ago, I made a startling discovery. I learned that my maternal grandfather—a family member my English-born mother rarely spoke of—had been a practicing psychic. That suddenly seemed to explain my early and abiding interest in psychic phenomena. But I've decided that even though I might have a genetic, intuitive advantage, I'm not all that different from anyone else who works at being good at what they love.

Make no mistake, I did work at developing my skills in order to become highly intuitive. And because I did, I can help guide you there easily and quickly. I know the shortcuts. All it takes from you is the same curiosity I had when I was a child (and when you were a child). It also benefits from an openness to the possibility of creating a better life through developing your own "sixth" sense.

Have I been able to "see into a person's life"? Yes. Have I amused, amazed, and astounded some of my clients? Definitely. Have I won the lottery? Well, yes—and no. (But more on that later.) What I have done most consistently is to help people like you learn some important things about themselves and their current situations, and then suggest ways to improve their lives. When my clients listen with open minds and hearts, they almost always learn something of value to them personally. That's what I wish for you as you read *The Complete Idiot's Guide to Being Psychic*.

William James, a famous American psychologist, said, "The greatest discovery of my generation is that human beings, by changing the inner attitudes of their minds, can change the outer aspects of their lives."

Developing your psychic abilities can definitely help you change your attitudes—and your life. I can personally vouch for that. And if you read this guide and apply what you learn, you, too, will find your life changing for the better. And you may even be helping other people to change theirs.

So now, open your mind—and your heart—and let's begin.

How to Use This Book

Ooops! Before you just jump right in, we'd like to offer some basic info to get you started. Here's how the book is organized:

Part 1: What Does It Mean to Be Psychic? presents an overview of all things psychic: its history, its science, and its current practitioners and what they do. We want to get you grounded in the basic facts about intuitive ability, including ways to recognize your own.

Part 2: Building Your Psychic Awareness focuses on developing your psychic senses. We offered a big clue in the title for this part: Awareness. Once you become aware of being surrounded—and infused—with natural intuitive ability, you'll find yourself opening up to whole new levels of experience.

Part 3: The Body Psychic describes the connections and interactions between your body, mind, and spirit. Indeed, you may come to see that your intuition is the connecting link between these aspects of yourself—and with the outer world.

Part 4: Beyond the Body Psychic offers more advanced steps toward involving your mind in the process of psychic development. Here's where we get into the fascinating facts about altered states of consciousness, visions, dreams, and communication between minds.

Part 5: Leaping the Barriers of Space and Time gets a pretty spiritual vibration going. We talk about sensing events before they happen, considering previous lifetimes, channeling messages, and accessing the second self. It's absolutely fascinating—and something you can learn to do yourself!

Part 6: More Psychic Phenomena talks about the sort of stuff you see on newsstands and on TV. It's far out, fun, and sometimes even freaky. There are down-to-earth tips for divining the future yourself, as well as trivia on the truth that's "out there."

Part 7: What the Future Holds: For You! offers insight on the predictions for the new millennium. It also includes what probably matters most to you: a chapter on giving your own readings. So, what are you waiting for—it's time to get started!

Extra Insight

Throughout this book you'll find boxes that explain unfamiliar terms, give you helpful tips, point out warnings or pitfalls, or give you further information. Here's what to look for:

From the ESP Files

These boxes present tidbits and trivia about the history and/or study of psychic phenomena.

Beyond Words

These boxes help you talk the talk. They'll bring you up to speed on technical terms we use in the text by giving you simple, straightforward definitions.

Intuition Hotline

These boxes make simple suggestions for using intuition in your own life.

Mixed Messages

It's often wise to see two sides of a situation. Some material that may sound pretty simple at first should be taken with a little caution: These boxes offer an extra warning.

Unsolved Mystery

These boxes bring you wacky, weird, and/or wonderful stories about various psychic phenomena.

Acknowledgments

Last, but certainly not least, we want to thank many tremendous people who have helped create or inspire this book. As we say later in the book, everyone and everything is connected: The hearts, minds, and spirits of all those who have come together to create this book are proof of that. May the light of the universe bless you all.

I would like to thank my husband Gary for all his support. I appreciate all the proofreading, shoulder rubs, dinners, and late-night discussions. Thanks also to my stepson Cliff Watson. I really don't read your mind, Cliff (most of the time). To my wonderful network of terrific girlfriends, Savita Brewer, Cheryl Gilman, Shiri Hughes, Marina Petro, Jean Redpath, Cheryl Richardson, Gayle Rosen, Barbara Selwyn, and Laura Walker. Thanks for all the cheerleading. You knew I could do this before I did. LaVonne, thanks for your good humor, great spirit, and terrific writing. It was fun to work with you.

LaVonne would like to thank the following people for their contributions to the book: Lee Walker for his expertise as a physicist and dreamer; Ruth Seeliger for sharing "the way"; K. Lavonne for her courage and encouragement; and Joanne Go for her inspiration and support. Big hugs go to Brian, Elizabeth, and Patrick for their patience, faith, and love (and sharing computer time!). A huge thank-you goes to Lynn Robinson, who always anticipated just what was needed next, whether it was extra information or enthusiastic support.

At Macmillan, Kathy Nebenhaus, Gary Krebs, Lynn Northrup, Robert Shuman, and Robyn Burnett all offered ongoing and invaluable support. We both would like to acknowledge Lee Ann Chearney of Amaranth for providing the vision for this book and for keeping us on track throughout. Thanks also to Suzanne LeVert for editorial guidance and for encouraging us "onward"!

Special Thanks to the Technical Reviewers

The Complete Idiot's Guide to Being Psychic was reviewed by two experts who double-checked the accuracy of what you'll learn here, to help us ensure that this book gives you everything you need to know about using your psychic talents. Special thanks are extended to Shiri Hughes and Belleruth Naparstek.

Shiri Hughes has been a practicing psychic and medium for more than 30 years. Now in her early 70s, she is grateful that her intuitive ability saved her life at least three times during World War II. Shiri studied astrology and metaphysics with the famous astrologer Isabel Hickey, then studied mediumship with the brilliant medium Sophie Busch. In 1970, the Spiritualist Church ordained Shiri as a minister. Today, Shiri teaches classes in the development of mediumship and psychometry, as well as gives readings to clients in which she uses clairaudience, clairvoyance, and, occasionally, clairsentience.

Belleruth Naparstek, A.M., L.I.S.W., is the author of *Your Sixth Sense: Unlocking the Power of Your Intuition*. A clinical social worker and psychotherapist who has practiced for 33 years, she is a nationally recognized pioneer in the applications of guided imagery for healing and nutrition, and the creator of the popular, 24-title Time Warner audiotape series *Health Journeys*. Ms. Naparstek lives in Cleveland where she writes, lectures, consults, and runs Image Paths, Inc., her audiotape production company.

Trademarks

All terms mentioned in this book that are known to be or are suspected of being trademarks or service marks have been appropriately capitalized. Alpha Books and Macmillan General Reference cannot attest to the accuracy of this information. Use of a term in this book should not be regarded as affecting the validity of any trademark or service mark.

Part 1

What Does It Mean to Be Psychic?

When hearing the question "What does it mean to be psychic?" most people picture an odd-looking peasant woman sitting behind her crystal ball, looking up ominously and saying, "I was expecting you." Well, times are changing. If you want to see what a psychic looks like: Look in your mirror—because you yourself are already psychic.

Now that you know that, you probably still wonder just what that means. Part 1 offers an overview of all that "psychic" can mean. We also approach it from the perspective of history, science, and psychology. And we show you how it's currently in use, in practical ways that make sense in today's world. First, let's start with what you want to know most: How do you know you're psychic?

Chapter 1

Are You Psychic?

> ### In This Chapter
>
> ➤ Confirming what you already know: You're psychic!
>
> ➤ Mysterious words for everyday events
>
> ➤ Discovering your source for psychic power
>
> ➤ Honing your psychic gift

Let's clarify what we suspect you already intuit: Everyone is psychic. And that includes you! In this book, which I (Lynn Robinson) have written with my knowledgeable and talented co-author LaVonne Carlson-Finnerty, we'll show you how to mine your special powers and use them in exciting and constructive ways.

Your psychic ability has been with you since the day you were born (or perhaps for centuries *before* you were born, but we'll talk more about that later). Everyone enters the world with an innate ability to sense information that seems to come from outside, or beyond, themselves. This ability manifests itself in many forms (almost as many forms as there are individual people). And it provides insight and information as general as a gut feeling and as specific as the details of a future event.

Most likely, at least one of the following has happened to you to one degree or another. Each is an example of a psychic phenomenon:

> ➤ You anticipate when the phone's going to ring—and you even know who's on the other end before picking up the receiver (and all this without the help of caller ID!).

➤ You constantly find yourself in the right place at the right time. For example, the person sitting next to you in the jury pool happens to be a piano teacher—and you've just inherited a piano!

➤ You buy a gift for a friend, only to discover that your friend's been looking for that item for some time without success, and hasn't told you (or anyone else) about it.

➤ You dream about a place you've never been before and discover, upon visiting it, that it looks just like you dreamt it.

➤ You're teamed up with a new business associate with whom you feel instantly comfortable. Before the end of your first meeting you're finishing each other's sentences.

But if being psychic is so common—if *everyone's* psychic—why don't we talk about it more often? For one thing, people in our Western culture aren't openly encouraged to acknowledge and train their intuitive skills. As schoolchildren, we busily focused on mastering our ABCs and 123s. Most of us have never been required to take an emotional or psychic IQ test! Yet, according to *Life* magazine, a recent poll showed that 60 percent of Americans believe they've had at least one psychic experience in their lives. For now, rest assured that you *are* indeed psychic, and that what you now need is the confidence to get started on developing this wonderful gift.

So, for starters, this chapter tells you the basics about what it means to be psychic. You'll find out about some psychic "stars" and other tantalizing tidbits of psychic trivia. And you'll discover a few more ways that your intuition has expressed itself, too.

Psychic, Intuitive, or Just Plain Crazy?

Perhaps the vocabulary of psychic intuition is another thing that makes accepting and discussing "psychic stuff" seem so...scary...intimidating...weird? Throughout this book, you'll encounter some words that will be familiar to you, and many that may not be. We'll introduce you to telepathy, clairsentience, ESP, psychometry, psychokinesis, remote viewing, channeling, precognition, the paranormal, the Gaia mind, and more. Don't worry about what they mean right now. Just remember that the range of words used to describe psychic phenomena is as varied as psychic experiences themselves. The study of psychic phenomena is called *parapsychology*.

These days, the term "psychic" means many things to many people. It's a word that's been around the block a few times, so it's carrying a bit of extra baggage. For one thing, "psychic" can refer either to the ability to transcend concrete knowledge or to a person who has this ability. Some people view the word "psychic" from a rather superstitious angle, giving it a negative or sometimes even evil connotation. It's not unusual for people to fear something that has no rational explanation.

When you're "being psychic," you're accessing knowledge without understanding how or why that knowledge is given to you. You just *know* it! Being psychic is all about trust—trusting that your source of information is more powerful than your own imagination, and trusting that it's there for your greatest good.

In the field of medicine today, we're seeing doctors embrace the power of the connection between our bodies and our minds to heal and nurture us. High-tech computer and biomedical advances are changing the face of medicine, but these breakthroughs exist hand-in-hand with a new respect for alternative medicine techniques such as acupuncture, chiropractic, and biofeedback.

Beyond Words

Parapsychology is a branch of psychology that studies psychic experiences. The term came into use in the late 1920s when the field's founder, J. B. Rhine, created the first institute for psychic research, The Rhine Research Center, situated near the Duke University campus in Durham, North Carolina.

Disciplines that combine mental and physical well being (such as yoga, meditation, and massage) are enjoying a renaissance of enthusiasm, and some medical schools are conducting scientific studies into the documented healing effects of prayer. Doctors and scientists agree that there's a lot they need to explore about how the health of one's psyche and one's soul influences their mental health and their physical health, which determines how long one lives as well.

It seems a natural progression that people are growing more accepting of psychic experiences. These days, when you hear that someone's had a vivid dream about a loved one who passes on unexpectedly shortly thereafter, you're probably a lot less likely to dismiss it as a coincidence and more willing to accept it as a psychic connection.

One reason why psychic experiences are hard to describe is because they occur in a nonphysical realm, which means that they aren't concrete. You can't touch them, feel them, or take them home to show mother. And it can be very difficult to prove them. One of the key lessons you'll learn from this book is to have faith—not necessarily in a Higher Power—but in yourself. The foundation of improving your psychic power is trusting in yourself. As the saying goes, "Trust your intuition."

In fact, I believe the words "psychic" and "intuition" are interchangeable. In my practice, for instance, I refer to myself as an intuitive reader. The word "intuitive" sheds a whole new light on being psychic, since it focuses on discerning truth through a direct, albeit unexplained, source of knowledge (as compared to receiving information from a supernatural force). "Intuitive" suggests that the information sent or received finds its origin inside one's self. So, if you work on developing your ability to think and feel intuitively, you're being psychic.

Unsolved Mystery

One of the most famous psychics of this century is Jeane Dixon. She has advised many performers and politicians throughout recent decades. Among her most famous predictions was that of President Kennedy's assassination. But she wasn't the only one with this foreknowledge: Kennedy himself reported a premonition of his own death.

How's Your Psi These Days?

Beyond Words

Scientists who study psychic phenomena created the term **psi** as a neutral (i.e. more scientific) way to refer to psychic experiences and abilities. Psi is a letter of the Greek alphabet, and the first letter of the Greek word *psyche*, which literally means "breath" in Greek and refers to the human soul. **Extrasensory perception** (ESP) means that you perceive someone's thoughts, situation, or issues in life without using one of your five "ordinary" senses.

Psi (pronounced "sigh") is the study of psychic phenomena from a psychological perspective. It's another term created in an attempt to talk about the abstract concept of being psychic. *The Journal of Parapsychology* defines psi as "a general term to identify a person's extrasensori-motor communication with the environment." (Whew!) The *Journal* was created by a group of researchers who were trying to prove the existence of *extrasensory perception* (ESP).

In general, psi isn't a word commonly used by everyday folks on the street (but it's sure the buzzword within the psychic community!). You might want to save it for an impressive opening line in a cocktail party conversation. But we want you to avoid getting too attached to *any* specific terms for the psychic experience, so that your mind will have more freedom to welcome and explore the many intuitive messages that come your way every day.

Do You Have the Vibes?

Admit it! Whatever you call being psychic, you've always been fascinated by the idea that you could know something without having been told about it by someone else. Like most people, you've always secretly wished you could read someone's mind—or predict when a catastrophe would occur—then avoid it and save the day, or get rich by knowing in advance what the stock market would do.

Well, you're not as crazy as you thought. Although most people, especially those without any training, cannot perform any of these amazing mental feats, everyone does have a psychic sense. And that includes you! (Besides, predicting the ups and downs of the stock market may be a misguided use of your psychic skills, anyway.)

I once asked a physicist if he believed in psychic intuition. His answer (the short one!) was "No." His long answer, however, reveals something interesting. This physicist postulates that psychic awareness relies on an accumulation of knowledge and the ability to predict outcomes successfully based on that knowledge. It's a little bit like playing the odds—the more inside information you have, the more accurate your choices can be and the more chance you have of beating those odds. So, according to our physicist friend, if you've got the vibes, you're consciously applying knowledge you've accessed and processed in an unconscious, unexplainable manner—that science has yet to catch up with.

Ever Had a Psychic Experience?

Since you're reading this book, we'll assume that either you or someone you know are among those 60 percent of Americans who've had an experience they'd call psychic. And now you want to know more. But if you're in doubt about whether you may be a bit psychic after all, consider the following questions. Chances are good you'll answer at least one of them in the affirmative. Without even realizing it, you're tapping into your intuitive side. Give it a try:

➤ Do you get hunches about things coming up in your life?

➤ Do you sense what is going on with other people's feelings?

➤ Have you ever known about future events before they happen?

➤ Do you feel physical sensations (knots in your stomach or an all-over heaviness, for example) that alert you when you're making a decision that's wrong for you? And do you honor those physical clues?

➤ Do you feel physical sensations (tingling or lightness, for example) that alert you when you're making a good decision? Do you honor the sensations?

➤ Are you aware of how your intuition speaks to you?

➤ Do you receive information through kinesthetic (physical) sensations, through more cerebral hunches, or through feelings and emotions?

➤ How often do you check in with your intuition when you need information?

Did you answer "Yes" to any of these questions? If so, this confirms the answer to the question you've been asking yourself all along: "Am I really psychic?" Doubt no more! The answer is "Yes."

In future chapters we'll talk about why you answered "Yes" to some questions, and how you can use each question to develop your psychic intuition. Everybody has a unique way of getting in touch with his or her own psychic abilities. Throughout this book, we'll help you discover the best ways to tap into yours. We'll give you insight into the various forms of psychic ability and help you understand where your special talents fit into this awesome, yet undeniably real, range of powers.

When first getting in touch with your personal psychic skills and strengths, be aware that there is a wide range of possible ways to receive information. Some people may feel a physical sensation in the body, others may experience an emotional change, and still others may hear a voice or see an image. The possibilities are infinite, because they are all unique to each individual.

From the ESP Files

Each individual gets psychic information in his or her own unique way. But there's more to it than that. Because for some individuals, the way the information arrives can change from one event to the next, depending on the situation. For example, if you're overly stressed, you may develop a headache as your body's way of saying to get some rest. If you're about to say "No" to the career opportunity of a lifetime, your stomach might tighten into knots. If you shouldn't take that walk in the park after dark, you may feel a prickly sensation at the back of your neck. If you're asking for intuitive guidance about a decision, you may get a warm feeling at the thought of a good decision—or maybe even a few words offering guidance or a good idea. Any or all of these things may occur—stay tuned for more details.

Separating Questioning from Questing

To start learning where your psychic potential fits in on a grander scale, you need to know where you're coming from. For starters, examine your existing attitudes and beliefs toward the amazing and mysterious world of psychic stuff. Chances are, you feel a mixture of curiosity, anxiety, fear, doubt, and eager enthusiasm when thinking about being psychic. All of these feelings are normal, especially when you're exploring new territory.

Think about all the input you've received over your lifetime about the psychic realm. The popular media tends to view psychic phenomena with an equal measure of suspicion and fascination. The popular TV show *The X-Files* taps into the public's strong desire to investigate the nature and truth of psychic experiences and events. In movies and on TV, though, psychic phenomena tend to be larger than life, often with supernatural or paranormal qualities attached (they do have to entertain, after all!). But harnessing psychic power in your own life is not so extreme, scary, or out of this world. Being psychic can be an everyday way of being, another part of who you are.

Traditional religions have a wide range of viewpoints on psychic matters, not all of them positive. Your own parents, depending on their religious backgrounds, probably downplayed psychic impulses or spurned them, for fear of putting "silly" ideas in your head. Yet each great religious tradition from Buddha to Mohammed to Christ has a tradition of prophecy and miracles. (We'll be exploring the rich history of psychic intuition in Chapter 2.)

How often have you stopped to think for *yourself* about what being psychic really means?

Mixed Messages

Beware of becoming overly eager in your quest for psychic intuition. Don't let wishful thinking or personal ambition convince you that desired—but possibly inaccurate—information is meant to be a psychic blessing. Positive thinking and affirmations can be extremely powerful, but they must be acknowledged for what they are—conscious and willful directing of your own thoughts.

The Soul Connection

Perhaps the intuitive messages you receive can be looked upon as gifts from the universe, offering to guide you along a clearer, smoother pathway. Perhaps they originate from an all-seeing and all-loving God who speaks to you through these impressions. Or perhaps they are entirely physical biochemical sensations, brought on by hormonal overloads of body chemicals that scientists are only just discovering. Experts have no answers to these ponderings. Explore your beliefs so that you can resolve any possible barriers that could prevent you from opening up to something new, such as your own incredible psychic potential!

Intuition Hotline

Always know that *you are in control*. While many psychics insist that the future is etched in stone, we believe that choices and decisions do matter. Intuitive information forms messages you receive from your higher self, offering guidance rather than an ultimatum. *You're* in control of your own destiny!

"I Know, But I Don't Know How"

A common expression among many beginners—and even masters—in the world of intuitive insight is "I know but, I don't know how." If you've ever had this sense or the impulse to express it, you're definitely on track. But what does it mean?

You've probably had a moment when you stopped short in your tracks, struck with a thought or idea that came from seemingly no where. Perhaps it had no relation to any topic you'd had on your mind at all, and yet the information later proved accurate. Once you gain a little experience with receiving intuitive information, you'll be able to say "A-ha!" with the full confidence that the information is something that comes from a source beyond your five senses. You may never be able to describe the inspiration for that source, but you can get better at recognizing and using this type of knowledge.

Intuition as Life's Teacher

A safe way to view intuition is as our souls' instructions, guiding us to make correct decisions for ourselves, according to our higher purpose in life. The messages we receive may give us information about how to proceed in our lives. Or they may provide insight into what lessons we should be learning from certain experiences, even painful ones. They offer suggestions for taking the next steps, large or small, along our path.

In addition to positive growth in our personal and spiritual lives, our relationships with others also benefit. Psychic insight can grant us greater understanding, empathy, and compassion for others. It informs us about our world in new ways, giving us a fresh perspective. I like to refer to intuitive information as "an instruction package for planet Earth." But don't worry too much about reading the entire world: Once you start seeing your immediate surroundings, the larger world will come to you.

Neophyte to Master: Honing Your Intuitive Talent

Remember one thing: Keep an open mind! As you begin tapping into your psychic information, you'll discover it's a hit-or-miss proposition at first. It may take you some time to sort out which messages are meant for you. Maybe you won't be bending spoons like Uri Geller from day one, but eventually you'll tune into the method of sending or receiving information that works best for you. You'll also start to get a good sense of when an intuitive message is truly coming to you—loud and clear.

Here's an image to help illustrate it. Envision your intuitive powers as a radio wave or radio signals coming from station W-PSI (or K-PSI if you're on the West Coast!). The power is always there, you just need to know how to tune in. For some, this tuning in involves a concerted learning effort; others may just happen to hit the best station right off the bat. With a little effort, anyone can soon gain access to a usable frequency. You just need a few lessons on how to fine-tune your psychic receptors.

Everyone Has the "Gift"

Everyone is born with some degree of psychic ability. It's not a sacred gift intended only for a few select geniuses. Just like studying piano or training as a soccer player, anyone can do it. Of course, the occasional prodigy does surface in these areas now and then, and the same is true with psychic abilities. But you can't all be Mozart, Pele, or the Amazing Kreskin—and you needn't expect to be.

As with any other skill or talent, the more you use it, the better you get at it. (If you dread the thought of practicing anything, here's some consolation: Practicing your psychic powers is much simpler than lugging a string bass to lessons or getting dressed for a hockey game.) And as you become more confident and in control of your intuitive abilities, the better able you'll be to trust your psychic insights when making major life decisions.

We've put together the following table of people who've relied on psychic experiences at one time or other in their lives. Soon, you may be adding your own name to the list!

Psychic Experiences of Famous People

Sir Winston Churchill	British statesman	Saved from death on more than one occasion by following psychic intuition, Churchill believed he was guided and protected by the guardian of his sacred cause.
Albert Einstein	Physicist	Is reputed to have formulated the Theory of Relativity while resting.
Henry Ford	Inventor of the Model T automobile	A believer in reincarnation, Ford was comforted by the notion that he had more than one life to get things right.
Morgan Robertson	Novelist	Predicted the sinking of the *Titanic*.
Edgar Mitchell	NASA astronaut, the sixth man to walk on the moon	After traveling in space, became fascinated by ESP and founded the Institute of Noetic Sciences.

continues

Psychic Experiences of Famous People, cont.

Arnold Palmer	Golf pro	Enters a trance state while playing golf: "It is not merely mechanical, it is not only spiritual; it is something of both, on a different plane and a more remote one."
Joan Rivers	Talk show host and comedienne	Traveled out of body to visit her daughter, who was residing in a city far distant from where Rivers was "sleeping" at the time.
Mae West	Actress	Possessed clairvoyant skills: "I don't imagine things and hear voices. I know something exists around me."

An interest in psychic ability is increasingly acknowledged by police departments. Thirty-seven percent of America's urban police departments report consulting a psychic at some point in investigations. Dorothy Allison, a well-known and controversial police psychic, led detectives to the body of a murdered girl near Niagara Falls in 1991. (Reportedly, Dorothy is now receiving information about the JonBenet Ramsey murder case.) In November 1995, the U.S. government revealed a 20-year Pentagon study of psi, showing that they used psychics as spies. Results of the government experiments reveal documented evidence of psychic functioning.

While you may not be able to locate your neighbor's missing dog or predict tomorrow's Lotto jackpot numbers, with effort and concentration, you'll soon find yourself accessing your own powers of psychic intuition. Over time, you'll gain confidence in what you "know" and you'll learn more about where and how that knowledge comes uniquely to you!

Practice, Practice, Practice

Now that you're convinced you have this tremendous gift, get ready to use it. In the upcoming chapters we include exercises to help you find the right psychic path for you. The next chapter gives you some insight into humankind's experiences with psychic phenomena over the centuries. (You might recognize your own abilities in some of the skills we describe.)

From then on, we focus on the many perspectives of psychic ability. Somewhere in there, you'll come upon a method (or methods) of being psychic that hits home for you. Try to be aware and open to this connection to your own psychic talent. We'll help you tune in to your intuitive side. And don't forget: Practice makes perfect.

From the ESP Files

Does psychic intuition run in your family? Just as musical virtuosity and athletic finesse tend to run in families, psychic talent also appears to have a genetic component. Indeed, research indicates that it seems to skip a generation. My family is proof in point: My grandfather contacted my mother late in life (he hadn't been in touch with her since she was 12) and revealed that he was a professional psychic. (To test this out yourself, give Granny a call and ask her if she's always had an uncanny knack for knowing stuff ahead of time.)

Let's start now. Sit quietly and comfortably in a straight-backed chair with your hands resting on the tops of your thighs, palms facing down, and your feet flat on the floor. Close your eyes. Breathe in deeply, letting the air fill your abdomen. Breathe out slowly. Repeat this for five deep, full breaths. Quiet and center your concentration on the breath flowing into and out of your body; feel your heart beating. Remember that in Greek, psyche or soul is literally "breath." An open, clear mind is a psychic mind. Stay tuned.

The Least You Need to Know

➤ Everyone—including you—is psychic.

➤ The words "psychic" and "intuitive" can be used interchangeably.

➤ Each individual has a unique way of tuning into his or her own psychic abilities.

➤ Our intuitive talents can provide guidance in every aspect of our lives.

➤ While developing psychic power is not difficult, the more you practice, the more accessible it becomes.

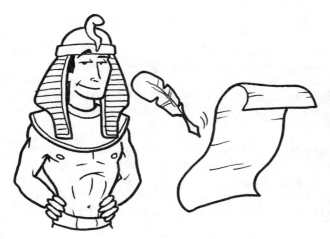

Chapter 2

Psychic Phenomena Through the Ages

In This Chapter

➤ Ancient origins of age-old practices

➤ Sacred sources of psychic knowledge

➤ Famous psychic seekers

➤ The future of soothsaying

Throughout the ages, every civilization has demonstrated a belief in a power beyond itself, beyond the human realm. The tremendous urge to understand this power has inspired artists and writers in every century since the dawn of time. Early cultures searched for gods in nature. This search led to great works of art, whole schools of philosophy, and to the doctrines of the world's religions.

Why are people so eager to get to know God? Of course, everyone wants to be a better person by getting in good with the one upstairs. But there's probably more to it than that, because—face it—human nature tends to be just a bit self-serving. What everyone also wants is an insider tip on what's coming up next, whether it's where to make your first million or where you'll spend your time in eternity. This desire may explain why the search for the divine tends to be deeply intertwined with divination—the practice of foretelling future events through supernatural means, prophecy, or intuition. In fact, "divine" and "divination" share the same root, which means "pertaining to god." When it comes to psychic phenomena, divination refers to seeing the future in three ways: through the supernatural, by prophecy, or with intuition. We'll show you what we mean in this chapter.

The Ancients

The earliest people were surrounded by nature. Instead of hiding from the elements in little pink houses, they faced the immense power of nature on a daily basis. They acknowledged that they were at the mercy of nature, and set out to both appease and understand the forces that ruled it. They believed their fates lay in understanding the forces and spirits of the natural world. They looked for signs and omens in the way the birds flew or the wind blew.

Shamans, medicine healers, and exorcists were viewed as outstanding members of their communities, people who had an inside line to the greater forces beyond. These living forces were capable of both good and evil. When someone was ill, people assumed he or she had been taken over by an evil force, and an exorcist was called in to cast out the evil. These specialists were revered, much as doctors are today—and they even made house calls!

Reading the Body

Babylonia is among the first civilizations with a recorded history. Situated in the fertile area where the Tigris and Euphrates Rivers meet, the culture began to take hold around 2000 B.C. As proof of its cosmopolitan sophistication, the world's first city documented accounts of reading animal entrails to predict future events. Maybe that's where the saying "gut reaction" comes from.

From the ESP Files

The reading of body organs is officially called haruspicy. Although the ancient Babylonians were the first to document their use, other civilizations also performed the practice. Voodoo practitioners used various animal parts as a means of divination or protection. The Incas in Peru and the Aztecs in Mexico tried their hand at it too, as recently as 500 years ago. Just goes to show that certain ideas transcend culture!

Here's an example of how an entrails reading worked (probably not something you'd want to try at home!). The Babylonians would begin by sacrificing a sheep, then removing its organs. A seer, or *baru*, would direct his inquiries to the various organs of an animal and get answers to his questions. For instance, each zone of the liver would signify something about the health and reign of the current king. If it had a long cystic duct, the king would have a lengthy reign; if it was swollen, he'd gain increased power. Divining by liver inspection—now there's an interesting specialty to get into! (Just look—and pray—for a sheep with a long, fat liver!)

Markings on the skin also offered important signs. This form of divination was practiced in early times in Egypt, Cyprus, Greece, and western Italy. From there, it traveled to Rome, where it was authorized by the state. The study of skin markings was probably the precursor of palmistry, as well as other newer forms of fortune-telling, such as *metoscopy* and *meliomancy*.

Beyond Words

Metoscopy is a form of fortune-telling based on analyzing lines on the forehead. **Meliomancy** is the art of reading moles to predict future events.

Consulting the Oracle

Just as the kings of ancient Persia read the entrails of animals, the rulers of the more recent Greeks, and then Romans, used their own methods to learn the future of their reigns. And as the formation of city-states grew more sophisticated, so did the rulers' need for a more subjective means of divination.

The terminology used when reading the palm descends from the mythology of the Greek and Latin gods. For example, the mound at the base of your thumb, referred to as Venus, indicates your personal inclinations toward love and physical beauty. For centuries, palmistry was studied among Europe's political and religious elite, and even taught in the universities. (Gives new meaning to the phrase "palming your notes.")

From the ESP Files

Chiromancy, or palmistry, goes back a long way in India's history, and has remained a favorite form of fortune-telling in southeastern Europe. It probably originated from the examination of entrails, but it inspired confidence because of the fact that palms are marks of individual identity. Even the Bible reflects a longstanding awareness of the practice in passages such as Proverbs 3:16, which states, "Length of days is in her right hand; and in her left hand riches and honor."

In Greece, the *oracle* brought the answer to this dilemma. Oracles offered divination in two forms: (1) the normal and interpretive, and (2) the frenzied and obscure. The normal was based on natural signs, such as observable behaviors in birds, fish, or—always a favorite—snakes. The frenzied was so-called because the prophecies were frequently revealed under the influence of sacred (often hallucinogenic) substances. These verbal messages mark some of the earliest predictions to come directly through a person using language (compared to the nonverbal signs of nature).

The best known and loved oracle was the oracle at Delphi. She is the one you all heard about in your history class on Greek mythology (which you always wondered why you needed to study). Actually, the title of "Delphic Oracle" did not pertain to a specific individual, but was passed from one high priestess to the next. (By the way, the oracle's symbol was the python, which probably harks back to the serpent in the story of the Garden of Eden.)

Beyond Words

Oracle refers to an utterance, which is often obscure, that is believed to come from a divine source, usually to foretell the future. It also refers to a person who makes the utterance or to a place where it is made.

These high priestesses, picked as virgins in the early days but later chosen from women over 50, chewed leaves from the sacred laurel plant before offering their prophecies. They also drank from an underground stream called Cassotis, which was believed to contain prophetic water but which also produced gaseous fumes. Both of these sources contained possible poisons, which may have triggered trances and eventual unconscious states in those who drank from them.

Mixed Messages

Even for the sake of a spiritual or psychic revelation, the use of hallucinogenic drugs, from organic mushrooms to synthetic lysergic acid (LSD), is a dangerous undertaking. Try quiet meditation for the safest results!

Messages spoken by the priestess during her inspired state were interpreted by individuals who were considered diviners—and also happened to be members of the elite families of Delphi. Of course, some historians suspect that these upper-class representatives translated the messages in ways that enhanced their power and wealth. We'll never know for sure, but one thing is definite: In the minds of the people, the words of the oracle of Delphi reigned supreme—and led them to great accomplishments as a conquering and colonizing empire.

Of course, Greece's conquests lasted only until Rome won out. And yet Rome had it's own form of the fortune-telling female: the goddess Fortuna. Although she had many names, depending on which province you were in, Fortuna was originally portrayed as controlling two ship rudders: one guiding to prosperity and one to misfortune. Later, she was pictured holding a scepter and sitting on a globe, with a bandage over her eyes. Although this suggests the image of Justice, Fortuna was believed to make her choices with no regard to laws of nature or man—whimsically, rather than logically. Perhaps she is an early forebear of Lady Luck.

Celestial Wisdom of the Stars

Almost 5,000 years ago, one of the earliest and longest enduring methods of foretelling future events was born: *astrology*. Ancient Sumer and Mesopotamia were famous for their astronomers, who not only predicted events by viewing the stars but also created the foundations of arithmetic used today.

In fact, they were so aware of the connection between the positions of planets and the passing of time that they created a calendar based on it—predicting the changing days, months, and years with great accuracy.

Much of our current knowledge of astrology comes from the Greeks, particularly from Ptolemy of Alexandria (a.k.a. Claudius Ptolemaeus), who lived at the beginning of the second century A.D. He is associated with the idea of "houses" in our astrological charts: The theory goes that each person's life can be divided into 12 categories, such as relationships, possessions, and creativity. The planet that appears in each of a person's house indicates how that person will handle that aspect of his or her life. Learning where the planets fit into your categories allows you to get a lot more specific about predicting your personal future. Ptolemy believed that celestial sources of information were far superior to any other in predicting important events for society as well as individuals (which is more scientific—and a lot cleaner—than reading entrails). Many modern astrologers, amateurs, and professionals alike continue to share this belief.

Beyond Words

Astrology is the art and science of foretelling the future by studying the influence of the relative positions of the moon, sun, and stars on human affairs. In contrast, astronomy is the science that studies the material universe beyond Earth.

Psychic Power in the Sacred Texts

Though many early forms of divination were based on natural signs or pagan practices, the development of written languages created ways to document psychic events and record specific practices. These lessons are often contained in the world's great sacred texts. Indeed, these experiences frequently form the foundation of their most famous stories.

Intuition Hotline

You can practice bibliomancy—fortune-telling by using a book, sacred (like the Bible) or secular—by opening the book at random and blindly placing your finger on a passage or simply taking note of the first passage your eye falls on. Then you need to divine (or interpret) what this special passage means to you.

Bible Stories: The Three Wise Men and More

The best-selling book of all time, the Bible, is filled with stories of heroes with powerful psychic abilities. Often these people heard voices, saw images, or had dreams—all of which led to prophecies that were realized at a future date. In short, these heroes predicted the future. Of course, Biblical text itself never refers to these abilities as "psychic," but they do fit the description.

Among the most obvious intuitive heroes in the Bible are those who received information through dreams. Remember the story of Joseph? He interpreted the Pharaoh's dream of seven thin cows consuming seven fat ones and seven thin ears of corn consuming seven fat ones to mean that the Egyptians would have seven plentiful years to store enough extra food to last through a seven-year famine. And that's exactly what happened. Joseph was known for having his own psychic dreams, too, which enabled him to predict (and often avert) future difficulties.

Perhaps the greatest visionary was Isaiah, who wrote many sections of one of the greatest prophetic books contained in what is now called the Old Testament. He predicted the downfalls of many neighboring nations, all of which came to pass. Isaiah also described an apocalypse that many people believe is yet to come.

Other spiritual leaders received direct verbal messages from God. Noah was told to build a big boat, which he did despite the ridicule of his neighbors, who then watched as he floated safely away when the floods began. Abraham also received verbal messages from God, as did Moses. Jonah heard a voice telling him to go to Ninevah as a prophet, and when he refused, a huge fish swallowed him until he was ready to change his mind.

Beyond Words

Paganism is loosely defined as any religion outside of the Judaic, Christian, or Muslim traditions. It typically involves *polytheism*, belief in many gods.

The New Testament begins with stories of various visions and portents. The best-known story is probably the one about the wise men, who traveled from the East by studying the stars. They followed a particular star that announced the birth of a king. Meanwhile, Mary was visited by an angel who foretold Christ's birth. And shepherds had visions of angels predicting his birth. The end of the New Testament contains one of the most prophetic scriptures, the book of Revelations. It is based on the dreams and visions experienced by Paul, who was converted to Christianity after experiencing a vision so intense that it caused Paul's temporary blindness.

As Christianity spread, it slowly incorporated the practices of *paganism* into its religious ceremonies. For example, people uttered Christian prayers as they gathered herbs for good luck. Gradually, practices that were not incorporated into the Christian religion—such as divination—began to be viewed as suspicious or superstitious.

This engraving, "The Dove Sent Forth from the Ark" by Gustave Dore, shows that Noah took the message he received from God seriously, building the ark to protect two of each species from a devastating flood.

As Roman rule diminished in the third and fourth centuries A.D., a philosophy called Gnosticism began to form. Its theories are close to what is now call the "occult." Gnostic teaching stated that the "stars are gods" and that only The Chosen (highest spiritual beings) are capable of receiving divine knowledge. As the Dark Ages set in, records of this and other ancient belief systems disappeared, leaving people in the dark about many aspects of these fascinating traditions.

Jewish Mysticism and the Kabbalah

At about the same time that the New Testament and Christian religions were forming, the Jewish religious tradition developed its own form of mysticism. The Kabbalah, from the word meaning "received love," is a mystical movement that also contains a magical side. It includes the use of amulets, charms, rituals, and combinations of letters and numbers reported to have sacred powers.

One of the Kabbalah's chief texts is the *Zohar* (meaning "Splendor"), which dates between the first and third century A.D. Considered the product of divine revelation, believers feel that the *Zohar* is a description of how a mortal can ascend to God as well as how God descends toward mortals. The *Zohar* contains numerological principles and describes a tree of life with 22 branches that are connected to 10 branching points, also called "spheres," which represent the godly qualities that one seeks to attain while in a physical form. Traditionally, only Jewish males over the age of 40 have studied the Kabbalah, but in recent years the information has become accessible to younger spiritual seekers, who have greeted it with enthusiasm.

The Eastern Tradition: Are You a Yogi or a Buddha?

The Babylonians weren't the only early culture to use body parts to predict the future. Ancient Chinese cultures began a body-reading practice that used bones (certainly animal and perhaps human under certain circumstances) instead of organs to get the inside scoop. They would carve questions to the gods in the bones. Then they heated the bones, which caused cracks to appear across the questions. The configuration of the cracks revealed the gods' answers, usually in the form of a "yes" or "no."

Another ancient form of divination, which has gained great popularity in the West recently, is the *I Ching* (a.k.a. *Book of Changes*). Dating back to about 2000 B.C., its predictions are based on 64 possible arrangements of six lines. This system probably originated from ancient diviners who dropped sticks and then gave a reading based on their positions when they landed. Today, special coins are available for that purpose.

Intuition Hotline

There are several readily available easy-to-read and easy-to-follow texts of the *I Ching*. You might want to try your hand at throwing coins, and reading the elegant and poetic interpretations of the results. You might gain some insight into your life and your future.

Meanwhile, Siddhartha Gautama (a.k.a. Buddha) was born in India around 563 B.C. At his birth, someone predicted that if he ever encountered suffering, Siddhartha would renounce the comforts of the physical world. For this reason, his well-off father protected him from seeing any type of suffering. But when Siddhartha became an adult, the inevitable happened. Siddhartha discovered suffering, and off he went to find out what to do about it.

For years, Siddhartha studied under yogis—men who practiced meditation and yoga as the main means to spiritual growth. Although these teachers were India's main source for spiritual gurus, Siddhartha eventually developed his own path to enlightenment. What he realized was that suffering is caused by desire, and that enlightenment comes through freedom from desire. The religion he developed, called Buddhism, spread from India to China around A.D. 100.

Yogis and Buddhists alike agree with the idea that a universal mind underlies and permeates everything, including space and time. This concept is one way of viewing the psychic realm—that seeing into another person's mind or into the future is simply tapping into the universal mind, the pool of infinite knowledge and information that already exists and is omnipresent. Perhaps this pool is the source of direct knowing, or psychic intuition.

Certain sects of Eastern mystics believe that the physical world is no more real than any that exists in the mind. By overcoming any delineation between these worlds, these gurus are said to perform feats of magic, such as walking through walls.

Mixed Messages

Don't try any of the physical feats attributed to yogis—walking over hot coals, holding one arm above one's head for several years—in order to consider yourself psychic! Leave them to the experts!

Psychic Masters: From the Middle Ages to Right Now

As you may have noticed, many records of amazing psychic events occurred around the turn of the changing millennium 2,000 years ago. Remarkable leaders—Buddha (early on), then Christ, and a little later Muhammad and Zoroaster, all visionaries and all referred to as prophets—lived at that time. These leaders both benefited from and added to the growth of ideas that were passed along the Silk Road between the East and West. And their brilliance survived the formidable Dark Ages that followed, an era that leaves a gaping hole in our knowledge of many subjects.

Now it's necessary to travel through time ourselves, to the late Middle Ages and the Renaissance, when another explosion of information and ideas occurred. This period of time offered fertile ground for the study of the psychic realm, as more and more people accepted psychic abilities as a fact of life, but began to insist on a scientific explanation!

Psychic Saint

One of the earliest heroes from this period is Hildegard of Bingen (a town along the Rhine River in western Germany). An abbess who lived from 1098 until 1179, Hildegard was able to find acceptance and respect as a mystic, preacher, theologian, medical writer, author, and educated woman. Hildegard began experiencing visions when she was five years old, joined a monastery when she was eight, and became head of her community at age 38. As an adult she wrote about 26 of her visions in the book *Scivias*. It was examined by a papal commission, which led to Pope Eugenius III accepting her visions as authentic.

In 1148 Hildegard received a vision telling her to found a new convent. When her abbot would not allow it, Hildegard became ill, a pattern that repeated itself throughout her life whenever she couldn't fulfill her visions. Eventually, the abbot relented and Hildegard built the Rupertsberg convent near Bingen. She later built another convent at Eibingen. Today, she has gained renewed popularity for her work as a writer, composer, and painter of illuminated manuscripts.

Psychic Prodigy

Another world-famous favorite among the religious psychics is also a female—Joan of Arc. Born in 1412, Joan heard even as a child what she later described as voices. These voices prompted her as a teenager to don armor and lead the French army against the English to end the siege of Orleans, her home town. After Joan suffered several defeats at the hands of the English, they captured her and returned her to the French theologians (who were English loyalists). They called her a heretic due to her ability to hear voices.

To save herself, Joan recanted her reports of the voices she heard and appealed to the pope. However, she was shortly returned to prison and raped by her captors, after which she withdrew her recantation and espoused renewed faith in her "voices," causing her captors to burn her at the stake as a heretic at age 19. A posthumous retrial in the mid–15th-century cleared her of heresy; it took only another 500 years or so before the Church proclaimed her a saint in 1920.

Nostradamus: Far-Seeing Psychic

Another famous visionary, probably the greatest yet known to humankind, is Nostradamus. Born Michel de Nostredame (Michael of Notre Dame) in Provence, France in 1503, he was the eldest son in a Jewish family that had converted to Catholicism. Like most people of means in his day, Nostradamus received training not only in all the classical languages, but also astrology and medicine. He became an astrologer and physician, and is reputed to have created remarkable cures during outbreaks of the plague in France.

Nostradamus didn't start to glimpse into the future until he was in his early forties. First he would receive premonitions and then experience visual flashes of insight. His early prophecies were rather insignificant, such as which piglet in the back yard would be served for dinner. But eventually, when his prophecies concerned more important matters, he began to publish them. His rhymed prophecies, published under the title *Centuries* (1555), brought him the favor of the French court. He wrote them in the form of four-line predictions, such as this one:

> *Like the great king of the Angolmois*
> *The year 1999, seventh month,*
> *The great king of terror will descend from the sky,*
> *At this time, Mars will reign for the good cause.*

Albrecht Durer, a contemporary of mystic Nostradamus, depicted the skies of the Northern and Southern Hemispheres in 1515, illustrating the blending of science, astronomy, and astrology at this time in human history.

As you can see, the wording is a bit vague, which leaves the predictions open to various interpretations—literally as well as figuratively (he wrote his prophecies in Latin, French, and Greek!).

Nostradamus reportedly predicted such events as the Napoleonic Wars, the American Revolution and Civil War, the assassinations of Lincoln and both Kennedys, World War II, the appearance of nuclear weapons, and space travel. He is typically portrayed as the archetypal magician wearing a big, black cape, a pointy magician's hat, and gazing with arm outstretched into a crystal ball. But that is not actually the case.

In order to make a prediction, Nostradamus did not rub a crystal ball. He placed a bowl of water on a brass tripod, tapped his wand into the bowl, and then touched it to his robe. He then gazed into the bowl to receive his visions, a process known as *scrying*. His clairvoyant senses proved to surpass the voices he heard in his early experiences. He died in 1566.

Beyond Words

Scrying is a fancy word for crystal-gazing, which involves looking into a reflective surface while deeply concentrating (what Nostradamus did). Although scrying typically uses a polished ball made from any transparent jewel, many other surfaces have been used too. Some examples include a hole filled with water (popular in Polynesia), a mirror, sword blades, rings, glasses of sherry, and even fingernails (now *that's* a good manicure!).

25

More Notable Paranormal People

Describing all of the intuitive people in history would be an impossible task. For one thing, the parameters of what is mystical, psychic, prophetic, or fraud are difficult to define.

For example, where do you place witchcraft in the psychic lexicon? Is it possible that many of the people who were proclaimed and persecuted as evil witches were merely psychic? Perhaps the Grand Inquisitors and judges of the Salem Witch Trials were simply afraid of the phenomena that they didn't understand and that's why they condemned those who practiced them so severely.

The following table lists a few of the folks who spoke up with some ideas that weren't always readily accepted by their peers.

A Psychic "Who's Who" for Recent Centuries

Tituba	1692	Slave and fortune-teller who confessed being a witch at the Salem Witch Trials.
Emanuel Swedenborg	(1688–1772)	Swedish mystic who defined divinity as infinite love; described out-of-body experiences; formed the roots of the 19th-century interest in the paranormal.
Franz Mesmer	(1734–1815)	Father of modern hypnotism; mistakenly believed that magnets and their fields produced the hypnotic trances he induced in his patients; also influenced interest in the paranormal.
William Blake	(1757–1827)	Mystical artist and poet whose visions guided his work.
The Fox Sisters (a.k.a. the Rochester Rappers)	1848	Two sisters (Kate, 15, and and Maggie, 12) whose seances invoked spirits to rap on and levitate objects; influenced widespread Spiritualist movement throughout 19th-century America.
Daniel Dunglas Home	(1833–1886)	Spiritualism's best-known physical medium; produced human levitation, body elongation, and spirit materialization.
Madame Helena Blavatsky	(1831–1891)	Made the Theosophical movement popular.

Harry Price	(1881–1948)	Founded the first British laboratory for scientific study of psychical phenomena.
J.B. Rhine	(1895–1980)	Founded the Parapsychology Lab at Duke University (1935); coined the term "extrasensory perception" and established use of Zener cards.
Edgar Cayce	(1877–1945)	Leading 20th-century American psychic; known for psychic healing.
Uri Geller	(1946–present)	Established acceptance of psychokinesis in the mid–20th-century.

Eye on the Century Ahead

Society's view of psychic phenomena has undergone tremendous changes in the short span of 100 years. For centuries, people "believed in" but feared every sort of mysterious power, but turned their back on these "superstitious fairy tales" when faced with the Technology Revolution. But as science began to reveal that everything is relative (and thereby possible but not definite or permanent), people once again turned to explore realms that transcend a merely physical plane.

When the Spirit Moves You

Just over 100 years ago, a new type of movement concerning the supernatural flourished. Called Spiritualism, it involved communication with spirits of the dead. The movement began in a small town near Rochester, New York, when a loud banging on the walls awakened a blacksmith and his two teenage daughters. As this disturbance continued over several weeks, neighbors were called in to witness the ruckus.

The Fox sisters, who had created elaborate methods to communicate with their spirit visitor, soon organized seances throughout the United States. These seances came complete with rapping sounds and levitating tables—the preferred mode of spirit communication. Many people claimed that they felt the hands of the spirits upon them. Theories abounded about what caused this rapping, including fraud, but the fact remains that the Foxes were never caught in the act of producing the raps and thumps.

Over the next 20 years the Spiritualism movement had 11 million people—30 percent of the American population—believing that life after death meant that the dead were able and willing to communicate with them. The movement became so rampant that 15 years after the first spirit visit to the Foxes, a bill was proposed in the U.S. Congress to organize a committee to investigate the Spiritualism phenomenon!

Unsolved Mystery

While Congress questioned Spiritualism's credibility, the President questioned its followers. A trance channel named Nettie Colburn, reported to be a medium for President Lincoln, apparently visited the White House many times between 1861 and 1863. Her guides told the president not to put off acting on the Emancipation Proclamation.

Spiritualism began to fade as technology and reason gained ground in the early 20th century. Meanwhile, curiosity about Spiritualism was growing in the scientific community. Several researchers in both the United States and Europe began to study psychic phenomena with experiments based on scientific principles. We'll talk more about that in Chapter 4.

A Very Special Case

Even while Spiritualism and the belief in unseen powers was fading in popularity, one man kept the faith in healing alive. Called "the Man of Miracles," Edgar Cayce (pronounced Casey) diagnosed tens of thousands of cases, over 30,000 of which he documented. Much of his healing ability seemed to focus on spinal disorders.

Cayce, raised in Kentucky, was not a trained doctor. In fact, he never completed his formal education. Yet he discovered his ability to offer a diagnosis and treatment while still quite young. At age 16 when he injured his back playing baseball, he went into a trance and told his mother what treatment to administer—which worked within 24 hours. His amazing abilities became more accessible to others after he underwent hypnotism with an expert named Al Layne, who continued to work with Cayce in future years. Throughout his life, he received information on healing while in a trance, yet could not recall it afterwards.

Eventually, a skeptical doctor named Wesley Ketchum underwent successful treatment by Cayce. His support brought Cayce to the attention of the American Society of Clinical Research in Boston. Their approval was followed by a *New York Times* article proclaiming Cayce's achievements as a healer. Despite his popularity with the public, the medical establishment continued its skepticism. Perhaps this was due to his often unorthodox treatment recommendations, including homeopathy, herbal medicines, electromagnetic therapy, and color therapy—many of which worked for his patients then and continue to gain credibility today.

The Year 2000 and Beyond

Now that pure logic has reached its pinnacle through computers, and technology has grown more controlled—and controlling—people are expressing a backlash against purely rational thinking. They are exploring new uses for age-old mental abilities, by using intuition for crime control, healing, and personal growth.

In the 21st century, technological expertise and eternal questing may finally combine to tap into sources of power that have not yet been realized. This combined effort is already underway in many research laboratories. Scientists are actively examining brain function during spiritual states, such as meditation, and dream stages, when the unconscious mind comes to the fore. Furthermore, scientists are studying communication between conscious minds, as well as between the mind and body. Curious? You'll learn more in Chapters 4 and 27.

As science reveals many longtime mysteries, people grow even more curious about the riddles they can't answer. And as computers take on many unimaginative tasks, scientists become free to delve more deeply into the aspects of the mind that defy logic and outsmart artificial intelligence. The mind provides us all with the greatest possible frontier for exploration. Beam me up, Scotty!

The Least You Need to Know

➤ It's human nature to seek an understanding of God and our future.

➤ Every religion and belief system has heroes who tap into their intuitive abilities, often as prophets or healers. The insights of many of these visionaries often lead to the creation of new religions.

➤ Throughout history, many psychic types have been greeted with suspicion or persecution.

➤ Exploration of all things psychic seems to ebb and flow, tending to be most popular during great explosions of ideas and information.

Chapter 3

What Can a Psychic Tell You?

In This Chapter

➤ What you can—and can't—expect to learn from an intuitive

➤ Different types of specialists, their fields and styles

➤ Finding the right psychic for you

➤ How to get a good reading—and know you've done it!

Psychics...without a doubt, they're probably one of the most misunderstood groups of professionals around. Indeed, most people expect to receive strange and unrealistic messages from intuitives (a.k.a. psychics)—everything from lottery numbers to the address of their next apartment.

This chapter gives you a pretty good idea of what you should and shouldn't expect from psychics. We'll ask you some specific questions that will help you get to know us—and yourself—a little better. After all, before you can get in touch with your own intuition, you have to start being honest with yourself. This chapter also shows you a little bit of what it's like to be on the other side of the crystal ball, so to speak—what it's like to work as a professional intuitive.

Reining in Your Expectations

I had a new client who said she needed guidance about a recent job loss. I agreed, knowing that I often get intuitive information about a person's aptitudes and career directions. But when the young woman arrived, she whipped out a steno pad as if to take dictation: She was ready for action!

After focusing for a few minutes, I talked to her about the employment problems she'd had in the past, as well as her general aptitude. I'd been speaking for only about five minutes when I realized that my client was actually tapping her foot—and with impatience! When I asked her if there was something else she'd rather I tune in to, she admitted that she didn't want to waste her half-hour on this kind of information. She just wanted the name and phone number of the next company she would work for so she could just go get the job and start work tomorrow!

To have this amount of faith in my intuitive powers was admirable, but far from realistic. (And what kind of impression would she make if she showed up at the corporate offices saying, "My psychic sent me!"?) Intuitives offer information that can guide you, but they exert no special control over your life or your future. They can help you to think and explore, but they can't make decisions for you. And would you really want them to?

Are Psychics Mind Readers?

The most common assumption people make is that intuitives can read minds. When I tell people that I'm a psychic, they often ask what I'm "getting" about them or offer me their palms. It often gets so uncomfortable, in fact, that I sometimes don't tell people what I do at all, but instead make a vague reference to working in counseling or education—the same sort of thing physicians might do to prevent folks from asking them to diagnose their symptoms at a party.

Unsolved Mystery

Back before satellites brought us the news live as it happens, people relied on word of mouth, which usually took several days to hear if something happened some distance away. In one case, Emmanuel Swedenborg, often considered the father of spiritualism, did not need to wait to hear unhappy news. On one Friday evening of September 1759, when he was in Germany, he reported receiving psychic knowledge of a fire occurring Sweden. He described minute details that later proved true—when early word of the disaster arrived from Sweden on Monday evening.

The thing is, it doesn't work that way—at least not for me. I'm not on all the time, and neither are my intuitive abilities. To give someone a reading, I must really concentrate on that person and that person alone. I then need to read and interpret the images that come to me, the emotions I feel, and the words I hear about the person or situation. This is not the case with all psychics: Some are awash with psychic impressions as soon as they enter a room—an exhausting way to live, I think!

From the ESP Files

A common assumption about psychics is that they look exotic and mysterious. Just so you know, I don't wear heavy makeup, lots of jewelry, a turban, or robes—and I don't carry a crystal ball! (In fact, I usually dress in business clothes at the office and look quite normal.) Many psychics, who usually call themselves "intuitive consultants," work in business settings. They help companies with hiring decisions, assist in predicting trends, or help the sales force increase their sales by "tuning into" the competition. They all look pretty normal. Not so different from you!

In fact, when I first started my practice, I found it much more difficult to maintain my emotional boundaries than I do now. That's partly because of the way information comes to me: I'm more of an empath (like the intuitives in the TV series *Star Trek*). I pick up information with my emotions and feelings. If someone came to me for insight into a difficult divorce, a job loss, or the death of a loved one, I experienced their pain, anxiety, and grief. By the end of the day, I felt like a limp dishrag! Even now, it's sometimes a challenge to balance my empathy with my objectivity about a person and the situation I'm reading.

Over time, though, I've learned to use what I call compassionate detachment. I still feel my clients' emotions and have compassion for them, but I don't completely take all of those powerful feelings into my soul. My mission really is to help my clients—and myself—to learn and grow from their experiences, as tough as those experiences may be.

But my way of doing things is hardly the only one in the psychic world. Indeed, you have much to choose from, depending on your needs, desires, and personal preferences.

Different Kinds of Readings

I used to drive myself crazy thinking I should be equally good at finding lost animals, diagnosing illnesses (medical intuition), or tuning into the spirit world to hear from the dearly departed. With time, though, I came to understand that each psychic has an area of specialty, or ways of receiving information that are stronger than other ways.

33

Intuition Hotline

Keep an open mind: Often, a reading provides information that appears to help you on one level but that applies to other levels as well. If you heed a message about tempering your anger with your boss, you might end up getting along better with your family and friends, too.

My specialty, for instance, is YOU. I do best when dealing with subjects more psychological or spiritual in nature: personal and spiritual growth, relationship issues, business trends, marketing ideas, and—don't laugh!—home inspection intuition, which I'll tell you about in the next section.

All About You

A common concern in our society is the sale or purchase of a new home; because of the expense and commitment involved, many people reach out for as much information as they can get, and sometimes I can help. Here's a real-life example of how I learn about individuals from information I gather about their homes—what I call my home-inspection intuition. A regular client (we'll call him Steve) was just finishing a session that largely concerned developing new strategies for working with particular clients in his advertising agency. Just before he left, he mentioned that he and his wife had made an offer on a house and wondered whether I could offer any insight.

I closed my eyes and immediately received a visual impression of a cracked chimney, a rotted supporting beam, and an area of rot on the north side of the roof beneath the gutter. When I mentioned all these things to him, he shook his head, saying that the inspector hadn't turned up any of these problems during his inspection. Steve called a few days later and reported that, because I'd had been so accurate about all the issues in his business, he'd decided he should get another home inspector to check out the information I'd given him about the house. Surprisingly (or not!), my impressions about the house were right on the money, and Steve saved thousands of dollars on its purchase price.

Of course, readings involve much more than psychic home inspection. An intuitive can describe to you what makes your boss tick, how you can motivate a certain employee, why your mother-in-law is upset with you, or how to instill more confidence in your teenager. Yet that same person couldn't help you find your lost cat or deliver a detailed message from your late Aunt Ethel. But that doesn't mean no one can!

If that's the type of information you're after, you can consult a different kind of psychic.

Mediums

The best-loved *medium* today is probably the psychic played by Whoopi Goldberg in the movie *Ghost*. Do you remember the scene where she discovers that she's actually talking with a ghost? She's more surprised—and terrified—than anybody!

Most mediums are better prepared than Whoopi was. They have come to terms with their special ability to communicate with spirits. Their purpose is to relay or interpret messages between the currently living and the spirits of those who have gone before. They may hear the spirit speaking to them, or receive symbolic, emotional, or visual impressions of information. We call psychics who work in this way mental mediums.

Another kind of psychic who brings information from the next world to this one is called a channeler. These psychics achieve a relaxed, sometimes semiconscious or unconscious state (also known as a trance) so that a spirit can channel its own voice through the medium's body. Also known as physical mediums, channelers may fall into a light trance in which they are fully aware of their surroundings and the information they receive, or a full trance in which they have no awareness or memory of the experience.

Beyond Words

Using the word "medium" to describe a spiritual medium actually makes a lot of sense. Just as "medium" means "a middle state or condition" in the physical sense, a spiritual **medium** is someone who serves as an instrument through which another personality can manifest itself.

Like psychics in any other area of expertise, each medium has his or her own unique way of tapping into psychic abilities and perceiving spirit messages. In most cases, only the medium perceives the spirits, but attendees at several seances in the first half of the 20th century (when the Spiritualist movement was hot!) reported seeing spirit materializations—and even took some photos to prove it! This is a far cry from most modern mediums, who often don't perform ritual seances or use any devices, such as crystal balls or Ouija boards. Although some still follow these traditions, others, such as James Van Praagh, author of the best-selling book *Talking to Heaven* (E.P. Dutton, 1997), channel messages through their minds.

Police Psychics

Although psychics aren't mind readers, they're often called upon to provide information at crime scenes or to help find missing people. After following every available lead to no avail, police departments frequently try to unearth clues from beyond the physical world. In fact, a June 1998 article in *Life* magazine reports that 37 percent of police departments in large cities report that they've consulted psychics. Although they don't usually solve the crime quickly by pointing out the actual criminal, police psychics often offer information that contributes to the case's overall information.

Like all other types of intuitives, police psychics do not all receive information in the same way. Some receive mental pictures that they may not even understand themselves but which help lead the police in the right direction. For example, one police psychic envisioned the route a murderer followed to dispose of a body. Although she was not familiar with the local signs or turns in the roads, local police were—and found the body within hours. Other police psychics pick up on emotions experienced by either a victim or a culprit, such as reacting with fear when being near a certain place which turns out to be the crime scene. Still others hear words, see images, or receive other messages that offer clues to the crime or criminal.

One of today's best-known police psychics is Dorothy Allison. One of her successful predictions led police to find a body encased in cement near Niagara Falls. She predicted that in a reservoir near the falls they would find a dismembered body encased in cement. The police did indeed discover a body, although it was not the one they were looking for.

Another police psychic received mental images of rectangles arranged in a certain format, which she sketched for police. Once the culprit was caught, the police discovered that the rectangles marked the exact placement of where the murderer had buried his victims beneath his house. The murderer was John Wayne Gacy, one of the most prolific serial killers of our time.

Medical Intuitives

Individuals who have unique insights into a person's body and his or her need for healing are referred to as medical intuitives. These people may either diagnose a condition or offer suggestions for a remedy. Medical intuitives do not consider themselves gods or miracle workers. Instead, they are conduits for passing along information about healing that comes from beyond themselves. Although not all medical intuitives heal specific conditions, some do. These intuitives are called psychic healers.

Mixed Messages

If you're experiencing unpleasant or painful symptoms, your first stop should be NOT to a psychic! Get yourself to a doctor for a diagnosis and treatment, then see a psychic if you need more information or guidance.

One of today's most popular medical intuitives is Caroline Myss, who can determine a person's physical weak spots by calling up what she refers to as their files and reading them. Once she makes her clients aware of the problem spot, she provides suggestions for how to eliminate the emotional or spiritual cause of the symptom. In other words, she offers ways that they can change their lives to improve their health. Although she no longer works with individual clients, she continues to help others learn the intricacies involved in being a medical intuitive.

Individual medical intuitives work in many different ways—they certainly are not all alike. Some may sense where a person has a problem by experiencing the symptom in the same spot in their own bodies. Other medical intuitives use touch to diagnose a condition, while others use the power of the mind from a distance. We will discuss psychic helping and healing practices in greater detail in Part 3.

What Is It *You* Want to Know?

Most readings address relationships, careers, spirituality, family, health, and life lesson issues. I find that the more specific my clients' questions are, the more helpful I can be. When I first began giving readings, I wasn't sure how specific I wanted my clients to be about what they wanted to know, mainly because I wanted to believe that, as a psychic, I should just *know* everything. I soon discovered, however, that I was spending a lot of time in the reading telling people things they already knew, like "You have a husband and two children—a boy and a girl," or "You hate your job as a sales manager." I could amuse and amaze people, but—apart from providing simple entertainment—my insights didn't really help to guide or inform my clients.

I now realize I'd rather spend time giving people assistance with the deeper issues in their lives—the ones they struggle with, the ones they need insight about. I find much more helpful when a client says, "I'm having difficulty in my job as a sales manager. I would like to get some insight into how to work more effectively with my boss, as well as what you get about what I could do if I left this company."

Intuition Hotline

Making up a list of questions is great, but remember the old saying: Everything in moderation. I once had a client who came in with three pages of single-spaced, typewritten questions—and the amount of time I could spend on each one!

I read for people from all walks of life and from all circumstances. I recently gave a reading for a senior executive from an international company that is headquartered in the Boston area. We discussed what I saw as market trends in his industry, how he could boost production at an overseas factory, and how he could deal with a difficult boss who has a very autocratic management style.

Another recent client was a 65-year-old retired secretary who was distraught over a new relationship with a man her family didn't approve of. We discussed the specifics of what I intuited about the woman's family's fears and how she could talk to them about her situation and resolve some of the conflict.

A phone reading from California brought my next client to me. I spoke with a man who was six months into an entrepreneurial consulting venture that was turning out to be wildly successful—and he needed advice on how to promote himself to various prospective clients. We spoke several times over the next few months, discussing some of the potentials and pitfalls that I saw with each individual or company that he approached, how he could differentiate his business from others like it, and his strengths and weaknesses as a consultant.

All of these topics, and many more, can be addressed by an intuitive. And all of these individuals gained insight into their concerns. They were able to look beyond the overwhelming emotions connected to the moment and take a longer look at others, the future, and its possibilities.

Getting a Good Reading

Getting a good reading depends on two things: the right psychic and the right attitude. In the following sections, we'll talk about both of these. Let's start with the attitude—yours.

Basically, if you're going to spend time, effort, and money to see a psychic, you want to gain all you can from the experience. In order to do that, remain as open as possible to what you hear—even when you hear something that you may not want to hear or do not understand. Often, you'll discover that the comments you heard can help you in situations that you may not have known were coming. An attitude of openness and trust creates an open atmosphere where information can flow more freely.

From the ESP Files

A reading can provide much more than pat answers about what you should do next. In fact, many people use a reading to help them get in better touch with their feelings, much like a therapist would do. For instance, I do the readings more from a spiritual or personal growth perspective. I generally look at cycles that are going on in your life and give you an overview of what I see to give you some perspective. I use my intuition to help you make choices in your life. Sometimes you might find I confirm things you already know. That probably means you have a good sense of intuition yourself. Many people find it comforting to have an objective outside observer read a situation for confirmation.

In my experience, there are three types of clients that can make my job really difficult. First are those people who come only to test me: They sit with their arms folded across their chests and their legs crossed in a body language that signals, "I know you can't read me so don't even try." It takes an enormous amount of energy to read for someone who does that.

Then there are those clients who are completely passive, expecting me to decide everything for them. Such people tend to be very fatalistic, in effect saying: "Just tell me my future. Just tell me what you see." Because people have free will, they need to understand that their attitudes and choices make a difference in the outcome of events. Life is more than reading a script of the future.

Other difficult clients are those who never take action, even after gaining insight into their situations. I had one client who came to see me every year over a five-year period—and nothing ever changed! She was in the same job she hated, the same relationship that wasn't going anywhere, and in the same stand-off in a legal dispute. Each time I talked about her options, I told her that most of us are afraid of change and risk. Yes, it feels uncomfortable and scary, but this woman needed to do something or her situation would likely remain the same. (This isn't necessarily the rosy picture you want to hear when you go to a psychic!) I gave her intuitive information about the various relationships in her life, and even referred her to several professionals who could assist her with her concerns and support her through the changes she wanted to make. After the fifth year, I finally told the woman, in a nice way, that she should probably save her money and just listen to the tapes of the previous sessions!

But that's the bad news. The good news is that you can have a terrific and helpful session with a psychic as long as you come prepared and bring your open mind along with you. Here are some tips that might help you:

> **Intuition Hotline**
>
> What's a healthy time to wait between visits to an intuitive? We recommend waiting a minimum of six months, if not a whole year. For one thing, there's not always a lot of new news. And then you need time to let the lessons from your previous visit settle in. Also, we want to encourage self-reliance, not total dependence on your psychic.

➤ *Evaluate your expectations*. Before you visit an intuitive, decide what you'd like to get out of the reading. Do you want information about relationships, past lives, health issues, career direction, life purpose or life lessons, or spiritual guidance?

➤ *Write it down*. The act of writing down the issues or questions that concern you will help both you and the intuitive you visit.

➤ *Prioritize*. Many psychics will start with an overview of what they feel or sense about you, including giving you information about your present life, general lessons you are here to learn, future trends, or mental patterns that you play out. After that, you'll want to ask your most important and pressing questions first.

➤ *Go light on the details*. When you ask the psychic your questions, give just enough background to clarify your concerns. Too much detail will overwhelm the psychic with your own take on the issue. At the same time, give them enough detail so that you won't have to spend much of your session listening to data you already know.

What I've learned from my years of experience is that I can't fix everyone. People often come to me with very complicated situations, family histories, and psychological dynamics. Some clients have an unrealistic expectation that my words and insight will solve all their issues and dilemmas for them. I know that in the space of the half-hour to hour that I spend with someone, I may be able only to shed some light on the direction out of the pain they are in. Sometimes I can help by simply listening and acknowledging the difficulty of their situation. Many times I wish I had a magic wand to wave or, better yet, a Rip Van Winkle pill that they could take and wake up when the situation was resolved!

What, No Crystal Ball?

No, a psychic doesn't have to touch you, or even be in the same room with you, to intuit things about you—although some prefer this method. For instance, I give readings by phone to people throughout the U.S. and even internationally—only about 30 percent of my clients visit my office in Newton, Massachusetts, which is a suburb of Boston. The office is located in an upscale section of town, on a street lined with gourmet restaurants, coffee shops, boutiques, and antique stores. I don't have a big sign with "Readings by Madame Lynn" or a neon hand out in front. The office building is filled with psychologists, physicians, and social workers. Clients take an elevator to the second floor and turn left to get to my office door, which simply says, "Lynn A. Robinson, M.Ed.". Then they can have a seat in the waiting room and listen to classical music until their appointment.

My office looks like a big living room. It's filled with books and plants, a sofa, and a cozy chair. It's quiet, located at the back of the building, and looks out onto a porch. In the summer, it's overflowing with pots of petunias, begonias, and impatiens. I usually invite clients to sit on the couch, ask if they'd like to tape the session, and then explain a little about what I do before proceeding.

I just use my intuition when giving readings. I don't read palms or cards, or use astrology charts, but instead receive information in mental pictures or symbols, feelings or emotions, and sometimes in words. I usually close my eyes when I give a reading because it helps me to concentrate on the information I receive.

Not all psychics work in this way or in this environment, of course, but you shouldn't be surprised if the surroundings you find yourself in at your first reading aren't quite as exotic as you had imagined!

From the ESP Files

Many psychics, like me, perform successful readings over the telephone or through the mail. People are often puzzled about how I can do readings over the phone, but the truth is that I don't find the phone sessions to be any more or less accurate than the readings in person in my office. I believe I tap a Universal Source of information and can access that at any place or any time.

How to Choose a Psychic

So many different kinds of psychics are available. You can go to a medium, a tea-leaf reader, a numerologist, or a tarot reader—to name just a few types of intuitives. We recommend asking friends for a reference to a reputable reader. But it's also possible that the reader who was terrific for your friends may not be great for you. Another route is to observe your prospective reader first. If he or she teaches or lectures, you might want to go to the reader's class. It's also possible that the reader may have written an article or book on his or her philosophy.

Intuition Hotline

The key thing to remember when choosing a psychic who's right for you is what you're looking for: Think about what you want to get from a reading. Many intuitives are excellent at what they do, but they may not all be right for you.

Following are some questions to consider asking the psychic when making an appointment for a reading. Keep in mind that the answers aren't right or wrong, they're a matter of personal choice. For that reason, you'd be wise to write down your own preferences for each answer before you talk to people, so that you can keep track of who most closely matches what you're looking for.

➤ Do you believe that the future can be accurately predicted? Do you feel you have any free will?

_____

_____

The preferred answer to this question depends on whether you want someone to simply spell out your future for you (which is a bit unrealistic), or offer insights on what you can do to take greater control of your fate.

➤ How long have you been in business? Do you practice on a full-time basis?

_____

_____

Full-time professional psychics show both confidence in and dedication to their work. If they've been around for awhile, they've probably got a loyal client base who knows they do good work.

➤ Do you have any specialties, such as career help, relationship predictions, and so on?_____

_____

This is entirely subjective on your part. Do you want insight into a certain area? If so, what is it and can this intuitive provide that?

41

➤ What tools do you use (astrology, tarot-card reading, palmistry, crystal-ball gazing)? _____

_____

This is another totally subjective question, based on what you, the client, feel comfortable with or desire.

➤ Do you want your client to bring questions? Do you prefer a certain kind of question? Is there a limit to the number of questions?

_____

_____

Because I believe in addressing the issues that the client feels are most important, I appreciate any psychic who takes this approach. Of course, I can only answer as many questions as time allows, and if I feel led to focus more on some than on others, I will follow my intuition. But it may help you sort out your priorities by listing all the questions that matter to you.

➤ Can you offer insight on specific people? Does it help if the client brings pictures of these people? Is an item of jewelry or some other object helpful?

_____

_____

Most intuitives are happy to have any additional connection to help inspire and spur their intuition forward. Most will encourage a client to bring along whatever helps evoke any impressions of that person.

➤ Can I take notes or tape record my session with you?

_____

_____

Confident and open intuitives try to avoid a sense of secrecy and mystery. They want to allow you an opportunity to review what you both learned in the session.

➤ May I bring a friend? _____

_____

Most intuitives would want to know whom you are inviting, and then probably say "Sure." But don't fault them if they don't give the green light. Some may prefer to focus on you and your mind, without the possibility of distraction or interference from someone else.

➤ How much do you charge? _____

_____

Although prices can vary tremendously, a one-hour session usually falls in the range of $50 to $150.

➤ What kind of training or background do you have?

_____

_____

Intuitives can develop their abilities in many ways. Although there are no set criteria, you might feel reassured to know that they studied at a certain school or with certain teachers. But the most important thing is that they are open and expressive about how they work. You want to know that they will be upfront with you, so that you can feel a sense of trust.

➤ Have you always been psychic? Do you consider it a gift or do you feel that anyone can develop it? _____

_____

This is another subjective question, which really depends on your personal preference. If you feel you'll trust someone more who's been in touch with his or her psychic side longer (since early life), then that's something you'll want to look for.

These questions aren't arranged in any special order and clearly you won't need to ask all of them. We suggest that you pick the four questions that hone in on the information that is most important to you. Then when you call people, ask the questions that matter most to you first. Over the years, I've had several people spend more than 30 minutes asking questions about my sessions and then cancel—or simply not show up for—their appointments.

If the psychic's answers don't match up with your preferences as you go down your list of questions, you won't need to take up any more of the psychic's time. Just thank him or her and bow out gracefully. In general, try to be respectful of the psychic's time when asking questions for an initial appointment.

Once you've made an appointment, treat it as you would any other commitment. If you can't make it for any reason, please call and let the reader know so he or she can schedule someone else in your place. (I've had a few folks who didn't call to cancel their appointment because they figured I'd "just know"! Then there was the guy who kept calling for an appointment but wouldn't leave his name and number because he wanted to see if I was good enough to intuit his number.)

About Psychic Hotlines...

Psychic hotlines have become extremely popular—and controversial—since business began booming in 1984. That's when the psychic hotline companies got carte blanche to use infomercials to advertise on late-night cable TV. Late-night viewers tend to have troubles that keep them up at night and are lonely enough to want someone to talk to—and who better than a psychic?

But not so fast. There are some problems. Although psychic hotline companies are not forced to publish their financial statements (a policy that releases them from public accountability), according to an unofficial survey published in February 1998's *Harper's Magazine,* 70.2 percent of phone-psychic users belong to minorities and 48.3 percent are very poor. Yet the price per minute is approximately $4.00.

Hotline psychics are often called into question for using an interrogation technique called *cold reading.* It relies on making insightful statements that could apply to anyone, and on repeating information that a person may have unconsciously alluded to in an earlier part of the conversation. For example, the statement "You handle stress by becoming angry at others" could apply to anyone, but when you hear it you think about an instance when you have done just that. Any response you make could later be brought up in a way that seems highly insightful. Yet there's no way of proving whether a hotline psychic is on the level or not. Most likely, they cover a broad spectrum: Some are highly intuitive and others are less so.

Beyond Words

Cold reading is an interrogation technique that police detectives often use. It works by making a seemingly insightful comment that could actually refer to just about anyone, and then observing how the interviewee responds.

Internet Psychics

You can find many people and organizations involved or interested in psychic phenomena on the World Wide Web. In the case of psychics, the Web site provides you with more information about them than a simple psychic hotline does. A Web site may include information on a psychic's background, a philosophical statement, and maybe even the psychic's picture. (Check out my Web site at **http://www.lynnrobinson.com**!)

Having background information is helpful, so use it to help you sort out what feels right to you. Some psychics may prefer to write back and forth to you and then e-mail you a reading; others may suggest using a chat room; still others, such as myself, prefer to schedule an appointment over the phone. I recommend the more direct type of personal contact, so you can sense your comfort level and rapport with the person who's doing the reading. If you'd like to take a peek at the wide variety of information on the Internet, you'll find a list of Web sites in Appendix C.

Trusting Your Own Intuition

No psychic is perfect. Giving a reading is often a very inexact science. It often involves interpreting different types of data, including feelings, impressions, and images. Remember that your own feelings can count as intuition, too. If you receive a reading that doesn't feel right to you, trust your own intuition and get a second opinion from another reader.

What to Watch Out For

Unfortunately there are some unscrupulous people in the psychic reading profession, just as there are in any discipline. For instance, one psychic who worked in the Boston area for many years had a particular scam that has been repeated with minor variations in other areas of the country. She definitely was a gifted psychic, but she used her ability to take advantage of others—until the police caught her in a sting operation.

I learned about this psychic through a client, a woman in her thirties who worked as a secretary at a local university. One day she showed up in my office for her appointment and promptly burst into tears, sobbing that she had lost all her money and she was still cursed.

After I helped to calm her, she explained that another psychic had given her some very accurate information about her family and thereby won her confidence. The psychic then gave her some information about her lack of relationships and told her that she was cursed and would never marry unless the curse was removed. Of course, the psychic had the key to removing the curse: Pay her ever-increasing amounts of money to speak with the spirits that could reverse the bad luck.

You may think this was just a naive young woman. But over the next several months I heard from several well-educated, intelligent men and women who had fallen victim to this scam. The psychic was an extremely charismatic woman who received between $500 and $10,000 from each of my clients alone.

Above all else, trust your own intuition! If you aren't comfortable with the person or the person's answers, don't make an appointment. Above all, stay away from anyone who promises to cure all the problems in your life with one easy reading.

The Courage to Change

Change can come in at least two forms: walking away from something old that no longer suits you, or walking toward something new that appeals to you. Both of these apply to meeting with a psychic.

If you have met with someone previously and you still don't feel comfortable and confident with that person, consider looking for someone who does make you feel at ease. On the other hand, if you've always felt anxious or afraid about seeking psychic guidance, perhaps you'll consider checking into it.

And if you're someone who has found a particular intuitive whom you feel comfortable with, then make an effort to follow his or her advice. An intuitive is guiding you along an ever-changing path, so don't be afraid to take your steps in a positive direction.

Whether you are new to the intuitive world or not, you probably will feel more confident with a professional's help in understanding where you're at and confirming where you're heading. A professional can encourage you to trust your own intuition, too. But if you're still in doubt or have the kind of mind that always asks "How?", then turn to Chapter 4, which explores what science is saying about being psychic.

The Least You Need to Know

➤ Many types of intuitives are available who can provide many types of information, which is accessed through various means.

➤ Get in touch with what you want to know—before you see a psychic.

➤ Not every psychic is ideal for every client. Don't hesitate to look around for one who's right for you.

➤ Trust your own gut reaction to what you're hearing.

Chapter 4

Mind Over Matter? What Science Has to Say About Being Psychic

---

In This Chapter

➤ Studying psi phenomena as a science

➤ Who's researching and how

➤ What we're learning about the brain

➤ How experiments are helping us

As we discussed in Chapter 2, artists, prophets, and philosophers have been talking about psychic phenomena for ages. Indeed, the sacred *Vedas*, written in India thousands of years ago, state that it is an illusion that individual minds are separate from each other, but that, in fact, our minds can cross boundaries of time and space to access information.

Today, science is finally catching on to—and trying to catch up with—these ideas. But whether or not the source of psi is something sacred (as the yogis would claim) does not currently concern scientists all that much. Rather, their focus is first on proving that psi exists, and then defining exactly what it is. In this chapter we take a look at how science regards psychic phenomena.

The Science of Parapsychology

When professional researchers of psychic phenomena refer to what they are studying, they use the word psi, which we introduced in Chapter 1. Psi is the first letter of the Greek word *psyche*, which refers to the breath, soul, and mind. (Hence, it is the root of the word psychology, the science of the mind.) The scientific study of psi includes areas such as telepathy, precognition, clairvoyance, and psychokinesis.

Modern science's early attempts to study psychic phenomena actually began over a century ago. In response to the highly popular Spiritualist movement, various scientists organized groups to investigate reports in that area. Numerous scholars founded the first, the Society for Psychical Research, in 1882 near Cambridge University in London. This organization focused on examining, and whenever possible debunking, the most famous mediums of the day. It established certain research standards and kept copious records.

Its counterpart, The American Society for Psychical Research, was formed in 1885 and remains America's longest standing organization with documented reports of psi research. It has an exhaustive library of information on almost every experiment conducted on just about every type of paranormal phenomena. You can visit them in New York City or look them up on the Web (**http://www.aspr.com**).

From the ESP Files

Among the world's earliest scientific researchers of psychic ability was Upton Sinclair, author of *The Jungle* (1906) and Pulitzer Prize winner for his conscientious critique of social ills. Yet in 1930 he broke from his usual realistic writing style to publish *Mental Radio,* a book that documented hundreds of experiments that confirmed his wife's ability to see telepathically. The investigative methods and their results were so impressive that Sinclair's friend, Albert Einstein, wrote the book's preface in praise of their scientific validity.

Who's Studying Psychic Phenomena?

A number of individuals and institutions are keeping their eyes on psi, and for a number of very different reasons. From the U.S. intelligence agency and the advertising industry to religious leaders and hardened skeptics, what's going on in the scientific world of psi is getting some widespread attention.

Scientists of all kinds, especially those poised on the cutting edge of physics, are wondering how psi reflects what they are finding in the areas of quantum mechanics, complexity theory, and chaos theory. Social and behavioral scientists are investigating how the implications of parapsychology (which we defined in Chapter 1) have affected the development of individual personalities as well as cultural identities and social progress. We'll talk more about that in the next chapter. For now, let's look at what's going in the "hard" sciences to study this invisible one.

The Parapsychology Research Labs

The first American research facility devoted to the scientific study of psychic phenomena was the Rhine Research Center, formed in 1927. Situated next to Duke University in Durham, North Carolina, it remains greatly respected for its high standards, state-of-the-art research techniques, and remarkable results. Now referred to as the Institute for Parapsychology, it is a leader among several highly reputable psi research science labs.

Following in the footsteps of the Rhine Research Center, several new psi research labs have formed over the past few decades. Here's a list of other leading psi research facilities:

Intuition Hotline

The Internet contains amazing amounts of information on state-of-the art research, much of it provided directly by the research facilities that are currently exploring it. For further details, check out the list of Web sites in Appendix C.

➤ Anomalous Cognition Program, University of Amsterdam, The Netherlands

➤ Cognitive Sciences Laboratory, Palo Alto, California

➤ Consciousness Research Laboratory, Palo Alto, California

➤ Consciousness Research Laboratory, University of Nevada, Las Vegas, Nevada

➤ Department of Psychology, University of Hertfordshire, U.K.

➤ Eotvos Lorand University of Budapest, Hungary

➤ Division of Psychiatry, University of Virginia

➤ Mind-Matter Unification Project, Cambridge University, U.K.

➤ Koestler Parapsychology Unit, University of Edinburgh, Scotland

➤ PEAR Laboratory, Princeton Engineering Anomalies Research Lab, Princeton University, Princeton, New Jersey

➤ Institut fuer Grenzgebiete der Psychologie und Psychohygiene, Freiburg i. Br., Germany

➤ SRI (Stanford Research Institute) International, Palo Alto, California

As you can see, the scientific search for psi knowledge is not limited to a specific region or country. Its study has spread worldwide.

The Physics of Psi

The verdict is still out on what's really going on in the world of physics in relation to psi. Of course, scientists always strive to create a theory to explain what makes everything tick, and how it all fits together. Some skeptics think this puzzle about how the universe works may never be solved, while some scientists believe psi may be able to help solve it.

One of the more popular theories today relies on principals of quantum mechanics. The idea is that all matter is made up of tiny bits of energy called quanta. These bits come together to form atoms that, in turn, vibrate at a unique level for every person and every thing. This level of energy vibration, called a frequency, is like a fingerprint that leaves its mark anywhere you've been. And anything that is part of you or closely associated with you (perhaps even your thoughts) also contains this mark. In that sense, your presence can spread much more broadly than your physical body.

From the ESP Files

One maverick scientist who is raising lots of uncomfortable questions about the implications of psi on traditional science and its experiments is Rupert Sheldrake. His recent book *Seven Experiments That Could Change the World: A Do-It-Yourself Guide to Revolutionary Science* (Riverhead, 1996) explains his viewpoints. You can even help him with some experiments when you visit his Web site (**http://www.sheldrake.org**).

Another modern theory, posed by the British physicist David Bohm, combines relativity and quantum theory. The idea is that everything is made of energy. In essence, everything *is* energy, which runs throughout the entire universe simultaneously. This energy contains a deep level of consciousness that interconnects between everything, including an implicate (unseen) and explicate (physical) order. Regardless of whether this material or energy is consciously aware of its presence, this underlying conscious energy permeates and affects everything all at once. It is able to manifest itself in both the material and energetic realms via a means of holographic movement.

This idea challenges the long-held belief that existence occurs on a linear plane, in only one place at only one point in time. Using mathematics, Bohm theorized that time and space do not really exist, except as constructs that people agree to. In essence, everyone and everything is part of a *nonlocal reality*, meaning that events that are far from one's awareness can, nevertheless, have an effect on them. This principal allows for the possibility that psi works by transcending the boundaries of space and time, creating the interconnectedness that yogis and philosophers described 5,000 years ago.

One thing that physicists and psi scientists agree on is that physics and psi probably follow the same set of natural laws. But at the moment, no one school of thought about physics is agreed upon as true beyond a doubt. In general, even most psi researchers aren't ready to come out proclaiming that psi has all the answers. Rather, they suggest that it may lead them to the best questions to ask in order to understand a wide variety of issues and concepts.

Beyond Words

Nonlocal reality refers to the scientific concept that events distant from someone can, nevertheless, affect them. The term "nonlocal mind" is often used in psi circles to refer to accessing a vast, eternal mind that transcends space and time.

What Inquiring Scientific Minds Want to Know

Psi is fascinating to study because it calls so many basic beliefs—scientific and otherwise—into question. Just when you think you're past the adolescent questioning phase and feel convinced that you've got it all figured out, some bizarre synchronicity or flash of insight occurs that gets you started thinking about the nature of reality all over again. Many scientists feel much the same way: Psi isn't possible to explain, but it's definitely out there. They can't just ignore it, so what can they do to make sense of it?

To start the search for what psi means, researchers tend to divide psychic phenomena into several primary areas, and then pick one on which to focus their study. Those primary areas for possible research include:

➤ *Telepathy*, involving the study of direct mind-to-mind communication

➤ *Precognition*, studying the transfer of information about future events that could not be inferred through any known way

➤ *Clairvoyance*, studying the transfer of information about faraway places without using the normal senses

Mixed Messages

Although psi scientists study a wide variety of topics that many scientists might consider "out there," they definitely have their standards. A word of advice: Don't ask a psi scientist to fill you in on certain phenomena, such as vampires, Bigfoot, or alien abductions. This can really offend their sensibilities.

➤ *Psychokinesis*, involving the study of mental interaction with material items, whether animate eor inanimate

➤ *Biological psychokinesis*, involving the study of mental interaction with living systems (for example, healing from a distance)

All of these areas call traditional knowledge and assumptions into question. For physicists, these subjects indicate that people may lack a basic understanding about space and time, and about how energy and information travel. For biologists, these subjects raise questions about what possible senses people may have that they aren't even aware of yet. Psychologists may work to reexamine the ways that the mind, memory, and perception work.

Predicting Outcomes

Psychic researchers use various ways to study psychic phenomena. Certain techniques have been tried and disregarded while others are continually developed in an effort to find foolproof ways of proving the existence of phenomena that defy the ordinary senses. Understandably, this is an especially difficult task in the paranormal arena, which comes from a realm beyond one's visible, concrete senses. Yet the scientific method is based on hard proof and criteria must meet high, objective standards.

In a way, this hard-proof approach creates a sort of catch-22: The phenomenon is unseen and almost impossible to measure, yet researchers relentlessly pursue the search for evidence and the perfect way to prove it. In doing so, they almost always fail and thus the validity of even the pursuit of this knowledge is questioned by skeptics.

If you're tempted to join the skeptics in questioning the results of psi studies and the scientists who conduct them, stop and consider some of the greatest scientists of all time. Galileo, Newton, and Einstein—all knew their ideas were valid even in the face of ridicule (and sometimes persecution) from their contemporaries.

Just as Einstein was able to prove his theories with mathematical formulas, modern psi researchers attempt to demonstrate the validity of their ideas through the use of statistics and probability. These methods offer a numerical basis for judging the likelihood of the results of their studies. This type of numerical evidence is necessary because not everyone is open to—or trusts—his or her ability to perceive psychic information as a personal affirmation of proof. This is especially true of skeptics, who have closed rather than open minds.

Even highly intuitive folks do not perceive psychic information on every level, but rather in the area of skill they have developed. For these reasons, psychic researchers strive to provide hard data via numbers, whenever possible.

From the ESP Files

Over a period of 16 years, a majority of Nobel prize-winning scientists acknowledged that they tapped into their intuition when making their discoveries. According to a 1995 article in *Intuition Magazine*, 82 of the 93 winners said they believed in scientific intuition, while only 11 denied, or expressed doubts about, its existence. But during the interviews, even the skeptical scientists recounted experiences that could only be described as intuitive.

Common Experiments to Test Psychic Ability

Over the years, researchers have focused on certain experiments to help them detect and prove psi. They continually revise the experiments in an effort to weed out any possibility of getting false or biased results. We'll describe three main types of experiments here:

➤ Ganzfeld experiments

➤ Remote viewing experiments

➤ Random number generator (RNG) experiments

One of the better known techniques used to research psychic ability in individuals is the *ganzfeld* experiment. During these experiments, the subject is placed in an environment without sound, light, or other sensory input. You often see pictures of people being prepared for ganzfeld sessions: Their eyes are covered with half-spheres, that look like (and sometimes are) Ping-Pong balls. They wear microphones that enable them to constantly describe their impressions to the tester, although they are not given any feedback.

Once all external distractions are eliminated (as much as possible), the subject is sent information through psychic means. Usually another person telepathically sends the subject a picture of an image, while the subject continues to describe any images or feelings he picks up. By describing the image he is receiving, the subject enables the sender to improve her technique of sending information. Once the sending part of the session is over, the subject is shown four images, including what the sender was looking at and sending. The subject chooses the image closest to what he saw in his mind. Success is measured on whether the subject chooses the correct image.

Beyond Words

Ganzfeld is a German word, meaning "whole field." It refers to opening the inner mind by shutting out external data, such as light and sound. When these distractions are eliminated, the mind is more susceptible to picking up psychic signals. A **random number generator** refers to a machine that creates random sequences of electronic bits that are equivalent to "heads" and "tails." The patterns respond to changes in thought patterns by becoming less random. **Remote viewing** is the ability to use the mind to see a person, place, or object that's located some distance away and beyond the physical range of sight. This ability also enables one to witness events at a remote site without using the known senses.

Pure chance predicts that the correct image will be chosen one time out of four times, creating a 25 percent success rate. But the actual results of over 700 ganzfeld sessions, carried out by various labs, averages about 34 percent. This may not sound like a high number to you, but remember that it's a strong percentage above chance. Clearly, some sort of telepathy occurs among some of the subjects and senders.

Scientists use *remote viewing experiments* to measure whether subjects can obtain information without having a sender transmit it. One remote viewing experiment begins with someone who is not involved with the experiment selecting a photograph from a group of hundreds and setting it aside in a separate location. No one involved in the test sees this photo, but the subject then tries to describe its contents. This process may be repeated several times with various subjects and different photos during the experiment. At the end, a group of judges match up the subjects' descriptions with the available photos, to see how closely they meet the mark.

This test has been tried thousands of times at different laboratories over the past two decades, and the cumulative results indicate that sensitive subjects can perceive remote images, even without a sender involved. To add an interesting twist, some researchers have used a version of this experiment to have subjects describe photos that would be selected in the future—and they were right on target!

Unsolved Mystery

Professional remote viewers receive frequent requests to explain what happened in the tunnel on the night of Princess Diana's death in 1997. Although no one's yet been able to explain what happened that night, the princess's astrologer did experience precognition of her death. In two separate dreams, Penny Thorton saw scenes from the accident, which went unheeded by Diana. Nevertheless, the astrologer published her insights in the 1995 book *With Love From Diana*, which shows that her dreams, although brief, were accurate.

Another popular research tool in recent years is the *random number generator (RNG)*. These machines combine electronic and computer technology to measure whether the mind has an effect over the machine. Basically, the machine spits out a series of zeroes and ones in random patterns. The experiment aims to measure whether psychokinesis (using the mind to affect matter) occurs.

In one type of RNG experiment, a subject focuses his or her thoughts on trying to change the random distribution of the numbers. This is sort of like a high-tech coin toss, where you expect to get a 50/50 ratio of heads and tails. But using a completely computerized testing system eliminates the possibility that someone could somehow cheat by throwing the dice in a controlled way. This test has been repeated over three decades by more than 60 scientists, and has shown small but consistent results: The human mind can definitely change otherwise random systems.

Statistics and Psychic Ability

All of these experiments show that psi scientists are making progress in their research. For years, skeptics have resisted this notion by tearing apart individual experiments and claiming that this or that lab or researcher had biased results. Specifically, if one lab's results differed from another's, all the results were cast into doubt. However, one must understand the nature of experiments before criticizing too harshly.

In his influential book on the state of psi research, *The Conscious Universe* (Harper SanFrancisco, 1997), Dean Radin, Ph.D., defends the way that psi experiments are measured and compared to other sciences. He explains that two versions of the same experiment seldom come up with the same results. And this is true of the hard sciences as well as soft sciences. (It seems that the experiments school teachers have students follow from textbooks are among the few that have consistent results—and they don't always work either!) Furthermore, the same experiment that is performed with any variation, such as the number of subjects tested, may be evaluated according to a separate set of odds.

According to Radin and other scientists across many disciplines, the likelihood that every experiment may have somewhat different results makes repeated trials—by different people in varied places—especially important. It is the overall, combined results of many experiments that indicate what's really going on. The art of looking at these combined results is called *meta-analysis*, and it provides the key to putting soft sciences, such as psi, on the same turf as hard sciences. It seems the two types of sciences, when compared through meta-analysis, are subject to the same statistical laws for measuring effects that are greater

Beyond Words

Meta-analysis can be defined as the analysis of analyses, or the analysis of a group of studies about the same subject. It combines the results of similar experiments performed by various researchers to get an overview of the outcome.

than random chance. This system is showing that psi research has consistently been accurate over its decades of testing. As with any field of science, certain psi experiments show robust results, while others appear less significant.

Where Do We Fit In?

Okay, so scientists are finally proving what most people already know: The mind can reach beyond its physical boundaries. But what does that mean for those who aren't focused on science?

Think about the possible uses for psi. By seeing across space and time, historians could discover what really happened in the past, rescue missions could locate accident victims, and explorers could dig up lost treasures.

Using the mind to control living matter can be invaluable in the areas of both conventional medicine and spiritual healing. The study of the mind-body connection has shown people how to use their minds to help overcome cancer and chronic illnesses, conditions that traditional medicine remains unable to treat. We'll discuss this phenomenon more in Chapter 10.

By using the mind to control matter, people could invent more responsive machines and even robots that could act on their wishes. Of course, an obvious choice for a business based in psi is the casino industry—and it *has* researched its potential. (You can bet we'll be talking more about that in the next chapter!)

Of course, all of these scenarios are fantasies. A few of them may be close to happening, and others probably never will. And would we really want them to? There's plenty we can do with psi on a personal level. Indeed, using your thoughts to empathize with others and to create order in your own environment is perhaps a much more appropriate—and attainable—dream.

The Least You Need to Know

➤ Many top-notch, international academic institutions have psi labs.

➤ The same natural laws that apply to physics and other hard sciences also apply to psi.

➤ Brain research shows specific places and devices where intuition operates.

➤ When psi and hard science research are compared on equal terms, psi's results are as good as the best of 'em.

Psychology and Psychic Phenomena

The obvious place to look for information about intuition is the source of all thinking: the mind. Sounds simple enough—until you start asking what "mind" really means. Is it simply the brain, or does it include the thoughts that make up, and possibly transcend, the actual physical boundaries of the brain?

This question has inspired philosophers and spiritual seekers for millennia. Now it's enticing medical specialists, psychiatrists, psychologists, and psi scientists as well. These experts have begun studying all aspects of what is called the mind, including the brain, the subconscious and unconscious minds, and the joining of many people's minds together. In this chapter, we'll touch on various theories about psi's role in how the mind works.

When Great Minds Think Alike

We'll start by looking at how science is exploring ways that everyone is psychic even when they are not even aware of it. In this sense, people are not only all psychic, but all psychic *together*. The thought that all people are part of a single mind is not a new one, but finding evidence for this is a new area of focus. And finding evidence that shared thoughts can influence events on a worldwide scale is proving particularly challenging—with fascinating results!

From the ESP Files

A classic example of people putting their heads together comes from the New Testament. Remember the passage from *Matthew* when Jesus says, "For where two or three are gathered in my name, there I am in the midst of them"? This doesn't mean that a ghost will visit the people who are praying. Rather, it suggests that their concentrated efforts can tap into a greater power. Some people might consider this power telepathy, or even PK, enabling people to focus their thoughts in order to increase their level of spiritual consciousness and perhaps even their ability to affect the world. After all, isn't that what prayer does? Of course, other people might see calling prayer "psychic" as a heretical point of view...

Beyond Words

Psychoanalysis is a systematic approach for investigating the unconscious as a means of mental and emotional healing.

Carl Jung and the Collective Unconsciousness

Perhaps the first scientist to suggest that everyone's unconscious mind shares certain thoughts or images was Carl Gustav Jung. Born in 1875, Jung received his medical degree in 1900, then moved to Zurich to begin a career in psychiatry. A contemporary and a colleague of Sigmund Freud, Jung soon branched off and created his own school of *psychoanalysis,* one that had a much less traditional way of looking at the world and the mind.

Indeed, Freud and Jung held quite different views of the unconscious mind. While Freud, the father of psychoanalysis, taught that the unconscious expresses deeply buried personal experiences (based primarily on sexual urges), Jung proposed that the unconscious mind expresses a much deeper awareness that is shared by people with similar cultural traditions (and perhaps based on inherited genes). To reach these deeper levels, Freud practiced very personal psychoanalysis, while Jung studied the symbolism in dreams, art, myths, and language across many cultures and religions—and among more than 10,000 patients! Jung called this shared level of common symbols and knowledge *the collective unconscious*. As proof that certain symbols and thoughts belonged to a single source that each individual's mind can tap into, he referred to the shared symbols that keep cropping up in many cultures and languages, even when they had great physical distance between them. He called these symbols *archetypes*, and assigned some of them associations with certain meanings.

Here is a list of commonly recognized archetypes and what they represent. Recognize any from your own dreams?

➤ The Spirit—the opposite of matter; infinity

➤ The Wise Old Man—a primal source of growth and vitality

➤ The Trickster—the antihero; a mix of the animal and divine

➤ The Shadow—the primitive, instinctive side of ourselves

➤ The Divine Child—the true self; our total being

➤ The Great Mother—feminine mystery and power in its many forms

Beyond Words

The **collective unconscious** is a level of the mind believed by Jung to be inherited and to contain a reservoir of ideas, symbols, and archetypes that form the world's myths and belief systems. **Archetypes** are the common themes that arise from the collective unconscious and repeatedly appear as symbols in myths and dreams.

While Jung had loyal followers in his day, he faced constant criticism from the powerful forces in the Freud camp. Ironically, the past century has brought increasing skepticism of Freud's extreme devotion to the all-powerful sexual impulse, while many psychologists, anthropologists, and philosophers are exploring Jung's ideas with ever-growing curiosity and acceptance.

Field Consciousness Effects

Although the scientific world as a whole has changed vastly since Jung's early days, these changes largely support his theories. The scientific study of physics, for instance, has undergone a revolution from Newton's classical view of nature as fixed to Einstein's view that time and space are relative. Modern physics supports the idea that everything exists as waves, rather than as specific points in time and space. Another way of referring to these waves is "fields," which include time, space, and gravity.

Recently, certain scientists suggest that consciousness itself is a field. Like gravity, the field of consciousness has certain properties, including a force comparable to that of gravity. It could be that this force is similar to Jung's idea of the collective unconscious.

Research in this area of *field consciousness* is new, but ongoing. Psi scientists are researching the theory that when many minds focus on a single topic, they result in a measurable effect. Experiments have focused on showing that normally random results, and even physical effects, can change when many people focus their minds on a single event. As we discussed briefly in Chapter 4, researchers in this area have been able to measure results by the use of random-number generators (RNGs), computerized machines that indicate a definite change from randomness to order during moments of intense mental focus by an individual, or many, minds. This occurs when the machines, which normally spew out ones and zeroes in random patterns, suddenly start to spit out a higher ratio of a single number—seemingly in response to concentrated thoughts and focus of nearby minds.

Beyond Words

Field consciousness expresses the idea that mental awareness comes from a source other than our internal physical cells contained in our brains. Just as modern physics supports the concept that matter and time exist as fields, consciousness may also fit into this category.

In recent years, many labs across the world have been studying the phenomena of group mental focus. Dean Radin, Ph.D., as Director of the Consciousness Research Laboratory at the University of Nevada, Las Vegas, has both conducted studies and gathered data from many other studies to show the effects of field consciousness. Events that have been measured vary in their topic of focus, location, and the numbers of people involved, but they show surprising evidence that *something* occurs when many individuals simultaneously focus on the same event. The point of these machines and the experiments is not to indicate a specific outcome, but a change in randomness. In short, they show that thought alone, without any physical action affecting it, can create order out of chaos.

RNGs have been used to measure the public's focused attention during such well-known events as the Academy Awards in 1995 and 1996, the 1996 Olympics opening ceremonies, Superbowl XXX, and the O.J. Simpson verdict—all of which had millions of people viewing and focusing. During these events, random number generators were placed in various locations, such as near TV sets with different-sized groups of people watching them. The RNGs measured significantly high levels of order, meaning that the focusing of so many minds on a single event created an enormous amount of synchronization, or order, in the machines that were designed to maintain randomness.

This information about coordinated thoughts and consciousness may increasingly be put to use by advertisers, governmental leaders, and even casino owners. The potential power of this unity of thought adds a scientific basis to social activists' hopeful efforts to create change by raising consciousness. It also suggests a way that prayer may work to provide a powerful source of healing.

Gaia of the Mind

One theory that seems to support the idea that many minds are connected is the Gaia theory. The "Gaia Hypothesis," proposed by James Lovelock in the 1940s, proposed that the earth is actually its own entity, an enormous biological system that creates a single living organism. This idea infers that the earth has one shared mind that works together, even without people being aware of it. You can compare it to a beehive. Thousands of tiny insects all work together to form a common world of their own, even without knowing what their sisters on the other side of the hive are doing—much less what you, me, or the leader of China are up to. In a way, many of us humans are like that.

According to the principles of evolution, the earth as a living organism would do whatever is necessary to ensure its own survival. The idea that it "consciously" controls everyone's thoughts sounds far-fetched. However, people's minds may respond to the earth's needs in a unified way, just as the human body's nervous system may automatically respond to an emergency (or any stimulus) without requiring the brain's conscious thought. In effect, human minds may respond in certain ways, following trends or thought patterns, without making a fully conscious decision to do so. And this could be called psychic ability or intuition.

Your Brain: Psychic Central

Where does psi live? What is it, in a physical sense? It's possible that psi is another aspect of brain function, an additional perceptive sense that is somehow based in your physical brains. It's also possible that psi is a bridge that connects your physical brain to a nonlocal mind.

Psychology, in particular, can gain many new inroads through the continued study of psi. Because psychic ability is associated with the mind, the brain is a logical place to start studying what may be going on. And because psychology and neuroscience are relatively new sciences, every day scientists are learning more about how they interconnect.

The Split-Brain Theories (Ouch!)

In recent decades, one of the most profound discoveries in medicine won the Nobel Prize in 1981 for Roger Sperry. This brain researcher went beyond the conventional wisdom that the left hemisphere of the *neocortex*, responsible for reason and analytical thinking, reigned supreme in the brain. He revealed that the right hemisphere makes an equally important contribution, providing the power of intuition, as well as imagination, artistic creativity, and free association.

Beyond Words

The **neocortex** is the uppermost region of the brain, responsible for rational and higher thought.

A more recent theory, put forth by Paul Maclean, a brain researcher at the National Institutes of Health, is that the brain can be divided into three sections, each with a unique function, starting from the bottom up. He found that the basic brain, at the bottom, is the oldest (in terms of evolution) section of our brain, and is associated with basic animal instincts such as the fight-or-flight reflex. The second section is the limbic system, which is responsible for feelings and emotional attachments. Above that is the neocortex, the newest section of the brain, which Maclean and others credit with higher thought.

Regardless of which brain section you rely on at any particular time, each one learns information and adapts to it in a different way. Opinions differ on what part of the brain houses the intuitive abilities. Some people say that they are situated in the basic brain, which is linked with instinctual responses. Recent research suggests that intuition, with its ability to see in visual, symbolic images, is positioned in the neocortex, the higher, and more highly developed, area of the brain.

The human brain and central nervous system is as complex as any communication system in creation. It's no wonder that some scientists believe that our hidden powers of psychic ability lie within this labrynth.

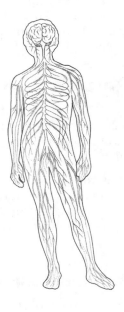

So, the brain's ability to connect to intuitive information seems to be housed in its upper-right corner. If only it were that easy to just knock on our noggins and get an answer to any question! But understanding how the brain is designed provides us with insight into how the transfer of information works.

An important theory about left and right brain hemispheres acknowledges that the interaction between the two creates the ideal mental state. To use our brain's abilities to their fullest, input from both hemispheres should be balanced to create an equal input of logical and intuitive thinking.

From the ESP Files

The connection between the left and right sides of our brains may explain one of the longest standing puzzles of humankind: why men and women seem to think differently. Using gross generalizations, women tend to be strong at reading emotions and communicating, while men tend to be more effective in compartmentalized, task-oriented areas. Researchers have found physical evidence that suggests why: The two halves of the female brain are more closely connected than those of males. Maybe that's why women have such a reputation for their accurate female intuition.

While the left brain is hard at work analyzing the facts, the right brain should be busy interpreting the data. Although we tend to focus on the rational functions carried out by our left brains, we can help to increase our right brain's input by participating in creative activities and meditation. This may explain why meditation helps us access our intuition…or maybe there's more to it than that.

Surfing the (Brain) Waves

In addition to believing that all the various brain parts should come together to create optimal brain function, some scientists point out the importance of *brainwaves* working together.

Beyond Words

Our brains constantly produce and give off electrical impulses. These currents of electricity are called **brainwaves**.

Our brains give off four types of brainwaves, called beta, alpha, theta, and delta. To make it simple (and highly oversimplified), here's a table to show you what they do.

Name of Brainwave	Where It Occurs Most	What It Does
Beta	Normal waking states	Maintains rational, concrete thinking
Alpha	Daydreams, fantasies, and visualization	Bridge to subconscious; improves memory and creative insight
Theta	Subconscious; dreaming sleep	Repository of creativity, inspiration, and memory
Delta	Unconscious mind; deep sleep	Gives restorative sleep; may access intuition and empathy

Although this looks fairly simple, our brains are always at various stages of combining these waves. For example, our theta waves are said to be the strongest—and the most helpful brainwaves—during meditation, and yet the process benefits us even more when they interact with the delta waves. Some scientists suggest that this blending of various brainwaves actually creates a brand new type of brainwave. Some followers of Eastern philosophies propose that the awakened mind, wherein a person is more fully aware of their spiritual existence, combines all four forms of brainwaves at once.

What Psychiatry and Psychology Have to Say About Psi

Intuition Hotline

For tips and exercises on easy ways to put your brainwaves to work for you, check out Anna Wise's book, *The High-Performance Mind* (Tarcher, 1995).

Until recent decades, many psychologists and psychiatrists viewed psi with skepticism and confusion. They were having a hard enough time trying to figure out the nature of creativity, consciousness, perception, memory, and learning. Were they supposed to be responsible for explaining psychic phenomena, too?

In recent years, the field has become more open to the idea that a connection may exist between psi and psychology. Some experts even suggest that psi be treated as any other aspect of the mind, such as consciousness or learning. Indeed, understanding psi may help explain how we perceive and process information on all levels.

Are You Psychic—or Crazy?

Why is it that when a child has an imaginary friend, she's called cute, but when an adult has one, she's called crazy? One of the world's most famous experts on mental health had regular conversations with his imaginary friend—as an adult. His name? Carl Jung, who readily revealed that his imaginary friend was named Philemon.

In some individuals, this ability to communicate with beings beyond their visible world extends beyond the imagination into the spirit realm. Mediums can do this, as do people who communicate with spirit guides or angels. And who are we to say that these unseen beings aren't real? Indeed, through the ages, mystics and prophets have been persecuted for claiming to see into realms beyond the invisible. Over the centuries, many people who talked about paranormal phenomena were imprisoned for being insane.

So how can we judge when someone's psychic— or just plain crazy? A common symptom of *pathological* and *schizophrenic* people is their inability to combine their impressions into a healthy, whole image of reality. For example, a person with multiple personalities perceives and reflects the existence of only one character at a time. They do not recall that they have another personality aside from the one they're experiencing. Yet a healthy person has a solid center that realizes the difference between the material and unseen worlds.

A similar situation occurs with schizophrenics who hear voices: They cannot distinguish what they hear in their mind from the facts they see in the material world around them. Interestingly, recent research by Robert Freedman at the University of California showed that schizophrenia is attributed to a genetic brain malfunction. The experiment, using a tonal sound given twice in quick succession, found that normal people block out the second tone, while schizophrenics hear it clearly. This connection between a physical malfunction and a mental one may be another hallmark that separates mental illness from a healthy imagination or highly tuned intuition.

Mixed Messages

The process of becoming open and aware to psychic power is called spiritual emergence. It can become overwhelming for some people, who may experience both emotional and physical disturbances, a state referred to as a spiritual emergency. Sometimes this disturbance may mimic a psychiatric emergency. An organization called Spiritual Emergence Network, founded by Christina Grof in 1980, is available to provide education and referrals to people with concerns about this issue. You can reach them at (415) 648-2610.

Beyond Words

Pathological refers to a deviation from a healthy, normal condition. **Schizophrenic** refers to a mental disease marked by withdrawn, bizarre, and delusional behavior.

Mitchell B. Liester, a psychiatrist in Colorado Springs, Colorado, researched the similarities and differences between pathological and psychic people. One distinction he makes is that people with pathological conditions are subject to a disintegration of their personality, while people with psychic experiences transcend their personality.

Psychological Research

Many of the same types of experiments used to come up with data for psi as a hard science are also used in psychological research. Two examples are the ganzfeld and remote-viewing experimental techniques described in Chapter 4. Often the physical and social sciences are exploring the same phenomena, just from slightly different angles.

In addition to studying the processes involved in extrasensory perception, psychological studies also may be directed at evaluating the tests themselves. Psi researchers tend to be extremely conscientious (perhaps because they often face unfounded accusations of fraud). They constantly double-check their results by repeating the tests, a process referred to as replication. Averaging and analyzing many experiments creates a more accurate view of what the results really mean. And testing the test also allows researchers in the area of psychology to question not only how mental information is learned and transferred, but also how the testers are perceiving that transfer.

Confused yet? Well, maybe we can shed some light by using a few examples of some studies going on today. A popular experiment pertains to the feeling of being stared at. A "starer" and "staree" are separated, while the starer can use a closed circuit video system to see the staree, whose nervous system is being monitored. Researchers have detected an decrease or increase in the staree's nervous system activity, corresponding to when the starer was told to direct calm or aggressive thoughts, respectively, toward the staree. Another twist on this experiment has the starer look at the staree with no intention, which also shows a change in the nervous system—but in a different way. Introverts showed a much higher level of stress when stared at than did extroverts!

Researchers at the University of Hertfordshire in Hatfield, England, are looking into the psychology of deception. Using written tests, polygraph machines, and observation, they're exploring how deceit is used in business and criminal fraud, everyday lying, military deception, scientific fraud, conjuring, psychic fraud, and self-deception. By looking at the results, the researchers analyze behavior and also consider how the mind handles information. They also use the results to show psi scientists how to use more accurate psi testing methods, and how to work with people who report psychic experiences.

These same researchers are also examining the psychology of luck. The experiments study how people look at and believe in luck, and the role that their beliefs play in a great variety of events and in their self-perception. Such studies raise questions about how our thoughts shape our self-image, as well as if we might be able to use our minds to overcome both random events and matter. Just think: You'd have to be a pretty powerful psychic to have your directed thoughts win out over several million other people who are also fervently wishing and willing to win their state lottery!

Unsolved Mystery

One morning last summer I awoke from a dream with a group of six numbers repeating themselves in my mind. I asked my husband if he knew how many numbers were on the state lottery tickets. He answered that there were six. I couldn't think of any rational reason I was hearing repeating numbers, so I asked him to play them in that day's lottery game. I remembered to ask him about it a couple days later. He confessed that he had forgotten to play on the day I had had the dream. Instead, he played them the day after. When we looked at the newspaper to determine the lottery winners, we had the right numbers but on the wrong day. If he had played it on the day the numbers came to me, we would have won $5 million dollars. (P.S. I stay married to him anyway!)

Psychic Gambling—It's a Crapshoot!

So, if intuitive types can use their minds to control matter, why aren't they striking it rich at the game tables? Or creating a monopoly on the state lottery?

While some statisticians state that it actually *is* possible to beat the odds at the gambling tables through psychic finesse, maintaining that level of finessing is where it gets sticky.

Casinos are carefully designed to be distracting, using both sound and visual effects to keep you on your toes. Such influences affect the players' ability to concentrate on the game, as well as their ability to remain levelheaded. You see, a big part of actually taking home some winnings is knowing when to go home—that is, to quit when you're ahead. If a highly trained intuitive could consistently concentrate—and sense when to quit—he or she might be able to make a mint. But it's hard to make a career of that because intuitives are, like the rest of us, human, with human desires and urges!

So far, we have no documented reports of casinos hiring psychics to watch from afar and affect the outcome. And the odds of that happening are unlikely, because most people who get in touch with their psychic senses tend to become focused on more pure pursuits than self-centered objectives like gambling. Furthermore, specific numbers, including lottery numbers, are generally not the type of information that your intuition delivers in a straightforward manner (although it can sometimes happen).

From the ESP Files

Do you remember the character played by Dustin Hoffman in *The Rainman?* Although he had trouble adapting to the outside world, he was brilliant with numbers. He was also good at focusing on only one thing at a time—and he won big in Las Vegas! Some psi psychologists suggest that a genius of this sort, referred to as a savant, actually has ESP that is highly developed in one area. For the character Dustin played, it was numbers.

Well, now that you know where scientific study stands, it's time to try a few experiments of your own. The next part of the book is designed to help you get in touch with your own abilities to perceive intuition. Once you get a sense of that, you'll see how your own experience can transcend all of the experiments that science can offer.

The Least You Need to Know

➤ Scientists are putting together theories on the interconnectedness of all minds.

➤ Physical evidence in the brain indicates that certain areas and states are most accessible to intuition.

➤ Psi may actually be a type of mental process or state, such as memory, learning, or consciousness.

➤ Traditionally skeptical, more psychologists are beginning to research connections between psi and awareness.

Part 2
Building Your Psychic Awareness

Hearing about someone with highly developed psychic senses is pretty fascinating. But sometimes you wonder how that person got from where you are now to where he or she is today. Part 2 tells you how to start developing your own psychic abilities.

A major hint is: Be aware. Your intuition is sending you information all the time—you just need to start noticing it. First, we'll help you figure out what type of abilities you're inclined to have. Then we'll help you ascertain what level your skills are at right now. We'll show you how to open up and tune in to greater reception to your psychic equipment.

Chapter 6

How Do You Receive Psychic Information?

In This Chapter

➤ Different ways of receiving psychic information

➤ Exploring your compatibility with each psychic mode

➤ Discovering which mode works best for you

An important first step to building your intuition is paying attention to how you as an individual best receive information. We each have a dominant mode or combination of ways to receive psychic impressions, and understanding what works for you is a key to opening up your intuitive insight.

If you're a beginner, think of the ways that you normally receive information through the five senses. If you usually find yourself thinking in images, your psychic skills probably work along the same lines. The same principle applies for those of you with a keen sense of hearing, and likewise for physical touch and even smell. Even taste can make an appearance on the psychic scene.

This chapter will get you to start focusing on where your special abilities lie. Becoming aware of your natural inclinations will help you tap into an easy psychic source for yourself. If you want to explore more than one pathway, that's fine, too. You certainly should take some time, at some point, to follow your curiosity. But starting with the easiest way first is more direct, and may help you get to any others faster in the long run.

Clairvoyance: Your Inner Vision

Clairvoyance comes from the French, meaning "clear seeing." It refers to the power to see an event or image that appears in the past, present, or future. This type of sight usually does not occur with your physical eyes, but instead with your inner eye.

Beyond Words

Clairvoyance, from the French meaning "clear seeing," is the ability to perceive things that cannot be seen with the physical eye. It also refers to keen perception and insight.

For example, I was preparing to give a reading to a new client named Esther. When I closed my eyes, an image of a huge umbrella immediately popped into my mind. I saw it quite distinctly. In my mind's eye, the umbrella stood in the corner of the room, tipping over. While I often receive symbolic intuitive messages, I couldn't make any sense whatsoever of this falling umbrella. Not knowing what else to say or do, I simply told Esther what I'd seen.

To my surprise, Esther shrieked, "Oh no! That can't happen!" She then explained that she owned an event management business and intended to put on a huge promotional function—held under a tent—for her largest client the following week. All of the buffet tables were to be decorated with umbrellas! "They can't fall over. It would ruin everything!" explained Esther.

From the ESP Files

Among the various types of psychic vision is auric sight, which pertains to the ability to see auras. We call the energy emoted by every object, living and otherwise, an *aura*, and each aura has a different color and different characteristics. Certain people have the ability to see these auras, which we'll talk more about in Chapter 11.

Because I don't believe that everything is predestined, I suggested that Esther tie down the umbrellas securely and, while she was at it, secure the tent itself with extra rope and fasteners. Esther called a week later to say she'd arrived at the event early in the morning and "battened down her hatches," so to speak. When she returned a few hours later, all of the other tents had blown over in a sudden windstorm. Esther's was the only one left standing!

Sometimes the images received through clairvoyance are literal images, such as the umbrella blowing over. Oddly enough, this image was so literal that only Esther herself could understand it. On the other hand, many images are symbolic, and need to be interpreted by the person who personally receives them. Whether they are literal or symbolic images, they usually do not appear outside the intuitive's own mind or inner eye.

Many people think of the term "inner eye" as a figure of speech, but the yogic tradition also uses the term "third eye." According to the Eastern tradition of *chakras*, wherein certain areas of the body influence energy flow in specific aspects of our lives, the third eye is the seat of clairvoyance. Located in the center of the forehead, it is the screen that receives visualizations, whether in the form of visions or imagery. Although a person may not feel that a picture literally appears in his or her third eye, the concept provides a slightly more concrete way of thinking about this ability.

When the process of clear seeing occurs inside one's mind, it's called subjective clairvoyance. But clairvoyance may reach beyond sheer visualization as well. In some instances, intuitives report seeing physical manifestations, which they call objective clairvoyance. (If you aren't up for any visits from unexpected guests, never fear. People who have developed this ability are rare and you probably aren't one of them.)

> **Beyond Words**
>
> **Chakras** are centers of energy located between the base of the spinal column and the top of the head. To healers or others who can see or feel the chakras, they are vortices or funnels of energy. They serve as a place of interconnection between the body and the spirit.

Clairaudience: Your Inner Voice

The translation for *clairaudience* is "clear hearing." *Webster's New World Dictionary* defines clairaudience as "the act or the power of hearing something not present to the ear but regarded as having objective reality." Clairaudience can include hearing sounds, such as music or ringing, as well as voices. Like clairvoyance, clairaudience can be divided into two types, objective clairaudience, which occurs in the real world so that anyone can hear it, and subjective clairaudience, which occurs only in one's mind.

When people hear voices, they can get confused about this form of intuitive information because it often sounds like their own, inner voice (which is sometimes referred to as self talk). Through practice, you can discern whether you're hearing psychic information, self talk, simple wishful

> **Beyond Words**
>
> **Clairaudience** is the ability to hear sounds that aren't accessible to the physical ear but seem to have objective reality.

thinking, or an expression of something you're afraid may happen. One helpful hint for distinguishing the source is that, generally, intuitive impressions come through to you in a very kind, loving, and helpful manner—something your self talk often doesn't do.

Mixed Messages

Certain types of schizophrenics also report hearing voices, and if you start hearing voices out of the blue, your first stop should be your doctor's office. We also recommend that you make sure you're truly hearing psychic information before acting on your premonitions. And whatever you do, don't try anything dangerous because you think it's based on your intuition!

I once experienced this form of intuition while giving a reading to a young woman we'll call Cathy. We had been discussing her difficult relationships with men, which had been quite emotionally painful to her. Cathy feared that she would always make bad choices where men were concerned, and felt quite hopeless about this.

As I tried to gain some insight on this issue, I heard a very insistent voice in my head saying "Read her the quote! Read her the quote!" As I heard this voice, I also saw an image of a page of inspirational quotes I keep in my file cabinet. Because the quotes didn't really have anything to do with the reading (or so I thought), I was a little confused. However, the impression was so insistent that after apologizing to Cathy for the odd interruption, I did what my intuition suggested. Feeling drawn to the third quote on the page, I read it to Cathy along with the author's name.

When I looked up, Cathy was crying. Since the piece wasn't particularly moving, I was surprised at her response. After a moment, Cathy told me, "The man who wrote that...I lived with him for 8 years." She went on to explain that their relationship hadn't been all bad, and that relationships could have positive aspects after all. Although she didn't go off in search of this long lost love, Cathy renewed her sense that relationships didn't have to be hopeless and decided to take a more optimistic look at future possibilities.

Those psychics who receive information in this auditory way claim that they have a particular "psychic ear," meaning that either the left or right ear is the dominant one for receiving their psychic auditory impressions. Clearly, they are hearing a sound, rather than sensing a thought, as we discuss next.

Clairsentience: Your Inner Sensing

Clairsentience is commonly considered "clear thinking" or "clear knowing." *Webster's* defines it as the "ability to perceive things out of the range of ordinary perception." This is the type of information that makes us say, "I know but I don't know how I know." It may come to you as an "aha" moment or as new information that makes such perfect sense that you feel like you've always known it (and you probably have).

Although clairsentience does not fit the mold in that it isn't directly related to one of the other five senses, it is the most common way that people receive psychic information. That is, most people have received information in this way, whether they knew it or not. They may have described it simply as intuition, not connecting it with the psychic aspect at all.

As mentioned earlier in the chapter, this clear knowing is my predominant mode of receiving information. For instance, one of my clients recently had some trouble with his boss and needed advice about how to work with her more effectively. To help focus on the person in question, I asked her first name.

Beyond Words

Clairsentience is the ability to perceive information out of the range of ordinary perception. It's translated as "clear thinking" or "clear knowing."

I closed my eyes and said the woman's name to myself, then immediately sensed someone very angry and controlling. I also received a symbolic, visual impression of this woman coming toward me an ax—the term "battle ax" immediately leapt to mind! When I related all this to my client, he started laughing. The boss was apparently known in the office, not so affectionately, as the Battle Ax Boss. I then went on to describe some effective strategies for dealing with her.

Trusting Your Gut: Your Physical Knowing

Although there isn't an official word for clear touching, the kinesthetic or physical mode of receiving information definitely exists. It doesn't refer to an external physical touch, as much as your own internal physical responses when sensing information. For example, if your stomach is in knots after you make a decision, you're probably receiving intuitive information through your body that your decision was wrong. In fact, this experience is probably where the expression "following your gut instinct" comes from. Sometimes, feelings come from touching an object and, by doing so, tapping into its past, a technique called *psychometry*, which we'll discuss in more detail in Chapter 7.

Beyond Words

Psychometry is one type of intuition that involves psychic feeling going beyond the inner world to the outer, physical one. This sense involves the ability to touch an object and thereby tap into its past and its owner's past. It works when you pick up the vibrations that accompany the object's past.

Other types of physical knowing also occur. Husbands of pregnant women experience sympathy pains, and some medical intuitives feel someone else's pain in the same spot in their own body. Headaches may also express psychic information, warning that you are overstressed and need to slow down.

So Close You Can Taste—or Smell—It

Some people also receive intuitive information from tastes and smells. They may get a bad taste in their mouths when facing an uncomfortable situation or when something doesn't seem right. Or they may smell smoke as a warning signal for impending trouble.

Some people know when they receive a psychic insight because the insight is accompanied by the scent of roses. Other people find they smell something familiar and specific—like their grandmother's perfume—when receiving intuition. Indeed, scent often triggers a more immediate and realistic psychic response than any other sense. (The reason for this is that the scent-reading nerve cells are both primitive, and so somewhat simple, and closely positioned to the part of the brain that processes them.)

From the ESP Files

Remember *Remembrance of Things Past?* That's the classic novel by Marcel Proust, who got a whiff of a French pastry called a madeleine, then saw his life flash before his eyes. Whether Proust experienced his memory through his third eye or his regular type of memory is impossible to know, but many people know the feeling of being carried instantly back in time when they smell a certain scent.

Finding Your Niche

Now that you have a better idea of what types of intuition are out there, here are some clues about where to start finding yours. But *you* need to do the legwork—by answering these exercises thoughtfully.

Information-Gathering Exercise

Here's an exercise to help you figure out your dominant mode of receiving information. It may seem a little open-ended, but that's how this exercise works.

For that reason, you should consider this an information-gathering exercise, not a final, definitive statement about your abilities.

Remember a time when you had an accurate intuition about something. Describe that experience here:

_____

_____

Did you just "know"? Describe your perception here:

_____

_____

Did you receive a flash of insight? Describe that perception here:

_____

_____

Did you have a physical sense in your body? If so, where in your body? Describe that experience here:

_____

_____

What did the experience (no matter how it presented itself) feel like? Describe that feeling here:

_____

_____

Did you interpret it as a positive or negative impression? Describe that perception here:

_____

_____

Did you hear a voice or have an auditory impression? Describe that perception here:

_____

_____

What did it sound like? Describe that perception here:

_____

_____

Was it your voice? How did you differentiate it from your normal self talk? Describe that perception here:

_____

_____

Did an image come to your mind? If so, what was it? Describe that perception here:

_____

_____

Did you get a symbolic representation of your answer? Describe that perception here:

_____

_____

Was there a smell associated with your insight? Describe that perception here:

_____

_____

As we mentioned at the beginning of this exercise, it is intended to be open-ended. We just want to help you start thinking about how you access your intuitive insights. But now that you've answered all of these questions, what do you think is your main mode of receiving intuitive information?

_____

Meditation and Intuition Exercise

Although not impossible, it's unlikely that you'll be open to getting psychic impressions when you're busy—physically or mentally—with other things, especially at the start. You'll be most open if you're in a relaxed state, which you may be best able to achieve through quiet meditation. Before you begin this meditation, think of a question you would like some intuitive information about. Phrase the question so that it evokes more than a "yes" or "no" answer. Following are some examples:

➤ "What could I do to enhance my psychic abilities?"

➤ "What could I do to improve my relationship with (name)?"

➤ "What are some ways that I could increase my income?"

Once you feel comfortable with how the question is worded, try the following technique.

1. Close your eyes. Take a deep breath and relax.

2. Visualize the sun over your head, glowing radiant and warm.

3. Imagine the light from the sun flowing through your body, filling your head, down through your neck, across your shoulders, down into your arms, through your hands, and then into your fingers. The light fills your chest, back, belly, and hips and flows down into your legs, feet, and toes.

4. Imagine the light is bathing every cell with healing and calming energy. The light also brings knowledge and wisdom.

5. Now visualize this light flowing down through your physical body and out around your body. Feel it soothing and relaxing you.

6. Take a deep breath in and slowly let it out as you say the word "Relax." Begin to slowly count from 10 down to one. As you do, imagine you are becoming more and more relaxed.

7. When you arrive at the number one and you're in a deeply relaxed state, ask your question. Allow yourself to be open to any information that comes in. Pay attention to your feelings, symbolic impressions, and any physical sensation or words that come to mind.

Intuition Hotline

Take your time when it comes to receiving intuitive information. Many people in my classes find the answers come to them after—sometimes hours after—they come out of this meditation. So don't be discouraged if you don't get an immediate response.

As you begin to make an active effort to practice some of these exercises, you'll start to notice that information comes to you more often, even when you aren't expecting it. As you become more used to these occurrences and receive confirmation of what was

Unsolved Mystery

Former Beatle John Lennon is said to have had clairvoyant abilities. Indeed, he had a premonition that he would be shot. He even claimed that his paranoia about being murdered was the cause of the group's break-up. Despite his fears, he said, "I believe in life after death. I believe that death is not an end but a beginning."

actually intuitive compared to what was wishful thinking, you'll become more comfortable. You'll also build confidence—and that good old trust we keep talking about.

Daily Observation Exercise

Here is an exercise to help you get in touch with that "everyday occurrence" type of intuition we just mentioned. Even when you don't take time to sit and meditate, this exercise can help you become more aware of the amazing intuitive stuff going on around you. Which is really what intuition is all about: raising your awareness.

1. Pay close attention to what your intuition is telling you as you go about your day. Check in with it often.

2. Ask your intuition questions, such as: "What should I do in this situation?" "What do I need to know about this?" (Remember that you may get the answers from a variety of sources, including feelings, words, images, body sensations, and so on.)

3. Act on the information you receive. If using your intuition is new for you, try using it in relatively low risk situations at first.

4. If you don't understand something, ask for clarification. You may not receive information immediately. Remember that developing this skill, like any other, is about practicing. You may not be perfect at first.

5. If the information doesn't feel right or you aren't ready to act on it—don't!

6. Write down the guidance you receive. It is helpful to look back at what you've experienced from time to time to see how accurate your guidance is.

We'll talk more about keeping a psychic journal in Chapter 7. For now, remember that your intuition is always there to guide you and provide you with encouragement and information. Learn to trust it!

Let Your Intuition Decide Exercise

Whenever you have a decision to make this week, stop and tune into your intuition. This can work for the smallest matters as well as the grandest. For now, focus on a larger type of decision that you need to make this week, but try to apply these steps to smaller ones, too, as you go along.

What decision do you need to make? Describe it here:

_____

_____

Write down all of the impressions you receive about this decision.

Describe your emotional/feeling impression(s):

_____

Describe your physical impression(s):

_____

Describe your auditory impression(s):

_____

Describe any other impression(s):

_____

What does this information tell you about the decision you hope to make? What does it tell you about how you go about making such decisions? Are you beginning to trust your instincts?

Assessment Exercise

If you took the time to complete these exercises, we're certain that you're much more aware of your recent decisions and the process you followed for making them. But did this process change the outcome of your decisions? Think back on that a little more.

How did your decision turn out? Describe the results here:

_____

_____

Which of your impressions were most accurate or most helpful?

_____

What is the dominant mode in which you received this information?

_____

Can you isolate anything that helped you separate a true psychic insight from a false one?

_____

Is there anything else that you noticed about this decision-making exercise?

_____

We hope you feel comfortable with how your decision turned out. If not, did you sense an uneasiness when you moved forward with the decision? If you feel good about your decision, what helped confirm your comfort level? That's something you'll want to focus on when you're looking for future intuitive insights.

Whether or not you feel absolutely great about your insights and abilities, acknowledge the possibility that answers come to you from many more avenues than you may ever have expected. That's the best start for someday discovering where those avenues lead—and letting them take you along with them.

Now that you have a sense of how you receive information, you'll want to gain a better sense of where you're at right now. The next chapter contains a great big "You Are Here" sign. As you continue your quest to get in touch with your psychic side, knowing where you're at now helps get you more centered on the psychic path.

The Least You Need to Know

➤ Understanding how intuition is received is a first step toward building it.

➤ No one way of receiving information is better than another: We all receive it uniquely.

➤ Finding the form of intuition that works best for you may help you tap into your abilities more easily.

➤ Pay attention to how you normally perceive information: This offers a clue into how you might receive psychic insight.

➤ Don't pressure yourself to feel attuned to a specific method right away. Let nature takes its course.

Chapter 7

How Psychic Are You Right Now?

In This Chapter

➤ Figure out how intuitive you are

➤ Classic psychic exercises for added insight

➤ Tune in to what's really going on

➤ Document your journey with a psychic journal

Well, now that you know that you're psychic and even understand a bit better how you're inclined to receive this information, the question is: How psychic are you really? Your present level of psychic awareness is an individual and personal matter. There's certainly no contest going on here, so there's no point in working for a competitive edge. But knowing where you are now helps show you where to focus your practicing efforts.

In this chapter we'll offer some basic clues to knowing where you are in terms of your intuition. We'll also include several exercises that allow you to sample different types and uses of psychic ability. You'll probably discover that your method for receiving psychic information (which you focused on in the previous chapter) matches up with the type of exercise that works best for you here. Try it and see!

Determining Your Psychic Personality Profile

Just as people have certain personality traits in their personal and social lives, they have traits in their psychic lives. They may carry on a relationship with their intuition that seems to come from outside of themselves (for example, through clairvoyance or clairaudience). Or they may feel that their information comes through highly internal processes (such as clairsentience or simply knowing). And how they react to the information also reflects their psychic profile. Whether they remain silent about their sense or talk it openly, the way they sense and respond to psychic information is individual for everyone.

To help you get in touch with whether you are a psychic introvert or extrovert, we include the following exercise. It offers you one last opportunity to fine-tune your sense of how you receive information, which applies to your psychic personality profile as well:

Exercise for Confirming Your Dominant Psychic Sense

Read through the next paragraphs once to fix the images in your mind. Next, close your eyes and experience the imagery with all your senses. In order to do this, you may find it helpful to ask a friend to read it to you, or to record it on a tape recorder and play it back as a guided imagery. Here goes:

Close your eyes, take a few deep breaths, and relax. In your mind's eye imagine yourself at the beach on a beautiful, warm summer day. You hear the gulls calling to each other in the distance. You hear and see the waves as they gently meet the shore. You find yourself walking along, feeling the healing rays of the sun on your skin. The salty sea air floats around you as the breeze blows. Take your shoes off and experience the sand and then the wet, cool ocean on your feet. You hear a child laughing behind you and look to see that he is building a sandcastle. He yells to his brother to come and take a look.

You're feeling calmer and more relaxed as you stroll on the beach. You notice you're getting thirsty and see a lemonade stand a short distance away. You approach it and smell the citrus smell of the lemons wafting through the air. You buy a cup of the ice cold, tart liquid and take a sip. Taste it in your mouth and feel it slide down your throat.

Now open your eyes and record the results:

Could you **see** the sandcastle, lemonade stand, and the ocean?

_____

Could you use your sense of **touch** to feel the sand, the ocean water, and the cup of cold lemonade?

_____

Could you **smell** the sea air, the lemon's citrus scent?

_____

Could you **taste** the lemonade?

_____

Could you hear the **sounds** of the child or the gulls calling?

_____

What emotions did you **feel** as you walked along the beach?

_____

Was one or more of your senses easier to access than another? Which sense do you think was dominant for you?

_____

As you continue your sensory exploration, be aware that your strengths are likely to lie along the lines of your dominant sense as you defined it in Chapter 6. Trust the information that comes to you along that pathway.

Concentrate! More Psychic Exercises

Getting a handle on your psychic self doesn't have to be difficult. Many methods exist for helping you delve into your intuitive side. We'll describe several of the better known ways of testing and measuring psychic ability in just a moment.

Before you can get down to the nitty-gritty, however, you must first concentrate on clearing your mind. Concentrate on clearing your mind? Is that a paradox, or what? But the idea is to focus on tapping into your intuitive side and then opening up to allow information that you can't necessarily control to come to you. To do this, try these three steps that seem to work, in various forms, for many people (and they should remind you of the meditation exercise you performed in Chapter 6):

1. Choose a calm place and begin to breathe deeply.

2. Focus on the spot just between and above your eyes, which is the location of your third eye.

3. Acknowledge to the universe (or to your chosen Higher Power) that you are open to receiving information and are willing to wait for it.

4. Once you feel peaceful and open, you can simply wait for information to come to you, or you can direct your focus toward whatever exercise interests you, such as one of those that follow.

Zener Cards: Sending, Receiving, Even Anticipating

As we discussed in Chapter 2, a great deal of hoopla surrounded the practices of channeling, spirit rapping, and seances around the turn of the 19th and into the 20th century. In the cause of giving psychic phenomena serious attention, Dr. J.B. Rhine from Duke University in North Carolina initiated the first scientific investigations into what eventually became known as *parapsychology*—the branch of psychology that deals with psychic phenomena. He was the person who coined the term ESP or extrasensory perception.

Beyond Words

Psychokinesis (PK) is the ability to use the mind to move objects without touching them. **Materialization** refers to making an object appear from out of nowhere. **Out-of-body experience** (OOBE) is a feeling that you are outside or separate from your body. Often, an observer sees his or her body while remaining separate from it.

We've already defined ESP in Chapter 1 as the ability to perceive someone's thoughts, situation, or issues in life without using one of your five ordinary senses. But that encompasses a wide array of more specific skills, including telepathy, precognition, clairaudience, clairsentience, and clairvoyance. It also includes a number of closely related phenomena, such as *psychokinesis* (PK), *materialization*, and *out-of-body experience* (OOBE).

Dr. Rhine, along with his colleague Dr. Karl Zener, set out to conduct an experiment that would measure ESP and, in particular, telepathy. One of their research tools became known as Zener cards and, although other tests and procedures are also used, they remain important tools today.

Each Zener card is blank on one side and has a symbol printed on the other. Instead of the traditional suits, there are five Zener symbols: a red cross, a green star, a black square, an orange circle, and blue wavy lines. Each Zener card deck contains 25 cards, with five copies of the same five symbols in each deck.

To test telepathic transference of information, a sender shuffles the cards in preparation for turning them over one at a time. Upon turning over each individual card, the sender concentrates on sending the image on the card telepathically to the receiver, who is in another room. The receiver's task is to identify each card image as it is sent, making a note for each on a tally sheet. At the end, the results are counted up: A score of more than one in five indicates that something has occurred beyond simple chance. Dr. Rhine believed that having more correct answers than would come about simply by guessing indicated some degree of ESP. He repeated these experiments again and again to reduce any possibility of mere chance causing the outcome.

The five symbols on the Zener cards are a red cross, blue wavy lines, a black square, an orange circle, and a green star. To use the cards illustrated here, make an enlarged photocopy and use markers or pens to add the proper color to each image. Have fun!

 Create Your Own Zener Cards

You can conduct your own Zener-card experiment at home. Here's an easy way to make your own cards—and put them to use!

1. Purchase some blank, white 3" × 5" index cards. Draw the five duplicates of each of the five Zener-card symbols with colored felt-tip pens or crayons on 25 of the cards.

   Again, the five symbols are a red cross, a green star, a black square, an orange circle, and blue wavy lines.

2. Choose a partner and determine who will be the sender and who will be the receiver. Sit in different rooms. Both of you should get into a quiet and relaxed state of mind.

3. The sender shuffles the cards, picks up the top card, and concentrates on that image for three minutes. The receiver visualizes the image she receives and writes it down. It's generally best to just go with the first image you get. Don't try to figure it out or keep changing your mind.

> **Intuition Hotline**
>
> To find out how you best receive psychic information, pay attention to how you receive the image during the Zener–card test. Ask yourself these questions: Does the image come in a flash? Do you see the symbol? Do you get a feeling or impression that one image is correct over another? Do you feel you're simply guessing? Remember that there's no right or wrong answer here; you're simply opening your awareness to your own mental processes.

4. When the sender completes three minutes with each card, he should ring a bell or clap his hands to indicate the start of another image. The sender and receiver should not talk about any of the results until all 25 cards are completed.

Now check your results. The odds in pure chance would result in you getting five right out of the 25 chances. A higher score than five out of 25 shows that you have a more advanced degree of ESP. If you consistently score well above average, then you are quite psychic!

Psychometry: Can You Feel It?

You may remember when we discussed psychometry in Chapter 6. The term is derived from the Greek words *psyche*, meaning "soul," and *metron*, meaning to "measure." The concept of "measuring soul" refers to the idea that every object possesses certain vibrations that reflect its inner essence, which can be read when one is open to it.

This type of intuition is often referred to as "seeing with the fingers." It enables you to pick up information about an object's history through holding or touching it.

The theory for how psychometry works says that every object possesses vibrations that reflect its entire history. When you are open to sensing these vibrations, you can pick up on the object's past. This ability applies to places as well, so that you can tune in to past events when you are receptive to the vibrations of the place.

Many psychics consider psychometry a form of clairsentience, which is perhaps the most common form through which most people receive psychic information (see Chapter 6). For this reason, teachers often recommend that beginners focus on developing psychometry as a first step. This ability can be mastered within several months, and lends itself to a natural progression toward learning more challenging skills.

Psychometry Exercise

Here's an exercise to get you started. Begin by choosing a few objects that you would like to receive psychic information about. Good choices are a handwritten letter, a piece of jewelry, a metal object such as a key, or some older object, such as an antique vase. We recommend you try this with something that has had some history to it, meaning that it has been held or used by someone. For example, you won't get much information from a form letter from your insurance company, but a letter from your grandmother will have an energy that you can pick up on. Note that a piece of clothing or fabric will work only if you know it hasn't been cleaned, so you might want to avoid trying that at first.

Try to choose objects that a friend or relative can give you factual information about after you've practiced the exercise. Their knowledge allows you to get some verification of your accuracy when you're finished.

Arrange the objects on a table in front of you. Sit in a comfortable position and close your eyes. Take a few relaxing deep breaths. Choose an object and hold it in your hand. Concentrate fully on this object. Don't rush. Pay attention to images that come to your mind. You may receive fragments of information. They may come in words, feelings,

Mixed Messages

When first trying out your psycho-metric skills, keep it simple. You'll want to narrow down the amount of information you get, so you won't be overwhelmed with too many images. For this reason, stick with reading personal objects that have always belonged to one individual.

symbolic impressions, or a physical sensation. If you get a strong impression that is upsetting to you, try to shift your perspective to be an *observer* of the information and not an *absorber* of it. Your purpose is to pick up on the vibrations of the object and to receive a description of its owner.

Unsolved Mystery

Carl Jung maintained great credibility by always insisting on the search for scientific evidence and documentation. Even when he experienced clairvoyant moments that he could not explain scientifically, he still managed to get evidence. One of these occurred shortly after the death of a friend, when Jung was in bed thinking about the funeral. Suddenly his friend appeared, not as an apparition, but as "an inner visual image." This image led Jung to follow it in his "imagination," whereupon he took Jung to his home's library and pointed to a book on a high shelf. The next day, Jung visited the house in person. After he climbed up on a stool, he clearly saw the book, just where it had been the night before, entitled... what else? *The Legacy of the Dead.* Aside from the fascinating title of the book, the book's placement was just as it had appeared to Jung telepathically.

If you're doing this exercise with a friend, verbalize any information you receive. If you're doing it on your own, jot down your impression or keep a tape recorder running. Don't try to intellectualize or remain rational at this point. You might even feel like you're making things up. Don't worry about that: The time to analyze the content is after you're through. Stay open. You may want to hold the object in your other hand to see if the information you receive is any different. Record any and all information you receive. Repeat this process with all of the objects you have chosen.

When you're through, you may want to shake or wash your hands to release any of the vibrational impressions that came from the objects you were holding. Once you've done that, check your psychic information against the known facts about this object. How did you do?

You'll probably be surprised that you actually perceived some of the information correctly. But you don't have to be! Many intuitives believe that this information—and much more—is always there for you, just waiting for you to tap into it. And every time you practice psychometric exercises, you will be able to tap into this ability more easily.

Remote Viewing: Very Creative Visualization

Remote viewing has made headlines in recent years, as details of the Defense Intelligence Agency's Stargate program have emerged. The CIA acknowledged this clandestine program in 1995, yet a great deal of secrecy still surrounds it.

Beyond Words

Remote viewing is the psychic ability to witness events at a remote site without using the known senses.

Remote viewing was pioneered by a group of scientists in a government-sponsored program at Stanford Research Institute International (SRI) in California. Participants were taught to enter an altered state of consciousness, then trained to view places, situations, and people at a geographic distance in order to gather information. The government used this data to gain intelligence information on everything from distant activities and events to descriptions of weapons stockpiles. In other words, the government practiced psychic spying!

One insider from the operation, David Morehouse, described his experience in his book *Psychic Warrior: Inside the CIA's Stargate Program* (St. Martin's Press, 1996). Morehouse was initially a commander of Ranger Company, an elite combat unit. In 1987 he was shot in the head during duty and, though he recovered physically, his injury brought a disturbing psychic wound. He had recurrent dreams telling him that he had chosen the wrong path, and that his was a path of peace.

He kept these dreams secret: Exposing them would have ended his career. Several years later he was recruited for a top-secret unit requiring that he undergo a battery of psychological tests. During these tests he confessed to both the dreams and disturbing out-of-body experiences he was having. He expected to be given his walking papers, but to his surprise he was shown a file marked "Top Secret/Grill Flame." The folder contained references to "viewers" and "monitors" who seemed to be seeing or visiting a site in nonphysical form.

Morehouse was given more and more information about the psychic espionage program, learning that it had been in existence for 24 years. It was known by the names of Scanate, Grill Flame, Center Lane, and Stargate, to name a few. He joined the program and began a 10-month training session.

He learned to enter an altered state of consciousness and to take mental journeys to other places. He would write down information about what he saw, tape-record it, and sketch it according to strict guidelines. He was discouraged from interpreting what he saw or using his imagination to elaborate further. Eventually he reached what he calls a "philosophical impasse with the unit." He believes that remote reviewing is a gift to be used to further humankind, not to be used as an espionage tool.

Today, several laboratories as well as independent consultants are researching remote viewing. Its use certainly transcends espionage. In fact, you can try it right now by following this simple exercise.

Remote Viewing Exercise

For this exercise, choose a target place that you wish to visit. This should be a place that you don't know.

If you're by yourself, choose a place you can visit in the near future to confirm your accuracy. Keep a tape recorder on to record your remote viewing experiences.

If you're with a friend, try to remote view a place familiar to her but not to you. This might be your friend's office or her relative's home. Your friend can ask you questions about the remote viewing site and you can relay the impressions out loud as you experience them. Ask your friend not to comment on your accuracy or inaccuracy until after the exercise is completed. She should take notes during the exercise so you'll both remember the points to discuss later.

After choosing the target place you wish to visit, get into a comfortable, relaxed position and close your eyes. Take several deep breaths and exhale each one slowly. Imagine that you are floating gently out of your body and moving to the site you have chosen. Begin to notice and describe the details of what you see around you. Here are a few things to look for:

➤ What buildings do you see? Are they brick, concrete, or painted? Is there a street? Is it paved? Is it busy?

➤ Is there a park or a body of water? Are there people around?

➤ If you're in a building, what does it look like? What color is it? What do the furnishings look like? Are there any unusual objects that catch your attention? Are there windows? What shape are they?

Take your time. Move slowly. Stay aware of your surroundings. When you've finished with one area, you may want to move on or go back to an area you've already looked at. Depending on the site you have chosen, your questions may vary.

Once you finish your exploration, move back to your physical body. Take some deep breaths, wiggle your toes and fingers, stretch, and mentally come back into the room.

If you're working alone, write down all the impressions you received so you can check on their accuracy later. If you're working with a friend, ask for her feedback on your remote viewing.

Keep in mind that with many of these practice exercises you are learning new skills. Many people feel that they are making things up and are then surprised to find they were highly accurate. Be willing to take a risk, even if it means being wrong. Don't expect to be perfect. (Even the experts aren't!)

How Perceptive Are You?

Picking up on intuitive information has a lot to do with being open to it and aware of it when it comes. Sometimes you or others may receive information that seems normal enough, but if you pay attention you may see that it is actually unusual. The information can come to you either as a surprising extent of knowledge or an uncanny skill to receive it quickly.

Dr. Daniel Cappon is a Scottish-born psychiatrist, environmental expert, and author who has identified 20 skills that naturally intuitive people have. He divides the skills into two categories: *input* skills and *output* skills.

Based on his list of these skills, Dr. Cappon has devised an IQ test that measures intuitive ability. It's much too long to include all of it here, but we want to offer some insight. The input skills include 10 skills involving the ability to take in information quickly, without many clues. Among these skills are:

➤ Quick visual perception (the ability to spot danger in the blink of an eye)

➤ Quick visual location (the ability to spot things quickly, such as a familiar face in a group photo)

➤ Accurate estimation of time, dimensions, or weight

➤ Quickly taking in a whole scene and remembering the details

The 10 output skills involve acting on information quickly, even with a minimum of background information. Here's a sample of these skills:

➤ Knowing the best time to intervene in a situation (such as when to play the stock market and when to quit)

➤ Having hunches that often prove accurate

➤ Describing what's already happened, without having any outside source of information (finding out after you've described something that it did occur as you saw it)

According to these descriptions, James Bond—who somehow knows everything from the instant he walks into a room (or before)—is extremely psychic. (That's an idea that's not so far-fetched, once you know that the U.S. government engaged in psychic espionage.)

From the ESP Files

Intuition Magazine, which featured information about Dr. Cappon's tests in its 1995 Issue #6, reports that his testers "discovered that intuitive people moved their eyes differently than others. They zigzagged over the entire picture, while less intuitive people moved their eyes in slow uncertain circles, until they focused, usually on the wrong point. And, as people learned to be more intuitive, their eye movements changed, following more of the zigzag path." For more information on Dr. Cappon's research, check out his book *Intuition and Management* (Quorum Books, 1994).

If you're interested in a fun way to assess where you're at, Dr. Cappon has created a board game for that purpose. (You can buy it by calling (416) 792-2072 in Canada). In addition to his game, Dr. Cappon has devised several exercises for testing your own intuitive ability at home. Here are two of Dr. Cappon's homegrown tests. Try them yourself.

➤ Ask a friend to draw an image on a paper and then cut it into six or seven pieces, sort of like a puzzle (but with straighter edges). Make sure that your friend doesn't let you know what he drew ahead of time! Then ask him to scatter the miscellaneous pieces in a random arrangement on a table. As soon as you look at the pieces, ask your friend to time you—but you're allowed only seven seconds! If you can identify the image in seven seconds or less, consider the experiment a success!

➤ Ask a friend to select several sets of photos that you haven't seen. Each set should include photos that show a sequential event (for example, a building before and after it is torn down). Your friend should time you, allowing you to look at each photo for just seven seconds. The catch is that you will try to predict what the second picture will show after seeing only the first one. If you can do that, consider the test a success!

Learning to Focus

The idea of *focus* can mean many things and can be applied on many levels. But the key to understanding—and doing it—is making a mental effort to be aware. To put this into context, consider the psychometric exercise we talked about earlier. If you hold a watch in your hand, you can definitely *focus* on its physical traits. But once you've done that, allow your attention to move a little higher to a level beyond what you can sense in the physical realm.

Just as you can focus your thoughts on the material world, you can also focus on a less tangible one. Following are a few ways you can become more attuned to psychic experiences that are constantly occurring all around you. Once you open up to noticing them, you'll begin to see how abundant they are.

Beyond Words

Webster's has nine entries to define **focus**, but the most relevant for our purposes is "a central point, as of attraction, attention, or activity." Another entry says merely "to concentrate."

Paying Attention to the Subtle Message

Messages from your intuition are often very faint or indistinct at first. And because we're so used to hearing our negative self-talk, we often drown out our own intuition. It's not called your still, quiet inner voice for nothing!

When you're just beginning to tap into your intuitive cues, you may have difficulty differentiating between your intellect and your intuition. One way to tell the difference is to note if you are experiencing any fearful or anxious thoughts. When information comes from your intellect or negative self-talk, it's often based on thoughts of guilt, feelings of fear, or a need to protect yourself from a perceived threat. Guidance from your Higher Self tends to come through in a way that makes you feel peaceful and balanced; it is always encouraging and positive. Think of it this way: Your intuition "speaks softly"; it's your intellect that carries "a big stick."

Beyond Words

According to the *Webster's Dictionary*, synchronicity is a coincidence of events that seem to be meaningfully related.

Synchronicity

A common saying is "Synchronicity is God's way of remaining anonymous." Carl Jung coined the term "synchronicity" to describe "a causal connecting principle" that links mind and matter. He believed that an underlying connectedness draws everything together, and that meaningful coincidences cannot be explained by cause and effect. Rather, synchronicity seems to draw everything together with a sense that something bigger is happening out there—and it seems to have everyone's best interests at heart.

Many times your inner knowing helps you to arrive at the right place at the right time. Indeed, events come together with such precision that you may feel launched on some preordained course. When you are in the benevolent flow of synchronicity, you know you are trusting your intuition. Here are a few samples that many people can relate to:

➤ You've just applied for a job in a company where you really want to work—and a long lost colleague calls and tells you she was recently hired there.

➤ You have a dream about a favorite uncle. In the morning you receive a call to tell you he died the previous evening.

➤ You pick up the phone to call your sister and discover she's already on the line—having called you at the same time.

Many people may brush these experiences aside as mere coincidences, but there's nothing mere about them. They are all examples of synchronicity. Whether we know it or not, they happen for a reason.

My friend Elena is a seamstress who received a suit for alteration from a client. After the client left the shop, Elena reached for a pair of scissors and accidentally knocked a soft drink onto her client's suit, staining it irreparably. Elena was horrified. She prides herself on her professionalism and integrity and always takes great care with her client's clothes.

She decided that she would have to find the same fabric and remake the suit. She went to four fabric stores. She found the fabric in several places, but it was always the wrong color or shade. Finally she went to a fifth store in a very out-of-the-way place and again had no success.

She was about to resign herself to having to confess to her client when she decided to pray and ask for guidance. Elena has a very irreverent manner of prayer. She went into a corner of the store and said, "Okay, God. Listen to me. If you want me to remake this suit, you're going to have to show me where to get this fabric!" A few seconds later the bolts of fabric she had been leaning against toppled over. Guess what? The fabric she had been seeking was right there. Her client was thrilled with the beauty of her "re-tailored" suit, and none the wiser.

Did You Get It?

As you increase your awareness, you'll improve your ability to hear your "still, small voice" and to recognize the signs of synchronicity. But until you gain confidence in your ability to pick up on these subtle cues, here are a few exercises to help clue you in.

 Tuning-in Exercises

In each of the following exercises pay attention to how you receive your psychic input. It's just as important to pay attention when you're wrong as when you are right. And try to enjoy practicing these psychic skills—just for fun!

➤ Next time you're at a bank of elevators, see if you can intuit which one is going to arrive next.

➤ As you're coming out of a sleep state in the morning, see if you can get any impressions about the day's news. (No fair cheating with the news on your clock radio!)

➤ Try to name who's on the phone when it rings. (And Caller I.D. doesn't count!)

➤ Try to see if you can intuit some of the headlines for the next week, month, or year. And keep a list in your journal (which we'll talk about next). (Who knows? You may be called by the *National Enquirer* and asked to list your predictions!)

➤ Pay attention to what you intuit about the business trends in your industry this year.

➤ Play a guessing game with your radio. "Name that tune" *before* you turn on your radio. You may be surprised at how often you get it right!

Any time you find yourself getting one of these everyday occurrences right, give yourself a pat on the back for tuning in on target. You're getting there!

Intuition Hotline

If you find that you're good at predicting business trends you may find yourself in a new career. This intuitive skill, called business forecasting, is highly sought after.

Your Psychic Journal

How did you do with these exercises? If you're like most people, you'll find that you get better and better at tuning in and recognizing your psychic ability the more you put it to work.

In order to keep track of your progress, as well as record all of the interesting experiences you're bound to have, we suggest you start keeping an psychic journal. Purchase a small notebook that you can carry with you to record all that you learn. Record any of your own thoughts or impressions as well as the topics we suggest.

This book contains lots of fun exercises, quizzes, and games to help you become more psychic. Many times we'll ask you to explore your attitudes and beliefs, as well as to write down your psychic impressions. By writing in your journal each day, you'll begin to see how often you receive intuitive information. (In fact, you may want to revisit some of the earlier chapters, particularly Chapter 6, and write down some of the results of the exercises described there.)

Here are a few tips to help you get started on your psychic journal. We want to help you keep accurate notes while charting your progress. You'll be amazed someday when you look back at how far you've come!

➤ Record synchronicities and coincidences. Sometimes the information you record will not seem immediately important. In retrospect you may see that you had a clairvoyant experience about the future.

➤ Don't edit or censor the information you receive. You learn as much from your mistakes as you do from your successes. Also, time may tell you that you were more right than you could ever imagine.

➤ Feel free to draw pictures of any images you receive, or to write down any dreams that come to you.

And remember: Every time you write in your journal, always note the date. This offers a whole new way of understanding the information when you look back at it someday.

As you pay attention to the amazing psychic events surrounding you, your mind will begin to open up and realize an ever-expanding consciousness. To help you get in touch with this, the next chapter sets you on a path toward your inner journey. It's a lifelong journey that takes as much energy as you are willing to put into it—and transforms that energy into your ever-growing self.

The Least You Need to Know

➤ Simple psychic experiments can get you started on a path toward discovering your true intuitive skills.

➤ Focusing your mind is an essential part of getting in touch with your intuition.

➤ Don't underestimate the power of your intuition: If you suspect it's there, it is.

➤ An important way to acknowledge and learn from your intuition is to keep a psychic journal.

Chapter 8

Opening Up to Your Psychic Self

In This Chapter

➤ Learn to be true to yourself

➤ Discover the basic keys to meditation

➤ Make contact with your special guide

➤ Open your mind to new types of messages

Whether already deeply in tune with our intuitive sides or just starting out on our journeys, we all pause occasionally to wonder where our psychic ability comes from. Does it come from a divine source that resides outside ourselves? Or is it our own inner awareness, rising up from the hidden depths of our unconsciousness? Every intuitive will answer this question in a slightly different way, according to his or her own unique experience.

What each of us perceives as the source of our psychic gifts is based on our own personal beliefs. And just as personal is our journey to explore this source. In this chapter we'll focus on your inner journey, the one that leads you closer to discovering who you are and how you'll relate to the unseen world.

The Psychic Journey Within

Every one of us must face our unseen world and its new lessons on our own terms. It's extremely unlikely that a fully materialized ghost, like Jacob Marley who visits Ebenezer Scrooge in Charles Dickens' *A Christmas Carol*, will tap us on the back and tell us to clean up our act. Rather, we receive only lessons and insights that we're prepared to take in.

Intuition Hotline

Although it's rare to hear that someone receives a wake-up call in the way that Ebenezer Scrooge did, many people do report visions of or visits from loving spirits. The famous psychic healer Edgar Cayce described seeing an angel when he was a boy, an experience that is not uncommon among children.

One way to let the universe know you're ready to receive, and to affirm that fact yourself, is to prepare your mind. Getting your mind to slow down and then focus on staying empty is no easy feat. In fact, the challenge is so great that many spiritual leaders have devoted their lives to mastering this ability. A few examples of those who searched long and hard for a quiet mind are Buddha, Yogananda, and the Dalai Lama.

So why, you may ask, have humans evolved such a high level of intelligence only to have to empty our minds to achieve a higher level of consciousness? Well, to step up to that higher level, we need to step outside our individual, ego-oriented ways of perceiving things, which brings us right back to our psychic sense: To understand more about the unseen world, we need to keep our minds open to receiving information in ways that transcend the physical world.

From the ESP Files

Even physical exercise helps to prepare and quiet your mind. By letting off some steam at the gym (or anywhere else), you can release unwanted blockages of stress and anxiety that interfere with clear thoughts. Why do you think yogis have had such good luck getting in touch with their spiritual sides? They're stretching their energy channels and opening up their chakras as they twist their bodies into yoga postures!

The true masters of the open mind—Buddha and the Dalai Lama, for example—recommend a few practices that have stood the test of time. These include meditation, mantras, mandalas, and the classic wisdom, "Know thyself." This is a phrase that resounds throughout many schools of philosophical thought. It is often credited to Plato, who included it in his writing. But it actually made its debut on the marquis of the temple of Apollo at Delphi, that favorite hot spot for oracular insight.

Honoring Your Inner Voice

The intuitive journey is exciting on many levels. Not only does it introduce you to the possibility that whole worlds exist that you hadn't previously imagined, it also gets you in touch with your inner self. Getting to know your thoughts and understand your feelings is a gift in itself. But sorting through this personal information, also helps you distinguish what comes from your intellect and feelings and what is really intuition. All of these levels come together to make up what you call "yourself." You must learn to recognize which part of yourself is taking control when you're seeking information or trying to make a decision.

In order to access your higher consciousness, you may first need to get to the bottom of how you're feeling emotionally. If you begin to meditate and a certain thought keeps tugging at your mind, maybe you need to deal with that first. This could actually be both your emotional *and* intuitive sides telling you that you need to address the issue. However, if you've taken care of the big stuff and little, annoying preoccupations keep needling their way in, then you'll appreciate meditation and other mental tools for helping you focus.

Using your tools for inner guidance will get you to a place where you can hear what your inner voice wants to say. Once you ask for direction and get a clear sense (if not a strong verbal message) about what you should do, then follow it. That's what understanding your intuition—and honoring your inner voice—is all about! Trust your intuition and it will take care of you.

Mandalas

One of the more visually oriented ways to approach a higher plane of consciousness is by using a *mandala* to meditate. These beautiful, usually circular, designs draw your eye to their centers, which helps your mind focus during meditation. When creating a mandala, the artist tries to coordinate her personal circle with the universal circle, reflecting how her own life fits into the larger whole.

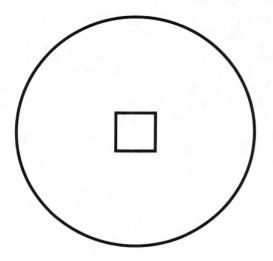

Here's your chance to create your own mandala. Use this template to get you started.

This art form is often associated with Tibetan-monk artists who spend hours creating them out of multicolored sand. Navaho Indians create similar sand-painted mandalas on the ground for healing ceremonies. Mandalas actually transcend many cultures, times, and places. Indeed, Carl Jung, the father of modern psychology, considers mandalas to be the ultimate symbols for uniting our inner and outer selves.

The labyrinth pattern on the floor of Chartres Cathedral (now reproduced on the floor of Grace Cathedral in San Francisco) is another type of mandala.

Mantras

If the visual doesn't do it for you, maybe a sound-oriented way to approach a higher plane of consciousness will work. One such method uses a *mantra* during meditation. Repeating a particular word or phrase, which usually has a sacred connotation, throughout the meditation helps to keep the mind focused.

A common Sanskrit mantra is "om nama shivaya," which roughly translates into "I honor the Self in all." The Hebrew word "shalom" (meaning peace) is commonly used as a mantra. Other frequently used words are "love," "beauty," "peace," and "God." Any word that is sacred to you or evokes a special feeling of a quality you seek to develop is a good word to try out.

Beyond Words

Mandala is Sanskrit for "circle," but it alludes to something like "the circle of life" on a cosmic scale. Technically, a mandala is a schematic drawing of the cosmos characterized by a concentric arrangement of geometric shapes, each denoting an image or attribute of a deity.

Meditation

As discussed in previous chapters, meditation helps you receive intuitive guidance because it puts you in a state where your mind is relaxed and less distracted by everyday details. Over time, a daily meditation practice of 15 to 20 minutes will work wonders to replenish your body, mind, and spirit.

Many people talk about how great meditation is. But if you haven't tried it, you might be inclined to ask, "What's the big deal?" In fact, in today's busy world, taking time to do doing nothing *is* a big deal. But when you meditate, you aren't really "doing nothing." Meditation can:

➤ Open you up to a higher energy source and recharge you.

➤ Reduce stress and anxiety. (You'll gain a calmer and more peaceful approach to daily life.)

➤ Improve your health and general well-being.

➤ Help you tap into a source of spiritual guidance that can direct you in your daily life.

➤ Assist you in finding a source of creative ideas to help with decision making.

Most people find it easiest to meditate before they begin their day. Others like to practice at the end of the day. Try different times to see what works best for you. Despite how busy you are, make time for at least 15 minutes a day. Choose a time when you're most likely to be undisturbed and remember to turn your phone ringer off and your answering machine on, so you won't be interrupted or worried about missing anything.

Keep in mind that meditation is a learned skill: You're training your mind to be still—and that takes effort, because your mind usually likes to jump around in a manner that many meditation teachers have described as a "drunken monkey" or refer to as "monkey mind!" Meditation means learning to focus your mind on one thing. This may be your breath as it moves in and out of your body, or a mantra or mandala.

Here's the meditation that I use when I want to connect with my intuition:

1. Sit in a chair with your back straight and your shoulders relaxed. Your feet can be on the floor or you may sit cross-legged, whichever is more comfortable for you. Fold your hands in your lap and close your eyes.

Beyond Words

Mantra is Hindu for a word or formula that is recited or sung. The sound is intended to resonate in the body and evoke certain energies during meditation.

Intuition Hotline

If you're uncomfortable with the term "meditation," try thinking of this as a time for stillness, quiet time, or even prayer. William Wordsworth called meditation "A happy stillness of mind." It really doesn't matter what you call it—just do it!

2. Take three slow, deep breaths. Inhale and exhale slowly.

3. In your mind hold a picture of a beautiful, light-filled scene. Imagine that your whole body is filling up with this white light. (Pause.) Picture every cell being bathed in white light, filling you with peace. This light holds all the wisdom and love from the universe.

4. See the light completely filling you and surrounding you. You may even imagine it filling the room you're in.

5. For 10 to 20 minutes simply pay attention to your breathing. Watch your breath in your mind's eye, going in and out of your body. If your mind wanders, gently bring it back to watching the breath. Continue to feel the light growing radiant and warm around you. Imagine its connection to a Higher Source.

6. You may find a mantra helpful to use during this meditation. You can simply say, "Peace," "Om," or "God." Do whatever feels right for you if it helps you with the meditation and your focus.

7. When you are nearing the end of the meditation, ask your intuition if there is a message for you and listen for an answer.

8. You also may say a prayer for a person or situation, or simply ask for continuing guidance on an issue about which you may need insight.

9. End your meditation by visualizing the light being sent to a person or situation that could use its help.

Some people also like to say "Thank you" or "Amen" at the end of meditation. Whether you choose to do that, or follow this meditation to a T, or pursue your own path, don't worry—there's no right or wrong way to meditate. It's a very personal practice, and whatever works for you is fantastic!

Learning to Breathe

Breathing may seem like the simplest thing to do. In fact, it was our first act after we exited the birth canal. And yet many masters have spent their whole lives trying to get it right—perhaps *because* it was their first act when they exited the birth canal. Breathing is the essence of life. It is so basic that when we do it we access our most basic selves.

In the past half century, more Westerners have tried to learn the techniques for breathing and meditation that Eastern yogis have studied for millennia. In recent years,

Beyond Words

Holotropic breathwork originated with psychiatrist Stanislov Grof and transpersonal trainer (a specialist in developing the holotropic method and helping others use it) Christina Grof. This powerful approach to self-exploration and healing combines consciousness research, psychology, Eastern spirituality, and mystical traditions.

psychiatrist Stanislov Grof has developed a method that combines breathing and meditation in a new way. Called *holotropic breathwork*, it helps individuals enter an unordinary state of consciousness for psychic healing by using a combination of evocative music, accelerated breathing, energy work, and mandala drawing. Aspects of this meditation method involve exploration of the inner self, transpersonal dimensions, and spiritual opening.

Opening Up to Your Guides

I believe that everyone is born with a guide who is with them throughout their lives. Some people have additional guides who come to help them in a specific lesson they need to learn or with a certain project they want to accomplish.

More and more people report having guides, and some feel confident that they have more than one guide at a time. There are many different kinds of guides. They are here to help people, and are available when people ask for help. People can perceive their guides in various ways. Some people describe their guides as angels. Others experience their guides as an energy or a light, or even a warm, loving feeling. They don't always hear words or see a vision, but get a feeling.

Guides are your friends. They are here to love, support, and encourage you. They are wise teachers, and they often give you information through your intuition. At first, guide-provided intuition doesn't feel much different from other types of information you receive. But once you learn to recognize it, you can easily see when you're receiving extra special insight. In addition to offering information for spiritual growth and healing, guides provide information about your creative endeavors, such as music, art, and even writing.

When I was a small child, I discovered my guide sitting at the foot of my bed one night. She seemed very real to me and it puzzled me that other people didn't see her as I did. She appeared as a beautiful woman in a white robe. At my young age I simply referred to her as "the lady." She was always very comforting. I felt, and feel, profound peace whenever she is with me. I didn't so much hear her talk as I felt her presence and still do. I frequently ask her for insight about clients as I do my readings and for information about projects that I'm working on.

Mixed Messages

Keep your guides close! Although there's no rule that you can't talk to other people about your psychic experience, limit your sharing to those who are understanding and respectful. In case someone isn't kind, you could find yourself feeling defensive about a positive, very personal experience. Once you have a sense that you have made a connection with your spirit guide, cherish the impression.

Not everyone will experience their relationship with their guide in the same way that I do. Indeed, "guides" may be just one way that some people conceptualize the intuitive information they receive. Everyone that does so reports that a common trait: The presence of one's guide creates a sense of being filled with love and light. If you do not sense the presence of a guide, do not bemoan the fact: It may not be the ideal path for you. However, if you're interested, we provide exercises to help you explore the possibility that you too have a guide to help you receive and interpret intuitive information.

Making Time for Peace and Joy

One of the ways that your intuition speaks to you is by directing you to joy and peace. Writer Brenda Ueland has coined a term she calls "moodling." She defines it as "long, inefficient, happy idling, dawdling, and puttering." We rarely give ourselves time like this, and may even think of it as laziness.

When we're our most busy selves, bustling around complaining about the direction our life is taking, we're most in need of moodling. Such preoccupation prevents our intuition from breaking through the minidramas we've created. We need to slow down to hear the still, small, quiet inner voice again. That voice will show us how to bring our lives back into harmony.

The following exercise gives you three steps to help you realign your awareness of inner joy. First, recall what's worked for you in the past, then open yourself up to where you're at in the present, and then see what amazing changes can come along.

Expanding Your Inner Joy

1. Think of three times in your life when you experienced inner peace. Describe them here:

   _____

   _____

   _____

2. Close your eyes, take a deep breath, and relax. Ask your inner self what would bring about greater joy and serenity in your life. Pay attention to any images, feelings, and body impressions you receive. Write your guidance here:

   _____

   _____

   _____

3. Based on the above information, what steps could you take in your life right now to bring about more joy and harmony?

_____

_____

_____

Be certain to take time every so often to simply "Kick back and smell the roses." But if you think you need a "quick fix," come back to this exercise. It will help you come back to yourself.

Creating an Inner Sanctuary to Meet Your Guide

Your inner sanctuary is a place you can go in your imagination to receive psychic guidance and assistance. You may perceive this information as coming from your own intuition or from a spirit guide outside of yourself. Some people have what they think of as an inner guide that is connected to their intuition. Whatever way you experience the information is okay. For now, picture that it comes to you in a safe haven in your mind's eye. But how do you get there?

I've designed the following meditation to help you take a psychic journey to meet your special guide. The easiest way to perform this exercise may be to have someone read it to you slowly or to read it yourself into a tape recorder and then play it back. Otherwise, you may be distracted by the act of reading as you attempt to meditate. Here goes:

 Meditation Exercise for Meeting Your Guide

1. Close your eyes and allow your physical body to become relaxed and comfortable. Allow your conscious mind to drop any cares of the day. Inhale deeply through your nose until your abdomen rises. Hold your breath for a moment, then exhale slowly through your nose. Continue breathing in this way for a few moments. Focus your attention on your breathing. Feel your breath coming in. Rest. Feel it go out.

2. Let yourself begin to feel relaxed and open.

3. Allow yourself to enjoy these feelings. Let your breathing move to a comfortable, relaxed rhythm. Tell your feet to relax. Say in your mind, "I am relaxing

Intuition Hotline

Try using guided imagery tapes to get you started. Experiencing guided imagery on tape frees you to relax, close your eyes, and focus on the words and the images they evoke. If you would like to purchase the *Creating an Inner Sanctuary* guided imagery audio tape, see the order form at the end of this book.

my feet." Feel the muscles become loose and relaxed. Relax your ankles. Say in your mind, "I am relaxing my ankles." Relax your lower legs. Relax your knees…your thighs…your pelvic area. Take a deep breath and imagine that breath flowing into your abdomen and relaxing that area. Now imagine it flowing into your chest…your back. Your neck is relaxing…your shoulders. Feel the relaxation flowing into your arms, and down into your wrists, hands, and fingers. Now relax your jaw. Let it drop. Relax the muscles around your mouth, your tongue, your eyes, your forehead, and your scalp. Take another deep breath and relax still further.

4. Count from 10 slowly down to one. As you do, feel yourself moving into a more and more relaxed yet alert and open state of mind. Let yourself enjoy a feeling of floating and moving weightlessly through space. Feel yourself traveling toward an illuminated, light-filled area. In your mind's eye, find yourself in a beautiful natural scene filled with the sights, sounds, and smells of a lovely day. The sun is warm on your skin and you have a feeling of relaxed safety, comfort, and peacefulness. This might be a setting in the mountains, at the seashore, by a lake or stream, or in a meadow. Accept whatever scene feels most peaceful to you and go there.

5. When you find your special place, you might want to imagine a house, a small cottage, or some other form of shelter there. You may want to place crystals, incense, magic talismans, plants, or flowers around your sanctuary. An altar might feel appropriate. Create and arrange things there for your convenience and enjoyment. You may even want to have a high-tech sanctuary and imagine a computer where you receive guidance. Or a large screen upon which your guide appears. Do whatever works for you. You can change and refine your sanctuary as you practice this exercise in the future. Your sanctuary is a place in your mind that you can return to at any time to receive intuition information for yourself and others.

6. Explore your environment. Allow your awareness to encompass the colors, textures, shapes, and spaces of your sanctuary. Notice any sounds you hear and notice the general feeling of this sacred place you have created. Be aware of any feelings or impressions you receive.

7. Take another minute to explore your environment.

8. Now, beside your sanctuary is a path. You may not have noticed it before. As you see it, your attention is drawn to a being surrounded by light that is approaching you. As it approaches, you feel your heart opening and you are filled and surrounded by a wonderful feeling of love and acceptance. This is your guide. Your guide steps toward you and greets you warmly. Your guide has been waiting for you. Allow this guide to be whatever it will. Allow it to emerge into your awareness without any assistance from you. Become aware of it's qualities, form, and appearance. You may experience the particular

essence of your guide as a scent, a feeling, or even a light being. Your guide may be male or female or may be perceived without gender or form.

9. Find a comfortable place for both of you to sit. Ask your guide for a name. Your guide responds: My name is

_____

10. Ask your guide if there is a message for you and listen for the answer.

11. Ask your guide the following questions:

    a) How can I work with you to develop my intuition?

    b) What is my life purpose?

    c) What steps can I take right now to enhance my life?

    d) [Your own question.]

12. When you feel you have completed your aim, bid goodbye to your guide. Know that you will easily be able to connect with your guide any time you want.

13. When you feel ready, open your eyes and return to your normal consciousness. Wiggle your toes, flex your legs, and stretch your limbs like a cat waking from a nap.

To evaluate your experience, take out your journal and respond to the following questions (or respond to them right here!).

➤ What did you experience during this exercise?

_____

_____

_____

➤ Describe your sanctuary. (Many people like to draw or paint a picture.)

_____

_____

_____

➤ What was your guide like? Did you receive a name? Don't worry if you didn't. It may come later.

_____

_____

_____

Look back at the four questions that you asked. What information did you receive? You may get more information as you write down your answers now.

How can I work with you to develop my intuition?

_____

What is my life purpose?

_____

What steps can I take right now to enhance my life?

_____

My own question was:

_____

The answer was:

_____

You may not have received answers immediately, and you probably don't know yet whether they are right for you or not. But keep your eyes peeled, because you're sure to be getting some answers soon—and probably in some unexpected ways!

A Willingness to Be Wrong

Whether you're a total beginner at developing your psychic awareness or an experienced pro, you probably already know that there's always something new to learn. And anything new always involves a certain amount of risk. When opening up your psychic insight, the risk may feel greater because there's nothing tangible or visible to confirm your impressions. But that doesn't mean you're alone.

In my "Developing Your Intuition" workshops, I use this exercise to help people discover how much they really know, after all: I have each person sit with a partner they don't know. I ask them to look at each other, and then use their psychic abilities to access information about their partners. Part of this partner exercise is to see what you receive psychically about your partner's work, career, and interest.

After I introduce the exercise I always hear at least one person in my class moan, "I can't do this. Everyone else can. I can't! I don't know how." I ask them to *be willing to be wrong*. If they feel like they are making up the information, so be it. This is intended to be a practice exercise to help them develop a skill. Sometimes people can gain just as much knowledge from how they received wrong information than they can from receiving correct information.

I had one student who started complaining that she "wasn't getting anything" about her partner. I asked her to make something up, to just pretend to be psychic. She exclaimed, "Bees! Bees! I just get bees!" I looked over at her partner who sat there quietly with his mouth agape. He stared at her and finally stammered, "I run an apiary." (In case you didn't know—and who would?—an apiary is a bee farm.)

Unsolved Mystery

The best-selling author Neale Donald Walsch puts an interesting spin on receiving inspired insight: He goes straight to the Big Guy Himself. In his book *Conversations with God: An Uncommon Dialogue, Book 1* (Putnam, 1996), Walsch explores his life and spirituality through a series of internal written dialogues between God and himself. While Walsch explains that God is directing his hand to record His sacred side of the conversation, some people claim that the words come from Walsch's own higher mind. Others, namely skeptics, consider the source his "imagination." But if book sales count as a vote of confidence, then Walsch and God are definitely on close terms. What do you believe?

Another, even stranger story started the same way with a similar recalcitrant student. She seemed quite agitated because her psychic information about the partner's career didn't make any sense. I explained that many times intuition works because we know something but we don't know what we know or how we know it. I encouraged her to be willing to be wrong and to tell her partner what impression she received. Reluctantly she said, "I see a head being cut open and love being poured in." Are you ready for her partner's answer? He was a neurosurgeon who practiced psychic healing!

Taking a risk is part of learning. And being willing to be wrong can even be the key to being right!

Psychic Energy Protection

Often, people may feel awestruck or even afraid of their newfound insights on the amazing power associated with psychic ability. Fear is a tool that many people rely on as a defensive strategy for facing anything new and difficult to understand. Part of your inner journey is coming to terms with this fear, sorting out why you're afraid, and learning ways to help yourself adapt.

When you begin to develop your psychic ability you may feel that you are much more sensitive to the energy around you. Have you ever walked into a room and the tension was so strong that you could "cut it with a knife"? You may pick up intense emotions from others more easily and begin to experience them as your own.

As people open up psychically, they often find themselves in situations in which they feel that things are not as they seem. At my former job, I had a secretary who seemed overly pleasant and agreeable. But whenever I entered her office, I began to feel impatient and irritable, when just moments before I had felt up and cheerful. I couldn't figure out why I felt that way, because there was no apparent reason. I rationalized my reaction for some weeks, but couldn't shake the impression that something was wrong. I later learned that she had been spreading rumors about me in an attempt to get me fired and take my position. This is a form of *psychic attack.*

Beyond Words

A **psychic attack** occurs when someone is willfully and consciously sending you negative energy. In all likelihood, this energy does not come from someone who has developed his or her psychic skills—just a regular person who thinks negatively about you.

How can you avoid having your energy adversely affected? You can strengthen your own force field by maintaining a positive attitude. When your own thoughts are full of joy, happiness, and hope you are less apt to feel the effects of others' negative thoughts and attitudes. Have you ever had a really bad day and everybody around you seems to just add to the awfulness of it? The theory is that "Like attracts like." When you feel up and full of energy, you attract a similar positive energy from others. The more loving, optimistic, and hopeful you feel, the more your up energy attract others of like mind.

Even on our best days, intuitives often feel a need to separate themselves from a flood of psychic information. We want to be able to turn it off when we're ready to rest. As a way of separating myself from my everyday life, I practice a number of meditations before I see clients. I usually do the one described early in this chapter. Here are a few more techniques; try them and then decide what works best for you.

If you are an empath who often picks up on others' feelings and energy, try this helpful technique:

Imagine yourself enclosed in a bubble of white light. The light fills you and surrounds you with energy and peace. See this light flowing down to you from above. Say to yourself, "Only that which is good and needful may enter."

If you are feeling drained by someone close to you, try the following method of strengthening yourself:

Visualize an intense, bright blue globe of light above your head. It explodes like fireworks so that the bright blue lights shimmer around you. Feel the energy that the light draws to you. Say to yourself, "I am energized and strong. I attract only good."

If you are going into a difficult negotiation or situation, first define the outcome you would like to create. Then try this visualization:

Imagine yourself standing under a waterfall of energy. Think about the qualities that you need to have for this difficult situation. Do you need power, strength, love, or courage? Visualize the energy in the waterfall pouring the quality you desire through your body, soaking into all your cells and then surrounding you. See your guide there to help you and add to this energy. Imagine the challenge you are going into and see yourself successful and all parties feeling good.

As in most areas of intuitive growth, there is no right or wrong way to create a sense of safety and confidence. And like most areas, exercises that appeal to your dominant psychic sense are also those to practice for strengthening your abilities.

How Does Your Guidance Speak to *You*?

Learn to go within and seek the guidance of your inner self. It may speak to you through small glimmers of insight, flashes of knowing, or whispers in your thoughts. It always shows the next steps to take, a new direction in your personal and spiritual growth. Intuition does not explain, but simply points the way. If you use it every day, your sixth sense will flourish and greatly enhance your life.

As we continue our journey, we'll show you additional ways to understand what your intuitive guidance is telling you. In Chapter 9 we'll progress from opening up your psychic self to fine-tuning your psychic tools. As part of this, you'll learn how to keep your skills in good maintenance—and use them for practical purposes.

The Least You Need to Know

➤ Meditation is a great way to open up to your higher self.

➤ There are many methods and tools for meditation—choose what works best for you.

➤ You have a special guide to help you grow and heal, and you can take the initiative to contact your guide.

➤ You can learn to protect yourself from negative energy and foster the positive.

Chapter 9

Tune Your Psychic Instrument

In This Chapter

➤ Refine your psychic perceptual skills

➤ Put your intuition to work for you

➤ Feel inspired—and stay that way

➤ Take a new view of time

Okay. Now you've amazed yourself with your own ability to tap into an amazing source of energy and information. It can be such an enlightening experience that all you want to do is sit and meditate. Or you may have drawn a blank and are still wondering, "So, what's the big deal?"

Whether you're awestruck or unimpressed, you have lots more to learn. You can definitely dig deeper to gain greater insight and awareness. And that's what this chapter is all about: helping you tune in to and further refine your psychic potential.

Tuning in to Station W-ESP

Tuning into your intuition is much the same as tuning your radio dial to your intuitive "station." Is your receiver on the right frequency? Your intuition is constantly transmitting information to you, which can provide you with valuable input about the choices you make, your direction in life, the friends you meet, and the happiness (or lack of it) you feel—if your dial is set clearly and you listen to what you hear.

Don't ignore your intuition. Paying attention to your inner insights is the first step in making sure you are properly tuned. Your first attempts may be met with a bit of static. Rest assured that with practice you can count on receiving the needed information at the right time so that you can act on its wisdom.

Using Your Psychic Abilities

In psychic circles, common wisdom says that intuition is here to guide us in our spiritual healing and growth. Often, issues that affect us deeply may express themselves in other areas of our lives. For example, tremendous amounts of stress or tension may show up in the form of a headache or some other illness.

That means that getting in touch with what ails you on a spiritual level can help clear up difficulty in other areas of your life. For that reason, you shouldn't judge, discredit, or ignore the psychic information that comes to you. Even when you don't understand why it's there, you would do well to accept it and trust it. That information can help you in every area of your life, from work to family to friends and more.

In Business

Because psychic ability is often seen as an aspect of our spiritual side, many people assume that it just doesn't blend with business. Nothing could be further from the truth. In fact, business is a huge part of all of your life, so why not use every tool available—including your intuition—to make it as positive and productive as possible?

From the ESP Files

Research has found that people who are highly successful in their careers are often highly intuitive. I have many clients who consult me on business matters, ranging from hiring new staff and motivating current employees to marketing their products and services and foreseeing trends in their industries. One client asked for my impressions of a woman named Susan, whom he was about to offer a senior executive position. My sense was that she had incredible organizational skills, handled complex financial dealings with aplomb, and was self-motivated. All of the traits William wanted for someone in this position. The bad news was that Susan wasn't very good at communicating with others, or at motivating people working for her. William decided to hire Susan, but changed the position so that she had fewer people reporting to her. He also implemented twice weekly meetings with Susan, so that they had built-in opportunities for communication.

Your intuition can help you improve your business skills, including the areas of:

➤ Forecasting trends

➤ Predicting stock fluctuations

➤ Planning strategy

➤ Making decisions quickly and effectively

➤ Managing effectively

➤ Overseeing transitions

➤ Understanding and motivating employees

➤ Predicting promotions and politics

➤ Knowing clients' needs

➤ Becoming more competitive

Any type of business atmosphere can make good use of these business skills—some more than others, depending on what you do. If you work in the financial arena, you can learn to trust your intuition about investment decisions. If you work in marketing or sales, you might get hunches about when to approach people and how. Researchers, engineers, and troubleshooters can gain amazing insight into technical problem solving. Managers can gain insight into motivating their staffs, as well as understanding problems, both professional and personal, that may be hurting their employees' performance.

You can also use your psychic ability to make personal decisions about career paths and job changes. If you're not happy with the job you're in, your intuition might help you get in touch with the source of your difficulty more easily, find out how colleagues view you, or better understand what makes your bosses and coworkers tick—all of which can help you do your job better and, thus, feel better about it. Even if you're currently happy at your job (and you just might be one of those lucky ones!), you can attain a keener awareness of how to appreciate what you've got, improve your surroundings, and make your efforts even more fruitful.

Any and all of these abilities can come to you, the psychic searcher, when you open your mind to the possibilities and express your desire to sharpen your skills and gain further insight. Your intuition can accomplish this in many ways, including dreams, sudden insights, and even subtle accumulations of logical information. If you'd like a little nudging in one of these directions, check out the decision-making exercise a little later in this chapter.

In Relationships

Who can say which areas of your life concern you more—your work or your personal relationships? Of course, your work involves relationships, but your way of handling them—and of using intuition in regard to them—is different. You definitely pay more attention to the emotional issues—past and present—involved in personal relationships. And your intuition is the perfect tool for helping you tap into deeper feelings, including both other people's and your own.

All people both men and women have an incredible fascination about what makes other people tick. Often people experience a great deal of pain when someone close to them is doing something they don't understand. What I do as an intuitive is step inside someone's skin, so to speak. I try to see the situation from his or her point of view. I try to feel what he or she feels. I give a voice to the feelings, concerns, and troubles that both the client and whoever he or she is asking about is experiencing. Then I try to present a plan of action to resolve the situation. You can undergo a similar process when you tap into your own intuition.

From the ESP Files

About 85 percent of my clients are women. Generally women want to talk about relationships (of all kinds) first and work second. Men usually want to talk about work and career directions first. When we have a few minutes remaining at the end of the session, they ask about their relationships! For example, a man might start with questions such as "My boss just refused to promote me and I don't know how to handle the situation or him," or "An employee who reports to me has become moody and depressed. What's wrong and can I help her?" A woman might start with questions such as "My husband is distant and preoccupied. Do you have any idea what's going on with him?" or "My sister has stopped speaking to me and I have no idea why she's upset." Of course, these questions describe a general tendency that fits a stereotype—not every woman and every man fits this mold!!

Take a minute to think about the types of relationships you're in, whether they're romantic, friendly, family, professional, or something else. How can your intuition help you improve on these? Often, it works by helping you gain insight into the other person's way of thinking, so that you can understand his feelings and get a sense of what motivates him. Once you know where that person's coming from, you can take tremendous strides to connect and communicate with him.

I have a client who is involved at a high level in her religious organization. Despite everyone's good intentions, her colleagues often have differences of opinion that prevent them from working well together. One day my client asked me to help her end a stubborn standoff taking place in the group. Using my intuition, I was able to explain the viewpoints of one of the leaders, along with his reasons for rejecting the group's plans. My client and I discussed ways to show him that she empathized with his views but had suggestions for effective compromises.

Oddly, the day after this conversation I heard the leader on the radio, expounding on the very same viewpoints that I had explained to my client. If you're wondering about the outcome of their conflict, this situation didn't have an easy solution. The information I provided helped everyone in the opposing group understand the other group's leader from a different perspective, which helped the lines of communication remain open for everyone. The two sides are still working out their differences, and they consult me occasionally to help with the newest step toward progress.

Your intuition also keeps you in touch with your own needs and what you can do to help yourself in relationships. A classic example of how this comes in handy is when new relationships form. I've had various female clients come to me after about a year of dating new men with the sad news that they had chosen the wrong person. And yet, when they look back at their first few dates, these women can usually remember a point when their inner voice told them, "This is not a good relationship to pursue." Despite hearing these inner alarms, many people choose to ignore their intuition. Often, because they have made mistakes in the past, they have become afraid to trust their own judgment. Once you are attuned to your intuition, it can act as both a warning signal and a confirmation sign that your own judgment is intact.

Unsolved Mystery

Did you know Elvis isn't the only musician credited with coming back to life? Liberace was once spotted returning to Earth on February 19, 1989, by the folks in the village of Fyffe, Alabama. They reported seeing a glittering, 12-foot-tall Liberace, along with his equally oversized piano, descending to Earth from a banana-shaped spacecraft. He played several of his popular tunes on a glowing piano. Thousands of people witnessed this phenomenon, which has yet to be explained.

One simple area where I always apply my intuition is in choosing the professionals who will work for me, such as doctors, dentists, and even my car mechanics. Many parents rely on intuition when it comes to choosing the best schools or teachers for their children. While certain educational arenas are ideal for certain students, they fail others. By understanding how two people will get along and how they will motivate each other, you can better decide the direction to follow for a long-term decision. In addition, you can understand how to present information about new transitions to others, so that change can be much easier for you and everyone else involved.

Many intuitive people believe that each person that we come in contact with is there to teach us something specific. For example, a child is teaching her parent patience, while the parent is teaching her child discipline. Even an angry boss can teach us something, whether it's the importance of being on time or the necessity of ignoring displaced anger because it doesn't belong to us. But if you're not quite sure what to think of someone, try the decision-making exercise described in the next section.

In Decision-Making

Many of us panic when faced with making a significant decision—and sometimes even a small one—in our lives. Often we can't seem to find a clear "yes" or "no" answer. We write endless lists of pros and cons. We discuss it with our friends and families. We often scurry about trying to gather as many facts about the situation as we can...and then we end up feeling even more confused than when we started.

Following is a process you can follow to take advantage of the intuitive input your psyche can give you when making important decisions. Intuition is not meant to replace logic and rationality. Rather, intuitive input simply adds information—about yourself, as well as the world around you—to your decision-making process.

1. *The Preparation Phase.* In this phase, you research your problem. For starters, write about the decision you are trying to make. Gather as much data as you can about the issue. Declare a firm intent to make your decision. Learn as much as you can about yourself and your response to the issue. This lays the groundwork for the intuitive information to come through. Frame the decision in the form of a question, "Should I take this job with XYZ Company?"

   Here's an example from my experience:

   Before I started my psychic reading business I was an operations manager of a software company. I was giving readings for friends a few hours a month. A writer for the Boston Globe *newspaper heard about my readings and asked if she could book a session with me. Several months later she wrote about her experience. Her article produced such a response for my services that my phone was ringing off the hook and I had to hire a secretary.*

   My questions for my intuition were:

   ➤ *Should I stay in my job and forget the readings?*

   ➤ *Should I leave my job to start a psychic reading business?*

   ➤ *Should I attempt to do my job and the readings?*

   I did as much research as I could during this phase. I found out about renting an office, setting up a business, getting insurance, and finding secretarial help. I spoke with other psychics in the area. I also spoke with my boss about my job, the future of the company, and how he saw my role in it. I gathered data.

   Want to hear what happened next? Read on through the transition phase.

2. *The Transition Phase.* This is the toughest part for most people. It's the stage during which you're waiting. It often feels like you're doing nothing. It's a time, however, to let the solution to your dilemma percolate. If you're a believer in guides, angels, and other helpers of the universe, you may want to think of this as a time that they are gathering resources, connections, and synchronicities to bring about your answer.

Try to enjoy a little down time. Take care of yourself. Get a massage. Take the day off. Meditate or do yoga. Relax. Sleep more. It's often difficult for your intuition to get through the usual busyness of your mind. Do anything that helps you slow down.

Now, back to my example:

I am an action taker, so I hate this waiting phase. I prayed about the decision. I asked for dreams, any form of guidance. I meditated. I wrote in my journal. I asked for a sign to indicate the direction I should take. I played out various scenarios in my mind and tried to feel out my response. I felt scared of the risk. Would it work to have my own business? Could I do this full-time? Could I make it on my own? What about benefits and security? I also felt excited by the idea of change and the possibilities it presented. Meanwhile, I continued to do my software job and give readings. I waited.

Sometimes, if you're not sure what decision to make, waiting is the best strategy. Allow time for your answer to come to you. If you feel you're in a time crunch, create a bit of quiet time away from your usual busy routine to allow a sense of inner calm to come your way.

3. *The "Aha" Phase.* If you've followed the first two steps with the clear intention of receiving intuitive input about your decision, the next step will happen all by itself. The answer may come in a dream, by a continual inner nudge toward a certain answer, or sometimes by a simple inner certainty about the right decision. The answer may come when you least expect it—and most need it. See the way it happened to me:

My answer came in a dream. In my dream I was out on a beautiful lake. I was taking in this glorious scene when I noticed that I was in canoes. That isn't a typo. I had one foot in one canoe and my other foot in another. The two canoes were going to opposite ends of the lake. I immediately woke up and laughed. I couldn't continue to try to go in two directions! I instantly understood that I couldn't possibly hold down my software job and give my readings. The answer became clear.

Your information may come to you in a similar way, or much differently. Just remember to trust it, as well as trust in your reading of it. It's a special delivery message just for you, so don't take it for granted or feel afraid to act on it.

4. *The "I Know I Made the Right Decision" Phase.* When you've made the right decision you usually feel relieved, excited, and maybe even calm and peaceful. Often events start to click into place for you. This is part of the synchronicity we talked

about in Chapter 6. You find yourself wanting to move into action. You may receive more nudges from your intuition about what to do next as the new path unfolds for you. Pay attention to the feelings of excitement or positive anticipation that usually come with this phase.

And to finish the story:

I was amazed at the coincidences and synchronicities that followed my decision. A friend had an office that she was thinking about subletting and I took it. Another acquaintance had just come back from several years abroad and needed a temporary job. She became my receptionist for awhile. Everything clicked into place as more clients called and referred their friends. That was 13 years ago—and I've never regretted the decision.

It's important to separate the fact that you made the right decision from the normal amount of anxiety that the actual change may bring about in your life. Most of us feel a little anxious when we make a change. We may have to move, leave a job and friends, or undergo some other unsettling event. Remember that there's always a learning curve in any new situation but someday you can look back and say, "Piece of cake!"

Here's an exercise with a few specifics to get you started with your psychic decision-making process. Give it a try.

Intuitive Decision-Making Exercise

1. What is the difficulty or challenge that I'm experiencing? Describe the situation here.

   _____

   _____

2. What am I learning from this situation? There may be a quality that you are learning to develop, such as courage, patience, or forgiveness. Describe any of your thoughts and feelings here.

   _____

   _____

3. What outcome would I like? Sometimes we get so focused on the problem, we forget to ask ourselves what we really want. Pay attention to anything in the present that feels exciting, that makes you joyful, peaceful, or calm. Describe any thoughts and feelings here.

   _____

   _____

4. What steps can I take toward achieving this outcome? Sometimes we reach our goals by a series of small steps. Think about your answer to #3 and state some actions that will take you closer to the outcome you want.

_____

_____

Sometimes it takes a little time to see how all of our concerns and details work themselves out. But look at it as an adventure. Making a decision means taking a step in a definite direction, which always involves a little risk. But go for it! One day you'll turn a corner, and find yourself saying, "I've never regretted it" for the rest of your life.

Using Your Personal Psychic Symbols

When you're working or waiting to receive intuitive information, don't overlook what might be right in front of you—literally! These messages can come in many forms, such as dreams, natural events, unusual statements coming from someone you'd least expect them to, or a phrase or passage of text that jumps out at you.

Your life is filled with messages that appear at every turn, and yet you often don't even recognize them. Or if you do realize that they're intuitive signs, you don't always know how to figure out what they're trying to tell you. For that reason, you'd be wise to sort out what symbols you associate with certain words or concepts.

Intuition Hotline

In her book *Everyone's Guide to Using Psychic Ability* (Weiser, 1995), Betty F. Balcombe suggests a fun way to get a reply when you're stuck. Write yourself a letter describing all the details of your problem. Then drop it in the mailbox. As soon as it comes back to you, just sit down and answer it. You'll be impressed by your own good advice.

Here's an example of how you can use symbols to gather intuitive information. If you are meditating and ask for guidance by saying, "What should I do to have more energy?" The symbol for a *change in career* pops into your mind. You realize that your work has gotten stale of late and decide to seek the advice of a career counselor.

You've been bothered by the fact that you've been having difficulty with a coworker whom you used to get along with. You wonder if you have done anything to offend her. You ask for guidance, saying, "What is going on with my coworker and how can I fix the relationship?" You receive a symbol of a broken heart. You recognize this as your symbol for a love relationship that has ended. Suddenly, you understand what may have happened to your coworker and decide to be more compassionate toward her.

From the ESP Files

Certain psychics use flowers as symbols in various ways. They may associate visions of certain flowers with certain feelings or occasions. I teach an exercise where I ask people to imagine their class partners to be flowers, symbolic representations of their partners. If someone psychically sees an image of a lone flower separate from all others, that person might extrapolate that his or her class partner is alone or lonely. If someone sees an image of a flower towering over other flowers, that person might make an interpretation that his or her partner is a leader. I had a person in my class who saw a weak-looking flower as a symbol of her class partner. She exclaimed, "I think you need fertilizer!" It turned out her partner was trying to get pregnant!

Here's an exercise to help you define your personal symbols. Go down the list and write down the first response that comes to mind for you. If symbols come to you in images rather than words, feel free to draw your symbols instead.

Discovering Your Psychic Symbols Exercise

Subject	Your Symbol
Work	_____
Education	_____
Marriage	_____
Money	_____
Home	_____
Health	_____
Travel	_____
Friends	_____
Divorce	_____
Career in healing	_____
Change in career	_____
Musical ability	_____

Change in location _____

Vacation _____

Someone who is shy _____

Someone who is controlling _____

Teacher _____

New situation/change _____

Fall _____

Spring _____

Spirituality _____

Ambition _____

Family _____

Love _____

Nature _____

Power _____

Other _____ _____

Other _____ _____

Once you've completed this list, you might also want to add other images that come to you in the future, whether they're new categories or revisions to old ones. Just don't cross out any records of previous associations, since one concept can have more than one symbol. You may soon have an extensive guide to much of what's going on in your mind.

What to Do When You're Stuck

What if you're keeping your eyes open, and you still can't see any sign of psychic guidance? Is it possible that you've had a taste of the "other side" just long enough to get you interested, and then make you wonder about it for the rest of your life? Not likely!

We've given you lots of exercises to work with (and will give you lots more)! Remember that not all of the ideas and concepts will work for you: Everyone responds differently. But keep practicing, take small steps, and have fun with this.

Mixed Messages

If you find you continually get stuck in feelings of fear or anxiety when you make a decision, something other than intuitive input may be going on. Susan Jeffers' wonderful book, *Feel the Fear and Do It Anyway* (Fawcett, 1993), is immensely helpful and uplifting for anyone trying to get unstuck and take action.

125

Aside from the big picture, make sure that you're taking care of the small stuff too. Do your research on any decision you need to be making. Write your thank you notes to the people who count. Make sure you exercise, so your thoughts and energy get flowing. Go on a walkabout around your neighborhood so you see a different view of the reality that surrounds you. Dance, jump, punch a pillow. Just stop taking yourself so seriously! Remember the saying, "Angels can fly because they take themselves lightly."

When You Don't Get Information Right Away

Keep in mind that you're still learning, and learning patience—with yourself, as well as your circumstances—may be a big part of your current lesson. Remember that everything takes time.

Many facts and forces may need to come into play before the path becomes clear. For example, you may be waiting to hear about one job possibility because another—even better!—job is about to become available somewhere else...maybe at a level or company that you never dreamed you'd have a shot at. This takes us back to that old adage that we keep sending your way: Trust your intuition.

But if you're really restless, here's something you can do to get some answers about what you think, feel, dream, and imagine. Ready for this amazing advice? Here goes: If all else fails...flip a coin. Not what you were expecting to hear, huh? Well, try it anyway.

Not-Your-Typical-Coin-Toss Exercise

1. Think about the decision you're trying to make. Form it in your mind as a "yes" or "no" question. "Should I take the job with XYZ Corporation?" "Should I apply to graduate school now?" "Should I stop dating John?"

   _____

2. Take a coin and flip it. Heads indicates yes. Tails indicates no. Okay, what was the answer?

   _____

   But wait! There's more to this exercise.

3. Think about how you felt about the answer. Were you disappointed? Relieved? Did you get a thrill of excitement through your body, or a knot of fear in your stomach? Admit it, did you immediately want to flip the coin two more times and try for best two out of three? (Or have you actually done that already?)

   _____

Any of these responses is an example of your intuition speaking to you. Your response gave you information about the answer to your decision. So often we expect our intuition to be a booming God-like voice saying, "LYNN: TAKE THAT JOB AT XYZ CORPORATION—NOW! GO GIRL!"

It's more likely to speak through subtle feelings, inner nudges, or physical sensations. When you learn to pay attention and act on these responses, they can be just as loud and clear as a booming voice.

How to Get Your Energy Moving Again

Sogyal Rinpoche, author of *The Tibetan Book of Living and Dying,* said, "Practice [intuition] consistently, so when you're in the heat of the battle, when you need it, it will be there for you. But you have to practice." Even when you feel at a loss for what to do, always continue to practice.

Practice includes many of the opening techniques we talked about in Chapter 8. Meditation and breathing are among the top two for many people, while exercise, praying, *chanting*, and *contemplation* help others. But in order to keep practicing, you need to stay motivated, or get newly motivated.

Here's an exercise to get you in touch with what motivates you.

> **Beyond Words**
>
> **Chanting** is the singing of a short simple melody or even a few monotonous notes. It often involves repetition of the same words or sounds in order to attain a spiritual state. **Contemplation** involves deep thought or reflection as a type of meditation or prayer. For example, one focuses their thoughts on a single concept, such as peace, as a way of reaching a more spiritual state.

Accessing Intuition for Success Exercise

1. Bring to mind a time in your life when you received something you *really* wanted. This could be a career change, a relationship, a house, a car, a family, or anything else of your choosing. Write this down.

   _____

2. What were the factors that made you successful in achieving this goal? Did you take action? Did you pray? Did you just think you were lucky? Did you have to work hard to get it? Did you have to let go of trying to get it to happen? Write anything that comes to mind about this.

   _____

3. What were the obstacles involved in achieving this goal? Were you discouraged? Did friends and family tell you not to do it? Was there a block that you had to overcome in yourself first? Write anything that comes to mind about this.

   _____

4. Imagine that you have a wise being looking out for you. This being knows you want more prosperity, peace, love, success, and ease in your life. Close your eyes and ask this wise being what you should do to bring more of these qualities into your life.

_____

5. Ask your wise being what you should do when you feel discouraged.

_____

Getting in touch with why you're blocked and what you need to do to remain motivated can help you immensely. You can learn much about yourself by understanding why you aren't moving forward. Remember, your intuition is always giving you an opportunity to learn.

Take Time for Inner Guidance

Life doesn't always go in a straight line even when we're doing everything right. Just as nature has seasons, cycles, ebbs, and flows, so do our lives. Our task as spiritual human beings is to learn how to love and forgive, experience peace within ourselves, be of service, and have compassion for others. The universe has many ways to help us learn those lessons in our schoolroom called Earth.

Time and Psychic Impressions

The problem with time isn't that we don't have enough of it: It's that it doesn't exist—but we still don't understand that it doesn't exist. Sound crazy? Well, some people actually believe that the commonly accepted idea that time exists in a straight line is nonsense.

Where's Einstein when you need him? His relativity theory is what got a lot of people thinking about this. Basically, modern physics is showing us that time does not exist only at one place at one point in time. Time is not fixed, or a given. But this idea is not new to many psychics, including those who lived long before Einstein. Like Nostradamus.

Those special psychics who can look back into history to see past lives or peer into the future at upcoming events are actually tapping into time at different points along a continuum. Or rather, at different points along continuums on different planes. Of course, we can't prove this—with words, anyway. Mathematicians are working on it, but meanwhile, just ask your psyche to show you.

How to Speed Up an Event You Want to Create

"The greatest discovery of my generation is that human beings, by changing the inner attitudes of their minds, can change the outer aspects of their lives," proclaimed psychologist and philosopher William James (1842–1910). This certainly presents a good argument for free will. It also shows us the power of our minds.

Creative visualization is built on James' type of thinking. If you think about what you'd like to achieve in your life, you can do just that. For example, if you want to own a brand new car, picture yourself in that car, happily driving it off the lot and waving to your friends as you drive it home. Be aware that using this technique works best when you place yourself in the picture. If you just picture a beautiful car that's empty, it will stay that way, and so will your driveway.

I've found that my clients who are clearest about what they want to create achieve their goals much more quickly. Those who feel unsure of their goals, feel they don't deserve them, or believe they may be unattainable, slow down or even halt the process of manifesting their desires.

Painting a picture of what you want to achieve works in various ways. For one thing, visualization sends a signal to your intuitive side about what you want. Then your intuition can begin to put the moves in motion that will make your desires become real. But don't expect your intuition to do it all alone. That's where the second part, taking action, comes in.

Beyond Words

Creative visualization is the process by which the creation of a visual image promotes a desired outcome. This image is often called to mind during meditation or deep relaxation.

Your tasks are to focus on your goals and then act on your intuitive impulses. Pay attention to any clue from your intuition that may help you achieve your goal. You may have a sudden impulse to call a friend. Call! You might feel drawn to read a certain book. Read it! You may have a sudden impulse to speak to the person standing next to you in line. Talk! Action and intuition work off each other to accomplish your goal. Your intuitive "Higher Mind" can see the overview of what it needs to do to pull all the events together to help you accomplish what you want.

Similar to visualization are *affirmations*. These positive verbal expressions also send a message to your mind indicating what you want to achieve. When you choose a positive affirmation always use the present tense, so that your changes can take place now, rather than some in the far-off future. For example, say "I am open to my intuition and easily act on it's wisdom," instead of "I *will be* open to my intuition…."

Beyond Words

Affirmations are statements that create a reality or truth through frequent repetition. We often hear about positive affirmations, which people repeat to improve their situation, but negative thoughts that we repeat often also work as affirmations—bad ones.

I used affirmations and visualizations to help start my business. My positive affirmation was, "I have a successful, full-time psychic reading business." My visualizations included a full appointment book, my answering machine with lots of calls from clients, and an image of a beautiful office with a smiling client. It all happened!

Slow Down the Pace in Your Life

You probably know people in your life who always appear confident, organized, and serene. These people never appear frazzled—they never seem to be overwhelmed if their computers break down when they're on a deadline or the carpools don't pick up their children in time for school. Their desks don't look like they require an archeological dig to find a piece of paper. What's their secret?

The key to remaining calm is being aware of what's going on in the big picture around and beyond you. In a crisis or period of frustrating feelings, stop panicking and ask yourself, "What am I learning? What could I have done—and what can I do in the future—to prevent this situation from happening?" Your answer may include learning to say "No" to things that drain you, focusing on bringing into your life the things that make you happy and give you energy, or questioning whether you really need to do more and have more. A popular book that can help you get in touch with these principles is *Simple Abundance: A Daybook of Comfort and Joy* by Sarah Ban Breathnach (Warner Books, 1995).

Staying centered helps you to live in the moment and be open and aware of all the messages that are coming your way. At the very least, you'll learn to get your priorities straight. At best, you'll attain a level of awareness that can connect you directly to the force that keeps us all living and loving. Stay tuned for more on how intuition works with our life force in Chapter 10.

The Least You Need to Know

➤ You can use intuitive information to help you in every aspect of your life.

➤ Learn to understand your own set of psychic symbols.

➤ Getting in tune with your intuition is a process: Be patient.

➤ Changing your view of time helps you gain control.

Part 3
The Body Psychic

Many people think of psychic abilities in terms of the mind alone. The body contains the brain, but the brain helps to move the body. And we suspect that still something else empowers them both: the spirit.

Part 3 talks about the connections and interactions between the body, mind, and spirit. We talk about a life force that appears to underlie and motivate all of existence. This force can create healing, which can be inspired by prayer. We recommend ways to strengthen your physical, mental, and spiritual access to this powerful and positive force.

Embracing the Life Force

The ancient gurus of the Eastern world knew several millennia ago what Westerners have just begun to learn in the past few decades: The body is intricately connected to the mind, emotions, and spirit. This connection seems fairly obvious to most of us, as it did to the ancient gurus who acknowledged it without question. But doubt remains here because most "scientific" Americans are waiting for that most Western of traditions: proof.

Everybody now accepts the idea that stress can lead to illness, while exercise and eating right improves health. Why? Because numerous studies have proven this to be true, which led doctors and other traditional healthcare providers to finally put forth these ideas. Meanwhile, alternative health researchers continue to make inroads into "new" connections between body, mind, and spirit. Within a few years, some of these "radical" ideas are likely to be accepted as conventional wisdom—and will then be promoted by the medical establishment too. In this chapter, we'll take a look at how the mind and body interact, and where the psychic side comes in.

East Meets West

"Mind and body are inseparably one," says Deepak Chopra in *Ageless Body, Timeless Mind* (Harmony, 1993). Born in New Delhi, India, Deepak Chopra, M.D., is a highly acclaimed medical doctor, trained as an endocrinologist, who has brought alternative health to the attention of mainstream American audiences through his best-selling books. Clearly, millions of Americans are ready to hear and learn more about healing of the body, mind, and spirit.

From the ESP Files

The term "dis-ease" has become popular in recent years among people in alternative health areas. Interestingly, this term was originally created by Norman Vincent Peale, the minister and author who wrote, *The Power of Positive Thinking* (Simon & Schuster, 1947). The idea behind it is that body illnesses are linked to uneasy emotional or spiritual states. In Louise Hay's book *You Can Heal Your Life* (Hay House, 1984), the author supports this theory by including a chart that lists a health problem and then matches it up to an emotional issue that causes it. This may be an oversimplification; the reasons for physical illness are complex. But listening to the clues that your body exhibits can help you examine any part of your life that may feel out of balance. Illness can be a catalyst for positive change, guiding you to a path of learning that opens up tremendous opportunity for both personal and spiritual insight and change.

Deepak Chopra, himself, is an interesting symbol of the coming together of the Eastern and Western cultures. His upbringing in the East has given him great insight into the ancient teachings and in-depth beliefs of the Indian gurus. In particular, his background involves the study of the highly spiritual form of medicine called *ayurvedic medicine*. His familiarity with Western medicine and culture enables him to translate the abstract Eastern ideas into everyday Western ways of thinking about things. In essence, he is not saying a lot that's new—except to Westerners, who are eager to hear it. So...what is this message about body-mind connections anyway?

Tapping Ancient Energy Sources

The idea underlying much ancient spiritual philosophy—including those connected with Christian, Jewish, and native American faiths—is that a universal life force runs through everything, including each and every person. It fills both the body and the mind, and provides people with the energy and drive to move through their lives. Because this vast force constantly runs through people, it also connects them—their bodies, minds, and spirits as a single entity—to the greater, universal life force that runs through everything surrounding them. In this way, the yogis and Buddhists are accurate when they say, "All is one." (It sounds like the Three Musketeers were on to this too.)

China's Chi

Ancient Chinese medicine calls the universal energy that flows through the body, *chi*. It flows through the body's vital organs, bones, bloodstream, and other parts along a network of pathways called *meridians*. The body contains 14 major meridians, each of which passes through many parts of the body.

Although chi cannot be seen, measured, or tested, healers who know how to work with it help move it through the body properly. These people believe that too much or too little chi in a certain body area—created because of a blockage of the flow of chi—can lead to stress and eventually disease. Some healers use acupressure or acupuncture to release excess energy that collects at specific points along the meridians. By releasing and directing the flow of chi through the body, they can balance any excesses that cause blockages and build-ups of stress.

Beyond Words

Ayurveda comes from two Sanskrit words: ayur, meaning life, and veda, meaning knowledge; combined they mean "the knowledge of life." Ayurvedic medicine is considered to be the oldest known natural healing system, but it is more than a medical science. It is intricately interconnected with close observation of nature and its relationship to man through meditation. This practice has formulated spiritual truths that have been imparted from guru to disciple for over 5,000 years.

Beyond Words

According to ancient Chinese medicine, **chi** is the body's vital life force. The Japanese call it ki. **Meridians** are pathways that carry chi throughout the body.

According to the principles of the ancient Chinese practice of QiGong, also known as chi kung, the flow of "qi" or "chi" energy through the body is facilitated through performing specific movements, breathing exercises, and manipulation of pressure points. "Chi" flows through the body's vital organs, bones, bloodstream, and other parts along a network of pathways.

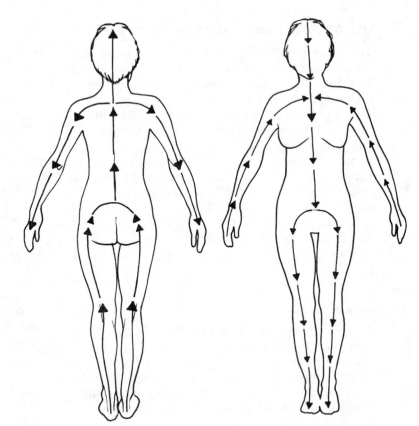

Beyond Words

According to the Indian yogic tradition, **prana** is a form of energy that animates all physical matter, including the human body. **Nadis** are passageways of psychospiritual energy thought to work like vibrating energy currents.

Yoga's Prana: Balance Your Chakras

In India, the word *prana* is used to refer to the energy that flows through the body, as well as all matter in the universe. It is not a form of consciousness or spirit, but a form of pure energy that animates the mind, as well as the body. Similar to the ancient Chinese beliefs, prana moves along pathways of the body.

In yoga-speak, prana flows through 10 currents, or pathways, called *nadis*. The three major nadis are positioned along the spinal column. When inhaling, one carries prana down the right side of the spine. When exhaling, another carries prana up the left side of the spine. The movement of prana between the two sides of the spine creates a current that moves prana throughout the spinal column. The seven chakras (which we introduced in Chapter 6) are positioned as major energy points along this pathway.

So why are we telling you all this? Because these ancient beliefs about how energy travels through the body correspond to how modern medical science tracks the movement of messages throughout the nervous system. Not too shabby, eh?

Nervous System Connections

Today, magazines and medical journals are filled with studies that show how our mental states are linked to our physical conditions. Though this idea is becoming more generally accepted, theories abound on how this body-mind process operates— even among those within the fields of alternative health and psychic healing. The possibilities are endless.

Intuition Hotline

Want to hear more about how the body and emotions interact? Check out Mona Lisa Schulz's book *Awakening Intuition* (Harmony, 1998). In it, she offers her observations as a neuropsychiatrist and neuroscientist, as well as a highly acclaimed medical intuitive.

Here's a general overview of what many modern intuitives and psi researchers think is going on within the body and mind. Some suggest that a field surrounding and including the body is composed of information about the body and what has happened to it. This information is stored along body pathways that may extend beyond the brain (contrary to the accepted idea that the brain alone stores all memories). This body memory may even be stored in the individual cells.

Mona Lisa Schulz, a practicing medical doctor who is also a medical intuitive, is a strong proponent of the idea that memories are encoded in the body itself. She explains that certain emotional situations cause the release of chemicals that travel through the body (as well as the brain). These experiences, via the chemicals, leave an imprint on the molecules that make up the tissue in an organ system within the body. Dr. Schulz reports that certain emotional issues affiliated with certain types of situations, leave their mark in specific organ areas. These organ areas actually correspond to the seven chakras, or emotional energy centers, of the ancient Eastern traditions. The following table shows you how certain emotional issues correspond to specific body areas.

Emotional Center	Body Area	Personal Issues
First	Blood; bones; hips; spine; immunity	Family issues; support; security
Second	Pelvis; lower back; sex organs	Relationships; drives
Third	Stomach; GI tract	Self-esteem; work
Fourth	Heart; lungs; breasts	Emotional expression; partnership
Fifth	Neck; throat	Personal expression
Sixth	Eyes; ears; nose; throat; brain	Perception; thought; morality
Seventh	Muscles; genes; connective tissue	One's life purpose; divine awareness

Dr. Schulz emphasizes the point that physical symptoms of illness can actually be a blessing. They are signals from our intuitive side telling us to pay attention to an emotional situation that needs to be resolved. Schulz feels that these emotional issues need to be addressed in order to help them flow freely through the body, rather than becoming blocked in certain spots. Sounds a lot like an emotional version of how chi works, huh?

How the Body-Mind Sends Messages

Our bodies have an intuitive language that sends us messages in a variety of ways, including bodily sensations, emotions, dreams, visions, and symptoms of disease. We've talked in Chapter 6 about bodily sensations and emotions as a form of clairsentience, and we'll talk more about dreams and visions in later chapters. So now's our chance to explore symptoms of disease as body signals for what's really ailing us—that is, emotionally and spiritually.

When medical intuitives give readings, they have access to the information about a client's condition. This usually includes the emotional dilemmas that are connected to the physical difficulty. Depending on how he or she receives the information, each medical intuitive intakes the information differently. For example, Mona Lisa Schulz sees a more literal picture of the affected spot as it would look in the interior of the patient's body. Modern medical intuitive Caroline Myss, on the other hand, sees a light, or energy, surrounding the patient, with darker areas that mark trouble spots.

Unsolved Mystery

Edgar Cayce, the famous healer who practiced during the first half of the 1900s, kept records of treating over 30,000 patients—a majority of whom were actually located long distances away. During each healing session, Cayce would go into a trance state; then his unconscious mind would begin the diagnosis with the words, "Yes, we can see the body." He attributed his ability to diagnose so accurately to his ability to see each of the patient's cells as being conscious. Each cell would thereby relay to Cayce (through his unconscious mind) what was causing the trouble for them.

Although these people have developed and shown tremendous skill at reading the body's information, you can do it too! You can start by listening to your own body talk to you. First, you'll want to understand the many ways that it can send you signals, so you'll know what to be on the lookout for. Following are a few different—and perhaps surprising—ways that the body works to communicate with you.

Gut Feelings

The area around the stomach has always been considered extremely important in the Eastern system of chakras. Now it has gained newfound importance in Western scientific circles as well. Indeed, in 1996 *The New York Times* reported that scientists had found that the body has a second "brain"—in the stomach! It is actually a network of neurons, neurotransmitters, and proteins called the *enteric nervous system*.

The enteric nervous system, and its interacton with the brain in the head, is so complex that it's become a new field of study called *gastroenterology*. Experts in this area propose that early forms of tubular animals had a single brain located in their gut, because their efforts for survival were food oriented. As animals developed, pathways out of the gut extended to a newer brain, used for more complex needs (such as sex). Eventually the connection between the two brains shrunk to a cable, the vagus nerve.

Beyond Words

The **enteric nervous system** is a primitive brain located in the layers of tissue lining the esophagus, stomach, small intestine, and colon. It connects directly through a vein to our main brain (the one in our heads). **Gastoenterology** is the scientific study of the enteric nervous system by medical specialists.

139

Some alternative health practitioners suggest that this second brain acts as the body's brain. Similar to the awareness that informs our minds of our thoughts and emotions, the body's brain tells the body about all that it is sensing and learning. Because this body brain harks back to our earliest evolutionary urges to survive simply by eating, it is probably deeply connected to our survival instincts. This may explain why we sometimes get gut feelings about decisions that affect our safety and survival—even when it may pertain to our jobs (and not life-or-death situations).

In a Heartbeat

The heart is more than a muscle that pumps blood. Similar to the gut, it appears to have its own minibrain system, an intelligence system that helps determine the effect that mental and emotional reactions have on your health. It works through a collection of neurons and nerves in the heart that carry impulses between the heart and brain.

The connection between the heart and brain is a two way street: The heart gets signals from the brain (and central nervous system) and vice versa. When you're calm, the rhythm of the heart sends an even and steady signal to the brain. When you get frightened or tense (in particular, during emergencies), your heart's signals become erratic and the brain picks up these interrupted signals and puts the body on alert. In this way, the heart actually controls the brain's cortex, which is responsible for higher mental function, organ function, and perception.

Considering that the heart and gut have their own minibrains, it's easy to imagine that our other organs and body parts may have brains as well. Certainly, our skin contains a system of picking up signals and passing their messages throughout our body to our brain. So try to start paying attention to what your body is thinking—and what thoughts it's trying to pass along to your main brain.

Mixed Messages

Learning to recognize your body's messages is a great way to keep yourself abreast and attuned to problems when they're just beginning. But don't ignore your urgent health needs in the hope that your intuition will tell you what to do. Be mindful of health emergencies. And don't forget to go for your regular checkups too!

Trusting What Your Body Knows

We all have an area in our bodies that I call our "intuitive early warning system." It's that nagging physical symptom that tells us something is out of balance in our lives or in our bodies. It's usually something relatively minor, such as a mild stomachache, a pulled muscle, a slight headache. It's our body's way of telling us, "Warning! You're on overload. Caution ahead!"

Here's the way that my intuitive health works and how I've learned to deal with it. My "early warning symptom" is a headache. My headaches used to overwhelm me: I would have to cancel my sessions with clients because the pain was unbearable. Since I believe that the body's symptoms are often a message about something that is out of balance, I finally decided to pay attention to my own body's intuition.

One day when I had the beginnings of a headache, I sat down to meditate. I imagined that I could give the pain in my head a voice, and I was determined to hear it and heed it. To my surprise, I received a rush of information, "You're always doing too much. You need to slow down. You don't have to do everything. You can lean on other people sometimes, you know! You don't always have to be strong!" It was true. I'm a doer. I like taking on the challenge of accomplishing big things—and I haven't always known my limits. I am usually independent in the extreme, so I have difficulty asking anyone for help. This experience was the first time that I had connected those issues with my headaches.

I've now learned to pay attention at the first inkling of a headache. I immediately ask myself two things:

➤ What can I let go of right now?

➤ What can I do to nurture myself?

I can't say that the headaches are entirely a thing of the past, but their frequency and intensity have greatly diminished. And so has my stress level!

We all just need to keep in mind that a disease is not our enemy. It may be a messenger from our intuitive guide who is trying to get our attention. It can be an incredible gift of wisdom that leads us onto a new path.

Trusting What the Earth Knows: The Life Force of Nature

According to the ancient sages who understand the workings of the life energy, or life force, or chi, we are all born with a certain amount of this energy. We can recharge ourselves through our interactions with the earth, sunlight, air, food, drink, and positive relationships with others.

Getting in touch with these natural forces helps us gain a connection with them, and with our place in the universe. This provides us with yet another way to become better attuned to all the information that surrounds us. We can intake the energy and insight that the earth provides and release our prayers or thoughts of grateful acknowledgment for our place in the grand scheme of things. In the language of the yogis, this gratefulness could be called "love."

Now that we're getting a closer look at how our bodies work in relation to our minds and the universal mind, what are we going to do about it? Chapter 11 will explain the basics of healing, which will then lead us on to chapters that look at new pathways for using intuitive energy to help others, as well as ourselves.

The Least You Need to Know

➤ Eastern medicine has many traditions that reflect what modern science is now discovering about the body.

➤ A vital, energy force runs through everything, connecting our bodies and minds.

➤ A healthy flow of our emotions corresponds to a free flow of vital energy through our body.

➤ Our body's physical condition can give us information about our emotional state.

Chapter 11

Psychic Healing

In This Chapter

➤ Healing begins from the inside out

➤ Sensing the energy that permeates the universe

➤ The colors of the energy that surrounds everyone

➤ Moving the energy of the life force

Believe it or not, we all have access to an awesome universal energy source. In fact, everyone and everything is one with that source, and is made of energy. Sound crazy? Well, that's what Einstein was saying: Energy equals matter. And that's what people are.

Psychics who have a strong sense of this energy are able to work with it in many ways on many levels. They see that it exists for everyone in body, mind, and spirit. With a little guidance, you can see and sense this energy as well, and learn to balance these levels within yourself. You too can begin to improve your flow of energy, to soothe your inner selves, and create harmony in all that surrounds you. This is the beginning of psychic healing, which is the subject of this chapter.

Feeling Better: Spiritual Regeneration

The word regeneration means to be made over again in a new form; *spiritual regeneration* refers to a spiritual rebirth. Christians might use the term "born again"; Buddhists might call it the "awakening." Regardless of what you call it, a newfound awareness of the spiritual side of life can give you a fresh outlook, improved attitude, and new sense of purpose in life. These changes may be so profound that your life will never be the same again.

Beyond Words

Spiritual regeneration refers to a spiritual rebirth or religious conversion. It suggests that a person is made over, usually in a new and improved condition.

This sort of conversion experience is certainly nothing to fear. It's actually a wake-up call to start looking at how valuable life really is and how important a part— you play in it. Not everyone needs to save the world, foresee future problems and solutions, or heal thousands of sick and dying people. But everyone can do something to help improve, and thereby to help heal, the world that surrounds them.

An important place to start healing is within yourself. Get in touch with how you're really feeling. Does your stomach hurt on days when you have an extra cup of coffee and two extra donuts? Then listen to what it's telling you. Do your eyes hurt in the morning after you've stayed up too late watching TV? Then get a grip on the remote control: Turn off the tube! Do you sometimes feel overwhelmed by too many feelings flooding through your mind at once? Then try taking regular time out to meditate or somehow get your feelings centered. You can start right now by taking one deep breath, and then another....

Getting in touch with your emotional state is a great place to start changing your life. If little things annoy you but you're not sure why, sit still in a quiet place and breathe deeply. When you think about the annoyances, try to isolate where the tension builds up in your body. That's a big hint about what types of issues are trouble spots for you. (Check out the table in Chapter 10 to see what body parts correspond to certain emotional issues.) So what do you do once you realize where your energy's getting stuck? Read on for some insight into how the body moves and directs energy, and how you can help get it moving too.

Auras

In the previous chapter we talked about the vital life force as an energy that flows through everyone. When this energy is flowing smoothly, all is well. But when it's not, every aspect of your life can become out of balance. Understanding this energy and its flow is a big step toward creating balanced, harmonious lives. Many alternative healers, some of whom are called energy healers, work with this energy. Some can feel it (as a form of clairsentience) and others can even see it (as a form of clairvoyance). This field of energy that surrounds each living organism is referred to as an *aura*.

What Is an Aura?

Webster's dictionary defines an *aura* as "a subtly pervasive quality or atmosphere seen as emanating from a person, place, or thing." (Is this intended to be vague, or what?) In intuitive-speak, the aura is a vibrating field of energy (often perceived as light) that pulses around and through the body at all times. In religious renditions of sacred events, you've seen them painted as haloes around holy heads.

Basically, the aura is a luminous atmosphere that surrounds all living things. Many believe that this energy both enters and leaves through the vortices of the chakras. The energy is denser the closer in to the body you get and thus perceptible, but it extends outward in infinite directions and comes in from infinite distances as well.

Many believe that this field around the body is an electromagnetic field, which may even conduct electricity through the water contained in the body. While surrounding the body, this field protects you and also helps you sense others' feelings and allows others to perceive your true self. The aura can be perceived through feeling, "sensing," or seeing.

Beyond Words

An **aura** is the field of electromagnetic energy that permeates and surrounds every organism, both living and not living. The word comes from the Greek "avra," which means breeze.

Some people are wired visually to see auras more easily, while others can feel or sense them. Even people who don't seem to have a natural inclination for seeing auras can learn to do it, with practice. We provide a few exercises in this chapter to help you get started with seeing or sensing auras, but first let's talk about what's *not* an aura.

What's Not an Aura

Two optical effects are often mistaken for the aura. These are floaters and after-images. Floaters look like clear dots connected by thin lines. These commonly appear when you've been in bright light, especially sunlight. Basically, they're dead cells floating around in your eyes and showing up against a bright background.

After-images often appear when you've been staring at something for a long period of time. For example, if you keep your eyes focused on someone for a long time and then move your eyes away, you may see the person's lingering shape, often in an odd fluorescent color. You may be tempted to think you've had a revelatory glimpse of insight, but don't get too excited just yet. When you actually witness an aura, you'll know you've seen the real thing.

How to See an Aura

To begin to see auras, you can first train your eyes to see under ideal circumstances. For example, many people find it easiest to learn when the person whose aura they're trying to see stands against a blank, white wall. Also, auras are most vivid around the head, so that's the best place to look for a person's aura. Later, you may eventually gain the ability to see the aura around the entire body. You'll want to practice simple techniques such as these first, and then apply what you've learned in order to see auras around people. Here's an exercise to get you started.

Energy Field Exercise

1. Get into a relaxed position in a dark room. Leave the lights out, but don't worry about a little light coming in through the blinds or under the door.

2. Hold your palms up about eight inches in front of your face. Hold them facing each other, about one to five inches apart. Look at the wall behind your hands; avoid focusing directly on your hands. Move your hands in toward each other and back out (as though clapping), increasing the space, and then decreasing the space. Do you notice an energy building up between your hands? You may see a light or feel a pulsing or tingling sensation. This is your auric or energy field.

3. Now outstretch one arm at chest level and turn your palm up as though carrying a tray. Place the opposite hand about 10 inches above your forearm, with your palm facing down. Slowly move your hand closer to your arm. Pay attention to the feeling or sensation in your hand. Does it change as you get closer to your arm?

Intuition Hotline

Barbara Brennan is a healer, teacher, author, physicist, and leading authority on healing. If you'd like to learn more about auras, chakras, and more, check out her book *Hands of Light: A Guide to Healing Through the Human Energy Field* (Bantam, 1987). The Barbara Brennan School of Healing, in East Hampton, New York, is designed specifically to train people to be healers.

Once you're seeing your aura, you'll realize that it is made up of various colors. Most people emit certain colors that predominate in their auras, and yet these colors can change with their moods. For example, a person with a happy disposition may tend to have a bright yellow aura, but it could momentarily change to red if the person becomes angry. Someone else might have a red aura, suggesting that the person is often angry. If someone's aura has dark spots in a specific area, it may show that the person has an illness in that area.

What the Colors Mean

Within the bodies are seven major energy centers that correspond to the chakras. Each energy center is said to be like a wheel of vibrating, spinning energy. Auras penetrate and radiate from these energies. Expert energy healers, such as Barbara Brennan, perceive the aura as having a particular structure that corresponds to the shape and size of the body. She can see frequency bands, in the form of color, that radiate through and out from the body in seven levels, which correspond to the chakras.

Similar to Mona Lisa Schulz's theory that certain emotional and life issues correspond to the seven organ systems, energy healers believe that each of the aura's seven energy levels also corresponds to one aspect of life. The following table offers a brief summary of the auric colors, where they may originate, and what life aspects they may represent.

Auric Color	Chakra/Center	Life Aspect Corresponding to Color
Red	Base of the spine	Physical sensation, survival, and strength
Orange	Sacral	Personal emotions: sexuality, creativity, and healing
Yellow	Solar plexus	Mental state: personal thoughts of power, anger, or hostility
Green	Heart	Interaction with others: love and harmony
Blue	Throat	Communication, expression, and judgment
Indigo	Forehead	Inner vision, wisdom, and perception
Violet	Crown of the head	Divine purpose: destiny

Although these colors match up with the seven main chakras and life issues related to them, the aura is not seen as a row of horizontal stripes that starts at the top of the head and moves down to the feet. Rather, the layers surround each person's body in rings, similar to the layers in an onion when it's cut in half. When reading an aura, some experts believe that each ring of the aura, extending outward from the body, expresses a different aspect of the person. That involves a complicated level of expertise, so we won't try to confuse you with that here. For now, let's try the ABC's of aura reading.

Reading Auras

Learning to read and interpret auras has a lot of practical benefits. You can look at someone and quickly receive impressions about that person. Does that person hold a lot of anger inside, which is characterized by bright red in his or her aura? Or does that person have a blue aura, which indicates that he or she is generally positive and calm?

You can practice your newfound art by performing quick aura readings of people when you first meet them. After you get to know them better, check whether your first interpretations were correct. You'll learn that each person's aura has varying shades of color. If someone has a dull or dark aura, that person is likely to be depressed and negative. Conversely, if you see someone with a bright, shining, and glowing aura, you can assume that person is generally positive and upbeat. Try it for yourself! The following exercise will get you started.

Intuition Hotline

You can learn a lot about yourself by performing the Basic Aura Reading on yourself while looking in the mirror. Stand before the mirror, half focus your eyes, and pay attention to the colors that appear around you.

Basic Aura Reading Exercise

1. Find a partner and have him (or her) sit across from you against a white or light-colored wall. Placing a low-watt bulb behind your friend helps.

2. Observe your partner with half-focused eyes, which means try to avoid staring directly at him. Instead, direct your eyes more at the wall behind him. Focus your attention around the edges of your partner's body, in his energy field.

3. Ask your friend to move slightly. Do you see the colors move with him?

4. Pay attention to any colors that you see. Several colors will appear in different areas of the body.

(Note: Some people *feel* or *sense* the colors rather than *see* them.)

5. Report to your friend what colors you see.

6. Interpret what you see by using the earlier table. Are your observations making sense to your partner, based on what he knows about himself?

If at first you don't succeed, don't give up. Remember that, like any skill, aura reading may take time to develop. You also might want to wait for a better time to try this: Some energy healers perceive the energy field only when entering a meditative state. Maybe this technique will work best for you too. Just don't be afraid to try out whatever may work for you. And if you see something that confuses you, contact an energy healer, who can advise you on how to improve your technique or whether to seek help from a certified healer.

Drawing Auras

Once you've tapped into your auric sight and have your visual sense in high gear, you may not want to stop your observations to make notes. Rather, take in all the information you can and then draw what you see immediately afterward.

One technique is to draw a circle or oval to suggest the human shape. Designate the upper half of the circle as the head, since you'll probably get the strongest sense of the aura in that area. The lower half can represent the body itself. To analyze what you've drawn, look at the previous table and match the color and its physical position to the issues the person may be facing.

A similar technique uses paints. Try using watercolors to make a painting that shows a person's body, colored according to your response to his or her aura. This can work well for people who sense the aura, perhaps without seeing it. Your unconscious mind can work through your own creativity to reveal colors that you may feel but not see. Try this with a close friend, so you'll feel comfortable checking your response.

Learning about auras is a terrific way to get in touch with the natural energies that flow through and around the body. Sensing this energy can open you up to whole new levels of understanding. It can help you comprehend the connections between all the parts of the personality that create the individual person: the body, thoughts, emotions, and spirit. Healing ourselves and helping others may be possible only by balancing all these aspects of our lives—something that many healers are accomplishing through healing touch.

Healing Touch

Today, as more people question the traditional medical establishment and also gain an understanding of the mind and spirit's importance (in addition to the body's), alternative methods of healing are coming to the fore. Those who work with the auric field focus on repairing, balancing, charging, and clearing the energy field on many levels, including the spiritual, emotional, mental, and physical. As Barbara Brennan explains, "Anywhere in your personal experience where you are separated from your true self, it will show in the human energy field and will eventually, as a result of distortions in the energy field, cause a disease in the body. Either it will weaken the body so an infection can come in or it will cause disease."

Unsolved Mystery

Recent spinal surgery on a former Brazilian military dictator, now 79 years old, raises numerous questions about what's most important: the procedure, the practitioner, or the spirit behind it. The operation was carried out by a 42-year-old medium named Rubens de Faria, who was trained as an electrical engineer. When he operated, however, he channeled the spirit—and expertise—of Dr. Fritz, a German doctor who died during World War I. Together, they cut a tiny incision in Dictator Figueirido's lower back and then tapped it with a tiny tool. The patient, who went to Mr. de Faria because his doctors told him an operation would be too difficult, has recuperated wonderfully—as have the thousands of Brazilians who clamor to be cured by Mr. de Faria, a.k.a. Dr. Fritz, every week.

149

Other types of healing that involve touch share the common belief that to create change, or healing, the patient needs to connect to his or her true self. Whether the healers use "laying-on-of-hands," "healing touch," or "faith healing," they all involve the idea that the healer and patient are somehow connected on a higher, perhaps psychic, plane that opens an inflow of healing energy to the patient.

What Your Hands Know

Want proof that auras exist? They've been photographed! In 1939, the Russian scientist Semyon Kirlian developed a technique using film between two electrodes to show a bright corona surrounding his hand. (One guess what they call this: a Kirlian photograph! We'll talk more about Kirlian photography in Chapter 22.) Skeptics have tried to downplay his discovery by saying that it's photographing ionization, but they still can't explain the differences between living and dying leaves: living ones show bright auras, and dying ones show dull ones.

In addition to demonstrating that living matter is more vibrant than dead matter, the Kirlian images also show an interesting fact about healers: Their fingertips exude amazing amounts of vibrant energy. Healers seem to have some force in their hands that is full of life energy. Once you become extremely observant of auras, you can see this for yourself. Often, healers have a lot of heat in their hands, which is thought to come from this life energy as well.

Getting in touch with this life force is important to healing, as well as to developing intuitive abilities. And the key to connecting to the life force is meditation. Just as meditation helps many people develop their psychic awareness, it also helps them tap into their healing potential. In addition to opening up the auric sense, it can provide the awareness that is necessary for healing—both within ourselves and for others.

The Buddhists express their recognition of the integral connection between meditation and healing hands by using *mudras*. They use these specific hand positions during meditation to harness vital life energies. Various subtle hand positions represent and inspire certain states or conditions, such as compassion, fearlessness, or renunciation.

You've probably seen hand positions like these in paintings or statues of Buddha or his disciples meditating; you also might have noticed they appear in many Christian paintings too. Indeed, the mudra for prayer looks very much like the famous Christian artwork of two hands praying.

Beyond Words

Mudra in Sanskrit means sign. These subtle hand gestures are traditionally used in India's classical dances to represent certain feelings. But they also are used during meditation, as you can see in many artworks of the Buddha and other spiritual teachers.

These hand positions, like the yogic poses, are intended to help focus the mind. They are not considered, in and of themselves, to be a source of power. Similarly, most healers do not consider their hands—or themselves—as the source of healing power, but rather as conduits through which the vital energy of life flows.

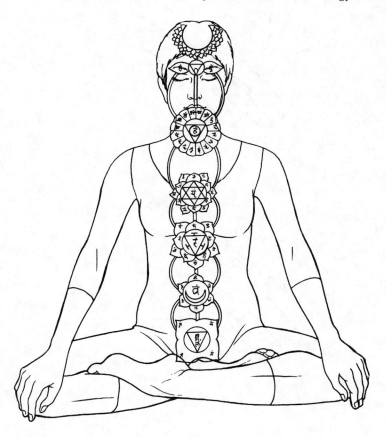

The seven chakras are called the base, sacral, solar plexus, heart, throat, forehead or third eye, and crown chakras.

The ahamkara mudra is a mudra for people who are unnecessarily passive and need some assertiveness training. This mudra is about asserting the ego and a sense of personal identity and individuality. The mudra promotes extroverted tendencies and is ego-transcending. The tip of the index finger extends beyond the thumb, asserting the self beyond the circle of OM.

The OM mudra (OM is the original sound of the universe and all that is manifested in it) is a mudra that merges the ego and the universe. All becomes one divine reality. The circle of self and universe perfectly closes as the thumb and index finger meet. This is a mudra of peacefulness and divine harmony or balance.

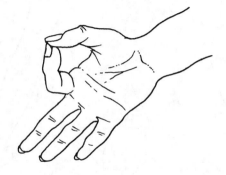

Reiki

One healing technique that is based on specific hand positions is growing increasingly popular in the United States. Called *reiki*, it is a simple technique that taps into the life force energy to help reduce stress and thereby lead to healing. It treats the whole person, including the body, emotions, mind, and spirit. A treatment creates a feeling of heat, tingling, or simply relaxation, and can result in feelings of peace, security, and well-being. In some cases, miraculous cures occur.

Reiki is said to have been an ancient healing art that was rediscovered, via visions, by Dr. Mikao Usai in the mid 1800s. It was brought to the West by Mrs. Hawayo Takata. Reiki was developed as a simple and natural method of spiritual healing.

Its practitioners learn the basic hand positions of reiki, but the ability to use it is transferred, rather than taught, to the student by the reiki master. The ability to use reiki is not dependent on intellectual capacity or spiritual development, and thousands of people have already learned to use it.

The source of this healing is hinted at in its name, which has Japanese origins. Rei can be interpreted to mean "universal" in the sense of all-present, or it can mean "spiritual consciousness," implying that its source comes from God or the Higher Self, and thereby knows all about each person, the person's problems, and where healing is needed. Ki is the same as chi, the life force that directly relates to how healthy a person is. If one's force is low or blocked, he or she is vulnerable to illness. If it's high and freely flowing, he or she is less prone to illness. It runs through every aspect of one's life, including emotions, thoughts, and spiritual life. Ki also is believed to be the source of psychic ability and healing.

Beyond Words

Reiki (pronounced ray-kee) is a type of hands-on healing, wherein a trained practitioner places his hands, using specific positions, on six points of the body. Doing this enables vital life energy to flow freely throughout the body.

While the practice of reiki does not require belief in any particular spiritual beliefs, it does involve principles of improving oneself and promoting harmony with others. These tenets are intended to help people understand that healing comes through the spirit, and thereby benefits from self-realization that leads to spiritual growth.

From the ESP Files

The Chinese have studied the flow of life energy for thousands of years. In fact they have writings that are over 4,000 years old, called the "Yellow Emperor's Classic of Internal Medicine," that list 32 different kinds of Chi or Ki. Practitioners of traditional Chinese medicine, believe that disease results when chi becomes blocked somewhere in the body and their treatments, including acupuncture, act to release chi and allow it to flow unfettered.

Intuition Hotline

If you would like to learn more, several good books can offer further information about reiki and its philosophy. You might want to check out *Reiki, The Healing Touch* (Vision Publications, 1991) by William Rand.

Mixed Messages

If you intend to practice healing techniques, please work under qualified supervision before trying to treat someone. If you seek alternative healing, check with a medical professional first, to ensure a proper course of treatment and for recommendations for qualified alternative health practitioners.

How to Use Therapeutic Touch

Another relatively new hands-on healing technique is therapeutic touch. It shares many of the same concepts of energy as other hands-on healing modalities, including the idea that healing comes from a universal life energy that flows through all living organisms and creates an energy field around their bodies. It is unique in its simple use of laying on of hands.

Dora Kunz, who developed therapeutic touch and brought it to the United States, believed the approach is based on the ancient practice of laying on of hands. She trained Delores Krieger, Ph.D., R.N., who then researched and documented scientific evidence that the technique is an effective form of healing. Krieger then trained thousands of nurses and other health care professionals, which has since brought the technique the respect of the traditional medical world.

The technique begins by having the practitioner center herself through a technique such as meditation. She (or he) then scans the body with her hands together, side-by-side, with her palms down and facing the body. Starting about five inches above the head, the practitioner moves her hands down the length of the body, feeling the energy from top to bottom, as well as both sides of the body. A practitioner senses various energy sensations such as tingling, heat, cold, heaviness, or a drawing feeling. She then assesses what type of imbalance she feels: loose congestion, tight congestion, localized imbalance, or an energy deficit. The practitioner then uses her hands to move the body's energy so that it becomes balanced. In this way, congestion is unblocked, so that areas with excess energy or an energy deficit receive the ideal amount of energy they need. Often, more than one session is needed for a complete diagnosis and treatment.

Therapeutic touch creates profound relaxation, helps alleviate or eradicate pain, and accelerates healing. It's known for treating common ailments, such as colds, headaches, stomach upsets, arthritis, burns, tension, and injuries, but has helped people with more serious conditions as well.

Therapeutic touch, like all hands-on healing methods, places an emphasis on love, compassion, and sharing of energy. With these healing methods, the emotional, mental, and spiritual interaction between practitioner and patient is important. The relationship must be personal, and yet the practitioner needs to remain somewhat detached—similar to the way intuitive counselors relate to their clients. Underlying all is a strong sense of caring, compassion, and love.

From the ESP Files

The alternative therapy industry is alive and well in the horse world throughout the USA, especially in the discipline of dressage, which is a spiritual enterprise when considered in its purist form. Among the active therapies performed on horses are acupuncture, acupressure, reiki, massage therapy, and communication. Some of the prominent trainers are psychic but do not herald this to the general public.

Fostering Compassion and Empathy

Helping to heal the world around you may actually be simpler than you think. Begin by paying attention to where help is needed. Once you start to really look at the people and things around you with an open mind, you'll be able to see the problems people around you are experiencing. You might notice a man walking with his shoulders slumped, as if he's carrying a heavy burden. He probably is. Someone whose face looks tired, tight, and stressed is probably thinking about something that concerns her greatly—physical pain, or grief, or hurt feelings.

When you start to really see what's going on in the world around you, don't be afraid to acknowledge and feel it. Accept that you have a gift—the gift of intuitive understanding. Many call it empathy, and what you do with this gift may be called compassion. It is not always necessary to run right in, shouting and waving a flag that screams, "I care." Indeed, overt expressions are rarely appropriate. Rather, take a deep breath and ask for guidance.

The ideal way for you to help people may not appear to you when you first realize their needs. Perhaps you'll have an opportunity to talk with them at some future date. They may want to pour out their hearts, and it's your job to just listen. Or you may never know exactly what troubles them, but perhaps what you offer can be as simple as a smile or a silent prayer. Any offering of compassion can be a form of healing.

At the same time, you'll come to realize that you are healing yourself as well, because each moment of awareness and empathy you share with another, and every blessing you offer that person, helps you appreciate all that you have and are.

The next chapter talks more about how we can put our empathy and insight into action, in ways that can be both simple and subtle, but astoundingly profound.

The Least You Need to Know

➤ Becoming aware guides you to healing yourself and others.

➤ You can learn to sense auras and interpret colors.

➤ You can learn to direct energy to help heal yourself and others.

➤ Truly looking at others is a simple way to learn compassion.

Prayer Is Psychic Healing Power

Healing takes place on many levels and comes in many forms. Faith healing, for example, depends to a large degree on the patient believing that the healer can mediate between him (or her) and God for healing. Psychic healing requires that the healer physically *do* something, such as manipulate energy, to help the patient. Spiritual healing involves a surrender of any division—spiritual or physical—between the healer and the patient, and the acceptance with unconditional love of the patient by the healer. With spiritual healing, healers make mind-to-mind connections between themselves and their patients, and then just allow a spiritual force to take action. These healers often report feeling an open and nonjudgmental love and acceptance of the patient, which is shared between the healer and patient and creates a pathway to healing for the patient.

You too can tap into this same openness to love, acceptance, and support that comes from the universe—or God, or a higher power, or whatever you call this force—to heal yourself and others—and that's just what we'll explore in this chapter.

Prayer and Science

Tapping into this all-powerful source of spiritual healing can have many names, but most people in Western society call it *prayer*. The relationship between prayer (and religion or faith) and science has changed greatly in the past few decades, ever since Einstein pointed out that there's not much difference between energy and matter. Until then, scientists pretty much agreed that what you see is what you get. The material world reigned.

Today, more scientists and doctors are beginning to acknowledge the power of the mind to affect the material world. Although the scientific community isn't quite sure what to call this ability, the spiritual community calls it God, or universal energy, or chi. Many religions call the effort to direct this force "prayer." And more scientists and medical professionals are looking at this force as a form of *distant healing*.

Beyond Words

Webster's defines **prayer** as "a solemn and humble approach to Divinity in word or thought." This definition expresses the importance of one's mental intention to connect with a force beyond oneself. **Distant healing** is healing that occurs through directed thoughts, such as prayer, even when the patient is not present. Distant healing can be considered a form of telepathy and/ or psychokinesis.

What Doctors Think About Prayer and Healing

One physician who is famous for his willingness to look into the possibilities of healing prayer is Larry Dossey, M.D. In his books, he describes his scientific quest to discover the relationship between healing and consciousness, and his exploration of the connections between medicine, mysticism, religion, and physics. In a recent TV appearance he remarked, "As a physician, I have had many experiences over the years that have led me to conclude that the world of clinical medicine is truly bizarre and unpredictable, and is a territory where almost anything is possible. Most of my colleagues, I feel, agree, for almost all physicians possess a lavish laundry list of strange happenings unexplainable by normal science."

While most doctors still don't write prescriptions reading, "Healing prayers, three times a day," more and more are willing to admit the connection of the mind and spirit with healing the body. Many Western doctors now prescribe visualization to patients with chronic pain and terminal illness—and admit their patients often improve after performing this powerful mind/body exercise. Study after study shows that patients without access to this type of technique and who express little hope of recovery or faith in healing seldom stage a comeback from serious disease. And almost every doctor agrees that getting well requires some level of optimism.

What Studies Show About Prayer and Healing

In 1988 at San Francisco General Hospital, Randolph Byrd, M.D., conducted one of the most frequently cited studies of the effects of prayer and healing. For 10 months, he studied 193 patients with heart disease, assigning people to pray for half of the patients and leaving the other half with no assigned prayer helpers. The patients who received prayers showed improvement rates 5 to 7 percent higher than their non-prayed-for counterparts. This group also required fewer antibiotics and diuretics, suffered from fewer cases of pneumonia, and suffered fewer deaths. Of course, this type of experiment contained many factors that were hard to control or measure, but it certainly got people thinking about the potentially powerful influence of prayer.

Recently, psi scientists have investigated the distinction made between *directed* and *nondirected* prayer. When you pray in a *directed* manner you have a specific goal or outcome in mind, as in, "I want my husband's tumor to go away." In this case, you're attempting to steer the outcome in a certain direction, such as curing a cancer or helping a stroke victim regain movement or speech. In nondirected prayer, you would not "tell the universe what to do" but rather leave it open-ended with no specific outcome.

Spindrift, a Salem, Oregon, organization concentrating on prayer research, conducted studies on plant life to answer the question about which prayer technique was more effective—mainly because scientists find they can measure the results on simple biological systems more easily than they can on humans. One such study follows how prayer practitioners can affect the development and metabolism of yeast cultures and the sprouting of bean and wheat seeds. In both exercises, they discovered that prayer helped trigger growth. Perhaps surprisingly, the nondirected technique was quantifiably more effective than the directed prayer technique, yielding double the results.

The results of the Spindrift studies suggest that a healer or a prayer (meaning someone who prays) is most helpful if he keeps his mind free of visualizations or specific goals. It appears that prayer is most effective when it focuses only on the patient and what he or she needs. In other words, to simply pray for what's best for the individual—to pray "Thy will be done" or "May the best of all outcomes happen for this individual or circumstance"—appears to be the most effective approach to prayer. Although this approach worked best in the Spindrift studies, it has not been tested widely with people and the jury is still out on the best way for you to pray for your own or someone else's healing and growth.

Intuition Hotline

Now you can pray—or at least connect to some pretty powerful prayer spots—via the phone or the Internet. To get a message to the prayer wall in Jerusalem, fax 011 0972-2-612-222 or contact Virtual Jerusalem at **http://www. virtual.com.**

From the ESP Files

EEG and biofeedback give scientists a hands-off, mechanistic method to simultaneously monitor mind activity and internal body functions. (An electroencephalograph (EEG) is a machine that records the electrical activity in the brain. Biofeedback is a monitoring device that patients use to gain voluntary control over an autonomic body function, such as their heart rate.) The mind's ability to affect the body may actually be a form of PK (psychokinesis), which psi scientists refer to as bio-PK or Direct Mental Interactions with Living Systems (DMILS).

Intuition Hotline

You can try your own prayer experiment at home. Buy two plants in the same condition at the same time. Put them in places of comparable light and "comfort" and give them the same amount of water. Indeed, the only difference is that you "pray" for one plant and not the other. Just be sure to put them far enough apart that your prayer doesn't "spread."

In addition, no evidence exists that people's prayers are sent anywhere or that any kind of energy is involved. Here's an interesting quote from Larry Dossey's book *Healing Words*, "If prayer does not go anywhere, then it may simultaneously be present everywhere, enveloping sender, object, and the Almighty all at once. Physicists have a word to describe a world in which information is not sent, but that exists everywhere all at once: *nonlocality.*"

Most scientists and physicians are not ready to accept the idea that all people share a single mind and source of energy. And yet shared thoughts definitely come into play when healing occurs through prayer. The source of this healing energy remains undefined, although it has been called many names over many millennia.

Are You a Doubter or a Doer?

Although you needn't believe in a specific God called by a certain name, faith and a true desire for wellness are important ingredients in many types of healing. Many people pray expecting that God will simply grant their requests. But it doesn't usually work that way. Prayer, with its built-in positive thinking, is a partnership. If you're always afraid to believe that it may work, you'll never even have a chance of knowing that it can.

Think of it this way: The odds of "winning" are better if you try to step beyond complete doubt. If you are in doubt and remain there, nothing can change. But taking action—even when you still have a few reservations—is the first step toward conquering doubt. Taking action requires at least a tiny bit of faith in the ability to improve and create change.

You're provided with many tools, but you have to use them. These tools include a strong intellect, to choose your goals and visions. You also have your imagination to see the kind of life and health you want so that you can begin to create it. You also have been given the gifts of decision-making, intuition, and your individual talents. You can use these gifts to create joy and happiness for yourself and others, or you can ignore these gifts, and run the risk of never seeing changes occur. The choice is yours.

The Chinese philosophical treatise called the *I Ching, or Book of Changes*, states, "Every event in the visible world is the effect of an image of an idea in the unseen world." In other words, you are what you think. So think positive!

The Power of Positive Thinking

As you've probably recognized from your own life, healing the body doesn't necessarily happen if the mind is unhealthy (or full of doubt) and vice versa. This body-mind connection can exert a powerful influence over almost any aspect of your life, from helping destroy deadly tumors to helping resolve a conflict at work that makes you feel ill at ease. Worrying and doubting is easy. Creating change requires some courage from you, both to let go of your skepticism and to take steps toward wellness and wholeness.

Beyond Words

Nonlocality is the idea in modern physics that a thing or a thought is not located in a specific region of space and time, but exists everywhere at all times. This view suggests that the mind is not limited to given places in space or time, such as the body or the present moment. It supports the theory that all minds are infinite and united in one whole.

Mixed Messages

If anyone suggests that you rely only on prayer for healing, don't neglect to check into other options as well. Prayer is a tremendous gift that you can offer to others and they can offer to you. However, the healing power of prayer may also guide you to an appropriate method of treatment, such as a skilled doctor. Answers to prayer come in many forms; healers who are in touch with that fact humbly recognize it and don't insist that theirs is the only way.

The first step to learning any type of healing is adopting a positive outlook. If you don't choose to express your power through prayer, you can still achieve an optimistic attitude by using your mind to direct your thoughts.

You can use strong verbal messages and visual images to direct your mind. These symbols penetrate your unconscious mind to become embedded in your brain and create new pathways of thought and action. They provide your intuition with new avenues for insight and opportunity. They express an openness to receiving all the exciting changes that your intuition has to offer. But how do you find the right words and images for you?

Creating Affirmations

Once you can picture the changes you want to create, strengthen this image with inner words. Putting words to your goals will help you more clearly establish them, as well as replace negative self-talk that would otherwise get in the way.

When you begin to work with your own personal affirmations, keep the following in mind:

Intuition Hotline

In order to make your affirmations more direct, active, and interesting, use strong verbs that show an action taking place. In grammar-school-teacher talk: Use active, not passive, verbs. ("The greatest good comes to me," not "I have great good coming to me.")

1. State your affirmation positively. ("I am full of health," not "I am no longer sick.")

2. State it in the present, as though you already have what you want. ("I have access to my own healing power," not "I will have access...")

3. Make it simple and succinct. A one-sentence affirmation is usually best. ("I am strong and healthy.")

4. Make it exciting. You want your subconscious and conscious minds to grab hold of it and want it. ("I am powerful and full of energy. I get stronger every day.")

5. The affirmation should be about you, not others. ("I am healing and accepting of prayer," not "I want people to pray for me.")

6. Make your affirmation something that is achievable. Avoid sabotaging yourself with a goal that seems unachievable. Choose a first step toward a long-range goal. For example, if your goal is to work out for three hours every day so that you look like Adonis by the end of two months, you may be sabotaging yourself. Try choosing more plausible time frames—and a physique that is believable to you.

7. Your affirmation should simply be a statement of what you want to create. It should not include the process by which you think you'll get there. This is important. If your goal is to be healthy and full of energy, state that.

Once you have a clear affirmation, let the universe figure out the miracles that need to happen in order to bring your goal about. Don't get caught up in the *how it will happen* part. Your task is to follow the nudges from your intuition that indicate the actions and steps you should take.

Creative Visualization

If you've ever spent an hour watching network TV (and who hasn't?), you know the power of visual images—and you know that advertisers know it too. The visual impact of images is even more noticeable in magazines, where perfumes and clothes are advertised with huge pictures and fewer and fewer words. So why can't you do your own internal advertising? Sell yourself on the idea of your own potential by painting a picture of it in your mind.

When you visualize, you form a mental image of what you want to create in your life. Everyone does this, whether they are conscious of it or not. It is a natural part of the imagination. For example, before going on a vacation, you probably visualize images of what that vacation will be like (which helps get you through that last horrible week at work before you can take off!). Before an engineer builds a bridge, he visualizes what it will look like when it's finished.

Before something is created in your material reality, you hold it in your mind. When you make an effort to do this consciously, it's called creative visualization (a topic we touched on in Chapter 7). You can use positive mental images of yourself and your life to create a better self-image and to improve your personal experiences. For example, if you want to lose weight you can hold an image in your mind's eye of how you want to look. You can imagine yourself as the thinner you in your mirror. You might picture your friends responding positively to the "new you." You can use your mind and ability to visualize and think of creative images of yourself looking and feeling slim, healthy, and full of energy.

Imagery is the umbrella term for this ability. When it is focused in a way that helps the mind and body work together to create healing or achieve any desire, it is called *guided imagery*. Much attention has been paid to guided imagery as a form of healing, or at least slowing, serious illness, because it was originally developed for that purpose.

Guided Imagery: The Mind As Healer

"Our emotions and words let the body know what we expect of it, and by visualizing certain changes we can help the body bring them about," says best-selling author Bernie Siegel in his book *Love, Medicine, and Miracles* (Harperperennial Library, 1990). This idea is the basic concept behind *guided imagery*, which enables you to improve your health, and your life, by imagining it in more positive terms.

Research shows that, performed properly, guided imagery can help lower blood pressure; reduce anxiety, depression, and physical pain; bolster the immune system; ease

Beyond Words

Guided imagery is a kind of directed daydreaming or meditation, which uses the imagination in a focused, directed way to achieve goals and desires. It was originally created to help the mind and body work together to create healing.

nausea during chemotherapy; lower allergic responses; and speed recovery from cuts, burns, fractures, and surgery. It also improves performance in sports and even certain types of mental activities.

When guided imagery is most effective, it encourages you to imagine with all of your senses. In addition to using images and thoughts, guided imagery involves imagining how things sound, feel, taste, and smell. Since sensory input is how the mind and imagination tend to take in information, guided imagery can go straight to the unconscious mind, bypassing all those words that can get in the way of direct communication between mind and body.

Another reason why guided imagery seems to be so effective at helping the body is because it involves the emotions. In fact, guided imagery seems to work best when using images that strongly affect the emotions. Similar to how images and other sensory input bypasses reason and travels directly to the unconscious mind, emotions also go directly to the unconscious mind. In addition, emotions carry a history with them that interacts with the body's systems. For example, if you imagine spending a happy, sunny day with someone you love, your body also re-experiences the same joyful, relaxed, and ecstatic physical responses.

Because emotions are so personal, everybody uses somewhat different ways of accessing effective images during the process. Some people prefer to follow imagery that someone else has created, while others create their own images. Under any circumstances, the important thing is to relax and let the imagination do the work. Of course, the more your practice, the easier it gets and the more effective it becomes.

Guided imagery works on the principal that images are events to the body. Sensory images are the language of the body, which it understands automatically and doesn't question. Belleruth Naparstek, author of *Staying Well with Guided Imagery* (Warner, 1994), explains that the first operating principle of imagery is, "Our bodies don't discriminate between sensory images in the mind and what we call reality." While images don't impact the body with the same intensity as real events, they create the same basic sense of experience. This sense, though perhaps a bit weaker than real experience, is nevertheless felt throughout the body.

When most effective, guided imagery occurs in an altered mental state similar to directed daydreaming, mediation, or self-hypnosis. In this state, the person gradually enters a state in which he pictures and experiences imagery that helps to heal or motivate him. A cancer patient may picture fighter jets shooting down harmful cancer cells, while an athlete may imagine a powerful puma giving her grace, speed, and strength. A person undergoing physical therapy may envision ideal childhood moments of running freely and then picture himself walking independently in the future.

This healing technique underscores the importance of imagination and creativity in accessing our higher minds, or intuition. It also reaffirms an essential point: You can use your mind to help heal and improve your body and your life.

The Sacred Psychic

We all have an innate wisdom or "knowingness" that we can access through our intuition. By learning to contact, listen to, and act on your intuition, you can directly connect to the Higher Power of the universe. It is always there to guide you and provide you with insight, whether you use it for healing old hurts or creating new growth. Your intuitive mind has access to an infinite supply of information. Your role is to listen to your intuition, trust its guidance, and learn to act on its wisdom.

Your life unfolds through the thoughts and beliefs you hold. Your inner guidance may not make sense to anyone else in the world. But when you recognize, nurture, and act on that guidance—such as many people do when they pray—it produces your dreams and visions.

Now that you've got a sense of how your mind can heal and improve your life, don't just take your body for granted. The next chapter explains how you can use the mind-body-spirit connection to its fullest by helping your body keep up with your mind. Just as your intuition nurtures you, you can in turn nurture it.

Unsolved Mystery

According to The *World's Most Incredible Stories* (Barnes and Noble, 1998), a busload of 54 Spanish pilgrims who had just visited the Blessed Virgin Mary vision in Fatima, Portugal, found themselves in the midst of a rather miraculous adventure. They discovered that their driver wasn't driving their bus! He appeared to be asleep but sitting in prayer, with his eyes closed and hands clasped, at the wheel of his bus that was hurtling 50 miles per hour through the streets. For 20 miles, the bus turned corners and changed gears, before pulling up safely alongside the road as the driver woke up.

One passenger, who had been a priest for 40 years, reported that, while the driver "slept," many passengers heard a clear voice come from his mouth that said, "I am your brother, Archangel Michael. God had the grace to drive the bus himself as a test of faith for our brother the driver." The bus driver remembers nothing except feeling an overwhelming compulsion to pray.

The Least You Need to Know

➤ Doctors and scientists are showing increased interest in the healing effects of prayer.

➤ Essential ingredients of spiritual healing are self-surrender and acceptance of others.

➤ Whether you call it prayer or not, you can direct your thoughts to change your health and life for the better.

➤ Your intuition guides you to a closer connection to the sacred.

Chapter 13

Getting in Touch with Your Body Psychic

> ### In This Chapter
>
> ➤ Your body: a psychic weather report
>
> ➤ Physical stress and psychic connections
>
> ➤ Building body health for psychic strength
>
> ➤ Reading your body's signals

Everyone's heard the saying, "Your body is a house of prayer." But what does that really mean? It suggests that everyone is a walking temple, or church, or sacred site, that is filled with fine ideals, pure intentions, and hallowed hopes. Sounds impossible, huh? Well, the trick is to notice the word "body." Your mind may often stray, but keeping your body under control may actually be easier than you might think. Your body is a good place to start learning the fine arts of discipline, control, and quietude.

You can't stop your thoughts from giving you the desire to have an extra drink, pick up a cigarette, or eat more ice cream, but you can use your body to help you become more aware of these temptations. In fact, your body is a very real, concrete boundary, almost like a fence that clearly points out that the border is being crossed: You can think about eating ice cream, but putting that spoon between your lips can set off an alarm that your thoughts have gone too far. In this way, your body can help your mind become more aware of where your thoughts have gained the upper hand and carried over into action. Similarly, your body can tell you when your emotions have gone too far, such as when your breath changes or muscle tension increases. In other words, your body can help you draw the line between your physical urges and your spiritual goals. This chapter will talk about the connections between your physical body and psychic awareness. Your body also provides insightful signs in the form of physical symptoms. Via symptoms, your body can give you clues as to what is going on in your life. If something is disturbing you—in your body, mind, or spirit—your body's signs will let you know, sooner or later. Sometimes these signs are a wake-up call to get back in touch with the Divine. After all, your body is part of that too, as well as a bridge to it.

How Are You Feeling Today? An Exploration

Does it seem like you're always running breathlessly from one task to another until you finally collapse on the sofa to unwind in front of the tube? Think of an ordinary day in your own life. Are you rushing to get the kids off to school, yourself to work, meet that deadline for your boss, or cram for exams at school? By the end of the day you're probably feeling exhausted, irritable, weak, fuzzy thinking, and wondering whether you should be checking in with your doctor—or therapist!

It's important that you listen to what your body tells you after such stressful days. Indeed, your body provides insightful signs in the form of physical symptoms about the way you live your life. Via symptoms, your body can give you clues as to what is going on in your life.

But for you to learn from your body, you've got to really listen to it. In this next exercise, focus your attention on how you're feeling today and what your intuition says about what makes you feel happy, energized, and excited about life. Take some time to really examine some of your day-to-day routines: Do they still work for you?

Paying Attention to Your Daily Intuitive Messages

Describe a typical work day:

_____

_____

_____

Think about the above scenario. What parts of your day feel boring, nerve-wracking, or stressful? Are there parts of your day that you dread?

_____

_____

_____

Think about your day again. What parts of it did you find fun, easy, and invigorating? What did you enjoy and look forward to doing?

_____

_____

_____

Obviously, it's better to have a day that is filled with joy, energy, and excitement than a day of disappointment and frustration. And once you become more conscious about what makes you feel that way, you've taken a big step in the right direction!

If you're like most people, you too often get caught up in complaining about what doesn't work about your life and forget to ask yourself what you really want. Here's your chance to do that. You might want to play some uplifting music to get you in the mood for this part of the exercise.

Close your eyes for a moment. Think about what you'd like your days to be like. Spend time daydreaming about what makes you happy. Is there anything you could change in your life that would make things easier?

Pay attention to any cues from your intuition. Is there an image that leaps to mind, or an inner voice encouraging a shift in perception? Perhaps you feel a surge of pleasure about a change you're considering. All of these impressions are ways that your intuition gives you messages.

Mixed Messages

Don't think TOO big when contemplating changing your life, otherwise you'll become overwhelmed. Instead, remember that small steps are often the key to success.

What information did you receive? Consider these ideas to be intuitive advice that offers you options for the future.

_____

_____

_____

Are you willing to act on the information? If so, what steps can you take starting today?

_____

_____

_____

When I've done this exercise, I've received information as mundane as "Go to bed earlier" and "Get more exercise." I've also received guidance about my business, such as when to shift my business to a new direction, whether or not to do more teaching and writing, how large a client list to maintain. Some of the suggestions my intuition offers make me feel a bit anxious because they indicate big changes. Yet time and again I find that when I don't act on this guidance, I start experiencing signs of stress.

Unsolved Mystery

Film star Shirley MacLaine is well known for her role as an explorer of psychic phenomenon. And she's learned to put mind-over-matter visualization methods to good use, too. She reports the story that she decided to overcome her fear of flying by visualizing a crash—while she was in mid flight. (Perhaps she assumed that if she faced the worst and overcame it, she could cure her phobia for good.) As we know, her plane never crashed, and she came out braver for the experience. But her friend who picked her up at the airport was terribly shaken after having a premonition that Shirley's plane had crashed. What the friend sensed was Shirley's mental experience, not her actual one.

If you're not sure whether you're hearing the message correctly the first time, never fear. You'll find that intuition rarely gives you the message just once. If you miss the message at first, you'll continue to see, hear, and feel nudges from your inner guidance system directing you toward the best path.

Stress and Other Physical Blocks to Psychic Awareness

We've explained earlier how the energy that flows through the body, mind, and spirit is all connected and comes from the same source. Intuition is one manifestation of that source. So to keep intuition flowing and insights coming, people must keep their bodies and minds free and clear of any blocks. A major block is stress.

Stress begins when you become tense in response to emotional upsets. Certainly an argument, insult at work, or outburst of temper can cause stress. But even minor annoyances can add up and become major sources of tension. Trying to pretend negative emotions don't exist by burying them and then acting happy doesn't work, because you usually bury them somewhere in your body. And this accumulated dumpsite later becomes the place where an illness takes shape.

In addition to stress (or in response to it), other problems can interfere with your healthy flow of life energy and intuitive information. Alcohol and other mind-altering drugs can become an escape route for many people who don't want to face the discomfort of emotional hurt. Other people pursue relationships with others as a form of distraction, even when the relationship may not be a healthy one. Anything—even TV—can be an unhealthy escape route if relied upon to avoid issues that need to be faced.

One problem with cutting yourself off from your feelings—physical or otherwise—is that you also cut yourself off from other areas of your life. For example, you may ignore tension in your neck that is telling you to slow down in your life before you become ill. Or you may avoid communicating with someone because of uncomfortable feelings, which gradually cause the relationship to weaken and possibly end. Something similar can apply with intuition: If you cut yourself off from feelings, you're likely to cut off your intuitive input as well.

Psychic Health

In order to keep energy flowing through you in a healthy way, you've got to release all of this built-up, pent-up, negative energy. Each of us needs to discover our own ways to clear out these blocks. Many people explore alternative health areas, such as acupuncture, reiki, and massage, to help themselves relax and open up. And everyone needs to develop regular healthy habits for handling emotional issues and daily stresses as they occur.

Body Basics for Psychic Strength

A few basic principles apply to all of us: Eat right, drink plenty of water, exercise regularly, get enough rest, and be honest with yourself. (Sound just like what Mom always used to say? Maybe it's the source of "mother's intuition" !)

It goes far beyond the scope of this book to offer you comprehensive information about diet, exercise, and stress reduction. It's really up to you to make an honest evaluation of your health habits and, if necessary, to take steps to improve them. That's especially true if you're trying to develop and use your psychic abilities. Remember: Your body is the antenna for intuitive messages, and if it's not in good shape, you probably won't be in a position to hear those messages well.

Maintaining good health is especially important if you're planning to help others heal, because you might start drawing on your own energy reserves and end up wearing yourself out. And what's the best way to recharge your reserves? Rest! Listen to your body when it's telling you to slow down, take a breather, or get to bed early! Feeling exhausted is a sure warning signal that you're doing too much.

To keep yourself healthy, strong, and disease resistant, take some time out to take care of your immune system. Supplements of vitamins, minerals, amino acids, and/or plant extracts are available to everyone. Seek advice on the best combinations of these supplements for you, which depends on what physical condition you're in.

From the ESP Files

Eileen Connolly, Ph.D., takes an esoteric approach to many psychic topics. In her book *Developing Your Psychic Powers* (Newcastle Publishing, 1990), she proposes that the color of the foods you choose to eat indicates your balance of energy, be it physical, mental, or emotional. These colors correspond to the aura-personal issue associations applied to auras (see Chapter 11). For example, eating lots of foods in the orange group, such as oranges and carrots, increases your energy and enhances your ability to cooperate with and consider others. Ideally, you should have a balanced color diet, but you may want to amend that if you want to improve specific issues in your life.

Mixed Messages

Some psychics choose to fast occasionally, for a few reasons. One is that the body expends more energy on digestion than any other body function. Occasionally reserving this energy allows a person to focus it elsewhere. Another reason for fasting is that it helps clear our systems, physically and psychically, by eliminating impurities that build up. But be careful when fasting! To make certain that you do it properly, be sure to check with your doctor first. And be sure that those people who are closest to you are informed of your decision. And by all means, drink plenty of water!

Of course, a big part of maintaining your immune system and body strength is eating properly. Just like everything else that's good for us, food follows the standard rules of balance and moderation. That means eating appropriate amounts of fresh fruits and vegetables, grains, proteins, and even fats.

Many psychics choose to adopt a vegetarian diet, based on the theory that we absorb the energy of whatever being we eat. The idea is that plants suffer less violent deaths, and therefore one does not take in as much bad karma when eating them. Your eating habits should be based entirely on your own urges and needs. There are certainly no rules for what a psychic can or can't eat. If you need to change in this regard, your intuition will let you know.

Everyone knows that water is essential to good physical health, but did you know it's crucial to psychic health too? Water is an excellent energy conductor, helping to keep the intuitive energy flowing smoothly through your body and between your mind and body. Think back over the recent days since you've started perusing this book. Have you noticed that you've been craving more water? That's your body's intuitive way of saying it wants to keep the energy flowing.

Of course, the obvious way to keep energy moving is to get moving yourself. Exercise is the best way to do that, and it's especially effective—in psychic terms—to get outdoors and breathe in the fresh air. Any contact with the outdoors and Nature gives the energy of the sunlight, air, and earth a chance to cleanse and energize you. In addition, Nature can help "ground" you if you begin to feel over-whelmed by *too much* psychic energy. In other words, take a reality break by getting in touch with the natural world!

Alternative Health Techniques

The field of alternative therapy, meaning ap-proaches to encouraging health or treating illness that are not considered conventional medicine, includes well over 100 different disciplines. And many of these disciplines of healing and growth contain various versions. When looking for one that's right for you, don't be afraid to read about

Intuition Hotline

Remember how your mom always told you to wash your hands? Not only is it a great way to remove germs, but it also helps wash away the "vibes." If you've been practicing healing touch or psychometry, wash your hands before and after. Water breaks the energy's charge that you detect when you touch the subject, so it's a form of psychic cleansing and protection.

and try several disciplines along the way. But the one that keeps coming back to your mind is probably the best one to actively pursue. If you're at a point where you want to help others heal, particularly through energy healing, you're sure to benefit from receiving some form of healing therapy yourself. This helps strengthen you and teaches you how to receive—as well as give—healing.

Certain *essential oils* are believed to help clear the mind to receive psychic insight, especially the expensive but effective jasmine oil and rose oil. Others that are commonly found include frankin-cense, lavender, neroli, eucalyptus, gardenia, honeysuckle, and sage. Usually only a drop or two of oil is used, by placing it in some type of burner.

Beyond Words

Essential oils are oils obtained from plants that retain the aroma and other characteristic properties of the plant. Their scents are used as perfumes, flavorings, and medicines.

In some cases, hands-on healers use a small amount of essential oil to activate the chakras in their fingers and hands. Sometimes they also apply them to their third eye. The idea is that these plant oils increase the healer's psychic perception of vital energy in the patient.

173

In order to increase the sensitivity of their hands, some healers receive hand massages or *reflexology* treatments, specifically on their hands. This helps to improve their overall touch sensitivity, as well as to reduce stress and increase inner strength.

Beyond Words

Reflexology is a form of hands–on healing based on the principle that every part of the body directly communicates with a reference point on the foot, hand, and ear. Massaging these points helps the corresponding body part heal by improving circulation, eliminating toxins, and reducing stress.

There are many wonderful forms of healing touch and other alternative health modalities that can help you feel more fit and less stressed, both in body and mind. But you can't talk about stress busters without going back to that old favorite: meditation. Many techniques and teachers are available to help you learn how to meditate in the best way for you, so we encourage you to pursue those. Meanwhile, no matter where you are or how busy you get, you can always take a moment out to breathe. This can instantly connect you to the free-flowing, vital power that includes your intuition.

What's Up, Doc?: Trusting Your Body

No matter how often you see your doctor or alternative practitioner, always take care to stay in touch with your own physical condition. Your health-care providers can't feel your symptoms for you, so it's your responsibility to bring them to their attention. But first you have to become aware of the symptoms yourself. To help you do that, try the following exercise. You can tape-record and later listen to the following words, have a friend read it to you, or read it through several times yourself before trying it on your own. You may want to have some meditative music softly playing in the background.

This also makes a good exercise for your psychic journal, particularly writing down what you receive about your symptoms. Describe *everything*. You may get a voice, an image, a kinesthetic impression, or even a scent.

Don't try to analyze your experience while you're in the midst of it, but instead wait until you have quiet time later. Remember, as with many of these exercises, you may feel at first that you're just making up your responses out of thin air. But stay with it and just write down everything that occurs to you. Don't judge it. You can try to write as you do the exercise, or remember your impressions and write them down later. Here goes!

Inner Physician

What physical symptom do you have that concerns you? Describe it here:

_____

_____

Sit or lie in a comfortable position and close your eyes. Take a few deep, relaxing breaths. Exhale slowly each time. Count slowly from 10 down to one and feel yourself become more deeply relaxed with each breath. If going to your inner sanctuary helps you to relax, you may want to do that at this point in this exercise.

Begin to gently focus on the area of your body that concerns you. Allow your attention to float there. Allow any images or sensations to come into your awareness. Imagine that your symptom has a voice. Ask it, "What is it you're trying to tell me?" or "What can I do to help you?" Write any information here.

_____

_____

Pause.

Do any feelings or emotions arise when you do this exercise? If so, write them here.

_____

_____

Pause.

What sensations arise in your body or the area of the symptom? Write them here.

_____

_____

Pause.

Is there anything else your symptom would like to reveal to you? Write it here.

_____

_____

When you are ready, open your eyes and return to normal consciousness. What have you learned?

_____

_____

Now think about ways that you could react differently when your symptoms arise. Describe several options here.

_____

_____

_____

I had one student who imagined an actual inner physician complete with white coat and stethoscope as her inner guide on this exercise. The guide gave her information about her symptoms and what to do to repair herself. Although she needed to see a doctor in order to receive treatment, her body made her aware of a potential illness. Your symptoms can help you stay healthy in a couple of ways. If they're severe, then they're telling you loud and clear to get to a doctor. On the other hand, small, infrequent twinges of pain or discomfort may be early warning signs: Heed them and take the time to get in touch with your inner self.

Psychically Attuning Your Physical Body

So far, we've talked about how the body, mind, and spirit are linked, and should be considered integral when approaching healing. But what if your physical body is doing okay? How can you improve your own emotional, mental, or spiritual state—even if your body feels fine?

Try the following meditation to get in touch with how good and connected you are actually capable of feeling when you open up to the possibility. You can begin this meditation in various ways. Choose one of the following:

➤ Go to your inner sanctuary.

➤ Take several deep relaxing breaths and ask for assistance from your guides.

➤ Get into a deeply relaxed state through meditation or guided imagery.

Once you are deeply relaxed, continue to the main part of the meditation:

1. As you inhale, straighten your spine and adjust your neck so that you can feel a flow of energy up your spine and out through the top of your head.

2. Imagine that a swirl of powerful white light is surrounding you and that you are floating upward toward a higher, finer vibration. As you imagine yourself rising higher and higher, you feel enveloped by feelings of love. (Pause).

   You feel enveloped by feelings of peace. (Pause.)

   You feel enveloped by feelings of compassion. (Pause.)

   You feel enveloped by feelings of courage. (Pause.)

   You feel enveloped by feelings of joy. (Pause.)

   You feel enveloped by feelings of wisdom. (Pause.)

3. Imagine these feelings flowing to every cell in your body, nurturing and healing you. If there is a place in your body you feel particularly concerned about, send these feelings there. You are now filled and surrounded by the emotions of love, peace, compassion, courage, joy, and wisdom.

4. Imagine that your physical body and its energy field are being healed through this powerful light.

5. See yourself in a future situation. Your body is strong, healthy, and full of vitality. You know that the light is healing you at a cellular level.

6. Continue to imagine a powerful, white light filling you and surrounding you like a cocoon of light. If there is a particular quality you would like to have more of in your life, imagine it pouring in upon you now, carried by the light. Imagine it filling and surrounding you.

7. When you are ready, return to the room in this cocoon of light. Sit quietly for a few moments.

Once you get a sense of how good you can feel when you're at your best, you'll want to stay in this frame of mind as much as possible. Feeling truly in tune with your Higher Spirit is a worthy goal to strive for. Go for it!

If you're curious about going beyond the body psychic and getting into something deeper…and deeper…check out the next chapter on hypnosis and other altered states of consciousness.

The Least You Need to Know

➤ Your body can help you get in touch with your intuition.

➤ Physical stresses can be a block or a stepping stone to psychic awareness.

➤ Getting in touch psychically with your physical symptoms can help you maintain your health—and help you heal others.

➤ You can conquer stress through healthy living—and some natural alternatives help too.

➤ Trust your intuition's warning signals and green lights.

Part 4
Beyond the Body Psychic

Once you have your beliefs about the body and mind connections sorted out, you're ready to gain a deeper awareness of how to transcend these expectations. Part 4 describes more advanced steps toward training your mind to access your less obvious psychic self.

We'll help you to understand the importance of accessing altered states of consciousness, from hypnosis to dreaming, to telepathy, and beyond. We also offer insight into the finer points of trusting your intuition and believing in yourself.

Chapter 14

Hypnosis and Altered States of Consciousness

In This Chapter

➤ Trance your way into your brain

➤ The power of suggestion

➤ Divine dictation

➤ You're in the driver's seat

For thousands of years, philosophers and scientists alike have recognized that thoughts can affect both behavior and bodily functions. But during the past century or so, great efforts have been made to learn if it's possible to actually *direct* these thoughts to influence the physical world. So far, the evidence indicates that the best way to do so is by reaching a state beyond normal, everyday consciousness.

Remember when we mentioned Franz Mesmer in Chapter 2? He's the doctor who invented the idea of putting patients in a hypnotic state during, or as a form of, treatment. That way, he could help them ignore pain during a procedure or help them relax if they suffered from anxiety. When Freud came along with his theory of the subconscious mind, the plot thickened. By the beginning of the 20th century, the pieces were in place for people to invent ways to direct the subconscious mind to control thoughts and, hence, behavior. We'll show you how you can tap into that power yourself in this chapter.

Going Into a Trance

A good way to help yourself become open to the power of suggestion is to help your mind escape the habits and beliefs of its normal conscious state. This "voice of reason," or logical mental state, keeps you trapped in old thought patterns, along long-established neural pathways, and thus closed off to new ways of thinking and intuiting. So what option do you have?

Beyond Words

A **trance** is an altered state of consciousness, marked by a heightened but narrowed focus of attention. It is also described as a state of complete mental absorption. Although some people describe a trance as a state between waking and sleeping, they are incorrect.

Intuition Hotline

If you would like to delve even deeper into altering consciousness to induce intuition, check out Belleruth Naparstek's *Your Sixth Sense* (HarperSanFrancisco, 1997). Her chapter on "Imagery to Access Psi" examines the components of intuition and replicates them with specific guided imagery exercises to alter consciousness and activate psi activity.

The answer that has come to shamans, visionaries, and mystics for millennia and to psi researchers recently is: Induce an altered state of consciousness. The word commonly applied to this state is "trance." A *trance* is really an umbrella term that covers any state in which the conscious mind "takes a backseat" long enough to let the subconscious mind come to the fore. Because the conscious mind usually creates a barrier to information that comes from other areas, a trance state allows you to have a more direct view of certain emotions and actions. This does not mean that it stops working or being aware of what's going on. It doesn't "shut off" the brain. It continues operating simultaneously with other levels of consciousness that are induced.

Indeed, alternative states of consciousness are based on consciousness with a different emphasis, wherein you become extremely conscious. "Taking a back seat" suggests that the rational, logical side isn't trying as hard as usual to run the show.

Several steps appear integral to achieving a trance state, including:

1. Relaxing
2. Concentrating
3. Turning inward
4. Focusing on specific sounds, words, or images
5. Choosing to change one's conscious state

Interestingly, taking these steps can help you achieve a variety of altered mental states all of which can fit into the category of trance. You can enter into a trance using any number of techniques, including meditation, communion, prayer, spiritual transcendence, and the best-known form of trance: hypnosis.

Going Deeper, Deeper...

Through the entertainment media, you've no doubt been introduced to *hypnosis* as a supernatural force that takes over a person's inhibitions and makes them do silly, embarrassing things. But hypnosis is not just a parlor trick; it is a useful medical and psychic tool used by health professionals around the world. At its heart, hypnosis is simply a state of intense concentration. When you're hypnotized, you're more alert and receptive to new ideas or suggestions.

Perhaps the biggest myth about hypnosis is that the person undergoing hypnosis gives up control of his (or her) own mind and is subject to the control of someone else, namely, the *hypnotist*. This myth has given hypnosis a bad rap. In fact, experts in the field of hypnosis propose that, although they make suggestions, all hypnosis is self-hypnosis and that its power lies in the mind of the person being hypnotized.

Hypnosis is actually achieved when the client reaches such an intense level of concentration that he (or she) blocks out any mental interference that distracts him from his focus. The physical process involved shows that his brainwaves slow down measurably, from the conscious beta waves to the subconscious alpha waves or perhaps even theta waves, which mark the dream state that you go through on your way in and out of deep sleep. (If these ABCs of brainwaves are confusing you, revisit Chapter 5, where we introduced them to you.)

Beyond Words

The dictionary definition of **hypnosis** refers to an artificially induced state resembling sleep, characterized by heightened susceptibility to suggestion. Experts on hypnosis, however, explain that hypnosis is actually a very natural state of mind that never involves sleep. A **hypnotist** is a guide, and ideally a trained expert, who directs and leads the subject into a hypnotic trance. A **hypnotherapist** is a hypnotist trained to help people use hypnosis to understand the sources of their problems and to create positive change in their lives.

In a sense, hypnosis is like guided meditation. You pass through a series of steps to go deeper into the unconscious, but actually hear every word during the process. Whether you enter a light trance or a deep one determines whether you experience other effects as well. A light trance may give you a feeling of being very relaxed or perhaps weightless, but otherwise may not feel all that different from the concentrated frame of mind you achieve when reading a good book. A deeper trance could create a euphoric state, or a state similar to being intoxicated—without the loss of control (or the hangover!).

Although the hypnotist remains fully conscious in a completely normal state of mind, the client's mind is free to soar to new levels of intense concentration. Free from the rational constraints of the conscious mind, you'll be able to heighten certain innate abilities, including your imagination, your memory, your creative tendencies, and your suggestibility. All of these abilities are closely linked to the intuitive side of your brain, which helps explain why hypnosis is such an effective route to psychic insight.

Hypnosis and Psychic Insight

Hypnosis can work with intuition in many ways. You can use it to improve your physical health and self-image, to resolve emotional conflicts, and to increase spiritual insight. Hypnosis makes these changes easier because it allows you to overcome your conscious mind's resistance to new ideas and its attachment to old beliefs. For example, a person who tends to eat chocolate bars when he's nervous could ask a hypnotist to suggest that he no longer crave candy when under stress. After explaining to the hypnotized client why too much candy could be harmful, the hypnotherapist might then suggest drinking cool, fresh water instead of eating chocolate when the craving comes on strong.

In the case of improving your physical health and mental attitudes, a hypnotist can help by replacing old thought patterns with new ones. This can apply to overcoming problems such as stress, insomnia, smoking, nervous habits, allergies, phobias, and more. For instance, a hypnotist with a client who wanted to quit smoking would access their client's unconscious mind. The hypnotist would then review the benefits of giving up cigarettes *before* suggesting a new behavior to replace the old one. Once the unconscious mind was convinced of the wisdom of not smoking, it would lend its support to the conscious decision to quit. Hypnotism can also help you improve in areas in which you're already strong, such as sports performance, public speaking, test taking, study skills, and more.

However, in order to overcome bad habits or achieve new goals, you often must resolve long-standing emotional issues—and doing so usually requires working with a hypnotherapist. Such professionals are trained to help you get to the underlying cause of problems, which are often deeply imbedded in memory because they are so painful. The pain will persist and continue to create new problems based on old habits unless you address the underlying cause.

One technique employed by some hypnotherapists to investigate the source of deeply buried emotional problems is *age regression*. Age regression involves guiding a patient's memory back to an early time in her life—or even before she was born—in order to uncover painful events or examine unpleasant emotions. Some people claim to remember experiences from past lives, another facet of psychic phenomena.

Mixed Messages

Don't experiment with hypnotizing your friends unless you've had professional training. Guiding the process effectively is more complicated than it sounds. And that goes for someone who wants to use you as a guinea pig: Tell her to seek appropriate training first.

Mixed Messages

Steer clear of untrained hypnotists if you're trying to resolve long-standing emotional issues. Without proper guidance, the messages you receive can be unclear or confusing, which can lead to further problems. Seek a certified professional if you decide to try hypnotism as a form of therapy. If you're not sure how to find a reputable hypnotherapist, you can call The National Guild of Hypnotists (603) 617-6179 for advice.

From the ESP Files

Experimental evidence shows that hypnosis is conducive to psi performance. In 1994, Rex Stanford and Adam Stein, psychologists from St. John's University in New York, performed a meta-analysis of 25 experiments conducted in 10 different laboratories between 1945 and 1982. The outcome suggests that a hypnotic state greatly facilitates psi performance: Hypnosis helped increase psi effects with odds greater than chance of 2,700 to 1. The control group of psi effects in an ordinary state showed odds of 8 to 1, which does not exclude the possibility of success due to chance.

On a simpler spiritual level, hypnosis can help you shut down the rational defenses of your conscious mind and open your senses to new sources of information. This information about personal and spiritual growth may be so wise and wonderful that you sense it must come from a source beyond yourself.

Muse or Myth?

We've all heard the ancient tales about creatures called muses who plant lyrics in the minds of great poets and otherwise inspire artists, musicians, and singers. Most of us view such a concept as pure

Beyond Words

Age regression is an application of hypnosis in which the client regresses to a younger age with the guidance of a hypnotherapist trained in this technique.

myth or the superstitious belief of ignorant ancients. And yet many modern psychics believe that their intuitive power comes from a higher source than their own conscious minds. Is this source the unconscious imagination or inspired guidance from a muse?

Even among intuitives, opinions vary about the source of the extraordinary information that comes to them, especially in creative areas. Some say that the source is the person's own higher consciousness or higher mind; others say that the person's higher mind acts as a bridge to spirit guides who provide inspiration. Reaching a conclusive answer to this question is probably impossible—and also unimportant—because each person has his or her own way of perceiving knowledge, relaying it, and describing it.

The important point to focus on is finding your own way to receive information. Once you reach an altered state of consciousness, whether through hypnosis or meditation, your mind is wide open and ready to learn. You can take in several types of information in several different ways. You may sense that you're gaining insight into your own personal and spiritual growth, receiving messages from spirits with specific advice for yourself or someone else, or even relaying images that can change the course of art, science, or the world.

From the ESP Files

In recent decades, the British medium Rosemary Brown has gained the attention of the musical world for her visits with the spirits of dead composers, who dictate new compositions to her. She reported that, at the age of seven, she was visited by the spirit of Franz Liszt, who explained that he was going to work with her. Other composers who gave dictation include Bach, Beethoven, Debussy, Chopin, and even Rachmaninoff. Interestingly, experts report that certain compositions are typical of the musicians' work when they were alive.

There are at least two ways to directly receive this type of information: *spontaneous drawing* and *automatic writing*. These skills are different than feeling highly focused and productive in your work. They require that your mind step aside and let your hands do the work. The less you think about it—or anything at all—the better. Which is why an altered state of consciousness, which sidesteps the rational mind, is so crucial.

Spontaneous Drawing

Anyone who puts herself (or himself) into the right frame of mind—an altered state of consciousness—can experience spontaneous drawing. Once your mind is free from rational explanations and judgmental demands (such as "my artwork must be beautiful"), you'll be better able to get to the true message that your mind is ready to reveal.

Before putting yourself in this frame of mind, prepare yourself for the artistic process. Get your pencils, chalk, or paints—or even clay if you're interested in sculpting— ready. Then meditate or reach a trance state and focus on a question or topic about which you want to receive insight. Keep your mind clear and wait. Once your hands begin to move, let them work independently of any rational efforts to control them. For example, if you feel a line looks out of proportion, don't worry about fixing it. In fact, if at all possible, try to avoid even looking at your artwork until your hands stop moving.

The point of this process is to let the unconscious creative side of your mind act freely. By doing so, you're likely to receive a symbol or image that gives you insight into an issue that's troubling you or a specific question that you've asked. In addition, some trained artists intentionally seek inspiration using this method to help them produce beautiful pieces of artwork. If that's your aim and you've been trained in a fine art, you may find that this method allows your skill to flow through your hands and into your work without requiring conscious thought. Whether you're an amateur or a fine artist, the point is to be spontaneous and have fun!

Automatic Writing

Automatic writing involves a process similar to the one that allows spontaneous drawing to occur. Although pen and paper have been the tools of choice in the past, modern mediums find that a keyboard works just as well. The important part is freeing your hands (and your mind) from conscious mental control, which may be difficult for people who insist on using proper grammar and punctuation. You've certainly got to let that sense of mastery go if you want to tap into your unconscious mind with any success.

Beyond Words

Spontaneous drawing and **automatic writing** are forms of creative expression thought to occur during an altered state of consciousness, when the rational mind is shut off and the unconscious mind steps in and takes control. Spontaneous drawing involves the creation of visual images or pictures, while automatic writing involves writing words. Writing musical compositions is based on the same process as these and, similarly, does not require a musical background or training.

Automatic writing comes in various forms. As we've mentioned, grammar and punctuation are not important. In addition, you may find that the words often run together and you may not be able to recognize the handwriting as your own. Many experts advise that you don't look at your hands at all, except to occasionally check that they're still writing on the paper.

When you've finished writing, take time to review your work carefully. The writing may begin as loops and curlicues that eventually take shape and form letters and words. They may come as phrases that stand out from other, unclear text or as symbolic words or images (more likely in the case of spontaneous drawing). Certainly, you shouldn't expect to have the Great American Novel on your first go-round—or ever, for that matter. Most messages tend to be private, offering you suggestions for personal improvement. These messages also tend to be direct, factual, and wise.

In many cases, automatic writing doesn't feel other worldly at all. You might approach it just as you would any type of informal writing. Sit down with your pen and paper, relax, and clear your mind. In fact, this is the perfect time to focus on that favorite project we've talked about before: your psychic journal.

Unsolved Mystery

One Australian medium named Ruth Bennett receives a special type of inspired writing, wherein the words flow rapidly into her mind and she simply records them. As the Minister of the Church at Windsor, she reports that entire sermons are sometimes dictated to her from a spirit guide. On one Sunday in the middle of her ironing, she stopped to grab a pen to take dictation. When she arrived at church that night, she unexpectedly had to take the pulpit, but luckily had the sermon she'd received from her guide that afternoon. It sure beat improvising!

Keeping and Interpreting Your Journal

Our higher mind or spirit guides can communicate with us in a myriad of ways. We've outlined many of these methods in the previous chapters. Automatic writing and drawing are simply other ways your intuition can communicate through you.

The main thing I try to get across to my students when they perform psychic exercises is that *they will feel like they're making it up.* Does it surprise you that—whether I'm giving readings or practicing automatic writing—I still feel this way; that my messages do not come from a higher spirit or even my own intuition, but that I make them up out of thin air? The only explanation I have is that psychic information seems to reside in a place in our brains that also holds our imagination—and so we often confuse the two.

This potential for confusion is why keeping a journal is so important when you're learning to receive intuition or communicate with your guide. The journal provides a way for you to evaluate the insight and inspiration you receive over a period of time. (It can even help you confirm that your unique insights were right all along!)

Here's an exercise that can help you get in touch with this ability when you're ready to write in your journal. Before you start, you may want to prepare some questions to ask. Or you can simply see what your intuition wants to communicate to you without any prompting.

Opening to Intuitive Guidance Meditation

1. *Sit quietly.* Do any exercise from this book you find most helpful for centering and quieting yourself (meditation, hypnosis, guided imagery, for example).

2. *Feel the light.* Surround yourself and fill yourself with light and ask that only the highest wisdom be present with you as you do this exercise. I say the following prayer:

   I fill and surround myself with the white light of the divine consciousness and of God so that only that which is good and needful may enter. I ask that God's wisdom be in my mind, on my lips, and in my heart.

3. *Breathe.* Sit and relax. Feel yourself becoming open. It's not necessary to meditate. Imagine that you are serene and receptive.

4. *Listen.* Your guide's message may come to you in a block of information or through a whisper. You may receive information through a series of images or pictures in your mind. You may have an impression of being loved or a feeling of physical warmth that flows through you. Ask for them to communicate to you in words so that you can write down the information.

Intuition Hotline

Choose a quiet time, when you're feeling relaxed, to practice contacting your spirit guide. Blocking out all outside stimulation will aid your communication.

5. *Write.* You may hear just a few words. It will seem like your own thoughts, but that's how guides communicate with you. I repeat: *You will feel like you are making it up.* With practice you will be able to differentiate between your own thinking and imaginings from those of your guide's. Don't force the words. You may have long pauses at first. Don't worry about making sense of anything as you write. This isn't the time to evaluate. Sometimes you'll hear whole sentences or receive a flood of information in thought impressions. Some people just get a few words at first. Stay in an open, receptive state and just listen. You may have the experience of knowing what you're going to write before you write it.

6. *Ask questions.* You can have a two-way communication with your guide. Ask your guide questions in response to the information he or she gives you. You don't have to write the question unless you want to. Just form the question in your mind and ask your guide telepathically. You may want to ask your guide's name and how you can best work with him or her.

7. *Evaluate.* As you practice your automatic writing and write the responses in your journal, it's important to evaluate your guide's information. Has it been helpful? How accurate is it? When you've acted on the guidance you received, have you felt better, calmer, more peaceful, and less stressed? You may want to ask for information from your guide that you can objectively evaluate. You might say, "I'd like information about my trip next month." "I'd like information about how to help my child with her schoolwork." "What steps can I take to improve my relationship?"

I believe that everyone has a guide for this lifetime. Sometimes a guide works with you for a specific purpose. It might be to help you with parenting skills or to assist you in a special project. You may have several guides, each with a different role in helping you. Expect that your guides may have different personalities, interests, or energies. Some guides are funny; others are stern taskmasters; still others bring a profound feeling of love and wisdom. Guides are there for every need. Don't be afraid to ask a guide to help you in a certain area of your life. Your guides like to be of service in whatever way they can be.

Mixed Messages

Avoid alcohol and mind-altering drugs when you're attempting to get in touch with your psychic side. By nature, these substances involve a loss of control, which is one reason many psychics avoid them. They recognize that altering one's state of consciousness is serious business, requiring concentration, responsibility, and free will. Alcohol also dulls and blocks energy and overloads the body with toxins that also interfere with psi.

Whether you feel your source of insight and inspiration is your spirit guide or your own imagination, don't hesitate to tap into this incredible power that comes through your creative process and imagination. But whatever you decide to call the source of this power, you're the one who's in control!

Who's in Control?

Whether you're working with a hypnotist or channeling your spirit guides yourself, you can choose to become fully conscious at any time during your trance. You may want to ask your guide for his (or her) name and information about what role he's to play in your life. One way to reassure yourself of the presence of your free will is to simply stop the process if you feel uncomfortable at any point. You *can* do that!

The same principal applies to hypnotism and other trance states. If you find you aren't comfortable with the suggestions that are coming your way, you can make the choice to come out of the trance. Remember that in these states you won't be unaware of what's happening to you. In fact, you'll be hyper-aware, which is why these states open us to our intuition.

In the next chapter, we'll talk about another altered state of consciousness in which we spend a large portion of our time: Sleep! Just as you can control other altered states, you can control this one, too, once you learn how. Read on for more info about mastering this amazing pathway to your intuition.

The Least You Need to Know

➤ Trances and altered mental states provide easy access to your intuitive mind.

➤ Hypnosis is an easy and direct way to connect to your unconscious mind and redirect your thoughts and actions.

➤ Altered states can improve imagination and enhance creativity.

Chapter 15

A Vision in a Dream

> ## In This Chapter
>
> ➤ The meaning of dreams
>
> ➤ The psychic side of dreams
>
> ➤ Controlling your dreams
>
> ➤ Understanding your dreams

Everybody dreams. Even those people who say, "I never dream" dream; they just don't recall their nighttime reveries. In fact, sleep research reveals that everyone has at least four or five dreams a night! What they still don't know is why dreams occur or where dreams come from within the brain and body.

Whatever their source, dreams have captured the imagination and attention of philosophers, scientists, rulers, and average citizens since history began. Writers and artists from every culture have documented dreams, and today scientists are doing the same thing. Some investigate dreams as a function of the brain; others explore them as psychic phenomena. One fact remains: The more they learn, the more they want to know.

Are you the same? Do you want to know what your dreams mean? Could they really be windows to your psychic world? We'll explore these issues in this chapter.

What Are Dreams?

Dreams remain an awesome mystery. They can be trite and serendipitous; they can be frightening and portentous; they can be structured and calming; and they can be all of these at once! Which makes you wonder what they're really about. Are they visions of an inescapable future? Insights into your emotional state? Warnings of possible disasters? Or discarded thoughts that your brain no longer has room to store?

Researchers are investigating all of these possibilities and responding with many different theories. Some say that no evidence exists to prove that dreams have any point at all. But most people find it hard to believe that we dream for no reason. They offer other possible purposes for dreaming, including (but not limited to) the following:

➤ Dealing with stress

➤ Preserving your mental and physical health

➤ Storing new skills and information

➤ Getting rid of superfluous information

➤ Leading you toward spiritual growth

➤ Receiving intuitive messages (last but far from least!)

From the ESP Files

For a long time, people thought that only a few dreams occurred in color, and that these dreams were superior to the rest. Not true! All dreams contain color, but many appear in a dim half-light, similar to moonlight. So, if you can't recall colorful dreams, don't just assume they're dull. Any dream has some sort of information to offer. Just spend a little time to delve deeper, and you're likely to find a wealth of insight, ready for you to reveal.

Before coming up with an answer to why people dream, researchers need to understand the processes involved in dreaming. The logical place to start is with what happens in the body and brain during sleep. By using electrodes to monitor brain waves, eye movements, muscle tension, and other physiological data, researchers can tell when people are dreaming—and then wake them up and ask them what was going on! (Sounds like a job every little brother would love.)

What's Happening When You're Asleep?

By monitoring sleep patterns, researchers have identified when most dreams take place. Most people follow the same sleep patterns every night, falling asleep and going deeper and deeper into a relaxed state for about the first 90 minutes. At that point, they enter a phase called *REM sleep*, which is marked by rapidly moving eyelids and dreaming. When researchers wake up their subjects during REM sleep, the subjects almost always report that they've been dreaming, and these dreams are often quite vivid.

Most people undergo REM sleep three or four times a night, following a 90-minute cycle. However, within each cycle, REM sleep lasts progressively longer: While the first period of REM-period sleep may last only 15 minutes or so, your final REM stage may last as long as 45 minutes. And since dreams correspond to REM stages, the average dream usually lasts between 15 and 45 minutes—15 minutes early in the night, and 45 right before you wake up.

Beyond Words

REM sleep stands for "rapid eye movement" sleep. This phase of sleep, when the eyelids twitch constantly, is most closely linked to the dreaming state.

But the time leading up to REM sleep and occurring between the cycles isn't wasted either. Although the other stages of sleep primarily serve to rest the body and mind, you may also have dream-like activity at this time, although it tends to be more mundane, similar to normal thinking, and less symbolic in content. In fact, only about 15 percent of subjects who awaken from non-REM sleep remember what they were dreaming, while subjects who awaken during REM sleep almost always recall something about their dreams. They also report having much more bizarre, illogical, and emotionally or visually charged dreams during REM. These "charged" dreams also may help the sleeper remember them.

Mixed Messages

Although sleep deprivation causes one to have an abundance of REM sleep and, hence, dreams, don't try using it as a way to experience more dreams. You'll just end up too tired to remember them.

When a person is sleep deprived, he or she definitely shows a need for more REM sleep. When that person does get a chance to sleep, he or she undergoes an effect called REM rebound, when the body tries to make up for REM time that is lost. This causes the person to experience much higher rates of REM sleep, with longer REM stages and fewer intervening sleep stages.

In addition to supplying a rich source of vivid dreams, the REM stage of sleep seems to meet other needs. In fact, the body and mind depend on getting a certain amount of REM sleep, and most scientists believe that dreaming is crucial to this process. As yet, however, no direct evidence inextricably links either physical or mental functions to dreams. So the question remains: What do dreams do? That question has baffled many of the world's greatest minds. But a few have offered some cogent theories about what's going on, including the granddaddy of psychoanalysis, Sigmund Freud himself.

Intuition Hotline

Don't be afraid that sleeping too well can adversely affect your ability to dream. In fact, the longer you sleep, the less non-REM sleep you experience. If you are well-rested and fall back to sleep, you have a good chance of returning directly to REM sleep. So don't stay up nights worrying that sleeping soundly interferes with your dream recall. Do your best to enjoy a good night's sleep whenever possible.

The Royal Road to the Unconscious

Freud called dreaming "the royal road to the unconscious." He believed that dreams carry hidden desires, using symbols to combine a person's longstanding wishes with their previous day's activities.

Freud was a big believer in psychoanalysis and felt that dreams could be interpreted only by a trained psychologist. His colleague, Carl Jung, contradicted him with the theory that individual dreamers were perfectly suited to interpret their own dreams because they were more likely to understand their personal dream symbols than would a psychoanalyst.

Of course, Jung had his own theories on what dreams are all about. As you may remember from Chapter 5, Jung developed the theory of the archetype, the universal symbols that every individual contains within himself (or herself), but which also shares in common with everyone else. Therefore, although dreams have meaning that dreamers can interpret, their content may involve information that extends beyond the dreamer's personal desires and anxieties. Although Jung did not believe that all dreams were truly archetypal, he suggested interpretations for several archetypal images. Looking at these (some are listed in Chapter 5) may help you decide whether you have had this type of dream.

Another, more modern, slant on dreams views them in extremely functional terms. A recent theory, for instance, postulates that while the body's at rest, the mind sorts through and processes all the information that it has encountered that day, and this process results in dreaming—either to store information or to discard it.

Obviously, the brain remains active even while the body is getting much-needed rest. Although no one can prove whether dreams are merely a last look at unwanted mental garbage, a way to work out deep-seated emotional issues, or a first glimpse at important information that is carefully stored for future reference, it appears that certain types of dreams transcend the everyday. In fact, certain dreams appear to hold keys to the past, present, and future realities, and when they do, we call them psychic dreams.

Psychic Dreams

What exactly is a psychic dream? That's a difficult question to answer mainly because almost all dreams seem to have a bizarre or ethereal quality that seems psychic even if the content is not particularly meaningful in this way.

Another problem is that it's often difficult to identify and document psychic dreams when they occur. For instance, some people—even though they can't recall the dream itself—are certain that they've had a psychic revelation when they awake. They may recall some specific words or simply have that sense of knowing that accompanies clairsentience. Unfortunately, by their very nature, these dreams are impossible to document or explore further.

Another sort of psychic dream involves perceiving information about another place or time that you can't validate until a later date. In this case, your dream may seem like a normal dream, except that it includes information that only later proves to have been predictive. And then there's the possibility that you may have psychic dreams of events that occurred in the distant past, and you simply aren't aware that you've gained a unique—and accurate—glimpse into history (yours or the world's). From just these few examples, you can see how difficult it is to try to pin down just what a psychic dream really is and what it may mean. Let's explore this rich world a little further.

Visions, Visitations, and Portents

Dreams that offer information about the future clearly appear to be psychic dreams, since this is information that you could not obtain without the aid of your intuition. This type of psychic dream, which offers information about the future, is the *prophetic dream.*

If you believe you have had a prophetic dream, you must write it down or otherwise document it, including the date you dreamed it, *before* the actual, predicted event occurs. By doing so, you can later prove that the information came to you as a foresight into the future. And having a written record also helps you keep track of how accurate your dream messages turn out to be.

There are three basic types of prophetic dreams, each requiring a different standard of proof, so to speak. Categories of prophetic dreams include:

➤ True precognitive dreams
➤ Foreshadowing dreams
➤ Dreams with subliminal awareness

Beyond Words

Prophetic dreams are those that pertain to sensing or predicting the future.

While prophetic dreams in general are more common than most people think, true precognitive dreams are rare. In addition to being documented, they must exactly match what actually happens in the relatively near future. Other types of prophetic dreams occur more often. A foreshadowing dream is less demanding in terms of proof: You must also have a record of date, time, and content of the dream, but the event predicted can resemble the dream in a less specific way and occur not immediately but within a reasonable amount of time. A dream with subliminal awareness must be recorded, but may include just one or two elements that come true within a relatively short amount of time.

Intuition Hotline

If you'd like to explore more about the dream world online, check out **http://www.dreamtree.com.** This Web site has lots of fun and fascinating information that might help you get better connected to the dreamier side of your unconscious.

Beyond Prophetic Dreams

A dream that predicts some clear cut future event is easy to label "psychic" because it is clearly prophetic. However, most dreams offer messages that are not so easily defined. Rather, they offer hints of deeper meanings, but leave the job of interpretation up to you. These dreams can be divided into general categories, including literal, displacement, and symbolic.

Another category of psychic dream is the literal dream. These dreams present information in literal, or actual, images. This information may come in the form of a visual image or verbal phrase that stands out and thereby helps you recall the dream.

For example, you may dream that a woman wearing a red Santa suit runs up to you saying, "I've lost it." You would be tempted to think this was a symbolic dream telling you to slow down your Christmas shopping efforts—until you're at the mall one day and the event actually occurs. Even if only one aspect of the dream later transpires in real life, such as seeing a woman in a Santa suit or hearing someone say, "I've lost it," this dream still qualifies as a literal dream.

Another sort of psychic dream is the displacement dream. In this type of dream, a literal image appears but in a different setting than it would be in real life. For example, you might dream that your mother gets a flat tire and has to walk home from the grocery store alone. After the dream you call her, concerned. She's fine, but tells you about her neighbor who had a flat and had to walk home from the grocery store. The event did occur, but the lead character was displaced (fortunately for your mother!).

Still another type of psychic dream is the symbolic dream. Although all dreams seem symbolic, these dreams gain added significance once the passage of time reveals their insightful images. For example, you could be searching for the best way to treat your back pain, which doesn't seem to be getting any better. You may dream of seven lights shining, accompanied by a voice that says, "Look at the seven lights." Upon awakening, it seems like an odd dream holding no particular meaning. But a few days later, you read in a book about the seven light-filled centers associated with the body's main chakras, and decide that you'll try energy healing as a way of treating your back pain. Only then does it occur to you how insightful your symbolic dream really was.

Unsolved Mystery

A classic case of premonition in a dream occurred in President Lincoln's own dream just days before his assassination. He described a dream wherein he wandered around the White House, which had a "death-like" feeling with sounds of "pitiful sobbing." When he finally found the source of the crying in the East Room, he asked mourners who was dead and was told, "The President, he was killed by an assassin." He was awoken by the loud sound of crying that had taken place within the dream. The remarkable prescience of Lincoln remains a fascinating enigma.

Considering how many different interpretations there could be to symbolic dreams, is it possible that all dreams are psychic and you just aren't able to discern their true meaning? There's no answer to this question at this point, except that time will tell. However, if you start to look at dreams in this sense, you'll certainly learn to value and respect each one much more than you have in the past.

Researchers at the Maimonedes Dream Laboratory in New York have done much in recent decades to hone in on psychic dreaming specifically. Montague Ullman and Stanley Krippner devised methods for testing ESP during dreaming—and showed high success rates. Their results suggest that dream telepathy is not that unusual, or that hard to do.

In various experiments, they had an awake "sender" look at a piece of artwork that contained a striking scene and then send this image to a dreamer. When awakened during REM sleep and questioned about their dreams, the dreamers frequently reported the image, or aspects of it, that the sender had relayed to them. According to expectations, the hit rate due to chance would be 50%. But the cumulated results of these experiments showed a much higher success rate of 68%. (Subjects had 102 hits versus 48 misses.)

The Maimonedes experiments inspired others to look at dream telepathy. For instance, a recent experiment by Kathy Dalton and two associates at the University of Edinburgh showed significant results in a clairvoyance dream experiment that did not involve a lot of high-tech measurement. They recorded the dreams they had each night in their own homes. The next morning, their dreams matched up with video clips that a lab computer had randomly selected and projected overnight, in a locked room. This research, though seemingly simple, suggests that dreams do indeed access a level of information that extends beyond the dreamer's own mind.

Psychic Knowledge? Or a Subconscious Detective?

So if you have a dream about an event that actually comes true, how do you know whether your dream was truly psychic insight or simply a coincidence? Is it possible that your subconscious mind picked up on certain clues, processed the information, and fed it back to you in your dreams? Ask yourself questions such as these before you decide whether or not your dream was truly prophetic:

➤ Did I receive any warnings (from other people or from the media) before I went to sleep that might have triggered my dream?

➤ Could I have subconsciously incorporated external noises I heard or other information I received while dreaming?

➤ Have I ever dreamed of this topic before? (Dreams with similar themes may be common for you. If so, the odds dictate that sooner or later your dreams are bound to coincide with real life.)

➤ Were there any unique details of the dream that identify the event in my dream as the specific event that actually occurred?

Knowing ahead of time that your dream will definitely come true is a rare occurrence. Only people who have had substantial experience with discerning their dreams can say without a doubt that they have seen the future. Unless you have a special gift for prophetic dreaming, you will probably have a difficult time accurately forecasting which dreams are true and which aren't. If you notice that you quite frequently have dreams that later come true , pay attention to any patterns that accompany these dreams, such as the way you feel upon waking from the dream or how clearly you recall the dream. Also, be certain to keep dated records of the dreams as soon as they happen, and share them with understanding people, who can support your documentation and also help you recognize patterns.

If you can't accept that dreams come from a psychic source that simply hands you insight on a proverbial silver platter, you can apply certain principles to help you get to the bottom of your subconscious messages. A leading spokesperson on the topic of dreams is that so-called "Man of Miracles," Edgar Cayce, who felt that individuals should take an active role in pursuing the impact of their dreams. He believed the purpose of dreams was to build up the mental, spiritual, and physical well-being for the "self-edification" of the body.

Cayce proposed that in order to interpret your dreams properly, you must study and know yourself completely. First, get to know how you feel about your dreams and what they can do for you. You must decide for yourself the purpose and function of each dream you have. Cayce proposed that all dreams serve one of two functions: either to help you solve problems and adapt to the external world or to awaken and alert you to new potential within yourself.

Next, you need to take inventory. Know your mind—conscious and subconscious—inside out. Be aware of your future plans, goals, interests, stances, and decisions. Acknowledge your hidden fears, longings, dependencies, and defenses. Understand the cycles, needs, habits, and stresses of your body. Once you gain this awareness, you can more accurately interpret your dreams and then see how they can help you improve mentally, physically, and spiritually. According to Cayce, whether dreams are psychic or not, they can give you tremendous insight into the power of your own dreaming mind.

Tapping Into Your Dream Power

The Chinese philosopher Chuang-Tzu once said, "One night I dreamed I was a butterfly, fluttering hither and thither, content with my lot. Suddenly I awoke and I was Chuang-Tzu again. Who am I in reality? A butterfly dreaming that I am Chuang-Tzu or Chuang-Tzu imagining he was a butterfly?" The philosopher made this observation in the 3rd century B.C., and people are still fascinated by this puzzle today.

Where do your dreams end and you begin? While your dreams occur totally within your mind, they require your full attention and actually become more real to you than your sleeping body. Of course, you can reassure yourself that you always wake up from a dream—an especially comforting fact if you're one of the millions who experience nightmares!

But have you ever experienced waking up but you couldn't move and couldn't understand why not? For this brief period, your mind's dream state was still in control and your conscious mind (with its ability to move your voluntary muscles) was not. Is there a way to extend this period when the conscious mind is aware but not quite in control—just long enough to let you have a closer look around dreamland? Some people can do this easily, and actually have cultivated the art of dream control.

Boosting Your Dream Recall

Before you can begin to analyze or control your dreams, you first must be able to remember them. This may sound difficult if you're someone who's unaware of your dreams or has never tried to recall them in a systematic way. Don't worry: Everyone dreams, and everyone can learn to remember their dreams. Here are some simple steps to get you started:

➤ Establish and maintain your own personal dream journal. At the very least, keep paper and pencil (or a tape recorder) by your bed, so you're ready to document any and every dream that comes to you.

➤ Write down any and every dream that you recall, including fragments and seemingly insignificant snippets. Do this as soon as you wake up!

➤ Before you fall asleep, tell yourself that you expect to dream, and that you want to remember your dreams. You can even make suggestions about what topic you want your dreams to cover!

➤ As much as possible, try to wake up naturally, without using an alarm clock. Because awakening from internal cues usually pulls you directly from REM sleep, you increase the odds of recalling your most vivid dreams. On the other hand, some people use alarm clocks set at 90-minute intervals, with the idea that they'll wake themselves up near the end of a REM sleep period. That may or may not work, however, since the timing of sleep stages is an inexact science at best.

➤ Remain quiet and still when you awaken. Keep your eyes closed and send your mind back to what you were just dreaming about. Don't start thinking about the upcoming day's activities.

➤ Recall your dream backwards. That is, remember the most recent parts first, then move backwards in the sequence of the dream events.

➤ Try to remember all of the dreams that you may have had. Then take a few moments to make any associations between your dreams and real-life events.

➤ Pay attention to dreams. Review records of your previous dreams often. Recall usually improves with interest and involvement, so think, read, and talk about your dreams.

Mixed Messages

Recalling your dreams during the day can be both good and bad. Yes, you want to be in touch with your dreams as much as possible, and should appreciate any opportunity that triggers more information or altogether new dreams. But don't let your daytime experiences tempt you away from recording your dreams as soon as you can in the morning. And when you do recall dreams, write them down right away—they will easily slip away as soon as you're distracted.

Of course, recording your dreams right after you wake up is crucial to remembering them. Don't say to yourself, "I'll write it down as soon as I get home from work this evening." The dream—or most of the details—will be gone. In fact, some experts estimate that the average dream is forgotten within 10 minutes of waking up.

On the other hand, once you get in the habit of writing down your dreams, you'll find that your recall increases at a tremendous rate. You'll probably record three to four dreams a week within your first two weeks and continue to record more from there. And if you start to feel that you're having too many dreams, then read the advice we offer above—and do the opposite! For example, as you fall asleep tell yourself that you prefer not to dream. And when you wake up, jump out of bed and blast your radio before you can remember anything. You get the idea. But it's hard to imagine anyone who would not want to know his or her dreams, since they offer an open door to one's own soul. We recommend that you actively value and accept each one.

From the ESP Files

Eric Maisel, creativity consultant and author of *Fearless Creating* (Putnam, 1995), suggests that the brain can accomplish a tremendous amount of work for you during sleep—as long as you invite it to. He suggests that by clearly phrasing a question that you want answered and then presenting it to your brain before falling asleep, your brain can present you with an answer in the morning. He recommends receiving this answer by writing down your thoughts on the matter first thing in the morning. He explains that sometimes you're presented with ideas that raise even more questions, and that is the point—to get at what's really going in your mind when your brain's unconscious processes are free to focus on the deeper issues.

Asking Your Dreams for Guidance

You can cultivate a sacred sense of your dreams by acknowledging each one as a gift from your intuition. Even when a dream does not seem to present some earth-shattering insight into saving the world, it can offer you a quick glimpse at some aspect of your life that you might want to look at more closely. Even when you're not certain what your dream means, the possibilities you merely guess at can provide you with enormous intuitive insight.

Intuition Hotline

Listen to your recurring dreams with special attention. They tend to focus on personal issues, and if you fail to understand the lesson of the dream well and continue unwanted behavior, the dream keeps repeating the message.

And with practice, you can do better than guess-work and observation. You can even help control the content of your dreams by giving your mind a specific task just before you fall asleep. You'll be suggesting what you'd like to dream about and asking your mind to give you information in specific areas of your life. Here are some steps to help you ask your dreams for guidance:

1. Before you go to bed, get your pen and paper ready beside your bed. Write down tomorrow's date. If you've been keeping a journal, read about the last dream you wrote down.

2. When you're in bed, relax and review your day in reverse. Think about what you did just before going to bed...how you got ready for bed...what you did this evening...coming home from work...leaving work...what you did at work in the afternoon...in the morning...and so on. Carry this through until you remember waking up and recalling the dream you had the night before. This process will help you develop a detailed ability to focus backward in time.

3. As you come closer to falling asleep, repeat to yourself continuously, "When I wake up, I will remember my dream about..." If you have clarified what you specifically want to know, insert the question that you would like your dreaming mind to answer. Avoid asking a question with a simple yes or no response.

4. When you awake in the morning, don't move or start thinking about the day ahead. Instead stay relaxed with your body in the same position and your eyes closed. Tell yourself that you want to recall your dream; then allow your mind to drift back to your dream.

5. Once you start to recall your dream, start writing. The idea is to write down whatever you remember immediately so that you're free to move on to remembering new material. If you find that you can't recall anything, be sure to write that down too.

When you look at what you've written, be aware of how you feel and which items you respond to most clearly and strongly. Underline these points, so that you can refer to them if necessary at a later date. These are the points that strike you as most relevant to your situation at this time. You may find that insights from several dreams can be put together to create a clear message for which you are waiting.

Beyond Words

Lucid dreaming occurs when the dreamer realizes he or she is dreaming. This awareness does not interfere with the dream's continuation, but may or may not enable the dreamer to direct the dream. Lucid dreaming—controlling the course of a dream—is a skill that can be learned.

Directing the Dream: Lucid Dreamers

Making suggestions for a topic you'd like to cover in a dream is a preliminary step toward actually controlling your dreams. Indeed, certain people have mastered this ability to direct the course of their dreams, referred to as *lucid dreaming*.

In A.D. 415, St. Augustine made what was probably the first written mention of lucid dreaming. Then, in the 8th century, the *Tibetan Book of the Dead* described a form of yoga that maintains full waking consciousness while in a dream state. This ancient art reveals an understanding of dreams as advanced as any proposed by today's modern researchers. The best known of these scientists is Stephen LaBerge—an accomplished lucid dreamer himself—at Stanford University, which has a famous sleep lab.

LaBerge's research offers the basis of what is now known about lucid dreaming. This dream state usually begins in the middle of a dream, but can also occur when the dreamer returns to REM sleep immediately after awakening. It happens when the dreamer realizes that what he or she is experiencing is not occurring in physical reality but in a dream. This awareness may be triggered by impossible or unlikely occurrences in the dream, such as meeting someone from far away in a strange place, flying, or creating objects with the mind, although some people lucid dream without having a specific cue.

Levels of lucid dreaming ability can vary greatly. Higher levels of lucidity allow the dreamer to realize clearly that every aspect of the experience is a dream, while lower levels involve varying degrees of awareness. In a high-level experience, the dreamer is able to manipulate the dream, and his or her actions within it. A dreamer's ability to imagine allows the dreamer to act out what he or she would like to do in real life or explore new possibilities.

Lucid dreaming can provide you with an important tool for achieving goals, relieving stress, rehearsing new behaviors, solving problems, finding artistic inspiration, or coming to terms with emotional difficulties. You can also direct it to help you access your intuition, if that's what you choose to do. Once you become able to control your dreams, you can then direct them to offer intuitive insight in certain areas. We'll talk more about how far you can go with this in Chapter 21.

Developing your skill at lucid dreaming is not all that difficult to do. But because so many various techniques are available, we suggest you explore the possibilities and decide which one will work best for you. In fact, Stephen LaBerge himself has written a book on the topic called *Lucid Dreaming* (Ballantine, 1990). That's a great place to look for more detailed information on how to learn lucid dreaming techniques.

Keeping Your Own Dream Journal

Whether you've experienced amazing moments of lucidity in your dreams or are working toward that by recalling simpler dream experiences, writing down your lessons definitely strengthens your dream connections. Here's the format I follow for recording my dreams; perhaps it will work for you too.

Date:

Dream title:

(Leave this space blank until tomorrow morning, after you have recorded your dream or dreams. Having a dream title allows you to easily look back through your journal to access any recurring themes.)

What was your day like?

(Write three or four sentences on the key events in your day. Emphasize any emotional highlights.)

Overview of issue:

(Write a few sentences here about the nature of a problem you are facing in your life. Describe some of the possible solutions and challenges involved with this issue.)

Dream question:

(After writing your overview, summarize your concerns into a one-sentence question. Try to phrase your question so that it evokes more than a yes or no answer.)

The dream:

(Write down any dream or dream fragments that you can recall. Sometimes you may not remember the actual dream but will wake up with the sense that something is resolved. If the dream itself eludes you, write about your feelings upon awakening.)

Dream interpretation:

(What thoughts and feelings do you have about your dream? What do you think it meant? Are there any parts of your dream that seemed particularly significant?)

Interpreting Your Personal Dream Symbols

Intuition Hotline

It's important to make your own associations of dream symbols before you consult outside sources about their possible meanings. However, after you have a clear sense of what your dream means for you, consulting a book may help you confirm your interpretation. *The Complete Idiot's Guide to Interpreting Your Dreams* (Alpha Books, 1998) offers an insightful overview of dreams, and their interpretations and symbols.

There must be a gazillion ways (or at least 10 or 20) to go about analyzing what your dreams mean. So, in order to avoid accusations of favoritism, we won't go into them here. The important point to make is that dream interpretation according to dream symbols is highly personal. What one person sees in one way might mean something entirely different to someone else. For example, you might dream of a flower and consider it to be a beautiful and positive sign; while someone who has allergies and or forgot to send their spouse flowers on a special occasion might consider a dream about flowers to be a nightmare.

When you see a symbol in a dream, don't run to Madame Divine's dream dictionary. Instead, go inside yourself to get clear about what the symbol means to you. Recall any previous associations with the image, as well as your current feelings about it. Make sure to understand your feelings, and always try to write them down. That way, if you do feel you must check out their symbolic meanings in some sort of reference book, you won't lose track of your own original impressions.

When trying to sort through your dream symbols and make sense of their meaning, remember to trust your intuition. Often it will give you a great big pat on the back, or some sign of recognition, when you come upon the correct interpretation of a dream. If you're trying to force an interpretation that's not accurate, your intuition won't let it sit right. And if you're trying to push away a message that you don't want to hear, it will keep coming back to you as the obvious choice. When you start saying, "No, that can't be it," then suspect yourself of being in denial.

Interpreting the messages that come from your dreaming mind can be challenging, but reading those that come from someone else's mind takes a whole new set of skills. So get ready to wake up and face the messages that are coming your way when you're fully conscious—via telepathy, a subject we take up in the next chapter.

The Least You Need to Know

➤ Dreams are a pathway of communication between the body and mind, which become active when the conscious mind shuts down.

➤ Psychic dreams take on many forms and may reveal messages about the past, present, or future.

➤ Not every dream is psychic, but they all contain a lesson.

➤ You can learn to control and direct your dreams.

➤ Recording your dreams strengthens recall and heightens insight.

Chapter 16

Telepathy: You're a Mind Reader

In This Chapter

➤ Telepathy: mind reading or imagination?

➤ Building your telepathic skills

➤ Measuring mind-to-mind messages

➤ Input from the natural forces

Telepathy may be one of the most common forms of intuitive experiences people have. For example, everyone can recall receiving a phone call or letter from a person they were just thinking about. Or giving a gift to someone who was about to buy that very item for him- or herself. Or sensing that a loved one is ill, and then calling to find out it's true. Perhaps these incidents occur so often because everyone has a special someone whom they are especially close to, whether it's their mom, dad, sibling, spouse, best friend, or maybe even their pet, and this closeness creates a special psychic bond between them.

But did you know that some information can be shared between total strangers or mere acquaintances? Well, psi scientists are seeing this occur regularly in experiments. They're trying to understand when and why telepathy works. They're trying to get to the bottom of what mind-to-mind communication really means, and what it can tell them. See for yourself what they've discovered in the pages that follow.

The Difference Between Telepathy and Imagination

If you have a knack for knowing what someone else is thinking, are you a gifted mind reader or just a good guesser? Answering this question is particularly tough when you're already close to the person to whom you're relating. For example, a mother and child have spent so many years together that they may recognize all sorts of unconscious clues and cues about each other's mental states and physical needs without even knowing it. So, how do you sort out cogent guesswork from true psychic ability?

A few characteristics appear to mark most telepathic experiences. For one thing, as we've mentioned, a close emotional connection between the people communicating serves to foster telepathic communication.

Secondly, most telepathy occurs spontaneously in moments of emotional intensity. That is, most people don't sit down and say, "Let's read our minds." Rather, telepathic moments are likely to occur during times of crisis, when the sender is experiencing strong emotions or sensations.

From the ESP Files

In his book *Telepathic Impressions* (University Press of Virginia, 1978), Ian Stevenson, a professor of psychiatry at the University of Virginia, collected information from various studies of telepathic communications. He found that 69.4 percent of the cases occurred between close family members, 28.1 percent occurred between acquaintances, and 2.5 percent occurred between strangers. Each of the cases used in this study were documented by witnesses who reported being told about the upcoming experience before any means other than telepathy could have come into play.

In general, telepathy seems to work best when transferring emotions, particularly strong ones, rather than thoughts. Another aspect of telepathy worth highlighting is its simultaneous quality: Telepathics share their thoughts at exactly the moment they occur—not before. This is especially common when people sense that someone they know has died. Usually, they experience this knowledge at the person's time of death, and thus they have no opportunity to physically see the person beforehand or to change the circumstances.

So, how is imagination different from telepathy? Imagination comes from within a person's own mind, and involves thoughts and motivations that never demonstrate having any basis in reality. Although imagination can seem like prescience or telepathy, you can categorize its results into two categories: *wishful thinking* and *projection*. When someone is indulging in wishful thinking but calling it telepathy, he may mistake his desperate wishes for psychic messages that do not actually exist. For example, a young man may believe he's received a psychic message from a beautiful woman to phone her, when it's only his desire to ask her out that's working on him.

With projection, a person may believe that the information she very much wants to receive—but doesn't want to take responsibility for—is telepathic. For instance, she may feel angry at Aunt Marge for expecting her to come to Sunday dinner. But because she feels too guilty to come right out and admit her feelings, she instead "intuits" that Aunt Marge is really the one who's angry. By projecting her feelings of anger onto Aunt Marge, she can feel justified about her negative feelings toward her—and less guilty about canceling the dinner plans.

But what about information that isn't emotionally motivated or physically disastrous? How can you be sure when someone, such as a business associate, is sending a simple message for you to understand or act on? The special ability of differentiating between telepathy and imagination, like any other skill, can be learned.

> **Beyond Words**
>
> **Wishful thinking** expresses personal inner desires, but may distort the perception of reality in order to make the desires seem like external truth. **Projection** is a psychological term that refers to attributing one's own personal emotions or traits to someone else; this is usually done in order to avoid facing one's own feelings or traits.

Building Telepathic Skill

Expert psychic communicator Edgar Cayce wrote about the ability to distinguish between imagination and telepathy, often referred to as *discernment*. Cayce felt that telepathy is more than mind-to-mind contact: It involves the influence of a spiritual force or power. So, one way to know if a message is telepathic is to determine whether it involves or improves an increased spiritual awareness. And how do you assess whether this spiritual

> **Beyond Words**
>
> **Discernment** in the telepathic sense refers to the ability to discriminate between personal desires, such as wishful thinking, and intuitive information.

Intuition Hotline

To test the theory that messages travel better between people who are emotionally close, practice sending telepathic messages to various people to whom you feel close. You can call them later, explain that you were conducting an experiment, and ask whether they had any thoughts about you or the contents of your message around the time that you sent it. Note whether you have a higher success rate with people to whom you feel closest.

awareness is involved? By constantly being in touch and attuned with your physical, emotional, and spiritual condition. This state requires complete honesty with one's self and benefits greatly from having a partner to work with to develop greater attunement to deeper levels of sharing and communication.

Cayce continually emphasized the importance of spiritual development to increase intuitive abilities. He developed an exercise to help two partners develop their skills of telepathic discernment. The idea is that both partners agree ahead of time to think of each other at the same time each day. At that time, each one should write down what he or she intuits the other is doing. Later that evening, they can compare notes. They should repeat this process for 20 days, after which their skills should be fully developed.

The key to Cayce's telepathic exercise is reality testing, which allows the participants to check whether and when their responses were accurate. This requires communication and sharing. Otherwise, a person could easily fall into wishful thinking, deciding that the other person is doing whatever he or she imagines.

Other intuitives, as well as recent psi researchers, have come up with other suggestions for effective ways to relay mind-to-mind messages. But one thing seems clear: Sending and receiving messages are two different processes. Performing each type of task requires your complete focus; don't try to do both at once. You'll experience sensory overload and be unable to relay clear information.

Receiving Messages

To practice receiving telepathic messages, prepare yourself in the way that many experts recommend. That is, work with a partner with whom you are already close. As your skills of receiving and discernment improve, you'll soon be able to apply your abilities to others you do not know as well. Also, remember to enter a relaxed or meditative state, so that your rational mind is quiet and your intuitive side is open.

Here are a few simple exercises to help you practice being the telepathic receiver. The first one helps you receive messages that have been sent by someone using a full range of sensory images to strengthen the image. The second one has them focus on sending visual images, which may or may not come though as clearly for you.

Receiving an Object Exercise

Get your paper and pencil ready. You and your partner should then settle into a quiet, comfortable position. It's fine to be in the same room together. Remember, in this exercise, you are the receiver and your partner is the sender.

1. Your partner, as the sender, should repeat several times—in his own mind—the name of a specific object, such as a vegetable, fruit, or flower. (Note that throughout this exercise, the sender does not need to have a real object present to look at, just his own mental version of it.)

2. After reciting its name silently several times, the sender should then experience the object in his mind. If it is a tomato, he should look at how red it is, smell its tart freshness, feel his teeth slice into it and the juice running into his mouth, and taste whether its flavor is sweet or not.

3. This whole process should take about 30 to 60 seconds. Then you can write down the image you perceived. If you don't see a clear image, write down any information you do get, such as color, shape, or smell. As we've said about other exercises, you may feel that you are making up your impressions, but don't let that stop you. Just try to have fun with the process.

4. Don't talk to your partner about what you sensed. Just let him see that you've finished writing so that he can go on to the next image. Repeat this process about five times. You can use five different objects of one type (all fruits such as an orange, apple, pear, banana, and grape) or a variety of objects (tomato, orange, chocolate, shrimp, and coffee). Food works well because it allows the use of smell and taste. (Don't try this exercise when you're hungry, or your wishful thinking mechanism may take over!)

5. Avoid talking at all during the exercise. When you've finished, then you can look at your notes together with your partner. Let him tell you whether you were on target or not.

Intuition Hotline

Another way—one that may be easier for you—to begin to learn to receive telepathic messages is by asking your partner to focus on sending you a color. He should let a specific color fill his mind, without attaching it to a specific object. For instance, if he chooses orange, he should just focus on orange, not an orange piece of fruit.

Once you feel comfortable with your success at the object-sensing exercise, try your hand—or rather, your mind—at receiving an impression of a visual image. This exercise is similar to the popular psi experiments, referred to as ganzfeld tests, that we mentioned in Chapter 4 and will talk more about later in this chapter. See how you do.

213

Receiving an Image Exercise

Get your paper and pencil ready. You and your partner should be in separate rooms, but close enough to hear a bell. Settle into comfortable positions in a quiet state.

1. Your partner should privately pick out about five different pictures from post-cards, magazines, or books. You should not look at any of them ahead of time.

2. Your partner should focus on one picture at a time, trying to think of nothing but that image. She should do this for about one minute, and then ring a bell.

3. Once you hear the bell, record your impressions of the image, whether you prefer to write or draw what you perceived. Don't be afraid to simply list or draw details, if a specific image does not come to you.

4. Your partner should allow you about 20 seconds to record your impressions. Or you can have your own bell to ring, to let her know when you've finished.

5. Repeat this process for all five images that your partner selected. Avoid speaking to your partner during this time.

6. When you've finished, look at your notes together with your partner. Let her tell you when you were on target, or not.

Mixed Messages

Don't try too hard when it comes to receiving telepathic messages—your anxiety will only get in the way. Instead, try to relax and remain open-minded and open-hearted.

Pertaining to these exercises, theories differ on whether you should stop and discuss each image just after sensing it or go through all five before stopping to compare notes. Basically, it depends on what you want to achieve. If you want to assess where you are right now without interrupting your concentration, go through all five images at once. If you want to develop your skills of telepathic discernment, stop to analyze which images transferred best—and why and how.

If you feel that you're not as successful as you'd like, don't be too hard on yourself. Remember that you'll often feel like you're just making it up. Be as willing to be wrong as you are to be right: You'll learn from your mistakes. Another factor may be your partner. It takes two to tango—and to talk telepathically. If your partner isn't focused or is having an off day, you'll be sharing that experience too. Keep in mind that, for both of you, this is a new skill, and as with any new skill, it takes practice.

Sending Messages

Interestingly, scientists seem to know more about who makes a good receiver than who makes a good sender. Perhaps they tend to focus on how people receive information because that's how they have proof that psi exists. For example, a sender with fantastic skills can't get his message across—and therefore can't be evaluated—if his receiver isn't effective. But that doesn't mean that sending isn't important. And you may have a special strength in that area.

To practice sending telepathic messages, prepare yourself in the same way that you would for receiving messages: Work with someone with whom you're emotionally close, and put your mind in a relaxed or meditative state. Check out these exercises and see how you do.

Mixed Messages

Don't rely on telepathy to meet new people! If you're shy, you may be tempted to send a telepathic message to an attractive stranger but, as you know, telepathy works best with people you already know well. The best way to start getting to know someone is to strike up a conversation—out loud!

Telepathic Telephoning Exercise

As a simple and fun experiment, try sending a telepathic message to a friend to call you. Pick someone who calls often enough that she wouldn't have to go out of her way to phone you, but not someone who calls you every single day, regardless (like your mother or your boyfriend). Sit calmly in a quiet place, close your eyes, and focus on the friend of your choice.

Say your friend's name in your mind and picture her clearly. You can even use words to tell her to call you. Then envision her thinking of you, going to the phone, and dialing your number. Envision this very slowly and distinctly, taking the time your friend would actually need to do this in real life and including every detail of the scene—even if you've never been there before. For example, imagine where her phone sits, how she would pick it up, and how her fingers look as they push the phone's buttons. Then hear yourself picking up the phone and saying, "Hello." The whole process should take about five to 10 minutes.

When you're done, write down the time that you started and ended the exercise. Then stop thinking about it. Your friend may not call immediately, but when she does, ask her what she was doing when you sent the message. Perhaps she was busy, but thought of you and waited until she was free to call. If you don't hear from your friend that day, give her a call the next day to see if the thought to call you did indeed cross her mind when you sent the message.

If you don't succeed the first time or two, don't worry. Try a few more times, perhaps without calling your friend to ask why you didn't hear from her. Then try the experiment with someone else. With this experiment, you can't lose. Whether you succeed or not, you'll save money on your long-distance phone bills!

Sending an Image Exercise

Here's another exercise designed to help you practice being the sender. Since effective sending can be more difficult to measure, we recommend checking your results for this exercise after each attempt you make at sending.

This exercise requires a little planning ahead. Select five or six pictures with specific images, which may come from magazines, books, or postcards. Don't let your partner see any of them. You may want to chose pictures that have an emotional content as these are easier to send and receive.

Plan for your partner and yourself to sit calmly in a quiet place at the same time, whether you're in the same house or in completely different towns. During this quiet time, you look at one image while your partner simply sits and waits.

While concentrating on this image, describe it with words in your mind and also look at every line, shape, and color. Then think about all the associations it brings up for you, whether good or bad. (Emotions are important for making an image have more impact on the receiver.) Continue thinking about the image for about 10 minutes.

Meanwhile, your friend should write down every impression he receives, visual, verbal, or emotional.

Try this exercise at various prearranged times for each of the five pictures. However, discuss your results after each one. Discussing the results shortly after the experience will help you understand what impressions you sent that did or didn't work, which will help you improve your skills.

The Ganzfeld Test: Ping-Pong Anyone?

While telepathy seems to work best between people who are emotionally close, psi researchers are afraid to completely rely on these relationships to prove that telepathy works. For one thing, skeptics could accuse the people who are communicating of somehow cheating. For another, researchers want to show that mind-to-mind contact exists on levels beyond the emotional. Whether they work with loved ones or strangers, researchers are finding that telepathy can be established, even in noncrisis, controlled situations.

A favorite method for investigating telepathy is the ganzfeld test, which we explained in Chapter 4. Remember the Ping Pong balls? In this exercise, the subject's eyes are covered and all external and body sounds are drowned out with white noise. In effect, the subject is deprived of any outside sensory distractions, which allows her to focus completely on an image sent telepathically from a sender in another room. Later, testers show the subject four images and ask her to choose the one that most closely resembles the image she received. If the subject picks the one relayed by the sender, her response is considered a hit.

In the 1980s, researchers revised ganzfeld tests (now called autoganzfield tests) in order to allow computers to control the experiments. Computers randomly select target images, show them to the sender and receiver, and then record the receiver's responses. These computer methods enabled researchers to have less hands-on involvement, which ensured that the transfer of information was not mistakenly occurring through the researchers themselves. Meanwhile, the senders and receivers continued to transfer information at the same rate: about 35 percent (remember that pure chance has a 25 percent hit rate).

These new experiments confirmed several earlier findings. For instance, they confirmed previous observations that creative or artistically gifted persons show higher rates of psi ability. A famous experiment, discussed in the *Journal of Parapsychology* in 1990 by Charles Honorton and his colleagues at the Psychophysical Research Lab in Princeton, New Jersey, tested students from the Juilliard School of Music in New York City as receivers. Their overall hit rate was extremely high: over 50 percent, among the highest ganzfeld hit rates ever recorded. This suggested that creative types are indeed highly intuitive—at least as far as telepathy is concerned. Theories suggest that perhaps such people deal better with information that seems less rational, an ability that may be due in part to their strong right-brain functioning.

From the ESP Files

In the now-famous Juilliard-student ganzfeld test, the group of highly artistic receivers, including drama, music, and dance students, showed extraordinarily high success rates of 50 percent. But the musicians proved to be real stars: They had a 75 percent rate of successfully identifying their target images. Obviously, telepathy isn't based solely on the visual sense.

Another category of people who tend to score very well on the ganzfeld test are those who have reported previous psi experiences, as well as those who are practiced at meditation or other altered states of consciousness, such as hypnosis. Researchers suggest that these individuals are good at several things that may help promote the telepathic process: relaxation, concentration, and tuning out distractions.

One other type of successful ganzfeld receiver has come to the fore: extroverts. These people may show successful results for a variety of reasons. One may be that they crave mental stimulation and therefore eagerly pick it up in the ganzfeld state. Another possibility is that outgoing types are simply more at ease in the experimental laboratory atmosphere, and therefore can focus more clearly. But don't worry if you're someone who tends toward the shy side: Many introverts have done quite well when allowed to take telepathic tests in the comfort and privacy of their own homes.

Unsolved Mystery

A prime example of telepathic communication occurred with the grandmother of psi research herself, Louisa Rhine (a psi researcher and cofounder of the Rhine Institute with her husband J.B. Rhine). She documented an incident in which she strongly sensed that her daughter Alice, who was working with the United Nations in Korea during the Korean War, would call her that day—even though international phone calls were extremely rare at that time and no plans were made for Alice to call. Louisa even passed up opportunities to enjoy activities away from home so that she could be there when the call came. Alice's first words were, "Hello, Mother, are you surprised?"

Ganzfeld researchers also use their more sophisticated measuring techniques to report new findings about how telepathy may work. The autoganzfeld tests show that higher hit rates occur when the target images consist of videotaped film sequences rather than still pictures. Are you surprised? Did you think that a moving target would be harder to capture? Researchers suggest that the videotaped images are easier to detect because they offer more information, use both the visual and auditory senses, inspire richer internal images, seem more lifelike, create a narrative structure that is easier for the mind to grasp onto, and evoke emotions.

Nature's Effects on Telepathy

When measuring telepathy, scientists have begun to ask whether they need to account for the effects of external forces. That is, could there be forces outside or beyond the mind-to-mind connection that influence how well the information travels?

Research has found that two natural factors do seem to affect the strength of telepathic messages. These forces are the Earth's magnetic field and the moon's fluctuating phases. In fact, the most recent research suggests that these factors work together to affect people in various ways.

It's Magnetic

Believe it or not, the Earth is surrounded by a magnetic field, referred to as the geomagnetic field. For years, experts thought that this magnetic force was too minimal to have any effect on human physiology or behavior. However, recent research shows that when the right mix of frequencies and patterns occurs, this geomagnetic field may indeed affect us in a variety of ways. (One theory even suggests that humans may have tiny traces of magnetic materials in their brains that operate similar to those found in homing pigeons' brains.)

What makes it possible to study these effects (in addition to lots of new technological toys) is that these geomagnetic forces fluctuate. So, when the forces show high levels of geomagnetic energy, industrial and traffic accidents tend to occur more often. As the magnetic force levels decrease, telepathic ability appears to improve—in both the emotional crises we described early in this chapter and in ganzfeld lab experiments. This correlation supports the theory postulated by many ganzfeld experimenters: that a decrease in external influences, whether from a subject's physical senses or the Earth's unseen forces, improves receptivity to psi.

It's Moonbeams

From ancient wisdom to present-day superstition, the belief that the full moon holds a power over people remains strong. And recent scientific research shows some correlation between lunar phases and certain human behaviors—including telepathy.

In a 1965 experiment, neurologist Andrija Puharich showed that telepathy peaked during the full-moon phase, was high during the new-moon phase, but was very low during the half-moon phases. While Puharich theorized that the effects were due to the sun and moon's changing gravitational forces, as evidenced by the tides, other scientists were exploring the geomagnetic effects brought about by the sun and moon's cycles. They found that geomagnetic forces also decrease during the full moon.

Actually, these theories do not necessarily conflict or refute the effects of psi. In fact, these findings support the same idea: that psychic ability, such as telepathy, seems to be strongest during full-moon phases and weakest during new-moon phases. For intuitive purposes, this means that psychic information may be more accessible during full-moon phases. But that doesn't mean you should forget about using your intuition during the new moon— it's always there to help you!

Intuition Hotline

Try this experiment to see if the moon affects your psychic ability. As you make entries in your psychic journal, draw the approximate phase that the moon's in somewhere near the date. Over time, look back and see if your intuition is strongest or most active during any specific moon phases.

As you develop your sense of intuition, you can practice using it to improve your mind-to-mind connections with others. You can sense when a business associate may have a question for you, and prepare yourself in advance. Or you may know when someone you love is in trouble, and make certain to be there to support him. There are many ways to use telepathy, but don't forget that many other types of intuitive communication are available to you too. The next chapter will take another look at ways you can get in better touch with your own internal senses. And then we'll start looking at how you use your intuition skills to tap into whole new realms of communication.

The Least You Need to Know

➤ You can develop your skills of mind-to-mind communication.

➤ Practicing open communication with people you are close to helps you sort out what's telepathy and what's not.

➤ Ganzfeld tests can teach us what makes telepathy work.

➤ Natural forces, such as the moon's phases, may affect how well information transfers telepathically.

Chapter 17

Trusting Your Own Psychic Intuition

In This Chapter

➤ Using intuition on a personal level

➤ Evaluating your life with intuition

➤ Creating positive change with intuition

➤ Checking in for reassurance

We've talked about ways you can get in touch with your intuitive side and interpret messages. We've discussed how information may come to you and how you can transmit it. But we haven't said much about what you can actually do with this knowledge. How do you make intuition and its messages useful in your everyday life?

As we've said, many intuitive messages tend to be personal to you. Putting these messages to use for you requires a little more finessing. You'll need to assess what your intuition is telling you that you're ready to do, and then take charge and actively direct your life in the direction you want to go—with your intuition always present to guide you. You can direct your thoughts and energy to move in a direction that's more in tune with what your intuition wants to do for you: improve your life and increase spiritual growth. We'll show you how in this chapter.

Intuitive Intelligence

Most people consider the sixth sense to be an extra sense in addition to the five known physical ones. But the term also includes an interesting pun. The word "sense" suggests a type of intelligence. And that's another way of describing what intuition is, after all.

Instead of being extremely rational and logical, like your educated, constantly thinking conscious minds, your intuitive intelligence acts on different—but nonetheless effective—principles. Here's a chart you can use to distinguish between the thinking that comes from the logical/rational side of your mind and that which comes from the intuitive side.

Logical/Rational Mind	Intuitive Mind
fragments	whole
limits	expansive
slow	in a flash
either/or	many options
judgmental	nonjudgmental
needs proof	trusting
critical	loving
controls	has faith
attached to outcome	detached
exclusive	inclusive
prompt	flowing
linear	flexible
expectant	still, quiet
complex	simple
driven	calming
"I should"	"I could"
doubtful	hopeful
categorizes	sees overview
self-righteous	forgiving
hesitates	courageous
sameness	diversity
sees limits	sees potential
values structure	open to possibilities

Both types of intelligence have their own type of good sense. Once you learn to bring them both into balance and equal use, you'll have a good chance at becoming something that people don't talk about very often: wise.

Information: Past, Present, or Future?

When receiving intuitive information, try to do so with an open mind and a broad point of view. Gaining fresh insight into past events or emotions can teach you how to change the way you are today, but you needn't consider it to be a reprimand or source of guilt. Similarly, information about future possibilities can reveal options and opportunities—not unchangeable inevitabilities. But taking a hard look at the negative side of what is likely to happen if you pursue a certain path may help you redirect your focus and take more positive action.

When I'm giving a reading, I perceive information about the past to my left, the present straight in front of me, and the future to my right. (Just to confuse you, I have a friend who gives readings and hers are just the opposite!)

Often, clients ask me about a hoped-for relationship. If I am immediately drawn to my left (the past), I assume that something has been unresolved in a past relationship and ask my intuition for information on that. I may ask my client for the first name of a person in a previous significant relationship and then give the client information that could help resolve the conflict.

When asked about a potential future event, I often see probabilities rather than certainties. Let me explain. I often see alternate paths or choices that someone may make. They actually look like strands of light going off into the future. Many times one of these paths lights up in my mind's eye. I interpret this to mean that this path is the most likely one for my client to take. Then I describe what I see as the outcome of this path. I also describe the other choices.

> **Intuition Hotline**
>
> Remember that receiving information is a highly personal experience. Although my friend and I perceive past, present, and future information based on certain locations (that is, coming from the left, right, or straight ahead), other people do not work this way at all, and can receive information in any number of ways. Strive to find the way that works best for you, without comparing yourself to anyone else.

Here's an example. I had a client I'll call Ruth. She sat down on my couch and asked quite bluntly, "Am I going to get a divorce?" She told me her husband's name was Bob. When I tuned into Ruth and her husband, I felt instantly that things were quite rocky between them. They had a lot of miscommunication and hurt feelings. I saw the paths of light into the future and unfortunately the one that indicated divorce lit up, which told me that their marriage was indeed in trouble.

For some reason, I felt a wave of sadness and regret wash over me as I related this to the client. I could see in my mind's eye that other paths of light, indicating other possibilities, were not completely dim. I asked my intuition if anything could be done to save their marriage.

I immediately received information about Bob, showing that he was filled with regret. I perceived him as a rather stubborn fellow who, I suspect, may have had an affair. I felt that he didn't want a divorce and was, in fact, quite distraught over this prospect. However, he had no idea what to do to communicate to Ruth that he loved her. The way he saw it, Ruth was angry with him all the time and he just wanted to avoid her at this moment.

I asked for guidance about what Ruth could do and how she could better communicate with Bob. As I was relating all of this information to Ruth, I could see that the strong light on the path to divorce was becoming dimmer and the light on the path to reconciliation was becoming brighter. I ended the session by giving Ruth a referral to a marriage counselor and reinforcing the issue of choice and free will. Later, she reported that she and Bob had stayed together and were making progress with a therapist.

Mixed Messages

When giving a reading about relationships, you may feel pressured to respond with an outcome your client considers positive, but stay open to the true messages you receive: Moving on may be the best option for him (or her), even if he doesn't yet realize it.

When I'm giving a reading about a relationship, I don't always focus on whether the relationship will work out (that is, have a "happily ever after" ending) or not. I ask my intuition about what my client needs to learn in the relationship. I think for me to say "Yes" or "No" takes away from all the learning that's part of a relationship. That learning may include ways to make a relationship work—or lessons about moving on.

Remember, intuitive information about the past, present, or future, arrives as a gift. You can accept it without thinking twice and just take it for granted, or you can refer to it often, pondering its uses for today and the years to come. Like a good guidebook, it's there to be questioned. So don't hesitate to go back and do that, again and again....

Beyond Words

Negative self-talk is the inner voice in your mind that creates a running flow of negative thoughts about yourself.

Using Your Sixth Sense

To fully use your sixth sense, you need to become more self-aware. You can do so by paying close attention to your inner dialogue—the voice inside your head that murmurs messages about your life and your self-image. So often when I give people readings I pick up on how much they put themselves down or engage in what is often called *negative self-talk*. This type of thinking drowns out what your intuition may be trying to whisper in your ear. It also defeats your hopeful efforts at trying to create positive change.

It's Not About Predicting the Future

Often, what we tell ourselves—about life in general or about our abilities and talents—becomes a self-fulfilling prophecy. I can make all sorts of wonderful predictions about your future, but if you go away from the session thinking "I could never do that" or "I'm not that smart (or lucky or educated or ambitious)," then there's no real possibility of change. Henry Ford once said, "Whatever you think you can, you can. Whatever you think you can't, you can't."

Your subconscious mind considers whatever words you choose to tell yourself to be the truth. If you tell yourself you're always unlucky, your mind believes it and creates the proof of that belief in your reality. What are some positive beliefs you hold that help you succeed? What are some negative beliefs you hold that hinder your success? Are you willing to change them?

From the ESP Files

Scientists have conducted research indicating that people who believe psi exists are more likely to experience it. On the other hand, skeptics that question the existence of psi have the greatest difficulty experiencing it. ESP tests clearly show believers scoring much higher than skeptics.

I am often aware of the power my readings have on the eventual outcome. While I encourage people not to take what I say as gospel truth, many do. They think they have a future that is etched in stone and that I have the ability to read it. Nothing could be further from the truth. We shape our future by the thoughts we hold, the dreams we dream, the beliefs we carry with us, and also by our willingness to make choices and take risks.

I have many clients I would define as successful in life. In many respects, they are the easiest clients to read for because they don't let a lot stand in their way. When they decide they want to create something, all of their positive beliefs engage to help them create their desired outcome. Here's a sampling of common beliefs I see that these successful people hold:

➤ "I can make things happen in life."

➤ "I love my work because I do what I enjoy."

➤ "My work and my life are the same."

➤ "People like me and trust me."

➤ "I trust my hunches and gut feelings."

➤ "I'm lucky. Situations unfold for me at the right time."

➤ "I believe there's enough for everyone."

➤ "I'm willing to take risks when I feel guided to do so."

➤ "I'm good at what I do."

➤ "There is a purpose and meaning to my life."

➤ "I enjoy being of service in my field."

When you hold such positive beliefs about life, then you're more likely to take the steps necessary to make your dreams come true. As part of those positive beliefs, your intuition is guiding you every step of the way. It gives you input, saying "Yes. This is a good decision" or "No. Stay clear of that direction. Go the other way." When you learn to pay attention to your inner sense, it leads you to greater joy and peace.

However—and this is a *big* however!—trusting your intuition does not mean nothing bad will ever happen to you. It means that you can make wiser choices, experience greater calm, and understand a greater purpose in your life—even during difficult times in your life.

Finding Your Inner Confidence

I try to give my clients hope for the future *and* the tools they need to accomplish their dreams. One of the most important tools is recognizing and accepting the power of your own words and convictions. Are you truly in touch with your core beliefs? You better be, because they really help to shape the way you experience life.

Creating change in your life may require you to modify or even eliminate some of your core beliefs. But first you need to know what they are. Take a moment and fill in the blanks in the following exercise.

Your Values and Beliefs Exercise

I believe that in order to have a happy life I have to:

_____

People who are successful are:

_____

People with money are:

_____

226

I believe that in order to get ahead in life you must:

_____

People who are poor are:

_____

To be spiritual you should:

_____

People who are psychic are:

_____

My worst fear is:

_____

My greatest hope is:

_____

My biggest obstacle is:

_____

My greatest strength is:

_____

One of the first principles in creating a life you love is to act "as if." If you start believing you have the qualities that you need in order to have a successful life, your unconscious mind won't know the difference and will start to draw new and positive experiences to you. Your intuition will provide you with information about going in the new direction that you have chosen.

Take some time out to answer the following questions. You don't need to write anything this time, just allow yourself to picture and imagine how you'd feel.

What would your life look like if you acted as if you were:

➤ Highly intuitive
➤ Confident and successful
➤ Extroverted
➤ Well-liked

Intuition Hotline

Be honest about your true beliefs. No one is judging you, and you certainly don't need to judge yourself. However, if admitting a certain belief or two bothers you, make a mental note and come back to that one later. Your intuition may be telling you that you need to work on this issue.

➤ Destined to succeed

➤ Full of energy

➤ Filled with creative ideas

➤ Courageous

Hold onto these images and feelings: They represent an exciting step toward creating inner confidence. The more you become familiar with your positive images, the more they will come to you naturally. This is just an early step toward replacing old negative thoughts with new healthy ones. Paying attention to your beliefs and to the way your inner dialogue supports them is another step along the way to creating what you want in your life.

So, now that you know what your current beliefs are, are you ready to decide how you'd like to change the ones that need changing?

Mapping Your Way to Guidance and Growth

We've talked a lot in this chapter about using your beliefs to create what you want in your life. What do you want—really want—for yourself and your future? If you're like most people, that isn't an easy question for you to answer.

In this exercise, you're going to create your own treasure map—one that can lead you to the greatest treasure you've ever dreamed of: your innermost dreams and desires for your life. We're asking you to work with symbols. Symbolic images are one of the primary ways that your intuition speaks to you.

This treasure map, or dream collage, is a visual representation of your hopes and dreams. Remember that book by Robert Fulghum, *All I Really Need to Know I Learned in Kindergarten* (Random House, 1988)? Well, this exercise will remind you of that! Get a large piece of poster board or foam core, a pair of scissors, some glue, a bunch of old magazines, and a few new ones. Go through your magazines and cut out words and pictures that inspire you. Pay attention to what excites you.

If you've always wanted to travel, for instance, cut out a picture representing your dream destination and paste it on your board. Same goes for a picture that represents an exciting career, or a perfect body, or a great relationship. Cut out and paste any photograph, drawing, or other visual representation of your goal or goals. Once you're done cutting and pasting, put your collage in a place where you'll see it frequently.

Creating and displaying your treasure map brings your secret dreams and desires, aims and ambitions, out into the open. As your eye catches it from time to time, you'll be reminded of that side of yourself that isn't always doing the expected, rational thing. With time, the strongest parts of that "secret" side will start to jump out at you. They'll remind you not only that they're there, but also that they're ready for you to start making them real in your everyday life. And you can turn to your intuition for help on how to create that reality.

Unsolved Mystery

Did you know there's a real "money pit" (not like the one in the Tom Hanks movie!) on Oak Island in Nova Scotia? This one involves stones with mysterious inscriptions alluding to treasure, and several layers of oak wood, each inserted about 10 feet below where the last wood appeared. Despite numerous attempts in the past 200 years—with treasure hunters digging down 150 feet to dig up the treasure—their efforts remain thwarted by an ingenious booby trap that always floods the pit. (Ironically, no one even knows what type of treasure—if any—the pit holds.) But the Oak Island pit does have something in common with the money pit in the movie: People have spent millions trying to get to the bottom of it.

Using Intuition to Change Your Life

Many people come to me with a vision of what they want to create in their lives—and, more often than not, they simply want me to affirm that they'll get it. The pressure to say, "Yes, you will get that new home, new relationship, new career, new car...," is enormous. But who wants to go to a psychic and hear that the relationship you just started is not going to work out or that you may become unemployed for a few months instead of promoted when your company downsizes?

I've always found it difficult to tell my clients that things are not going to work out exactly as they planned. I used to feel that I could devastate them, or at the very least crush their dreams. How is it possible to be honest about what I sometimes see psychically, and yet avoid forecasting failure?

I've prayed a lot about this one. I want to be able to guide my clients toward success—not just predict success or failure. Over time, I've begun to see a connection between someone's internal condition—what she's thinking or feeling—and what ultimately happens to her in reality. And you must keep this in mind as you explore your own intuition or, especially, if you visit a psychic for guidance. YOU are the are the architect of your world.

Intuition Hotline

Stating clear intentions is a powerful way to achieve goals. Affirmations are especially helpful in changing thought patterns and re-directing your life. If you would like to obtain a booklet and audiotape with a guided meditation and more affirmations on this topic, you can order my program called "Creating the Life You Want: Meditation" (side 1) and "Affirmations for Success" (side 2)," which is listed at the end of the book.

You create your life experiences through your beliefs, the images you hold, the guidance you follow (or ignore), and the actions you take. It is within your power to create a life you love.

People often come to me expecting to hear phenomenal predictions or witness miraculous events. I can tell them only what I see and provide them with what I understand to be the tools to create the reality they desire. The rest is up to them. One of my favorite quotes is from Lewis Carroll's *Alice in Wonderland:* "There's no use trying," Alice said, "one can't believe impossible things." "I daresay you haven't had much practice," said the Queen. "When I was your age, I always did it for half-an-hour a day. Why sometimes I've believed as many as six impossible things before breakfast."

I think that what the Queen was on to is a philosophy called *metaphysics*. It's derived from the Greek word *meta*, meaning "going beyond," and *physikos*, meaning "the physical plane." It suggests that a connection exists between what goes on in your mind, beliefs, and consciousness and what you create in your life.

Beyond Words

Metaphysics is a branch of philosophy that focuses on the basic philosophical principles of being and meaning.

Using Your Mind to Create Success

"There is nothing either good or bad, but thinking makes it so," says Hamlet. We believe that this principle can apply to how you approach your life. If you believe your life's miserable and will always stay that way, then it will. If you want it to improve and you start to plan those positive changes in your mind, then your new future has already begun.

But despite the best intentions, you'll still need to do more than wish and dream. I consider the following four steps as essential to achieving your goals and creating a life you love.

1. *Know what you want.* Have a clear vision or goal for what you want to create. Don't spend a lot of time figuring out *how* to achieve your goal. Just do what the Queen suggests to Alice: Believe impossible things!

   The universe has amazing tools at its disposal to help you create what you want. When you're honest and clear about what you want, your Higher Self takes the long view of the connections and situations that must occur before you attain what you ask for. It begins drawing together the people, opportunities, and events that you need in order to create what you want.

Your Higher Self finds opportunities for you and provides the necessary impulses for appropriate action, so that you're attracted to those opportunities—and they're attracted to you! Your feelings, hunches, and flashes of insight signal what actions to take. Your willingness to be spontaneous, follow your inner urges, listen to strong feelings, and act upon them can lead you to your goals.

2. *Believe in yourself.* I see that one of the biggest reasons people become unable to create the lives they want is that they lack self-esteem and self love. Do whatever it takes to start believing in yourself—see a therapist, work with your minister or rabbi, write in your journal. If you believe you're worthy of your goals and are capable of achieving them, you're well on your way!

3. *Know the "science" of creating/manifesting.* Thoughts, beliefs, and emotions help create your reality more than you might imagine. Researchers at the University of California discovered that individuals who believe strongly that they can change or control their destiny are more likely to persevere in a difficult task.

   I have a teacher, Tom, who taught me a valuable lesson: Whenever I spoke to him with any kind of limitation in what I said, such as, "It's so difficult to start a business in this economy," he would counter with, "If you say so." It annoyed me terribly at the time. But now, whenever I hear myself saying something in my mind like "I can't…" or "It's hard to…," I also hear Tom reminding me, "If you say so." I usually stop doing the negative thinking right away. Richard Bach addresses this issue in his book, *Jonathan Livingston Seagull,* "If you argue in favor of your limitations, you get to keep them."

4. *Start a plan of action.* I call this "putting energy out there." What one step can you take? Start. Do it. Then take another. Follow your inner guidance. What is it telling you to do? Is there anything that feels appealing or fun? Do that. Someone once said, "If you always do what you've always done, you will always get what you've always gotten."

Planning Your Ideal Life

As we've discussed, the first step in creating a life you love is to be clear about what it is that you want. I use the questions in the following exercise to identify my true thoughts and feelings, which I can later refine and expand if need be. You try it!

From the ESP Files

Psi research shows that the best research subjects are those who concentrate well. Various studies along this line of testing indicate that mental focus is a key factor in psi subjects successfully achieving the goals of the experiment. When using intuition to improve your life remember the importance of focusing on your goals.

Your Ideal Life Exercise

Write a paragraph about describing your ideal life in each of the first three areas. Choose two more that are important to you from the list in "other areas" and write about them also. Be as descriptive and specific as possible. The questions listed after each area are just to get you started. Follow your heart to write about what's important to you.

Work

(What would you do, even if you weren't getting paid for it? What kind of situation would you work in: Alone? Self-employed? A large corporation?)

_____

_____

Money

(How much monthly or yearly income would you like? How much money would you like to have in investments? In savings?)

_____

_____

Relationship

(If you are in a relationship, how would you like it to be different? If you are not in a relationship, describe what you would like to create.)

_____

_____

Choose Two Other Areas to Write About

(Physical health and appearance; creativity; home and possessions; "free time," hobbies; spirituality; family; education; community or volunteer work; travel; friends; associates)

1._____

_____

2._____

_____

Once you have your wish list, underline some of the most important words in each paragraph. This will get you started at creating your own written goal, or list of goals.

Your Goal

Write your goal(s) in two or three sentences here.

_____

_____

_____

Verbalize and Realize

Remember the list of suggestions we made in the "Creating Affirmations" section in Chapter 12? Those tips can help you to turn your goals into positive statements. Your intuitive mind can then interpret those as what your future is intended to be.

Following are some sample affirmations to help inspire you. This list of statements offers examples of affirmations that can help you reach your specific goals. You can create your own affirmations, or use these singly, mixed and matched, or as springboards to create your own personalized affirmations. In other words, use them in any way that works for *you*.

➤ My intuition continues to direct me in manifesting miracles in my life.

➤ Infinite riches are now flowing freely into my life and I deserve it.

➤ I find it easy to take appropriate risks and actions.

Intuition Hotline

Remember that intuition comes in many different forms, so stay alert to new ways that it appears to you. Once you get used to receiving messages in a certain way, don't always expect it to come to you in exactly that same way, or you may close off valuable opportunities for learning. It can come to you from a source as "solid" as another person (maybe even a stranger) who suggests a good idea, or from a source as ethereal as a dream. Because it's operating 24 hours a day, your intuition has a lot of leeway in its role as your internal guidance system.

➤ I love and trust myself. I make appropriate decisions for my career success.

➤ I trust my intuition and have the courage to act on its wisdom.

➤ I feel confident in all that I undertake, and I succeed.

➤ I use my abundance wisely in ways that are of service to my community and to the resources of the earth.

Write your affirmations here.

_____

_____

_____

Visualize and Realize

What will it look like to achieve your goal? Picture yourself living in the situation you want to create. Many people imagine their visualizations as a series of snap shots or slides illustrating the outcome they want to achieve. What three images come to your mind as a result of realizing your goal?

Write your visualizations here.

1. _____
2. _____
3. _____

Once you have a clear sense of your goal, go back and observe what actions appear to you as the steps you need to take to reach that goal.

Write down three things that you feel guided to do as steps toward achieving your goal.

1. _____
2. _____
3. _____

Following Through

Now that your plan is in place, don't look back. Don't second-guess yourself or give way to doubt. Trust that your intuition got you this far and that it won't leave you now. In fact, this is the time that it can really get into high gear and show you all it's got to give. But in case you have a tendency to second-guess yourself, here are a few guidelines to keep you on track:

➤ *Pay attention to your thoughts.* Listen to what you tell yourself about your life situation. Pay particular attention to your beliefs about your ability to achieve what you want. Erase negative self-talk.

➤ *Practice your affirmations and visualizations.* Practice these at least twice a day. Often, the morning and evening are the best times for most people to focus their thoughts.

➤ *Pay attention to what excites you.* Continue to think about what you would like to create in your life. Focus on what brings you joy in your life today and what may bring you joy in the future.

➤ *Take action.* Take action on at least three things that can move you closer to your goals/ visions/dreams. If you're after a new career, for example, call a job counselor, interview someone who works in your desired industry, sign up for a related class, or do some research on the Internet or at the library. Small steps count! By taking them, you're building a bridge to create the life you want!

Mixed Messages

Don't worry if your plan of action, or at least some steps along the way, seem less than wise (even silly)! Unless your ideas seem actually harmful, trust your hunches. Your intuition is guiding you to new pathways.

Intuition Hotline

As a way of keeping your affirmations in the forefront of your mind, try taping up affirmation "memos" around your home or office. They'll give you quick reminders, even when you're too busy to take time out to initiate the process of creating positive thoughts.

Owning What You Know

One important way to build confidence in your ability to carry through with your dreams and goals is to give yourself a pat on the back for opening up to your intuition. Following are some suggestions for staying in touch with the psychic side that got you this far along on your journey:

➤ *Begin each day by asking for guidance.* You might do so when you first wake up in the morning, when you're having your morning coffee, or even during your shower. If you need information about something specific, ask your intuition about that problem. Otherwise, ask for general guidance and wisdom.

➤ *Take time out every day for a 10- to 15-minute meditation break.* Experiment with doing it at different times of day, then decide which one works best for you.

Intuition Hotline

For the sake of maintaining a good habit, such as meditating, you'd be wise to get used to repeating the ritual at around the same time every day. This advice applies to any suggestion for touching base with your intuition on a regular basis.

➤ *Remember that your guidance may come in a variety of forms.* It may appear as an internal nudge to read a certain book or to call a specific friend. You may experience your intuition through a spontaneous feeling of joy when you do something that you love, which is your intuition's way of saying, "Do more of that!" You may get a gut feeling or another body sensation that indicates you're on the right or wrong track regarding a decision. Learn to pay attention to all the ways your guidance speaks to you.

➤ *Follow your impulses.* Be spontaneous. When you over-analyze something you may be arguing yourself out of your intuition's input.

➤ *Ask your intuition for help.* Get in the practice of speaking to it like a trusted friend. You'll be rewarded with an ever-increasing channel of communication in return.

All of these suggestions are intended to get you using your intuition as often as possible. Try to avoid using your intuition to get started on a new path, and then just forget about it and wander off on your own. Remember to check in with your intuition on a regular basis, just to make certain that you're still on track. You'll feel all the better for it.

Well, we hope we've guided you toward getting up a good head of steam when it comes to realizing your psychic side. And now that you've done that, you're ready to "break on through to the other side." Next, we're going to show you a different realm, one that transcends your own mind, your own life, and your own body. We're going to talk about leaping the barriers of space and time.

The Least You Need to Know

➤ Intuitive intelligence offers its own brand of knowledge and wisdom, which can create a perfect complement to your rational mind.

➤ Intuitive intelligence teaches valuable lessons, whether based on past errors or future possibilities.

➤ Glimpses of the future are not set in stone; they offer a chance to compare and consider options.

➤ Two factors are essential to creating change: choosing a goal and taking action.

Part 5

Leaping the Barriers of Space and Time

Wow! Time travel—right from the comfort of your own home! Forget about having Scotty beam you up: You can do it yourself through incredible journeys within your own mind.

Part 5 talks about some pretty far-out stuff, like sensing events before they happen, exploring previous lifetimes, channeling spirit messages, and getting to know your second self. It may sound strange at first, but when you think about it, these are just further steps along an ever evolving path of awareness and spiritual potential.

Chapter 18

It's the Vibes: Precognition and ESP

In This Chapter

➤ Perceiving beyond the senses

➤ Knowing the future

➤ Sensing the vibrations

➤ Taking it in or tossing it out

By now, you know that you can use your intuition to help you in the here and now—help improve your relationships, professional opportunities, and physical and mental health. You can tap into it as a way of understanding your emotions and overcoming enormous obstacles.

But that may not be all: You might also be able to use this power—the all-knowing, all-powerful, omnipresent force within you and throughout the universe—for insight into, and influence over, events outside of yourself. We call this power extrasensory perception, and that's what we'll talk about in this chapter.

The "Extra" in ESP

As defined in Chapter 1, ESP stands for extrasensory perception. The "extra" refers to the ability to receive or send information without using your normal five senses of sight, sound, taste, touch, and smell. It involves knowledge that comes via a nonrational pathway.

Intuition Hotline

Want to test your ESP? The Association for Research and Enlightenment, founded by Edgar Cayce, has a Web site where you can do just that." Check it out at **http://www.are-cayce.com/esptestintro.htm.**

Many experts typically divide ESP into three main categories:

➤ Telepathy (communicating mind-to-mind)

➤ Clairvoyance (seeing events or objects using an inner sense of sight rather than an external one)

➤ Precognition (viewing events before they occur)

Other experts, who really like to go into detail, add two more categories under the blanket term ESP. They are more pertinent to perception of the past than seeing into the future, but they're interesting to think about. They include:

➤ Retrocognition (seeing past events without using the five senses)

➤ Psychometry (learning the history of a particular object without using the five senses)

All of these categories share a common characteristic: perception that extends beyond the use of the five senses. Does that mean that they all add up to make up the one sixth sense that people commonly talk about? Or is it possible that people have many psychic senses, perhaps dozens or even hundreds, that extend beyond the familiar five physical senses? No one can answer this question (yet!), but it gives us a wide range of possibilities to ponder. On the other hand, certain skeptics insist that these phenomena are not unusual at all, and that a rational explanation must exist.

Beyond Words

A **hunch** is an unexplained sense of a future event or outcome. Although it is sometimes confused with the word "intuition," a hunch is just one way of receiving intuitive information. Therefore, all hunches are intuition, but not all intuition is a hunch.

More Than a Hunch

Those so-called realists out there might argue that there's a plausible explanation for having a *hunch*, the old-fashioned word for receiving information without conscious sensory input. But the key word here is "conscious."

These realists claim that a hunch may involve a combination of unconscious sensory input, past experience, and good judgment. For example, you might suddenly have an odd sense that a thief is about to attack you—without consciously realizing that you saw a knife glint in his hand. You also might have forgotten that you'd seen his face on a post-office poster several weeks ago. And perhaps you were already a bit tense because your shopping trip required going into an unsafe part of town.

Rationalists attribute this sort of foreknowledge to *inference,* suggesting that you knew the information all along and inferred (or figured out) a logical conclusion to the predicament. They call it unconscious inference when you are not aware of the conscious thought processes involved in bringing this already known information to consciousness. Here's another example: A regular fan of horse races could get good at predicting winners—not because she has psychic insight, but rather because she knows the horses and jockeys.

But what if a horseracing novice, who's never been to the track before or even glimpsed the sports pages, correctly guesses the winning horse? Or someone simply wakes up in the morning "just knowing"—or even picturing—getting robbed later in the day, even before he knew he'd be shopping in a rundown part of town? Rationalists call this *coincidence.* Optimists call it good luck or bad luck, depending. What do you call it?

Beyond Words

Inference is the process of deriving logical conclusions from premises assumed to be true. **Coincidence** is a striking occurrence of two or more events at one time apparently by mere chance.

Whether psychic insight or unconscious knowledge is responsible, however, the information you receive is still quite valid. Regardless of what you call it or where you believe it comes from, you can consider it a gift. When you receive it, take some time to either heed its warning or appreciate its insight.

Insight Into the Future

Intuitive insight about the future can come to you in a variety of ways, including:

➤ A vision of the future

➤ Words of warning or prediction

➤ A sense of knowing in the mind

➤ A feeling of warning

We're sure it's no surprise to you that these pathways loosely correspond to those generally used to gain intuitive insight in any area. After all, in some peoples' view, sensing the future is the quintessential type of intuition.

For some people, their impressions of the future are so strong that they know they've experienced something more than a hunch. This happens when someone can claim they've had that most definite form of proof: a vision of the event. Whether in a dream or in the mind's eye, sight creates a definitive image that remains evocative long after the image passes. People who experience future insight through sounds or words are less likely to be as confident of their predictions.

From the ESP Files

Prophecy can technically be categorized as foreknowledge that comes in the form of a vision or dream. Traditionally, its source is believed to be divine revelation. Prophecy has gained increasing amounts of attention recognition with the arrival of the new millennium. Depending on which prophet you believe, the end of the Earth is inevitable or a dawning of a new age of creativity, love and spirituality is on its way. What do you believe? We'll talk more about this in chapter 27.

With clairsentience (feelings about future events), certain insights tend to catch your attention because they arrive out of the blue, yet give a strong and clear sense of instantaneous knowing. Although this information can also pertain to the past or present, future insight usually strikes you as the strongest because you revisited it in your mind. That is, when the foreknown event actually occurs, you remind yourself of your previous thoughts or feelings about the future. In this way, future insights are reinforced in your mind, and therefore seem most common later.

Another familiar form of future insight involves fearful warnings or feelings about future events. Most people have had this experience, and it's not usually a fun one. We'll talk more about this later in the chapter. For now, let us introduce you to the technical name for foresight, or knowing beforehand.

Knowing It Beforehand: Precognition

Beyond Words

Precognition can be defined as foreknowledge or awareness of a future event before it occurs.

In our original discussion of the various meanings for ESP, we didn't mention yet another use for the term. Some people use the term ESP to refer specifically to *precognition*. What distinguishes it from other types of ESP is its relationship to time.

While telepathy and clairvoyance have to do with perceptions occurring across distance, precognition is extra special. It focuses on perceptions that occur across time—specifically, perceptions of future events. This leads us back to where we started the book: Precognition, or foretelling the future, is what many people automatically think of when the idea of ESP or psychic ability comes up. But it's not as simple as it sounds.

Precognition doesn't work as simply as just rubbing a crystal ball and then seeing someone's life pass before your eyes. For many people, precognition is completely unexpected, and certainly wasn't asked for before it occurs. In fact, people often don't know that they've experienced precognition until after their insights come true.

Precognition can also be hard to pin down because it is experienced in a variety of ways. Among the most common are through the emotions, brief inner glimpses through the mind's eye, or dreams. However, one aspect of precognition seems to stand out as its trademark: the sense of certainty.

Intuition Hotline

As a general rule of thumb for identifying true precognition, remember: The less likely it is that you could know the information ahead of time, the more likely it is to be precognition.

Sensing Emotions

Many people receive a strong sense or feeling that something's coming, but have little information about what it might be. They may recognize a precognitive experience only after the actual event occurs. A precognitive sense or feeling of a future event is called *presentiment*. A precognition of a negative or unfortunate future event is called a *premonition*.

Like telepathy and clairvoyance, precognition tends to involve people on an emotional level, particularly those with close emotional ties. Also like telepathy and clairvoyance, precognition seems to be notable when concerning potentially dramatic

Beyond Words

Presentiment is a sense or feeling about a future event. **Premonition** is a foreboding of an unfortunate future event.

or catastrophic moments, which naturally include extreme emotional states. Interestingly, this special ability to sense others' feelings, especially intense ones such as those associated with a crisis, also shows empathic intuitive abilities.

Whether in regard to others or yourself, a precognitive sense of danger is called a premonition. These forewarnings are an especially common type of intuitive ability for people to experience. A popular theory is that premonitions are an age-old evolutionary device, developed for self-preservation. If premonitions do indeed meet a basic evolutionary need of every individual, does it follow that intuition is an innate ability among everyone, and has evolved as a positive characteristic for survival and growth? That's a question we're all still pondering.

The warnings that come through premonition usually occur as intense feelings, rather than visions or calmer feelings that accompany a normal precognitive experience. Oddly enough, premonitions usually allow enough time to change the behavior or plans that could cause the trouble.

Information About Events

If you do sense that you have experienced precognition and have a little information about the event, try to follow up later. This will help you get a sense of whether your precognition was presentiment or foresight into an actual event.

A very specific aspect of precognition that refers to foreshadowing of future events is *second sight*. It suggests that you see actual future events through visions. People who have this ability are called *seers*. Second sight may also refer to remote viewing, which generally pertains to seeing places in their present state. We discussed this in Chapter 4 and will discuss it again in Chapter 22.

Beyond Words

Second sight is the ability to see future events. It is a general term that can refer to wisdom, or prophesy, or divination through the use of devices such as crystal-ball gazing or palm reading.

Another way that you may receive visual information about future events is through precognitive dreams. Of course, not all dreams foretell future events, but those that do are usually clear and easily recalled. Have you ever had an experience that seems familiar, but you don't know why? This may actually be a less clear recollection of a precognitive dream.

Ways You Can Experience ESP

You're all familiar with dreams, but how do you know when you're seeing into the future within these reveries? For that matter, you can ask the same question for visual images, sensed phrases, or strong feelings: How do you know if they actually reveal present or future events or if they are merely unexplainable episodes? Well, the obvious answer is: Wait and see. But along the way, you can learn a lot by paying close attention. (Keeping good notes in your psychic journal helps too.)

Psi researchers recommend the following tips for tracking your psychic predictions:

➤ Always follow up by finding out what actually happens in the future. That way you can track how well your feelings or visions predict the future.

➤ Stick with predictions of events that take place in the near, rather than distant, future. In other words, try predicting events that take place tomorrow or next week rather than those five years down the line. We'll give you some tips on how to do just that in the exercises that follow later in the chapter.

Next, we provide you with two simple exercises to help you get in touch with your precognitive ability. Try to keep the above two tips in mind as you explore.

Rising and Descending

Begin this exercise by getting in a relaxed, meditative state. For the first part of the exercise, count down from ten to one. As you do so, imagine yourself moving downward into your consciousness, as if you were walking down stairs or descending on an escalator or elevator. When you get to the bottom on the count of one, ask your guide to show you information about a newsworthy, well-known past event. Observe and remember your own feelings and sensations regarding this news.

For the second part of the exercise, again count down from ten to one. As you do so, picture yourself flowing gently downward into your consciousness on a feather, cloud, or magic carpet. When you arrive on the ground on the count of one, ask your guide to show you information on an upcoming event that will be noteworthy and possibly newsworthy too. Observe and remember your own feelings and sensations regarding this news.

An important aspect of this exercise is recording everything you experience as soon as you are done—and don't forget to date it. Over time you may see your new "news" come true, and you'll be glad you wrote your personal "headlines" down.

Creating a Screen

For this exercise, choose a screen on which to see tomorrow's information, such as a blank television screen or a calm pool of water. Position it in an environment you feel comfortable with and enjoy, and then sit back and relax, watching the screen. Try to picture tomorrow's headlines, or lottery numbers, or winners at the track. (We don't advise putting money on them—just check it out for fun!)

This exercise works best when you look for information in the near future on an area in which you have a specific interest. If you normally read the newspaper, envision yourself getting up and following your regular morning preparations before sitting down with the newspaper. Then open up your imaginary newspaper and envision the headlines. (If you don't normally look at the betting or sports stats, don't try to test yourself in that area. Just stick with the front-page news.)

As you experience shifts in time, make mental notes of how each one feels to you, or write them down in your psychic journal. When you're recalling the past,

Intuition Hotline

A Web site specifically designed for precognition and PK experiments is **http://www.fourmilab.ch/rpkp/other.html**. They ask you to access your intuitive foresight and write a description of what you see. They then randomly access an image to see how closely it matches your description. Like all good precognition experiments, they give you prompt feedback. All from the comfort of your own computer chair!

observe differences in how the days feel to you as compared to the way you perceive future events. Also pay attention to whether events that occur tomorrow feel different from those that occur a few years from now. Sense and assimilate the atmosphere, sounds, and physical sensations of various shifts in time.

Getting Comfortable With the Vibes

Have you ever noticed that children have a remarkable ability to perceive future events? Perhaps they seem to experience precognition more because they haven't been conditioned to avoid talking openly about it. They're innocent enough to freely state what they see without fearing what others think of them—or the tragic repercussions that may occur if their premonitions do come true.

Unsolved Mystery

The June 16, 1989, issue of the *Toronto Star* reported an unusual story about a girl and her doll. The youngster, Elizabeth, had an imaginary playmate she called "Betty Louty" whom she played and talked with for hours on end. When asked where Betty Louty lived, Elizabeth would say, "A long way away."

Several years later, while on vacation in Jamaica, Elizabeth and her family visited a market with stall after stall of handmade, identical straw dolls. Elizabeth noticed one doll on the top shelf of one stall, and insisted it was the doll she wanted. The seller mentioned that the lady who made that doll was no longer making them, adding it was "waiting there just for you." Elizabeth loved the doll, hardly ever letting go of her. Eventually Elizabeth's mom discovered a homemade label naming the doll's maker: Betty Louty.

On the other end of the spectrum from the openness of children is the skepticism of scientists. Most scientists have a problem with precognition because it doesn't conform to the standard law that cause *follows* effect. After all, that's the way time works: One thing leads to another. Right?

Well, not so fast. One theory (which hardcore scientists usually reject) is that every event, just like every object or person, contains certain vibrations. Accordingly, everyone has vibrations that you can sense, often without visual confirmation. You may still sense the appearance of new energy vibrations, or changes or interruptions in previous ones, even if you're turned completely away from the person when he arrives. These new vibes can set off your internal signals, making you nervous if it's a mugger approaching or bringing you joy if it's your best friend about to phone you.

Similarly, events as well as people may have vibrations. These vibrations can travel outward from the event, sort of like the ripples of a pebble that landed in a still pool. The concentric vibrations can travel backward in time and affect you by creating an imprint on your mind. The imprints from your regular day-to-day routine are not usually strong enough to be noticeable because they reflect your usual lifestyle. However, crisis events can create strong vibrations, perhaps like shock waves, that can travel backward and create a memorable impact on your mind, depending on how receptive you are.

With both people and events, the strength of vibrations appears to correspond to proximity. (As they say in real estate: location, location, location.) Just as you are better able to sense people who are physically closer to you, you may also be better able to sense dramatic events that are closer to where you are in the present time. Of course, these ideas are not proven; they're just one possible explanation. The important thing to remember about experiencing precognition is that you can choose how to react. We suggest relaxing and going with the flow of this special gift!

What to Do With Information When You Get It

Seeing the future can, understandably, set off all kinds of emotional alarms. Once you get past thinking that you're crazy, you immediately start to ask two questions "Why is this happening?" and "Why is this happening to *me*?"

In the face of a premonition, people may initially feel fear. However, if self-doubt or overwhelming confusion prevents them from taking action, they may begin to feel guilty. If a crisis does occur, often they're left wondering whether they should have done something to stop the event. And yet, the action to take isn't always clear, or possible to control.

Mixed Messages

Let go of the guilt. Many people who foresee unfortunate future events start to think that their thoughts actually cause unfortunate incidents to occur and are not an expression of a true intuitive sense. Learning to sort out the difference between the two can help relieve the guilt.

Consider taking action if the path to do so appears clear. Learn to trust your intuition. If you feel you can truly help someone, if at all possible do it without mentioning that your source of knowledge is psychic. To offer advice out of the blue, you need to be willing to be embarrassed; but you may look even more foolish if you go around telling people you're psychic. Find subtle ways to offer information instead.

If the solution does not appear clear, you don't have to consider it your responsibility to take action. Perhaps the information is intended as a lesson to help you, not a responsibility to fulfill. Many people who report experiencing precognition also report one of the greatest lessons that can come from it: spiritual transformation. Realizing that a source of knowledge exists—one that exceeds any power they previously believed possible—can dramatically change the life of the person who experiences it.

Often, people who experience revelations of intuitive insight begin to follow a spiritual path with a newfound belief and openness. By getting in touch with an infinite, eternal power, they begin to explore the grander scheme of what life is all about. That path leads many to explore the extension of intuitive knowledge beyond present lifetimes—to past and possibly future ones. Want to travel the path of a karma chameleon? Read on to the next chapter.

The Least You Need to Know

➤ You can receive information about the future in many ways and on various levels.

➤ Precognition involves a strong sense of "just knowing" that your intuitive insight pertains to the future.

➤ You can develop your ability for precognitive intuition.

➤ Accept information that comes through foresight as a gift, not a burden.

Been There, Done That: You, in a Past Life

Now that you know all about precognition (seeing into the future), how about checking out the past? Pretty pointless, as well as downright impossible, you say?

Well, science often takes centuries to prove what the ancients knew so well in the past. Indeed, the Hindi yogis and Buddhist teachers always believed that everyone has lived numerous past lives and will probably live many more, and ideally, we all learn and improve through each lifetime. But what makes all this work? That's what you'll learn in this chapter.

Karma Chameleon

What makes the world go round? *Karma*, or the law of cause and effect embraced by many Eastern traditions. (For many people, karma is a major part of their beliefs about religion and the afterlife.)

This universal law of cause and effect is based on the idea that all of your actions, and perhaps even your thoughts, will come back to you, sooner or later. For example, if you live a loving and kind life, those experiences will come back to you. But if you are cruel or vindictive, eventually you yourself will become victim to cruelty or revenge. Karma comes back to you both in this life and the next and probably the next. For example, if you punch someone in the jaw, your karma may well return to you then and there. And if you tend to lose your temper a lot, that kind of karma can carry over into other lifetimes.

For most people brought up in the Western, Judeo-Christian world, karma sounds like a system of justice and retribution. But here, once again, we run into that question of free will. Karma is not determined and judged by an external third party (God), who then punishes you. Instead, karma is affected by free will: You can choose how you want to live and act, and thereby what type of karma you create, from here on out. But what gets tricky is this question: Where does your existing karma, what you're living with right now, come from? To clarify, let's say you're a good person, but bad things happen to you—despite your ever-increasing efforts to be kind and helpful. What's going wrong? The "bad" karma that you accumulated in previous lives may be still catching up to you.

The Ancient Tradition of Reincarnation

The concept of karma makes more sense when you see it against the backdrop of *reincarnation*. This belief holds that each person's soul has passed through many bodies (or incarnations) and lifetimes. Each lifetime offers an opportunity for spiritual growth, greater consciousness, and creating better karma.

The idea of karma belongs to Hinduism, the world's oldest religion that dates back to 4000 B.C. (Interestingly, Hinduism's first written acknowledgement of reincarnation dates from about the same time that Pythagorus in Greece wrote about it: in the sixth century B.C., which means the concept is more universal than you might think.) Buddhism, an offshoot of Hinduism, refers to reincarnation as a "Wheel of Becoming" or a "Wheel of Birth and Death." This circular image suggests that the actions, or karma, you set in motion don't necessarily return to you in the lifetime that follows your current one. Karma need not bounce back so abruptly; the karma of a single deed may come back to you over the course of various lifetimes.

The important thing to remember is that karma is your teacher. Whether good or bad karma comes your way, you can learn lessons from it, thereby growing spiritually and metaphysically. According to the Buddhist traditions, once you've learned all the lessons that life has to offer (through as many lifetimes as it takes) you can finally escape the basic conditions of life—suffering and death—and reach *nirvana*.

But don't hold your breath for accomplishing that in this life. Almost everybody can count on going through (at least!) a few more lives before reaching perfection, enlightenment, and nirvana.

Preparing for the Next Life

So, you ask, what's the point of trying if the cycle of death and rebirth just keeps coming around? The idea is that with each lifetime you can make a little bit of progress. By facing the issues and challenges of each lifetime, your soul becomes spiritually stronger and wiser.

Beyond Words

According to Buddhist tradition, **nirvana** is the state of freedom from the demands of the physical world.

This symbol, known as Yin and Yang, represents the universal internal and external balance within each human body and throughout the entire universe.

In fact, certain schools of thought believe that a lifetime filled with great obstacles triggers the learning of greater lessons and thus promotes greater spiritual progress. If you're going through a particularly rough time, you might find some solace from that idea, as well as relief from some of your guilt or self-blame, old or new. For example, stereotypical thinkers may assume that being born into poverty means that you were "bad" in your past and have to repay debts. But it may mean that the impoverished person is a highly evolved being, who chose to lead a life of poverty in order to learn difficult lessons.

251

The idea that souls choose their next life is, of course, something no one can prove. But certain experts on reincarnation theorize that each soul gets to "regroup" between lives, evaluate its previous life, and then decide when and where it wants to be reborn. (Note that in this scenario the soul has free will; it isn't given orders by a third-party god.)

After looking at what it learned in the past life and deciding what it needs to learn next, a soul returns to the physical world in the form of a newborn baby. In effect, the soul takes on a new body like a person puts on a fresh set of new clothes. The new baby's parents, family, and socioeconomic status are carefully selected to enable the soul to overcome obstacles, learn pertinent lessons, and grow toward perfection. And just as the body has a fresh start, so does the mind. And the mind, as you know, can remember.

Intuition Hotline

Always practice loving kindness: Remember, the important thing about karma is how you handle what comes your way. Whether you're having an easy time or a challenging one, living a life filled with love and optimism is the safest way to ensure that your future karma is good.

Recalling Past Lives

But, you may say, how can the mind remember anything about past lives if it gets a fresh start? Clearly, the ability to recall these lives with our normal conscious minds is often quite elusive, which is one reason why the ancient sages suggested that we increase our levels of awareness through meditation and yoga. Doing so eventually enables someone to become aware of realms beyond her present surroundings and lifetime.

Unsolved Mystery

One theory that supporters of reincarnation suggest is that birthmarks in newborns come from wounds in a previous lifetime. Dr. Ian Stevenson, professor of psychiatry at the University of Virginia Medical School, has studied this theory as well as other aspects of reincarnation. He documented the famous case of an Alaskan Tlinget Indian named Victor Vincent. A year before his death, Victor told his niece that he would be reborn as her next child and would have a mark that matched a surgical scar on his back. When the baby, Corliss Chotkin Jr., was born a few years later, he had a birthmark in the same place and the same shape as Victor's scar!

Obvious possibilities for recalling past lives include recurrent dreams, clairsentient experiences when visiting certain places, and irrational fears of specific activities. When exploring some of these unusual phenomena, modern therapists have accidentally come upon a new method for evoking past-life recall.

Past-Life Regression Therapy

Many therapists around the world now practice a relatively new type of therapy based on the idea that lessons learned in past lives can inform the challenges faced in the present. Called *past-life regression therapy*, it's especially helpful in connecting traumatic experiences in earlier lives to the problems affecting present lives.

To resolve these interconnected past-and present-life problems, the therapist leads the client into an altered state of consciousness, usually through a form of hypnosis or progressive relaxation. The therapist then makes the suggestion to "go back to a time when this issue (phobia, fear, trauma) originated." The patient then has a spontaneous image or feeling that emerges, which indicates the appropriate lifetime.

A single session takes from 60 to 90 minutes. As the client, you're aware of all that happens—you'll feel like you're in two places at the same time or watching a movie in which you experience the physical sensation of the action taking place on the screen (sort of like homemade virtual reality). You remember all of it afterward, although most therapists also make a tape of the session for you to keep. The therapist will also discuss what your past life may teach you about the challenges you face today.

As you reveal the past-life problem, understand it, and work to mitigate its effects on your current situation, the past-life problem begins to fade away. In addition, it appears that the more past-life regressions you experience, the greater your ability to understand your current lifetime. This understanding helps you to release negative habits and beliefs. For example, someone with a severe *phobia*, such as a fear of water or heights, might well benefit from past-life regression therapy. He may discover that he drowned in a previous lifetime, and by doing so, release that life's fear and this life's phobia.

Beyond Words

A **phobia** is an irrational, unexplained fear. **Psychosomatic** describes a physical condition that is caused or influenced by the patient's emotional state.

It appears that certain types of emotional problems might be resolved rather simply and quickly through past-life regression therapy, and require fewer sessions than conventional therapy. Physical conditions that appear to be *psychosomatic* often begin to disappear with past-life regression therapy. On a much larger scale, past-life regression may help you discover what spiritual lessons you should focus on and which path to pursue in life.

Mixed Messages

Time your past-life regression therapy sessions with care. Experts vary on how long to wait between sessions: Some advise waiting at least six months between sessions to enable your mind and soul to integrate this potentially life-transforming information. Others insist on seeing people for a minimum of four sessions, all fairly close together, to allow time to process the information and then work with it. The amount of time between sessions really depends on what you and your therapist decide is best for you.

One psychiatrist who is a popular lecturer and author on the topic of regression and past lives is Dr. Brian Weiss. On his Web site (**http://www.brianweiss.com**), he describes his first experience with a client who began to recall past-life traumas in a regular therapy session with him. He made the suggestion to "go back to a time when this phobia began," assuming she would go back to a trauma in early childhood. To his astonishment and skepticism, she immediately began to speak of a past life. It turns out that the patient was just as surprised as Weiss.

The woman's memories seemed to hold the key to her recurring nightmares and anxiety attacks. But what erased his skepticism was that she began to channel messages from the times between lives that included remarkable insight about Dr. Weiss's family and his son who had passed away. The past-life therapy led him to become an expert at this very special type of therapy.

Getting a Past-Life Reading

A past-life reading done by a psychic is different from a past-life regression therapy session. Regression involves actually being regressed in time and seeing and/or experiencing the lifetime for yourself. Sometimes it can be like seeing it on television, and you keep a bit of distance from it. Sometimes you can feel the regression with all of the emotions that you experienced during that lifetime.

When I give people past-life information, I usually receive it in much the same way I receive information about the present. It comes in the form of images, feelings, and words. Usually a past life presents itself as something to resolve because it appears to be surrounded by some type of traumatic event. These events leave a very powerful imprint on a person's life, which they carry over into their next life. Sometimes, by becoming aware of these events, a client can begin to unravel answers to many questions about why they act in certain ways. Many clients have been able to reduce phobias by becoming aware of past lives.

One of my clients found a past-life reading extremely helpful in this regard. She wanted me to see what I read psychically about her six-year-old son, Sean, during the reading. Usually I tune in and see what I get in the present time about personality characteristics, life lessons, and soul qualities that the boy may be trying to develop in this life. It surprised me when I immediately got drawn to my left (this is the side where I get information from the past).

In my inner eye, I saw a scene of a past life. My client was a young girl, about 10 or 11 years old. She appeared to be responsible for her younger brother (her son, Sean, in this life) who was about four. I identified them as being in Eastern Europe; my impression was that they were part of a family of Gypsies. As the scene unfolded, I saw them at an outdoor market, and in a brief moment when the sister's attention was elsewhere, someone snatched her baby brother. My sense was that her brother had never been found again. She went through that life traumatized and guilt-ridden about her seeming irresponsibility in losing her brother.

When I opened my eyes again after relating this story I saw that my client was crying. Sobbing, she cried, "Now I understand!" She told me that she had been besieged with irrational thoughts that her son Sean would be kidnapped and she would never see him again. She had even sought out professional help to gain some insight about this. Nothing in her current life could explain these unreasonable fears, but when she put it in the perspective that she was responding to a past-life trauma, she was able to put many of her fears to rest.

From the ESP Files

One of America's most famous founding fathers, Benjamin Franklin, was a true believer in reincarnation. In addition to proclaiming his belief in his autobiographical writings, he prepared this epitaph for his tombstone:

"The Body of Benjamin Franklin, Printer, (Like the Cover of an Old Book Its Contents Torn Out and Stript of its Lettering and Gilding) Lies Here, Food for Worms. But the Work Shall not Be Lost For it Will (As He Believed) Appear once more In A new and More Elegant Edition Revised and Corrected by the Author." [sic]

Past-life information usually comes to me in a regular reading as an unresolved issue from the past. I present the information as an opportunity for the client to understand patterns that past-life events have influenced. It is my belief that past lives may or may not be taken literally. That is, I may actually be seeing a symbolic representation rather than a real event. I mainly try to access what the soul may have come into this life to learn.

If I feel that someone has a significant unresolved issue relating to a past life, I recommend the person try regression therapy. My concern with giving a past-life reading is that it doesn't usually help someone resolve an issue in a simple way. It's like a traditional therapist saying to her patient, "You have commitment anxiety because your mother wasn't emotionally available to you as a child." While that insight might be true, most patients don't walk away saying, "Oh now I understand where this issue came from. I'm fine now. No more commitment anxiety!" It takes more work, more understanding, and a great deal of patience to resolve the issue in a definitive way.

Although many people come to me simply wanting to know information about their past lives, I don't see the point of seeking that information just for fun. For one thing, most people have incredibly boring past lives. Very few people have led illustrious lives: Most of us were typical mothers, soldiers, or workers—not very exciting stuff at all. What's valuable is learning what's at the heart of the matter—what you learned spiritually and physically during those lifetimes. What qualities of soul and spirit did you enhance? Did you learn about compassion, or courage, or unconditional love? Maybe your lifetime lesson was about being patient or speaking the truth. Those are the aspects of a past life worth looking at.

Psychic Vibrations and Reincarnation

In the previous chapter we talked about precognition being one of the main categories of ESP. We also mentioned a less commonly known form of ESP, *retrocognition*. Both of these types of intuition involve the ability to transcend time to receive information without the use of the physical senses.

Some people may have dreams of, or otherwise get glimpses into, their own past without even realizing it. They may assume they're simply having a symbolic dream or dreaming of some historic moment that does not directly pertain to them. One reason they fail to recognize their "old" selves is that people do not keep the same physical appearance from lifetime to lifetime. Instead, they usually change gender, race, nationality, profession, and station each lifetime. Yet something always stays the same, and that something is the soul, spirit, or energy unique to each one of us.

> **Beyond Words**
>
> **Retrocognition** is considered a form of ESP, wherein one has an intuitive knowledge of past events. You can use clairvoyance and other psychic senses to receive retrocognitive information.

Energy Is Never Destroyed

Do you remember in the previous chapter when we explained that every event has a vibrational level that can resonate through time to create precognition? Well, every action or thought releases its own set of vibrations. Although the crises seem to make the biggest ripple, the day-to-day vibes also leave an impression.

These karmic vibes have been described as a spiritual-magnetic energy form. The word "magnetic" suggests what makes karma come back. If you send out a certain kind of karma, it comes back to you in some sort of inverted form: Acts of love for others comes back as acts of love for you. The same applies for negative karma; it too will come back to affect your life, perhaps as poverty, anger, or tragedy.

So how can you neutralize, or balance, negative karma? Don't react to it! In other words, don't recreate it or create new negative karmic energy you'll need to deal with later. Just absorb it, experience it, and when necessary resolve it with understanding and compassion.

So, what happens once you manage to clean up your karmic act and get your karma balanced in this life? Then you get to take it to a new level. When you exit the physical (or third dimensional) level, there's a fourth one, a fifth one, and so on. Each level of existence has its own type of energy vibrations.

Receiving Guidance from Past Lives

Since your karmic energy is always there, you can tap into it as a way of learning how to grow and finding out where to go from here. Accessing specific information, however, isn't easy: Basically, your conscious mind focuses on your current life, allowing your soul's input to come through only when you are asleep or in an altered state of consciousness, such as mediation. (Now do you understand why we keep advising you to meditate?)

Another theory on past-life recall attributes recollection of information to the magnetic energy mechanism of vibrations. This technique involves opening your mind and tuning into the vibratory patterns of the information you seek. When you send out a request for facts of a certain vibrational level or pattern, they come back to you as impressions via their magnetic energy.

According to many intuitives, including Edgar Cayce, access to past-life information is possible because it all still exists and is stored in the *Akashic records*. These omniscient records are like an ultimate, conscious computer data bank. They contain information about every aspect of every person's life, including body, mind, and soul.

Another theory goes that specific dates and details, whether from the Akashic records or not, may be forwarded to you by beings who assist you in your current incarnation. Some people call them guardian angels, and believe that they may even be tied to relationships in past lives. The source of this material—whether it's from a past life, a fantasy, early in this life, or anywhere else—is not so important. When it comes to resolving problems, many therapists say that they work with any material that the client brings up as a way of unearthing unconscious issues. Of course, not all therapists agree about this issue.

Beyond Words

According to Edgar Cayce and others, the **Akashic records** are a sort of universal memory bank or an invisible record of everything that has occurred in the universe, including details of every soul and every life ever lived.

Déjà vu: Here and Now or Then?

You've experienced it, haven't you? That feeling that you've already experienced something that is apparently brand new. A flash of "I've been here," "I know him," "I've done this before." Sometimes, even in familiar surroundings, you've had an inner glimpse of an event as though you've experienced it before. What you've lived through is something called *déjà vu*.

No one really knows where these feelings come from or what they mean. It could be one way you can connect with a place, person, or event from a past life. Another option is that the association comes via a dream or an out-of-body experience (something we'll talk about in Chapter 21). Any of these possibilities suggests an involvement of your psychic sense that moves you beyond your physical senses to connect you with a broader reality.

Beyond Words

Déjà vu is French for "already seen." It refers to a brand-new event that feels so familiar that it seems you've experienced it before.

Mixed Messages

Always seek your own truth and trust your own intuition when exploring any religious beliefs. Reincarnation is a fascinating topic, but you'd be wise to be skeptical of anyone who says he knows the only, absolute truth. Ultimately, the most important beliefs are the ones you know in your own soul to be true.

Karmic Caterpillars and Budding Butterflies

The process of understanding and changing karma can be compared to a caterpillar entering its cocoon. It may involve a long process of trying to grow and then waiting to become perfect. Through conscious awareness, you can create your own metamorphosis. Your intuition can help you get in touch with what you need to learn. It can even help you see yourself change and grow. After all, stepping outside yourself to see where you are, what the big picture is, and how it all comes together is really what ESP is all about.

Dreaming a Wake-Up Call

All through my childhood, I had a recurring series of dreams that had a nightmarish quality to them. I dreamed of a large mansion that I seemed to have lived in. Many times, part of the house would be burned and I'd find myself wandering through it looking for something I couldn't find. In one dream about this place, I was standing outside of it watching it burn to the ground. People from the village were also watching, but I was standing apart from them, distraught and sobbing.

When I was about 20 years old (in this life), I met a man about my age. At dinner one night, he casually mentioned that he had taken a class in reincarnation and experienced a past-life regression. This topic fascinated me and I asked him what he remembered. His first words were, "I remembered this big house…." Much to my embarrassment, I instantly burst into tears. I grabbed a piece of paper and drew out the floor plan of the house from my childhood dreams. It was the same house he saw in his regression.

What we were able to piece together from his past-life memory and my dreams were that we had been married in that life and had two young children. He discovered that I had been unfaithful to him with someone from the village and came to realize that he was not the children's father.

He had set the house on fire to punish me—without realizing that the children were inside until it was too late. He remembers that he killed himself shortly after this. I remember being ostracized by the townspeople. I finally left that area and lived a few more years, wandering from town to town before experiencing an early death.

After bringing this to light, I saw the young man again only a few more times (in this life anyway), and I never had the "Mansion Dream" again. But what I learned was that in that past life I seemed to be someone who judged others; a very wealthy woman who seemed to live apart from what I considered the common folk. I thought that my way was the best way, and that God was on my side and had rewarded me with this life of privilege. After the fire, I learned that all I'd really had going for me was my material possessions, that I had no true friends, no real meaning in my life, and nothing of substance on an inner or spiritual level. Soon, though, I found myself among the commoners to stay.

I believe that what that life gave me was an understanding of people from all walks of life and an ability to see things from all sides. It also made me look at the issues of forgiveness and judgment. I find all these lessons to have been extremely helpful in the work I do now.

Recognizing Karmic Life Lessons

To make yourself more aware of past lives and open to recalling them, try to take mental notes of your unique reactions to what's around you. Also, try to avoid judging yourself and what you see according to long-established belief systems (especially those that don't include reincarnation).

Regression Exercise

This exercise is designed to help you address an issue in your life—a fear of speaking your mind, a concern with commitment or decision making, or an inability to let go of an old relationship—that has been left unresolved.

Intuition Hotline

When trying to sort out whether an upcoming change in your life is simply repeating old karma or creating new, inquire within about how difficult it is to make the change. One rule of thumb is: The more difficult the change, the more likely it is that you're breaking away from old karmic patterns.

Usually the first thing that pops into your mind is the best issue for you to pursue. Write your issue here.

_____

This exercise uses a regression technique. You may want to tape it or have someone read it to you.

1. Begin by closing your eyes. Uncross your arms and legs. Relax. Take a deep breath and let it out slowly. Continue taking several more slow deep breaths and concentrate on your breathing. Then breathe normally.

2. Visualize a circle of white light forming in front of you. Now bring this stream of light through the top of your head down through your body from head to toe. Take the time to fill any spot in your body that feels dark or heavy. Saturate each area with the white light. Imagine this light flowing through you and then surrounding and protecting you.

3. Relish this feeling of being relaxed and safe. Allow a peaceful state of mind to flow through you.

4. Now imagine that you are being taken to a place where you will be shown your past life that most influences the issue that you are concerned about.

5. You are being taken to a temple. This beautiful building has a colossal double doorway placed squarely beneath huge arches and twin spires. A massive set of stone steps leads up to the entrance… Concentrate on bringing in every minute detail of its elaborate masonry… Now see yourself alone, poised at the foot of the steps, looking up expectantly at the doorway… Start climbing the steps; notice the rough-hewn granite as your shoes touch one step after another.

6. When you reach the top, stand beneath the immensity of the wooden doors. Breathe deeply, pause, and then stretch out a hand to feel the texture of the wood.

7. Open the doors and find yourself in a vast open room filled with light. The air smells of sweet incense, and you feel enveloped by the stillness, and the magnificence of the scene.

8. As you take in your surroundings, you notice you are not alone. A very kind, old man dressed in long robes approaches you and lovingly takes your arm and points at a door across the room. He walks with you and you precede him through the doorway and down a stone stairway. The steps are narrow and well worn, and they lead down to the cellars. Move down these steps; feel yourself descending deeper and deeper into the very foundations of the temple.

9. At the foot of the steps the old man explains that he is the guardian of the hall of records and he has been expecting you. He asks that you take a few moments to explain to him why you are here. You explain your quest for self-exploration and ask that you be shown a past life that will assist you in your self-understanding. The old man, bowing his head, listens attentively to your explanation and grants your request.

10. Now the old guardian beckons you to follow him. You seem to float behind the flapping tails of his robe as he sets off through the seemingly endless corridors, past shelf after shelf piled high with books. At last he halts before a door. He stands there for a few moments before pointing to another door he would like you to enter.

11. You are about to enter a past life when you walk into this room. You are completely safe as you observe your former self. Your guardian beckons you to open the door and walk in. As you do, you feel yourself changing as you step into a different time and place.

12. Take a few moments and observe who you are. Absorb what you see and feel—calmly, passively, and without emotion. In a few moments you will ask yourself some questions about what you are seeing; you will later remember everything you see and experience, but for now, simply observe your surroundings.

    What are you wearing?_____

    What fabric is your clothing made of?_____

    Are you wearing anything on your head?_____

    Are you male or female?_____

    What is the shade of your skin?_____

    What is the color of your hair?_____

    Are you inside or outside a structure?_____

    What does it look like?_____

    _____

    Is it night or day? Cold or warm?_____

    Are you alone or with someone?_____

    What are you doing?_____

    _____

    What language are you speaking?_____

    What country are you in?_____

13. As the scene in front of you continues to unfold, ask yourself the following questions:

    What did I learn in this lifetime?_____

    What did I NOT learn?_____

    What things was I good at in this lifetime?_____

    _____

    Do I recognize anyone?_____

    Who is my mother...father...husband or wife? Who are my significant friends? Do I have children? Who are they?_____

    _____

    What do I want to bring back from the past to enhance my present lifetime?

    _____

    _____

14. Now, as this past-life personality, complete these two sentences:

    "I will never..."_____

    _____

    "I will always..."_____

    _____

15. Allow yourself a few more moments to finish your viewing of this lifetime. Complete anything that is left incomplete.

16. Now you are ready go out the door you came through. Your guardian is waiting for you outside the door. He motions for you to follow him once more through the labyrinthine library to the stairway leading back to the light-filled temple. You walk behind the old man, climbing up the cellar stairs with him. He walks you across the grand hall that is filled with light to the door where you first entered the temple.

17. Now you step outside the beautiful, glowing temple and slowly descend the stone steps. As you move one foot before the other, you find that normal consciousness is slowly returning. By the time you reach the foot of the staircase, you are once more fully aware of your surroundings.

18. Take a moment to write in your psychic journal. Write down any and all details of what you remember. Do you feel you received an answer to your initial concern? If so, what do you feel you learned?

    _____

Did you learn anything new about yourself? You may or may not have had a tremendous revelation. Hopefully, you got a sense of where you'd like to start making some changes. If nothing else, maybe you can become more conscious of who you are, as influenced by—and separate from—where you are right now. That's another way to expand your consciousness!

Speaking of expanding your consciousness, get ready for a major growth spurt! Our next chapter is going to cover a topic that was hot 100 years ago—and is now back bigger and better before: the spirit world! It can definitely break down your barriers and broaden your horizons.

The Least You Need to Know

➤ According to reincarnation, everyone experiences an ongoing series of lifetimes.

➤ All action reflects the karmic law of cause and effect: What you do comes back to you.

➤ Each soul's lifetimes are especially designed to help a person grow spiritually.

➤ Your intuition can help you understand and learn from your previous lives.

Chapter 20

Channeling: Messages from Beyond

In This Chapter

➤ Contacting the great beyond

➤ Holding a séance

➤ Channeler or charlatan?

➤ Messages and meanings

Just because you can't see something right in front of you doesn't mean it doesn't exist, right? That's been the theme of this whole book, hasn't it? And the theme continues in this chapter, in which we discuss the possibility that the souls of people living and dead exist among and around us, available for consultation and information—available even to you if you know how to ask. The choice is up to you: Who and what do you want to know from the Other Side?

Communication with the Other Side?

According to those who are in the know, humans can communicate with ethereal beings on a variety of levels. Communication with spirits is called *channeling*. A person who communicates with spirits is called a *channeler*, or a medium.

Beyond Words

Channeling is the process of communicating with spirits who do not currently inhabit bodies. A person who communicates in this way is called a **channeler**, or sometimes a medium.

When we discuss channeling in this chapter, we're really talking about spirit-to-body contact: In other words, contact between spirits (either those of people once living or spirits that never had bodies) and living human beings. (Please note, however, that there's a difference between spirit-to-body contact and possession, which has a negative context. We explore possession in Chapter 24 and concentrate on the positive aspects of channeling here.)

All types of spirits are around and among us, and you generally attract those who have similar qualities to your own. If you're a loving person, for instance, chances are you'll attract a loving spirit to you. If you're a practical joker, you might find yourself communicating with a quirky imp. (This could be another aspect of your karma, which is yet another reason to try living in the most positive way you can to help you attract good karma and receive valuable spiritual guidance.)

Mixed Messages

The important thing to remember when exploring this world is that, in the spiritual realm, your free will reigns. You can always exert control, even if that means going to someone to ask for help in understanding what type of experience you are having. (We offer some resources in Appendix C.) Sometimes when people start exploring this realm, they can feel a little confused about what's happening, which is normal but unnecessary. Remember, any unwanted entity must obey your request to leave your presence.

The Process of Channeling

Before you can act as a channel, you must actively seek out guidance from a spirit. Indeed, a basic understanding within the psychic world is that each being, including you, has free will and that no spirit can force another, or be forced itself, to do something against its will. A spirit cannot communicate through a channeler unless the channeler agrees to it; in fact, the spirit must have an actual invitation from the channeler before it can enter. Although most people think that to communicate with a spirit, the spirit must be of someone they know or someone once alive, that doesn't appear to be the case.

Just as there are different types of spirits ready for contact, so, too, are there different ways to contact them. Although some channelers fall into a deep trance and wake up knowing nothing of what's occurred (as so often depicted in Hollywood), that's not the only process available. Some channelers are fully conscious during channeling and can even pause to attend to some interruption before continuing. In between are intermediary states of altered consciousness that are most effective for other channelers.

Channeling States

There are four main types of channeling that fall along a wide spectrum. All of these states, except for the first, involve an altered state of consciousness to some degree:

➤ Full-conscious channeling

➤ Altered-state conscious channeling

➤ Light-trance channeling

➤ Full-trance channeling

Someone who is a full-conscious channeler remains in his (or her) usual state of normal consciousness: He can move around, stop, and then restart the process. Altered-state conscious channeling occurs when the channeler feels fully conscious, but later realizes his focus was somewhat different from his normal thought processes. Trance channeling involves someone who seems to enter another realm. A light trance is less intense, perhaps occurring telepathically between the spirit and channeler's minds. A heavy trance involves the channeler's complete loss of consciousness, perhaps occurring when a spirit enters the person's body.

From the ESP Files

Jon Klimo, director of the doctoral program in parapsychology at the Rosebridge Graduate School of Integrative Psychology in Concord, California, and author of *Channeling* (North Atlantic Books, 1998), describes a form of entityless channeling, which he calls "open channeling." It does not involve any of the odd sensations that may accompany other types of channeling, but does include information that seems to comes from a greater mind than one's own. Could this be equivalent to clairsentience?

Although the historic stereotype portrays the channeler in a full trance, a new school of channelers (or at least a new group of those who are willing to talk about their experiences) is inclined to be more conscious while channeling. No one way is best for everyone. Each person's comfort level and increased spiritual insight are what matter most.

Is Anybody Home?

To begin with, the channeler offers an invitation—either through feelings or thoughts to the spirit world. No specific words need to be spoken (like the cartoon that says, "Hocus Pocus dominocus! The Spirits are about to speak!"). Some channelers may have certain phrases or rituals that they prefer to repeat in their minds, as a way to prepare themselves. In most cases, they simply express their intention to connect. Remember, a lot of contact with spirits is telepathic: Any words formed would more likely occur in silence and be transmitted telepathically.

Once a channeler opens himself up to receiving a message, he then begins the process of connecting. At this point, the channeler enters an altered state of consciousness, assuming that's his style. If his style is to enter a less changed state, he then opens the energy field that surrounds him to create a form of merging, or opens his mind to telepathic communication while remaining aware of what occurs.

After establishing a connection, a message starts coming through. At first, the connection may be a bit rough. But as the channeler and spirit begin to merge more completely, the information becomes clearer. If the channeler feels that the connection isn't right, he can ask for further clarification, visualize a better connection, or ask the spirit to stop "transmitting."

Certain channelers feel that the message is not strictly dictated by the spirit; rather, it is a melding together of the channeler and spirit. And because each channeler is a unique being himself, the message he relays has its own distinct character that is different from that of any other channeler. One analogy that may simplify this idea is that of a translator's work: Although the speaker offers information in a single language and format, each translator may translate it somewhat differently.

A Beginner's Guide to Channeling

Channeling is a skill you can learn, just as you're learning to develop other aspects of your psychic abilities. As you learn, though, it's important to remember that everyone has a different experience of what it's like to channel. Your style will depend not only on who your spirit guide or guides turn out to be, but also on your particular energy level, clarity, and focus. You may experience a feeling of expansive energy flowing through you, or a tingling or buzzing feeling throughout your body as you channel. Other channelers report a sense of floating upwards or of seeing lights and colors.

The message you receive may come in any number of different forms. Guides use images, feelings, words, and concepts to give you information. Many channelers report that the information is simply transmitted telepathically and you "just know" the answer. As a channeler, you are the person who translates the information sent to you from your guide. You may feel as if you've received a big block of unintelligible information and you must search to understand what it means and how it feels. Often, you'll feel the words form in your mind just at the moment you speak them. Or you may find that you're simply present as a vessel for healing energy—and words or ideas never come into play at all.

The following exercise will help you develop your channeling powers. Since it's a meditative exercise, you may want to have a friend present to take you through the process by asking questions to focus your energy. Soothing music may also help you deepen your meditative state.

Channeling Exercise

You may experience your guide as light or energy, male or female, someone you have known or someone you've never met. Your guide will help you with this exercise. She (or he) will adjust your energy and align her energy with yours. Your guide may change over time as you evolve and have different needs and questions. If you feel uncomfortable at any time in this exercise, just open your eyes and return to normal consciousness.

1. Sit comfortably in an upright position, either on the floor or in a chair. Make sure you're in a position that you can hold comfortably for 15 to 20 minutes.

2. Close your eyes and relax your body. Take several slow, deep breaths. As you slowly inhale and exhale, imagine your emotions, thoughts, and physical body becoming calm. Feel yourself slowing down and relaxing. Take a few minutes to relax deeply.

3. Feel and imagine light and love coming to you from a much higher dimension. Imagine it flowing to you, surrounding you and filling you. Feel yourself lifting to a spiritual, beautiful place that is filled with brilliant white light. Imagine that you are traveling in a bubble of light into the sky, floating through the stars. As you move higher and higher, you are filled with a feeling of perfect love and safety. Carry this feeling with you as you move higher and higher.

4. Adjust your posture to a position that allows you to feel open. You may want to move your arms, head, and shoulders so you can feel as expansive as possible. Slow down your breathing and imagine yourself opening up even further to all the love and hope that exists in the universe. Feel yourself floating higher and higher.

5. You may feel yourself growing warmer and feeling a buzzing or tingling sensation. Just notice whatever you experience. Take another deep breath and exhale. Imagine that your emotions are calm and balanced. Make the energy around you feel as beautiful as possible. Imagine that rays of love and joy are pouring down upon you. They open you up and make you appear radiant and filled with love.

6. Go as high as you can imagine, moving into finer and finer energy. At last you enter a high dimension that is bathed in flowing light. A doorway opens before you and many guides and masters are there to great you. They usher you forward into the light. They tell you they are taking you to meet your guide, who is right for you to work with. This guide has been especially chosen for you and he or she is closely aligned with you.

7. Your guide is coming to meet you. A path is being made clear as he or she gets closer. Your heart opens and you feel yourself being surround by an incredible feeling of peace and love. Your imagination is telling you all about what is happening around you. The other guides and masters slip away and leave you alone. At first you are simply adjusting to your guide's energy. Feel all the sensations, impressions, and images that flow through your mind.

8. Your guide is speaking to you telepathically. You find yourself hearing words and feeling sensations. Concepts may come flooding into your mind. This is your guide communicating to you. You can carry on a mental conversation with your guide. Ask him or her questions, then listen and feel for the response. The information may come to you in any of the ways that you may receive psychic information, including through images or sensations.

9. Ask your guide if he or she will continue to work with you to help you be more open to receive information and to be able to channel. Ask if you need to do anything to prepare to channel.

10. Ask your guide a question and see if you feel comfortable speaking the answers aloud. You may be more comfortable writing the answers or may choose to simply continue as you've been doing in speaking telepathically to your guide; whatever is easiest is fine.

11. Complete anything you need to say or do with your guide. Thank your guide and ask if you need to hear anything right now. Now take a deep breath and come back to normal consciousness. Open your eyes.

12. You may find it helpful to move around, walk, and stretch. If you still feel a bit spacey, go out for a walk for a few minutes and focus on your feet as they touch the ground.

Intuitive Hotline

For a beginner's guide on how to channel, check out Sanaya Roman's book *Opening to Channel* (HJ Kramer, 1987). For some terrific guided meditation how-to tapes on channeling, see the resource section at the back of the book.

Learning anything new takes practice to get it right. If you are doing this for the first time, don't be discouraged if you don't connect with a guide right away. If you simply succeed in feeling expansive, or experience a feeling of openness and compassion, that's great for a start. Remember that your guide will be using your own thoughts to transmit images, feelings, and concepts. We'll say again here what we say at each exercise: You will feel like you're making it up! Because your guide will be using your voice, your imagination, and your ability to translate the information, you may feel as if it is all coming from you. With practice you will have a clearer sense of your guide and feel his or her presence and energy.

As you continue to practice, you will begin to feel the guide as an energy presence that is different from yours. When a guide works with you for the first time, it is generally a very subtle experience. Nevertheless, you'll probably feel energized, focused, and filled with well-being during and after the experience.

From the ESP Files

If you ever want to take a vacation with your guide, Cassadaga Spiritualist Camp is just the place. Located in central Florida, it focuses on helping mediums use psychic techniques to get in closer contact with the spirit world. Established in 1894, the camp currently hosts about 100 full-time residents—and about 50,000 visitors every year—just counting the humans

There is another way to communicate with the spirit world: It's called a *séance*, and it's probably different from what you might expect.

Séances

If you're like most kids, you probably remember participating in a *séance*, maybe at a sleepover or a Halloween party. Everyone probably sat in a circle, held hands, and closed their eyes (except to peek). Then the leader would rattle off some hocus-pocus and you all waited for something spooky to happen. Of course, everyone probably scattered in sheer fright within seconds—way too soon for a visitor to appear.

Beyond Words

A **séance** is a meeting, session, or sitting in which a channeler attempts to communicate with the spirits of the dead.

As adults, most people still conjure up this image when they think of communicating with spirits. But actual séances are not the norm anymore; they've gone the way of most of the Spiritualist activities that started in the mid-1800s. New methods, which we'll discuss later in this chapter, have become more popular today. For now, let's look at the séance's illustrious past.

Hold Hands and Close Your Eyes...

Remember when we talked about the "Rochester Rappers" in Chapter 2? They were actually the Fox sisters, three young women who first brought public attention to the phenomenon of table rapping—the announcement of a spirit's arrival during a séance—in 1848. The enthusiasm for otherworldly evidence carried over to levitation of tables and other objects and led to the growth of the immensely popular Spiritualist movement in the later decades of the century.

Among the most famous mediums of the period was D.D. Home, whose reputation for his remarkable abilities and pristine integrity earned him a place in the history books. Reports of his demonstrations during séances include levitating his own body, having an invisible spirit play the accordion, and even having spirit hands appear in the air and pour water into a glass—without spilling a drop.

Another famous medium during this time was Nettie Colburn, the trance channel whose spirit guides advised President Lincoln. Between 1861 and 1863, Mrs. Lincoln called her to the White House to use her skills to present information and advice to President Lincoln on a wide variety of subjects, which he was known to have followed on many occasions. Her guides counseled Lincoln not to put off enacting the Emancipation Proclamation. She also advised him on ways to raise morale in the Yankee troops, which worked.

Lenore Piper, born in 1859 in New Hampshire, was a medium in Boston for most of her life. Known to be a consistently effective full-trance medium, she was investigated by the Harvard-educated philosopher and psychologist William James. He was later quoted on his experience with Mrs. Piper: "Science, so far as science denies such exceptional occurrences, lies prostrate in the dust for me."

Mrs. Piper channeled a physician named Dr. Phinuit, who apparently knew all about William James. During the hour-long session, the spirit relayed through Mrs. Piper the details of a recent letter James received from one of his New York aunts, the whereabouts of a missing waist coat, and a rug. Even the hardline scholar James was forced to admit, "Insignificant as these things sound when read, the accumulation of a large number of them has an irresistible effect."

Mrs. Piper eventually began working as the house medium for the Society for Psychical Research, where a private detective (hired by the Society) made certain that she received no nonpsychic information about the people she read for. No evidence was ever found to indicate that her exceptional information came from any source other than her spirit guides.

Of course, certain old-time mediums were probably faced with the temptation to make their sittings as exciting and dramatic as possible. In a sense, they were performers. Interestingly, certain mediums who were considered to be truly psychic, such as Eusapia Palladino, were also occasionally caught in the act of embellishing their demonstrations. Doubtlessly, this cast doubt on all the good work they—and their more highly principled—counterparts had accomplished.

Hoax or Heaven?

If you've ever looked through a book with old photographs of mediums, you've probably seen photos that show something that looks like goo oozing out of a medium's ear or nose. This "ooze" is called *ectoplasm*, an emanation of physical material from the spirit realm. Some photographs obviously are faked, making the whole idea seem pretty outrageous—which it is! But that doesn't mean it's not true. A few photos exist that look much more...ethereal. But what's even more amazing are firsthand accounts of people who have witnessed the appearance of ectoplasm.

Shiri Hughes, who is an expert in this area and provided expert advice to us in writing this book, reports witnessing four physical mediums over the course of 40-plus years of experience. She explains that a physical medium must be very strong physically because the process is exhausting; therefore they are most often (but not always) men. The medium sits in a chair at the end of the séance room, with a contraption of pipes, very like a circular shower-curtain rail, above him, from which are suspended heavy black velvet drapes reaching to the floor. This is known as the cabinet. (Participants are welcome to come up beforehand to make sure there are no trapdoors, no holes in the ceiling, and no hanky-panky.)

Beyond Words

Ectoplasm is an emanation of physical material from the spirit realm. A **physical medium** is a channeler who can make ectoplasm materialize.

The lights are turned off beforehand with the exception of one or two primary red bulbs, which enable participants to see the ectoplasm but does not frighten or upset the spirit forms. With the curtains pulled around the medium, the participants sing or say prayers, while the medium goes into a trance and the white ectoplasm is extruded from his body. The first such séance that Shiri witnessed was held by the medium Warren Smith, who had such extraordinary strength that the ectoplasm completely filled the enclosure where he sat. It bubbled up at the top of the curtains like a pot of boiling milk, and came dropping down on the outside of the curtains like huge, two- or three-foot blobs of freshly whipped cream. Nothing gooey, nothing messy, or repulsive, and it all vanished when it hit the floor.

Out of this cabinet walk loved ones from the spirit world, using the ectoplasm to form their body, clothes, and features. Your name is called when it is your turn to come forward, hands behind your back so that you do not touch the spirit. To do so could bring death to the medium, as the ectoplasm is believed to be his physical essence, which is now separated from him by quite a few feet. You hold a short conversation with your spirit and it then returns to the cabinet to allow another to come forward.

Shiri reports that at the last of the physical séances she attended, the spirit who came to greet her was her father-in-law. The resemblance was so startling that she exclaimed, "Why Walter, the likeness is so great I'd have known you anywhere!" To this he replied, "Well, my dear, we do our best. . ." Shiri emphasizes that ectoplasm, as well as physical mediums, are real indeed, if hard to find these days. She states, "One is never quite the same after attending one of these demonstrations."

Whether all séances are "real" or not, mediums and channelers certainly descend from a varied tradition of saints and scoundrels. Hildegaard de Bingen and Joan of Arc were probably channeling sacred messages as they led their personal and political battles. But they certainly had many less qualified—and less scrupulous—counterparts who were metaphorically run out of town before they could make it into the history books.

Intuitive Hotline

One way you can tell a spirit is present, with both the old-time mediums and new channelers who enter a heavy trance, is their change of voice. The channeled voice often sounds quite different and distinct from the channeler's own, and may have an accent that does not belong to the channeler naturally. But this altered voice is not a prerequisite for proving a spirit is present.

Doubtless a few swindlers continue to pretend to have better connections than they really do. For this reason, you are wise to doubt someone who claims to have all the answers.

One reason we keep stressing the importance of free will is so that you'll remember to use your own judgment. If you expect someone to give you all the answers about your life on a silver platter, your expectations are unrealistic, and if you pursue a channeler who will give you pat answers, you risk playing right into the hands of someone with dubious intentions.

In contrast to someone who gives you pat answers, a channeler who tells you what his impressions are and how he interprets those impressions is likely to be more realistic and thereby helpful. If you listen to his message and it makes some sense to you, and—sooner or later—offers useful insight, then you probably will feel comfortable with that channeler. If, over time, his messages do not become clearer for you, or do not seem to have your best interest at heart, take a hard look at what you're hoping to achieve by seeing that channeler.

What to Expect from a Channeler

As we mentioned, you can think of a channeler as a connection between the material and spirit worlds; a translator of the spirit language into the human lexicon. The original message may come in a clear, sequential order or it may come in abstract images. On her Web site (**http://www.sonic.net/~marina/channel/whatchan.html**), channeler Marina Michaels McInnis describes her impressions as a "thought ball, where concepts, thoughts, words, emotions, sensations, and images are all rolled up into a complexly interrelated whole, somewhat like a large ball of string...the task [is] to unravel that ball into a linear communication."

In order to be effective at sorting out this much information, and making some sense of it, a channeler needs to be flexible, intelligent, educated, curious, open-minded, imaginative, and even empathic. She (or he) needs to step outside herself and be willing and able to step out of her personal viewpoint to see things from various perspectives, and sometimes from various perspectives at once. This is important because the spirit world involves viewing information from different dimensions— beyond the third (physical) and even the fourth (time).

A channeler may offer information that seems baffling or, at best, irrelevant. But with time, the meaning of this information often comes to light as making a profoundly simple sense. For example, you may not understand now why you receive a certain message when something disappointing happens to you, and yet someday a better opportunity comes your way and the special message you received helps you put it all in perspective. This goes back to the idea that everything is somehow connected; a perfect pattern underlies apparent chaos. In many ways, channeled information isn't all that much different from that received in a regular psychic reading: It's just one more way that your intuition may provide you with information.

Who Do *You* Want To Talk To? (and Why!)

Spiritual beings who can be channeled exist on many levels. Some people refer to these levels as dimensions. The idea is that humans live in the third dimension, which is physical reality, and attempt to progress up through higher dimensions. Indeed, some people believe that spiritual beings can exist in more than one level, sort of keeping tabs on where they're at in each particular level simultaneously.

There is a wide range of beliefs about who spirit guides are and where they come from. According to who you believe, these may include human beings, aliens, enlightened masters, angels, gods and goddesses, universal powers that be, and possibly more. With all of these options, you start to get the idea that someone out there probably has a little free time to spend with you. And yet the point of any information they provide is spiritual awareness and development.

Channeling Loved Ones

When the idea of contact with spirits comes up, most people think of encountering loved ones who have died. According to a 1991 study by the International Social Survey Program, 40 percent of Americans responded that they had felt, at some point, that they had experienced some contact with the dead. Some people sense this as a feeling of a presence nearby, while others may hear or see the loved one.

One interesting theory is that people overwhelmed with grief have lower ego boundaries and more scattered energies, which creates a more open environment for spirits to approach. Many people feel solace and comfort when sensing that their loved one has passed to another realm and returned for a brief and reassuring goodbye. Others experience frequent visitations with their loved ones, involving a series of conversations or communications that help the still-living individual to build a new life and to release remaining negative feelings, such as guilt, regarding the loved one.

From the ESP Files

Dreaming is among the range of altered states wherein channeling can occur. For example, people have reported dreams that include an acquaintance giving a message, often about the acquaintance's death. When the dreamer awakes, he receives news that the acquaintance has just passed away—under circumstances that make sense of the message.

These experiences most often occur spontaneously, without the help of a channeler. In a sense, the individual is independently experiencing his or her own type of channeling with a loved one. People who are uncomfortable or confused by this process can seek professional therapists who are experienced at grief counseling.

Channeling Spirit Guides

A particular minister, who is known as a teacher in intuitive circles, was faced with the decision to retire early from her lifetime work at a prestigious institution. She secluded herself in a country house and spent several days meditating on the question. She eventually emerged—with the advice her guides had given her and a determined conviction to follow it.

When she announced that she was going to resign early, despite being one year away from getting full retirement benefits, everyone told her she was crazy. But halfway through the year, her department disbanded. She had been spared all the anxiety, disappointment, and bitterness experienced by many of her colleagues who had remained—and she gives her guides the credit for that. (And she still has a healthy pension to help her out financially.)

This woman contacts her spirit guides as friends and advisors, seeking their advice on any matter that concerns her. Her experience is rather like using intuition as a guide. Clearly, she has learned to trust their guidance, maintaining a very personal relationship with them and rarely channels for other people. When she does receive input regarding other people, she may try to help them with subtle suggestions, without telling them her source.

Unsolved Mystery

One highly intuitive woman experienced her own sort of Titanic tale. Shortly after gradu-ating from high school in the 1940s, she gave her high-school ring, which bore an unusual Egyptian symbol, to a young naval officer she was dating. On his next journey out to sea, his ship was wrecked and the newspapers reported that all on board had died. Several years later, she was married and went to a medium for a sitting. During the reading, the medium reported that a sailor was waving to her and asked her to contact his girlfriend. The woman, who grew up in a shore town, was confused by who the sailor could be—until he mentioned the ring with the Egyptian symbol. It turns out that no one else had even known that she had given him her ring.

In contrast, some channelers receive requests from their spirit guides to share their messages with the world. In 1963, Jane Roberts became the first channeler to do this in published form. With her channeled guide "Seth," she produced the bestseller *Seth Speaks*, as well as several other books, before she died in 1984. The public was ready to receive Seth's message of a multidimensional reality and each person's potential power to shape it.

Messages from the Spirit World

Jack Purcel is another channeler, well-known for his work with his spirit guide, named Lazaris (pronounced La-ZAR-is). He reports that his guide is like a best friend, and has written several books with his aid. Their guidelines on receiving and using messages are greatly simplified here:

➤ The teachings you receive should not create a feeling of limitation, or that you are less than you really are.

➤ The teachings you receive must be applicable to your life. They need to be useful in your personal and spiritual growth.

➤ You should feel happier, grow more joyful, and become more in touch with yourself.

➤ After receiving a message, you should experience more positive thoughts, feeling encouraged to adopt a more open approach to new ideas.

➤ The message consistently evolves in the same, positive direction. U-turns and sudden changes are not the norm.

➤ The spiritual entity has emotional consistency. Its moods and emotional framework should remain separate, not dependent on, your own.

➤ The power remains yours. You will never be asked to do something against your will or better judgment. If you feel this rule is being violated, question your source.

Once you feel comfortable receiving messages, your guides will inform you about what needs to be done. Generally, pursue a less aggressive course of action if at all possible. If you can offer advice or help without revealing your source, you are wise to choose that route. Stick with offering information in subtle ways and then trust the recipient's own intuition to help him or her apply your input in the best way possible.

True and trustworthy spirits are not busybodies. They have a purpose for contacting you and accepting your invitation to communicate. They may have a complex message or a simple reassurance to offer. Their lesson may be to open your mind to undreamed-of possibilities or to explore unknown ideas and feelings. The sense that you gain from this experience is likely to change your life forever; not necessarily leaving your established path, but becoming profoundly aware of it.

We will discuss yet another level of awareness in the next chapter. On this level, your spirit takes its own journey, rather than receiving spiritual visitors "at home." So grab your hat, and get ready to explore the realm of out-of-body experiences.

The Least You Need to Know

➤ Communication with spirits is called channeling, and is practiced by channelers.

➤ Channelers can work in various ways, but usually experience some sort of altered state.

➤ Channeling can be practiced privately for personal growth or with two or more people present to gain access to otherwise unknown information.

➤ Channeled messages should express a motive of spiritual growth.

Chapter 21

Out of Your Body

In This Chapter

➤ Your levels of existence

➤ Your second self

➤ Near-death know-how

➤ Out-of-body visits

"There are more things in heaven and earth, Horatio, than are dreamt of in your philosophy," says Hamlet. This statement certainly applies to your inner world as well, which, according to many philosophers and yogis, exists on many levels.

Many of us Westerners grew up with the idea that the individual exists on just two levels: body and soul. Other cultures and belief systems, from the Egyptians to the Theosophists, express the idea that each individual exists on several different levels—five, seven, ten, or more. As we'll show you in this chapter, traveling through those levels will allow you to explore yet another aspect of your psychic abilities.

Koshas: Yoga's Sheaths of Existence

The Eastern tradition of yoga is a good place to start a discussion of a human being's levels of existence. Within the yogic tradition is a tenet called the Sheaths of Existence, which divides various levels of being into the specific functions. Let's take a look:

➤ *Annamaya Kosha* is the sheath of the physical body, including the organs, bones, blood, and limbs.

➤ *Kamamaya Kosha* is the instinctual sheath, which senses the external stimuli through the sense organs, craves objects of physical pleasure, and acts to obtain desires.

➤ *Manomaya Kosha* is the intellectual mental sheath, involving memory, contemplation, experiences of pain and pleasure, and dreaming.

➤ *Atimanas Kosha* is the creative mental sheath, which contains unexpressed potential for future actions. It is responsible for providing solutions that come instantly, without mental effort or prior knowledge.

➤ *Vigyanamaya Kosha* is the sheath of intuition, including spiritual discrimination, ego boundaries, and personal strength. A person begins to sense the divine in this sheath.

➤ *Hiranyamaya Kosha* is the spiritual sheath, which includes the highest spiritual bliss that humans can achieve without losing their sense of individuality.

Anyone can strive to create a closer connection to any of these aspects within themselves. Other belief systems share similar ideas that the individual has several aspects of him- or herself called "subtle bodies," or rather selves that exist on a parallel plane. According to these theories, these aspects are all part of a larger consciousness. The theories emphasize the idea that the body itself does not contain these aspects. Rather, this consciousness contains the body, as well as the other levels, as just part of its manifestation.

The Astral Body: Your Second Self

A commonly recognized "extra" self is the *astral body*, also called an energy body. The astral body is made from the vibrations that make up the physical body. The astral body may also be called a double, because it is an exact duplicate of the physical body. The Theosophists refer to it as the "etheric double."

According to shamans and yogis, the astral body resembles the physical body but is made of a very fine and flexible material. Driven by emotions, passions, and desires, the astral body is thought to be a bridge between the physical brain and a higher level of mind. In certain ways, it is similar to the other types of altered consciousness that we have talked about. But it also offers a special ability: the most extensive travels you can dream of.

Beyond Words

The **astral body**, also called an energy body, is made up of a subtle field of light that encases the body. It is thought that when you're sleeping the astral body can separate from the physical body, which results in flying dreams.

From the ESP Files

Yet another level of subtle body is the shining body, which is made of light. This light represents the divine and its higher dimensions of consciousness. In this form, you may take the form of a single, condensed point of light. Sometimes, especially in mystical writing, this body is described as a flame, rather than a point of light.

From Unconscious to Conscious Projection

The astral body is capable of a very special type of travel. While leaving the physical body at rest, it can get up, walk around, and look back at its physical body, explore its immediate surroundings, and then journey to new places. What makes this experience really amazing is that you are fully conscious and in control throughout the experience.

This process of consciously leaving the body and traveling free of physical constraints is often referred to as *astral projection* or *astral travel*. Although many people use the terms interchangeably, experts distinguish astral projection as an awareness of separating the conscious mind from the physical body. With astral travel, an individual uses this conscious awareness to experience a sense of flying to new, nonphysical realms, as well as physical ones.

How the conscious mind disconnects from its everyday type of mental consciousness and separates from the body remains a mystery. It is difficult to prove what really happens during astral travel and, one way or the other, it doesn't really matter. Since astral travel is no easy task to master, whatever works for an individual who can make it happen is just fine, regardless of the process or what you call it. Indeed, experts say that naming or analyzing the process may only interfere with the process itself.

Beyond Words

Astral projection refers to becoming aware that your consciousness is separate from your physical body. For instance, people describe floating above themselves and viewing their bodies during astral projection. **Astral travel** takes astral projection a step further, allowing you to actually travel to a different locale while being conscious that you are not in your body.

Dream Journeys: Astral Travel

Just what *is* the process involved in astral travel? Experts agree that having a relaxed focus, such as with meditation and other forms of altered consciousness, helps you to reach this state. Concentrating too hard on achieving a certain goal, on the other hand, may actually interfere with the experience because of the conscious mental effort involved. As usual with altered states, the idea is to sidestep normal conscious awareness.

When preparing for astral travel, several steps can help you induce the experience. They include:

1. Choose where, or whom, you intend to visit. (Thinking of where you want to go, rather than focusing on simply leaving your body seems to work best.)

2. Pick a safe space to be in and lock the doors. Choose a place that you consider a sanctuary, and protect it both physically and psychically. Using the power of your imagination, create a shield of light around you and also envision yourself filled with light. Any time you prepare for astral travel, invoke whatever divine force or powers of good you believe in to protect you.

3. Find a comfortable position, either laying down or sitting upright in a comfortable chair.

4. Use progressive physical relaxation techniques, such as breathing, counting, meditation, or visualization, to relax your body but allow mental alertness.

5. Review your emotions and release any negative feelings of fear, anxiety, or guilt. Also, be aware that you have an inner skeptic, but you can ask it to step aside while you begin your journey.

6. Listen to a repetitive sound, such as drumming, a certain line from a song, or your own heavy breathing. Choose a sound that has positive or neutral connotations. (For example, if you dislike the Christian tradition, you may want to avoid listening to a tape of Benedictine monks chanting.)

7. Concentrate on a spot three feet away; you can gradually increase the distance. Visualize a gateway, such as a doorway or window that you have seen in a previous dream. If you're trying to visit a specific, real-life destination, visualize its doors or a similar image. Guided-imagery experience can help out here. (During your first few astral traveling experiences you may find that you don't get beyond the astral projection phase, which means that you may just feel or see yourself floating above your body.)

Mixed Messages

When your body is completely relaxed but your mind *is* aware, you may experience a physiological response called catalepsy, or sleep paralysis. During sleep, your brain deactivates the mechanism that moves your limbs, making your physical body feel heavy and hard to move. People tend to be most aware of this state when first falling asleep or just before waking up. The feeling may provoke a sense of anxiety, but it provides a perfect opportunity for astral travel.

From the ESP Files

Robert Monroe started the Monroe Institute in Virginia to explore altered states of consciousness. He believed people were highly suggestible to sound and that certain sound patterns could alter brain waves that helped people achieve a higher consciousness. He was best known for his books on astral travel: *Journeys Out of the Body* (Anchor, 1977) and *Far Journeys* (Doubleday Dolphin, 1987). Although he died in 1995, his institute remains famous for training people to have out-of-body experiences.

Once you have taken these steps, you may become aware that your mind is awake while your body is asleep. Try to calm your mind and thoughts in response to this realization. You may then hear a sound of roaring, sense a flashing light, and feel an electrical vibration on your skin. Any or all these can build until, suddenly, you hear utter silence and see complete blackness.

This is the final step before beginning your journey. Now you're ready to soar....

A Flying Dream...or More?

Next you enter the next phase of astral travel. All at once, your mind switches from its normal reliance on verbal thoughts to a nonverbal awareness. You witness all that happens, but experience no separation between thought and action. This phase contains certain helpful steps as well, which follow here.

1. Soon you realize that you are moving. You can move in an astounding variety of directions. Not just up or down, but spinning, soaring, or flying. And not just in one direction, but many at once.

2. You may grow outward in all directions at once, and then move inward again. You can experiment with this sense of expanding and contracting. You may feel this movement localizing around specific parts of your body, and can change this by changing your focus.

Intuition Hotline

Use visualization if you are unable to feel as if you can move freely while attempting astral projection. Imagine where you'd like to go and think of how you'd like to go there, but don't stick to simple walking or ascending directly upwards. Fly with flair!

283

3. Instead of seeing only in front of you, like normal, your point of view changes. You can also see in all directions at once; imagine yourself as being simply an eye or a sphere.

4. Once you get used to moving, you can choose to see or visit whatever or whomever you wish. However, you'd be wise to remember your etiquette. Although you are meant to feel at home in this realm and are free to be just about anywhere you can imagine, remember that you are a newcomer. You may not understand all that is going on, or be prepared to go everywhere. A little humility is always wise in new territory: Treat any being you meet with respect.

5. When you have completed your journey, just think yourself back to your physical body. Move your body until you feel comfortable back in your room and fully conscious. Take a moment to acknowledge whatever source gave you the protection that you requested.

From the ESP Files

One concept that keeps cropping up in astral travel is that of the silver cord. The Theosophists theorize that an infinitely long and strong cord connects the astral body to the physical one. You may or may not see or sense it during your astral travels, but many men and women from various cultures have. Their descriptions include "a coil of light," "a kind of elastic string," "a lighted cord," "a thin ray of light," "a thin luminous ribbon," "a beam of light," "a smoky string," and "a slender, slightly luminous cord."

Meeting other beings is a characteristic that makes astral travel unique. Although it may happen in lucid dreams (see Chapter 15), reports of this are rare. Otherwise, lucid dreams share many traits with astral travel. Indeed, some expert astral travelers enter or exit their astral travel through a lucid dream state. Not surprisingly, many people who are experienced with creating lucid dreams are also adept at astral travel.

The line between astral travel and lucid dreaming can become confused at times. In both, subjects are aware of being in an altered state and having an ability to control it. They are fully conscious and the world within their experience also maintains a certain consistency that adds to its feeling of reality. However, in both states, their world appears somewhat different from the real world and has many properties of an imaginary or dream world.

The main difference between lucid dreams and astral travel is that with lucid dreaming the subject fully realizes that he is dreaming, whereas as in astral travel, he feels that he has actually left his body. With a lucid dream, the subject begins the experience when he is clearly asleep; whereas astral travel can actually begin from a very relaxed awakened state.

As we say with all of the other experiences we have discussed in this book, write down what you experience. You can keep any astral travel information in your psychic journal, or a separate dream journal if you prefer.

Doubling Your Double

A special type of mental projection, which lends proof to the idea of body doubles, is *bilocation*. This occurs when a person—who is currently living and breathing—appears in two places at once and is equally "solid" in both places. They appear to be doing normal activities and may even speak to you. Historically, these travels were reported to occur when a person was not able to leave home but somehow "traveled" to a faraway locale to give an important message. More recently, Machaelle Small Wright in her book *Dancing in the Shadows of the Moon* (Perelandra, 1995) claims that she lives in two separate realities simultaneously, as two separate personalities living in two different time periods.

Instances of bilocation tend to occur with people who are mentally active, so full of ideas so that their minds are "divided." The idea is that someone may be thinking of one thing and doing another, causing his or her physical body to be in one place and the double to appear in another. Generally, bilocation is "accidental"; it cannot be controlled, or induced, in the way that astral travel can. In some cases, this occurs only as clairvoyance, when a person sees someone's unreal image as though it is actually there. In such a case, the image is projected by the "sender" rather than initiated by a clairvoyant receiver.

Beyond Words

Bilocation occurs when a living person is witnessed at a second location, while continuing to function normally in her physical body at her original location.

Activating Your Second Self

Experts at astral travel tell fascinating stories of their experiences. Some prearrange to meet fellow travelers—and compare notes the next day. Others travel to secret realms where they visit inner sanctuaries to study deep, spiritual insights. They can meet with teachers who help them learn, or spend hours researching ancient texts in unknown languages. And when they wake up, their clocks show that only a few minutes have passed.

In all likelihood, you won't be able to accomplish these feats on your first attempt. But here's an exercise to get you started on the astral traveler's path.

Exercise to Activate Your Second Self

1. While relaxing in a protected space, visualize your second self. Imagine it positioned just in front of or above you (depending on whether you are sitting or lying down), in the exact position of your physical body.

2. Carefully observe how your double looks. Check out the back of your head and body, as well as your lower half—parts of yourself that you don't normally see from a different perspective.

3. Allow your consciousness to move to your double. Begin to look through its eyes.

4. Look at your surroundings from this new perspective. Then move around the room, looking at everything from this new perspective.

5. Ponder what you would like to do next. You can stay close to home, by looking at other rooms in your own home. Or you might want to try reaching through your walls, and moving through your neighborhood. Or yo/`might venture even farther, perhaps farther than you can now imagine.

Intuition Hotline

Remember that you are always in control—and relax. Many people who are experiencing their first astral "flight" react with fear, which immediately brings them back to consciousness and ends the experience. If you feel yourself becoming afraid, remind yourself that you want to have this experience and will remain able to end it whenever you choose.

You may also want to visit a place or person who is normally far away through a process called *targeting*. This can be done by focusing on the image of the location or the person's face, then seeing it at the end of a tunnel. You then move yourself through the tunnel until you arrive at the desired place or with the intended person.

Beyond Words

Targeting is a technique for shifting consciousness during astral travel by focusing on a person or place in ordinary reality in order to visit.

Near-Death Experiences

Another type of altered consciousness involves the sense of separating from the body (and often traveling through a tunnel), but it stands out from astral travel in one big way: It does not require conscious control. We are referring to a *near-death experience (NDE)*.

In 1975, Dr. Raymond Moody, Jr. originated the term "near-death experiences" to describe the clinical death experiences of people he wrote about in his book *Life After Life* (Bantam Books, 1975). However, similar experiences occur that do not involve near-death circumstances. For example, saints, mystics, and others, who often pray or meditate, experience altered states of consciousness that have been compared to NDEs. But the great majority of these vision-like experiences come from those who have survived a close call with death.

What You See and Feel

Because of medical advances, more people are now able to have a close encounter with death and then live to tell the tale. These people share similar experiences, and their similarity is what makes them remarkable. Here's a list of traits shared in many NDEs:

Beyond Words

A **near-death experience** (NDE) occurs when a person who is considered dead experiences a vivid awareness of separating from his (or her) body. The person is eventually revived to reveal what he experienced.

1. As a person feels he is dying, he hears himself pronounced dead by a doctor.

2. The person hears a loud noise, usually a loud ringing or buzzing.

3. The person also feels herself speeding through a long, dark tunnel.

4. Suddenly, the person discovers she is outside her own physical body. However, she remains in her immediate physical environment.

5. The person sees his own body from a distance, watching the resuscitation attempt from this strange point of view. Emotional upheaval or detachment also accompanies this.

6. Eventually, the person collects himself and adjust to his unusual condition.

7. The person discovers she has a new body with unique powers, separate from the physical body she just left.

8. Soon, spirits of former loved ones appear.

9. A warm and loving spirit appears as a being of light, which asks questions. These are nonverbal and intended to help the person examine his life. Panoramic playbacks of major life events appear.

10. Gradually, the person approaches a border that seems to represent a barrier between life and death. For unknown reasons, she must turn back to an earthly life. Her time to die has not arrived.

11. The person resists returning, after glimpsing an afterlife of immense joy, love, and peace. But he returns to his physical body.

After having such an experience, many people have difficulty talking about it. For one thing, it is hard to describe with mere words. Also, many people they talk to cannot understand or believe the experience. And yet the person is changed forever.

From the ESP Files

The Gallup Organization and near-death research studies estimate that 13 million adults have had NDEs—in the United States alone. Worldwide, that number is much larger. NDEs are experienced by people of all nationalities, races, backgrounds, and ages. On the average, these people are no more or less religious than any cross section of the population, coming from agnostic and atheistic backgrounds as well as religious ones.

How NDEs Can Change You

Actor Kirk Douglas is reported to have had a near-death experience when a helicopter he was flying in collided with another aircraft. Douglas, with severe back and head injuries, was left fighting for his life and actually "died" for a few moments before being resuscitated. He states, "There was never a moment I was as close to God as I was then. I will never take life, things, or people for granted again. I'm more appreciative of being able to open my eyes in the morning and see those I love close by."

Those who have had an NDE show a dramatic change in their attitudes toward life and death. Surveys of survivors show that those having near-death experiences no longer express a fear of death. They also have a stronger belief in the possibility of an afterlife—or gain one if they previously did not believe in an afterlife. We cannot declare that NDEs prove that life exists after death, but they do suggest that consciousness continues, on some level, after physical death.

When asked about what the near-death experience taught them, they all share similar answers. They all seem to emphasize the importance of learning to nurture a true and profound love for others. And another lesson is to focus on trying to seek new knowledge, rather than limiting one's views. A person's values also may change: For instance, driving himself to get ahead financially or professionally may seem insignificant in the face of his revelation about the meaning of life. As we have seen, all of these lessons are important ones in the intuitive areas we have explored. Indeed, some who have NDEs report an increase in their intuitive and psychic abilities.

Have You Ever Had an Out-of-Body Experience?

Both astral travel and near death experiences are called *out-of-body experiences (OBEs)*. They share the sense that their duplicate body or second self has left the physical body behind and taken off on its own flight. Some subjects report seeing objects positioned in places that they could not have seen from the viewpoint of their physical bodies.

OBEs are actually more common than you'd think. Various surveys of how many people have had OBEs show different results, but their estimates range between one person in 10 and one in 20. Although OBEs can happen to anyone—including you!—most occur when people are resting, sleeping, or dreaming. However, researchers report that an out-of-body experience can happen just about anywhere; they've received reports of it occurring during high-speed motorcycle and airplane rides.

Are you wondering whether you've ever had an OBE? Or do you think you were just dreaming? Here are a few questions to help you distinguish between an OBE and a dream:

Beyond Words

Out-of-body-experiences (OBEs) are unusual and brief occasions when a person's consciousness seems to depart from her (or his) body, allowing her to observe the world from a point of view that transcends the physical body and bypasses the physical senses.

➤ Have you ever had the sense of being outside of your physical body?

➤ Have you had the sense of being outside your physical body and observing it?

➤ Did you have a tremendous sense of energy?

➤ Did you feel vibrations?

➤ Did you hear strange or loud noises?

➤ Did a sensation of bodily paralysis accompany the experience?

➤ Was the experience very vivid, resembling everyday waking experience more than a dream?

If you answered "Yes" to most of these questions, you probably have undergone an OBE. If you're still not sure, be aware that out-of-body experiences usually have an awesome impact on people who experience them. If you haven't experienced one, don't be afraid to keep trying. As we've said before, practice makes perfect.

Out-of-body experiences can be both awesome and intriguing, but don't get too carried away with the idea. The important thing to realize is that the point of an OBE, like any psychic experience, is to learn why you're having it and how you can grow from it. If you really want to have this type of experience, your dedication and perseverance will lead you there. But if you start to feel frustrated by your failed attempts, consider that this may not be the path for you. Explore other areas that have a greater pull on your imagination and energy.

Unsolved Mystery

Just a few years before Charles Lindbergh's famous transcontinental flight, skeptics would have been as unbelieving of its possibility as they are of astral travel. And yet, his 34-hour flight was more fantastic than many people realized—until 30 years later when he published his book, *Autobiography of Values*. In it, Lindbergh describes taking off without having slept much for days, so that by the 18th hour he was unable to stay awake. He reveals an experience whereby his mind separated from his body, and eventually blended with a greater consciousness, which became "one great eye, seeing everywhere at once." He was also joined by presences that helped him guide the plane. Although Lindbergh caught himself sleeping at the controls on several occasions, control of the plane was never lost and he landed within a few miles of his destination. In his first book to follow his flight, he made no allusion to the experience, except to title the book *We*.

And if you're beginning to think that astral travel is too far out there for you, get ready to come back down to earth. In the next few chapters, we're going to explore psychic phenomena that's more physical than the mental trips we've been taking. We're about to switch gears to psychic stuff that you can see, touch, and "talk to."

The Least You Need to Know

➤ Your physical body reflects just one layer of yourself, which actually exists on many more levels.

➤ A duplicate self can separate from your physical body and travel without the restraint of physical laws.

➤ This state involves an extremely clear and controlled level of conscious awareness.

➤ Near-death experiences do not require a sense of conscious control, but enable a person to separate from their physical body and see from new perspectives.

Part 6
More Psychic Phenomena

"Phenomena" is a fascinating word. It can suggest weird and wild freak shows or simply refer to things that can't yet be scientifically explained. According to this latter definition, life itself is a phenomenon. (And who would deny that life is phenomenal?)

Part 6 focuses on some of the more unusual—yet extremely popular—phenomena that people often call psychic. We start with ways that the mind has been used to move matter, such as metal bending and levitation. Then we talk about certain types of psychic "paraphernalia," and then devices that help with divination. We also have a chapter that touches on the media's favorite fun spots: ghosts, aliens, and other uninvited guests.

Mental Feats of Magnitude

Fantastic astral flights and infinite expansions of consciousness, space, and time—events and experiences that seem to occur in other dimensions and higher spiritual realms…it can all get quite ethereal—even overwhelming—at times. Maybe you've had about as much high flying as you can absorb for now. Maybe you're ready for an earthier view of that awesome energy.

That's what we give you in this chapter. We'll transfer this energy from an unseen realm to a physical reality by talking about ways that the mind is used to move objects, overcome physical obstacles, and affect matter in myriad ways.

Psychokinesis

As you've discovered, with the mental forms of psychic activity such as telepathy, clairvoyance, or precognition, the mind receives incoming information about people, objects, or events. In cases of mind over matter, the mind projects an influence outward toward other objects or people.

Psychokinesis (PK) is the general term for using the mind to control matter—without any technological help. Of course, mankind has devised all sorts of contraptions to manipulate and control matter in ways once thought impossible, but we're talking about control without using any outer, physical force. PK can include quiet activities such as prayer and healing or fantastic feats like table tipping, fire walking (ouch!), or that all-time classic—spoon bending.

Beyond Words

Psychokinesis (PK) can be defined as the ability of the mind to interact with matter.

Hey, Bend That Spoon

The most famous spoon bender to date is Uri Geller, the Russian whose phenomenal ability to mentally bend metal brought him world fame in the early 1970s. In addition to spoons, he could bend keys and stop wrist watches. Indeed, his PK abilities even affected these objects from afar: His fans in their homes at distant locations who tuned into his broadcasts reported having their broken watches start and perfectly good keys bent.

PK also began to attract everyday Californians—and party goers—in the early '80s. Jack Houck, a PK researcher—and party animal—is well-known for all the PK parties he's thrown, at least 300 since 1981. He started throwing these PK parties to check out his early findings that certain abilities are strongest when linked to a highly emotional event. (In Chapter 16, we mentioned that this same idea applies to telepathy.) In order to create an emotional event around attempts to induce psychokinesis, Houck threw parties—with games planned around mental metal bending.

Intuition Hotline

Choose your companions wisely—especially if you want to show off your psychokinesis abilities. Expert Uri Geller found that he did much better bending spoons and other objects when the crowd that surrounded him was upbeat and positive. Skeptical, negative people seemed to weaken his ability. Indeed, skeptics continue to debunk Geller and his feats. Nevertheless, he's still around: Visit his web site at **http://www.urigeller.com**, which is full of fun psychic tricks.

Houck refers to his most elementary experiment as Kindergarten bending, wherein novice "benders" apply the following steps to flatware forks that rest on the palms of their hands. If you're interested in throwing a spoon-bending party, we recommend you do a little more "research" first, but here are the steps Houck takes with his guests:

1. He asks the participants to use their mental abilities to concentrate on the spoon.

2. When the participant holding the spoon says, "Bend!" the other participants use all their mental powers to imagine the spoon bending.

3. Finally, they release their mental effort and allow the spoon to bend.

Houck reports that about 85 percent of the thousands of people at his parties achieved success at a Kindergarten bending level, the first of a series of experiments that go up to Graduate bending level. From these experiments, as well as others, he postulates that the benders find a period of a few seconds when the metal loses its structure long enough to become mangled. He describes a feeling of warmth that often comes from the flatware when it has reached this point of readiness.

Houck plans his parties to build excitement about these metal bending exercises. During the process, he actually encourages the bender and other party goers to make noise. The idea behind adding noise to the equation is to distract the bender's conscious mind and allow the PK force to work without interference. It also helps focus the other party goers (but not too intently) on the event.

Will Wishing Make It So?

Clearly, creating PK effects is more complex than simply wishing hard, clapping, or clicking your heels together. And yet, there's a certain side of it that requires *not* trying. The idea of letting go of the focus often comes up when discussing what makes PK work.

As in other areas where psychic skill comes into play, experts recommend achieving a state of relaxed concentration. In this state, which often occurs during meditation or hypnosis, the rational mind takes a backseat, allowing a deeper level of consciousness to direct the types of thought, or perhaps energy, that pass through one's mind. This process is quite different from wishing, which is based on a rational effort to direct very focused thoughts.

Levitation: Getting Off the Ground

If you thought astral travel in Chapter 21 sounded strange, what sounds truly fantastic is *levitation*—an activity that seems to exist only in Saturday morning cartoons. And yet the tradition of objects or people floating, or even flying, goes back a long way. For millennia, frequent flyers have included shamans, yogis, saints, sorcerers, and mediums.

There aren't many hard and fast rules about how levitation works. It can be spontaneous, but expert levitators can control it at will. The experience may last for just moments or for several hours. At séances where mediums actually become airborne, participants discover that touching the medium instantly causes their return to the ground. (Moral: It pays to levitate high above the crowd or very low to the ground.)

Beyond Words

Levitation is a PK phenomenon that lifts objects, people, and animals into the air without any physical means of support.

Most levitators go into a trance or other altered state of intense concentration. Within the Eastern traditions, mastering the ability to levitate involves secret breathing and visualization practices that tap into the universal life force or energy called "prana" or "chi." In short, learning to control and manipulate this force will enable you to defy fixed natural laws.

From the ESP Files

A French judge, Louis Jacolliot, was so fascinated by PK that he traveled to the East in the 1880s. In his 1884 book about the trip (*Occult Sciences in India and Among the Ancients*), he asked Brahmins to reveal their take on the source of paranormal phenomena. They responded that the "supreme cause" is the "agasa" (or "akasha"), "the moving thought of the universal soul, directing all souls..." Sounds like the Akashic records—that cosmic memory bank of all that has ever happened.

While historic records of levitating saints and sorcerers abound, there is little in the way of modern proof. In the 1960s, a Leningrad housekeeper and PK practitioner named Nina Kulagina was photographed levitating a small object between her hands. Similar photographs were taken in the early part of the 20th century, but proving their authenticity at this point is impossible.

Psychic Photography: Revealing Snapshots

A picture is worth a thousand words, isn't that the saying? Well, when it comes to proving the existence of psychic phenomena, photography is one way to go for reassurance. In Chapter 11 we mentioned *Kirlian photography*, a type of photography that shows the life force that emanates from all living things. In addition to measuring the energy that comes from healers' hands, it can indicate the health of each organ within the body. It has been used to show illness before it invades the physical body, to predict disease in plants, and to detect structural defects in various objects.

A much different type of psychic photography is called *thoughtography*, wherein an individual with this particular skill projects an image in his or her mind onto a negative. It's like saying that the camera reads the person's mind.

The most famous thoughtographer, who brought the art form into the spotlight in the 1960s, was Ted Serios. This quirky character would select an existing photograph from a book or postcard, concentrate on the image while showing great physical exertion, and then snap a photo of his face. Not surprisingly, many photos showed his blurred face, or appeared entirely black or white, but the occasional photo did show an image (or some portion of it) from the original photograph.

There are a number of theories on how thoughtography works. It could be that thoughtographers use psychic force to manipulate chemical particles on film, or they might be able to project an invisible image that the film picks up. The other possibility is, of course, that they're frauds and some of them certainly could be. On the other hand, some thoughtography experiments have been performed under stringent controls. Indeed, one Japanese thoughtographer, Masuaki Kiyota, worked differently than Serios: He produced several photos with the lens actually covered. Clearly, he was not placing some infinitesimally small image against the lens when the photo was snapped. This suggests that the power of thoughtography comes directly from the mind, not transferred through the psychic's face or through the light and shadows in front of the lens. Of course, psychic photography isn't for everyone. Indeed, it's probably one of the more offbeat specialties a PK practitioner can get into. But you might find it interesting to know about, and even fun to try your own experiment—if you ever have one last shot to use up on a roll of film.

Remote Sensing and Its Offshoots

In contrast to taking psychic photographs, *remote viewing* enables a person to perceive a distant image in his or her mind's eye. Although this perceptual ability originally applied only to seeing from afar, the more up-to-date modern term *remote perception* includes any type of sensory data perceived from a distance.

Beyond Words

Kirlian photography, a photographic technique developed by Russian scientist Semyon Kirlian. Kirlian used two metal plates as electrodes with a sheet of photographic film between them. When he put his hand between the plates and switched on the current, a high-voltage spark was released. When the film was developed, it showed a bright glowing energy field around his hand, which he named "bioplasmic energy. This glow also appears around other living objects, such as a leaf, but decreases as they gradually die. **Thoughtography** is a type of PK, wherein images supposedly imprint on photographic film through the power of the mind alone.

Mixed Messages

Don't believe everything you see, even if it's in a photograph. Unscrupulous people have and continue to tamper with negatives or even set up entire false photo shoots to display false psychic phenomena. Make sure what you're looking at has the stamp of approval from a known expert, such as professionals connected with the Rhine Institute.

Made famous in the mid-'90s when the U.S. government revealed using the technique in its espionage operations (discussed in Chapter 7), remote viewing has actually been a focal point of psi research since the 1970s. At that time, scientists Hal Puthoff and Russell Targ at Stanford Research Institute (now SRI International) in Menlo Park, California, chose to give clairvoyance more credibility by naming it "remote viewing."

Early experiments with remote viewing involved a subject staying in a room at the lab, while a group went out to a randomly selected target sight. The subject then provided a verbal or drawn description of the images of the site that they received. Independent judges then assessed how closely the subject's description matched the actual site.

These techniques have become more scientifically controlled through the use of computers and more rigid procedures. Researchers wanted to rule out the possibility that the subject could be using telepathy—by reading the mind of a person who visits or selects a target site—rather than true clairvoyance.

To do this, they give the subject a sealed envelope that includes a random, computer-selected set of coordinates for a specific target site; but they don't allow anyone to read the coordinates until after the subject describes the target. Even without any information about the site, remote viewers are able to correctly describe target sites—with success rates as high as those in the earliest experiments!

Beyond Words

Remote viewing refers to a person using his mind to visualize a person, place, or object located some distance away and beyond the physical range of sight. **Remote perception** refers to any type of sensory data perceived from a distance, such as sounds or smells.

From the ESP Files

Using the mind to move matter is one form of PK, but what do you call it when you make matter appear out of thin air? A miracle. Sathya Sai Baba, a guru living in India, has a worldwide following of devotees, including well-educated Western professionals. His modern-day miracles include materializing objects, such as jewels, from thin air and making meals appear out of sand. He also heals the sick, and always points to his spiritual purpose, "Spiritual love is central; miracles are small items."

Among the Stanford Research Institute's first subjects was a psychic named Ingo Swann. In addition to being skilled at remote viewing, he showed an ability to affect with his mind what he saw at a distance. In a particularly impressive experiment, he was able to create measurable changes in a magnetometer, a device especially designed to resist any change from external influences. Not only was this device enclosed in a vault in an eight-ton iron vault set in concrete beneath the building, but it was also protected by several layers of various metals and a supercooled electrical coil to shield against magnetic influences.

Interestingly, Swann's own early experiences with creating PK phenomena related to plants. He began by purchasing a small, unhealthy-looking plant and sending it positive thoughts. He claimed that the plant sent him telepathic messages about what it needed (more or less water, more copper oxide in its soil, for instance) through visual images. He then tried testing effects of negative thoughts on a different plant, by sending it untrue threats that he would poison it. Supposedly, the plant's health weakened at first, until it became evident that Swann would not carry out his threats.

Believing the reports of so many fascinating feats, whether as scientific experiments or personal pastimes, may be more difficult than actually accomplishing these feats. And yet, most people feel that at least a few of these amazing abilities are actually real. Science is coming much closer to proving their existence, but no one is able to prove how.

Physics? Magic? Or Intuition?

Theories on how PK works are about as numerous as the types of PK feats, ranging from physics to fraud. In fact, we can't even mention all the theories that physicists put forth because the scientists themselves don't even agree upon any one of them. But some scientists are beginning to see similarities between the bizarre events associated with psi and the workings of subatomic particles (bits of matter that are even smaller than atoms). Both appear to act randomly, without specific patterns.

Other researchers look at neutrinos as possible prototypes for how psi works. These particles move at the speed of light and may even pass through physical matter because they consist of pure energy. Some recent scientists extend this concept to theorize on the possible existence of psi particles, giving them names such as mindons, psychons, and psitrons. Pretty original names, huh?

Other scientists present ideas that do not try to specify physical mechanisms that make PK work. Some suggest that PK results from nonphysical energy, a psychic energy rather than a physical type. It may originate from a person's mind, or already exist, but is susceptible to the mind's mental manipulations or directions. Another theory is that some form of biological gas emanates from the body and forces an object to move. But various experiments have done a pretty good job of ruling out this possibility.

From the ESP Files

One famously documented séance involves a character called Philip. In 1973, a group of eight skeptical people in Toronto decided to create a personality, complete with details from his life story, from their own imaginations, and then try to conjure him up. And indeed they did! Philip appeared and communicated with them via table rapping, which they monitored closely to make certain there was no fraud. So what made a completely nonexistent character appear? The theory is that Philip was a product of the group's unconscious mind, creating a type of group psychokinesis.

We tend to lean toward another theory, which seems to have a strong following in the scientific community as well. It is derived from David Bohm's theory that combines the relativity and quantum theories, which we describe in Chapter 4. For an excellent overview of how these various theories come together, check out Chapter 5 of Belleruth Naparstek's book, *Your Sixth Sense* (Harper San Francisco, 1997).

What Can Happen When You Concentrate!

We've talked about how the body is made up of energy vibrations. This idea is not so hard to accept when you realize that the body is composed of gazillions of atoms. Atoms contain over 99 percent space, with their remaining miniscule particle of matter contributing less than 1 percent. That's a lot of empty space—and yet what holds it altogether and fills in the empty gaps is energy.

Unsolved Mystery

Fire walking is an ancient ritual that has been observed throughout China, Japan, Tibet, India and even the Mediterranean. For thousands of years, yogis and mystics throughout these cultures have been using methods of relaxed concentration to help them stroll—barefoot and pain free—over strips of 1,000-plus-degree embers. What may be even more astounding is that, since the 1980s, inspirational seminar leader Tony Robbins has led hundreds of Californians through the same process—and has survived without any lawsuits!

Each being and every thing has its own sort of "energy print" (like a fingerprint), which we call its vibration. These vibrations have rhythmic up-and-down patterns that move almost constantly. The catch here is the word "almost." Because when a vibration reaches the top or bottom of its pattern, it has a moment of potential rest. (This principle was compared to and referred to as a pendulum effect by physicist Itzhak Bentov.) At this precise moment of rest, called the "stillpoint," your vibration meets up with and matches that of the ultimate stillpoint.

This ultimate stillpoint is the original and ideal state of all vibrations. The idea behind this is that every dimension, entity, and object is interconnected at some level of existence, within a dimensional realm that is much different from just the physical world that we perceive. Rather than existing as hierarchical levels, they are multidimensional, where each ones fits inside another and they all interconnect. At the heart of it all, and running through everything, is the vibration that we're calling the stillpoint. Ironically, it seems to vibrate at such a high speed that it has no movement at all—which suggests that it includes the whole spectrum of vibrational speed and movement. And by having access to all vibrations, this state contains intimate knowledge of them all.

In a sense, all beings "blink" in and out of this vibrational state quite often. (It's estimated at around seven times a second for humans.) It happens so quickly that you aren't even aware of it on a conscious level. But the same part of your mind that sidesteps the conscious mind and taps into your intuitive side is aware of this stillpoint vibration. Indeed, that's how our intuition accesses information that we do not otherwise realize we have access to. But how does PK fit into this scenario? What makes it work?

Once a person is more aware of and attuned to her ability to tap into this stillpoint vibration, she attracts more energy to herself. In a sense, when opening to the new levels of vibration, your own levels tend to expand. This explains why simply opening up to intuition causes you to receive more insight and information. But with PK, after realizing the energy is there, a person must learn to direct it toward material objects.

From the ESP Files

Some researchers believe that psychokinesis and levitation were used in ancient times to erect large temples of worship and other structures. Some of the most famous edifices in the world are thought to have been erected using these psi skills. Among them are the Egyptian pyramids, Machu Picchu in Peru, Stonehenge in England, and the airstrips in the Nazca Plains. (These make bending spoons look easy!)

Before directing this energy outward, however, the key to controlling it comes from within. In order to become more closely aligned with it, you can practice making your vibrational level more closely match it. And how do you do that? Surprise! You meditate, or practice similar methods of altering consciousness—because these states create vibrational levels closer to the stillpoint. The more time you spend increasing these levels within yourself, the more closely connected you'll be to this tremendous vibrational force that permeates everything.

And what do you call this force? Well, if you're an Eastern yogi or mystic, you would call this energy prana or chi or ki. If you're a Western mystic, you could call it God. If you're a scientist, you might call it electromagnetic energy; if you're a psi scientist, you call it psi. Regardless of what you call this energy, it shows one interesting trait: It responds to what comes from within an individual, not from an external force.

Stopping Clocks, Breaking Computers...

When you begin to connect with an increasing range of vibrations and your own level expands, your influence may begin to spread even further. Just as becoming centered and focused helps you collect your energy and better control your environment, becoming scattered and frazzled can cause your energy to spread out willy-nilly. And because you interact and are interconnected with everything that surrounds you, your scattered energy can create similarly frazzled effects.

In other words, when your emotional intensity increases, so can your energy. And if you're stressed out, you might even see that things can start to break. This is a fairly common complaint from newcomers to psychic practices, who may not realize the value of remaining calm as much as possible—until they have to replace a camera, toaster, hairdryer, or a light bulb or two after their uncontrolled psychic energy breaks it.

I have a friend who is a healer and naturally exudes a strong energy field around her. She always sets off the alarms at the airport check-in systems. I haven't experienced any problems with watches or computers, but I seem to go through tape recorders, whether expensive or inexpensive, at a rapid clip. Obviously, the energy affecting these objects isn't always necessarily caused by stress. But energy associated with psychic experiences certainly has an affect on the objects around it. And you can bet that it affects people too.

We'll talk more about how psychic energy interacts with objects and events in the "real" world in the next chapter. We'll start with Ouija boards and move onto some homegrown forms of divination. Stay tuned.

Mixed Messages

If you notice that whatever you touch seems to break, don't panic! Whether it's because you're over-stressed or simply highly energized with psi, you *can* take action to minimize the damage. Just before touching something that could break (like any type of electrical appliance), pause a moment to calm yourself. To do this, try taking a few deep breaths or imagine being in a relaxing place.

The Least You Need to Know

➤ Your mind can exert control over matter—without the help of any physical force.

➤ Mental feats, including metal bending, levitation, and seeing from afar, are among the psychic phenomena related to physical force.

➤ Each individual's mind can tap into an all-present, unified mind that permeates the universe.

➤ Your own energy vibrations can affect objects around you, whether you are conscious of it or not.

Chapter 23

Psychic Tools of the Trade

In This Chapter

➤ Psychic paraphernalia, from boards to balls

➤ News from natural forces

➤ Information or imagination?

➤ Laissez faire or *fait accompli*?

We've been looking at how the mind moves matter, and at what might be moving the mind. It's fascinating stuff, but how can you translate any of this intuitive insight and PK potential into use in your own life? Of course, you start by learning to trust your own intuition. But if you'd like a little backup, or even just a fun way of conducting your own homegrown experiments, you can try playing with a little psychic paraphernalia. They may help you express your openness to receiving information and provide the tools for translating it.

Various devices can give you a few options for ways to tap into your intuitive potential. Many of these are especially useful when you are seeking specific information, such as "yes" or "no" answers to questions. In contrast, devices aren't all that helpful if you're seeking inspiration on an art project or insight into a complex mathematical formula. As you develop your intuitive abilities, you'll learn which methods work best for obtaining certain types of information; no one method is right or wrong. The important point is just to enjoy the experience, which is a more productive attitude for learning something as well! But just in case you're looking for an extra helping hand, we'll show you some options in this chapter.

Spell It Out: Ouija Boards

Among the classics of Spiritualist paraphernalia is the *Ouija board* (pronounced WE-ja). Depending on who you talk to, the source of the name could be either ancient Egyptian for "good luck" or a combination of the French and German words for "yes." Various people also claimed to have invented the board, which has been around for about a century.

Beyond Words

The **Ouija board** contains a planchette, a plate-like device designed to glide easily, and a larger base with letters, numbers, and words printed on it. People place their fingertips on the planchette as it moves across the base to spell out answers to specific questions.

The impulse to use this device came with the great popularity of Spiritualism after the Rochester Rappers (a.k.a. the Fox sisters) brought table rapping (the knocking on a table by unseen spirits during séances) to the fore in 1848. People used the table rapping as a way to spell out messages from the spirit world, with a certain number of raps corresponding with each letter of the alphabet. You can imagine how tedious it could be to talk with a spirit named Zebediah. So séance fans began looking for an otherworldly form of shorthand—and the Ouija board was born!

The Ouija board consists of a smooth surface (usually a round board) on which the letters of the alphabet, the numbers one through nine, and the words "yes" and "no" are drawn. Participants place a planchette, a smaller plate-like device equipped with a pointer, atop the board. During a séance, two or more people place their fingers loosely on the planchette, then ask a carefully worded question. Apparently directed by a spirit guide, the planchette's pointer glides around the board, pointing letter by letter to spell out an answer. Although the messages may appear a bit nonsensical at first, they eventually seem to flow more smoothly.

People who experience the phenomenon are amazed at how accurate answers can be, but usually emphasize the importance of wording the questions clearly. (Remember the oracle who promised the king that a great army would win the battle? The king mistakenly assumed the oracle meant *his* army. Needless to say, he was extremely disappointed when he suffered a devastating loss.) Foolish, impossible, or unclear questions lead to garbled answers.

If you decide to use a Ouija board as a way to communicate with a spirit guide, make sure to think through your questions carefully before you begin. Also ponder who you want to seek information from. If you seek valuable news from a specific entity, you'll need to make this clear. Like other psychic exercises we've described, we recommend asking good and loving guides for their protection, both before and after the session.

From the ESP Files

Do you recall Seth, the spirit guide who we mentioned in Chapter 20? He brought modern channeling into the limelight by communicating through Jane Roberts, the best-selling author. And can you guess how they made initial contact? When Jane and her husband found a Ouija board in the attic, and decided to try it out—just for a lark.

Some Ouija supporters suggest that the Ouija board enables otherworldly spirits to communicate freely, without having to work through the mind of a medium. Others would argue that the Ouija's spelled-out messages come from a part of the mind that sidesteps rational thought. Where the message itself originates, whether from a spirit world or one's deeply embedded personal intelligence, remains a fascinating mystery.

Going to the Earth's Source

While many people believe their source of spiritual or psychic information comes from the heavens, others believe it comes from nature and the earth underfoot. Do you remember when we talked about Gaia mind in Chapter 5? This is the idea that the earth is a living entity in and of itself, and each individual is just a smaller part of that greater level of consciousness.

Mixed Messages

Be careful who you connect with! Ouija boards have a history of being used for fun; they also seem to attract "fun-loving" (mischievous) spirits. Some experts claim that these tricksters are lower-level spirits, who may not have your best interest at heart. For this reason, some people discourage using the Ouija board at all. If you're still interested in exploring communication, you should always ask whom you are communicating with.

In that vein, some people suggest that other aspects of the earth—streams, rivers, grass, trees, rocks, and mountains—also have individual identities that fit into the grander scheme of the earth's purpose. In addition to providing tremendous natural resources, these entities provide great amounts of psychic power. Some followers of this theory claim that certain notable sites mark areas in which the earth's forces contain exceptional power, including Stonehenge, the Egyptian pyramids, and Buddhist monasteries.

But how do you discover these forces, know where they are, or tap into them? One way is by using the ancient intuitive art form of divining with sticks (or as they're called in their new and improved version, divining rods).

Dowsing

Ancient cave drawings going back 6,000 years show people holding forked sticks. The practice appeared in prehistoric pictures in places as diverse as Egypt, China, and Peru.

Dowsing for water would, understandably, be an essential use of divination for the early nomadic tribes who often traveled through dry territory.

Dowsing works according to the same principle surrounding psychometry. Like tuning into the vibrations linked to a certain object, dowsing tunes into the vibrational information regarding a specific place. A dowser performs the procedure by clearly formulating in his mind what he is seeking, then holding divining rods as he walks through his chosen area. When the dowser crosses a spot that contains the sought-after substance, the rods move. By walking back and forth near this spot, the dowser can ascertain the line that the water, or whatever material, follows.

Beyond Words

Dowsing is traditionally considered a method of detecting underground sources of water and other material by using divining rods. Although most divining rods are pre-made forked sticks with a single handle that splits in two, a tree branch in this shape also suffices.

Perhaps dowsing has survived from ancient times to the present because it has so many uses. Among its uses are dowsing for oil, minerals, lost objects, archeological sites, and even spiritual landmarks that may have been buried over time. Dowsing can also be done from afar by using a map and a pendulum—and in search of something far different from a bit of water!

Pendulums

Dowsing for information can be done with a *pendulum*. In addition to pointing out the location of physical materials on a map, pendulums can locate information within the human body (especially when it comes to pinpointing a site of disease), answer yes or no answers to specific questions, and even make stock market predictions. Anyone can learn to use a pendulum; the hardest part is asking an appropriate question and phrasing it properly.

Beyond Words

A **pendulum** is an object suspended from a fixed point that moves in response to a natural force.

Working with pendulums is a good way for newcomers to psychic ability to gain a sense of confidence. At his PK parties (which we described in Chapter 22), Jack Houck encourages people to try using the pendulum before bending flatware: It helps them tune into their intuitive mind, and also gives them confidence.

Pendulum Exercise

With very little practice, you can make this approach work, and see for yourself that you can get immediate feedback. You can even create your own pendulum.

1. Make a pendulum by attaching a weight or solid object to a string or light-weight chain that's about six to 12 inches long.

2. Hold it several inches above a flat, clear surface or clean sheet of paper.

3. Ask it a very basic question that you already know the answer to, such as "Is my name (fill in the blank)?" Note which direction it moves toward—that is your "yes" answer for the rest of this question session. Then ask a question that will clearly elicit a "no" response to ascertain which direction will mean "no" for the rest of the session. (This process should be repeated each time you begin a new pendulum dowsing session, as the direction for a specific answer may change with time.)

4. Prepare some questions that require "yes" or "no" answers. Try to focus on an issue or event that will not require a long wait before the future confirms the answer you receive (such as "Will my daughter grow up to be a doctor?"). Avoid formulating an ambiguous, frivolous, or insincere question.

5. Hold up the pendulum again, and then command it to be still. It should come to a complete rest.

6. Ask the questions you prepared. If you sense that a certain question is not getting a clear response from the pendulum, repeat the question, or try to reword it.

The same basic approach can be applied to map dowsing, if you'd like to ascertain the location of a person, object, or source of information. To do this, ask the whereabouts of something important to you as you move the pendulum over each section of a map. Gradually you will zero in on the location of the information in question.

Look Into My Crystal Ball: Scrying

Scrying is an old-fashioned practice of divination that involves staring into a reflective object, such as a magic mirror, crystal ball, or a still pool or bowl of water (as Nostradamus did). The act of keeping your eyes open while staring into a

Beyond Words

Scrying is the practice of divination that induces clairvoyance as you stare into a reflective surface and enter into a trance-like state.

shining, reflective surface works like a form of meditation or self-hypnosis—the prime state for opening your awareness to psychic insight.

Although Nostradamus used a bowl of still water as his reflective surface of choice, modern scryers most commonly use crystal balls, which are usually three to six inches in diameter. The ideal crystal ball is made of quartz, not glass, as quartz crystal is said to increase psychic energy. It should be placed (or held) against a dark background, such as a black velvet cloth. To prepare for scrying, darken the room, leaving only a candle burning.

When staring into the reflective surface of your choice, avoid using a hard, focused stare. Keep your eyes relaxed, don't strain, and gaze beyond the surface to the inside center of the ball. After much practice, a deep darkness may appear within the ball. After more practice, cloud forms appear, which eventually may be accompanied by colors or light. And after even more practice, images may begin to appear. As you become experienced, you can see an answer—including information from the present or future—in picture form when you gaze into the surface and ask a specific question.

Intuition Hotline

Limit your scrying session to 20 or 30 minutes to avoid causing your eyes to tear or burn. When learning to scry, you may notice that the area near your third eye begins to burn. This is actually a good sign—as long as you don't let it distract you.

Traditionally, images moving to the right are considered symbolic, and those to the left are considered actual occurrences. Another theory suggests that images that appear farther away occur farther away in time, but those that appear closer take place closer to the present time.

You will need to learn what is best for you personally. One thing to keep in mind: Scrying takes many hours of practice before a person can achieve any results. It is not for the fainthearted or impatient, and therefore has few practitioners. In general, scrying works best for people with a visual bent. It provides an image, then allows you to translate it in a way that makes sense to you. This explains why Nostradamus' descriptions seem rather flowery, Such as the one we included in Chapter 2. He saw visions of machines that didn't even exist yet, so he created his own verbal imagery to describe them. For those people who are visual, but prefer an additional verbal and metaphorical approach to divination, there is the tarot.

Archetypes and Metaphors: Using the Tarot

The *tarot* is surrounded by mystery; even its true origins are unknown. The earliest decks appeared in Italy in the late 1400s when they became part of a popular Renaissance parlor game. However, some historians believe that the images on the cards came from ancient Egypt and India, and that sages secretly preserved their sacred symbolism by placing them on playing cards.

Typically, psychics read the tarot to foretell the future. A seeker usually has a specific question or issue in mind when asking for a reading. The reader prepares herself through meditation or a similar relaxation technique. She has the seeker shuffle and cut the cards. At this point, the reader draws cards from the top of the deck and lays them out in a specific order and position, which are associated with certain aspects of the seeker's life, such as inner feelings, the past, the near future, and the environment.

Of the 78 cards, 22 are called Major Arcana and are symbolized by characters that suggest certain traits. For example, the Magician suggests self-control and taking charge. The Lovers suggest love, sex, and emotional success. The Sun suggests happiness, rebirth, and freedom. Where these cards are placed and how they relate to the others' placement is part of the interpretation. The remaining 56 cards are divided into four suits—Wands, Cups, Swords, and Pentacles—each with their own associations.

Along with its unknown origins, the way tarot works remains a mystery. While skeptics argue that cards are chosen randomly by chance, tarot readers raise the question of what "random" really means. They suggest that the seeker's intuition leads them to shuffle the cards in a certain way, which affects which card appears in what place during the reading. In addition, the seeker's intuitive guidance influences how the cards are read, just as the reader's intuition provides an appropriate interpretation of the cards.

Each individual has his (or her) own personal interpretation of what each card means, which usually comes from his intuitive sense. Because the cards are based on visual images, you can derive this personal interpretation without consulting books. Once you have a strong sense of what a card means for you, you can compare your impression to classic interpretations described in books. Interestingly, the two meanings—private and universal—tend to come together, linking your personal sense to symbols of a universal scale. This supports Jung's idea that all people share experiences that are represented by archetypal images.

Yet another method of divination exists that shares such a path of wisdom: the *I Ching*.

Beyond Words

The **tarot** refers to a special deck of 78 cards that are used as an approach to predicting the future.

Intuition Hotline

If you're just beginning to work with the tarot, you may want to start out using only the Major Arcana. These 22 cards have strong images and provoke associations. After you gain confidence with these basic, powerful cards, you can develop your skill with the more subtle Minor Arcana. If you'd like a good guidebook for learning more about the tarot, check out *The Complete Idiot's Guide to Tarot and Fortune-Telling* (Alpha Books, 1999).

311

Exploring the *I Ching*

The *I Ching* is a book that explains an ancient divination method practiced in China for centuries. First written down in about 500 B.C., the *I Ching* is also known as the "Book of Changes." It is designed to show how any and every event is susceptible to change. People who are well acquainted with the book claim that it seems to possess its own form of intuition: It adapts and expands its meanings in ways that reach its reader on whatever level they're at.

Beyond Words

The *I Ching* is an ancient Chinese book of divination that guides its user in casting coins and then understanding eight basic symbols, their pairings, and their interpretations.

When consulting the *I Ching*, a "reader" throws three coins and, based on the heads/tails positioning of six different throws, she can look their interpretation in the book. Using this interpretation, one can divine how a specific issue or event is likely to be affected by various actions. While showing the effects of these actions, the book also offers guidance as to what would be the wisest path to pursue. The *I Ching* is based on the principle that two basic forms of energy run through everything: yin (negative and receptive) and yang (positive and assertive). Each energy is represented by a line: Yin is broken and yang is solid (or strong). These lines are combined into sets of three to create eight basic symbols. These eight symbols, arranged according to a random coin toss, are used to create a series of 64 hexagrams. This pattern of hexagrams is used to do a reading. To understand how all of the symbols combine to create the meaning of each hexagram and influence the interpretation of the whole, the reader consults the *I Ching*.

From the ESP Files

If you really like numbers and want to learn an entirely different, mathematical approach to divination, check out numerology. This approach is based on the idea that numbers have a certain significance. For example, some numbers have been viewed as good or bad for centuries and throughout many cultures. The number 7 has been considered lucky; the number thirteen is thought to be unlucky. These beliefs appear in many cultures: In Italy and Mexico number 17 is considered the unlucky number. Numerologists believe that numbers reveal a great deal about an individual's destiny, life purpose, personality and fortunes.

Sound confusing? Well, like most methods of divination, *I Ching* gives you a certain amount to work with, then leaves the rest up to you. Mainly, the interpretation of what the message means is left to you—which is where your intuition comes in. After obtaining a reading, you may instantly recognize what you can learn from it. That's the familiar form of clairsentience: knowing without knowing how you know. On the other hand, you may perceive the message as a riddle. You will need to take time to ponder it and question yourself. In this way, you can learn to look at the situation from many perspectives, and to better understand your own motivations.

Charting the Stars: Astrology

A similar approach applies to another ancient form of divination: *astrology*. This is a way of studying the stars and planets, and applying the patterns of their movements to human actions. It is based on the idea that all action is reflected in similar actions on parallel levels or spheres.

Astrology has been compared to mapping the cosmos. The same cosmos that contains the movement of the stars and planets contains the pattern of human movement and action. To give an accurate reading an astrologer usually needs to know the exact time of your birth. Your birth certificate will have your time of birth if your parents don't remember. Often the hospital where you were born will have the records if you don't have a birth certificate. Where you were born also

Beyond Words

Astrology is the study of how the heavenly bodies influence human affairs.

has an impact on how an astrologer casts your chart. A good astrologer has ways to work around the lack of this information if you don't have an accurate record.

By knowing the exact time and location of a person's birth, a map can be made to show how they relate to and interact with the cosmos, as well affairs on a smaller scale. An astrologer uses the moment of birth as a center point to create a map, or chart. This 360 degrees on the chart are divided into twelve sections, or houses, that include various aspects of a person's life, such as his or her philosophy, family, intimate relationships, career, hopes, and friends. (On the following page we give you an example, using Oprah Winfrey's chart.)

Oprah Winfrey is an Aquarian. Oprah's Sun is in her fifth house, the house of creativity. Oprah's dedication to using her talents to benefit others is consistent with the Aquarian drive toward progressive thinking and humanitarianism.

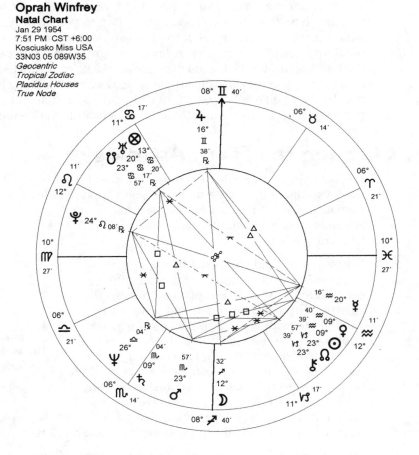

Oprah Winfrey
Natal Chart
Jan 29 1954
7:51 PM CST +6:00
Kosciusko Miss USA
33N03 05 089W35
Geocentric
Tropical Zodiac
Placidus Houses
True Node

By examining your relationship to these various personal aspects, you can better understand yourself and the actions you have taken. You can use your chart to see where your weaknesses and strengths lie, and to assess where these traits can probably lead you. But it's important to realize that your fate is not sealed in an astrological chart. By becoming aware of likelihoods, you can gain the opportunity to change them. Astrology is a complicated science, however, and one which goes far beyond the scope of this book. We suggest several books in Appendix B that can help you get started, including *The Complete Idiot's Guide to Astrology* (Alpha Books, 1997).

Using awareness to create an opportunity to change is the principle underlying all forms of divination. By gaining a larger view of who you are and by getting insight into deeper meanings in life, you give yourself the chance to change old patterns and unconscious habits. You help yourself to put your inborn gift of free choice to good use.

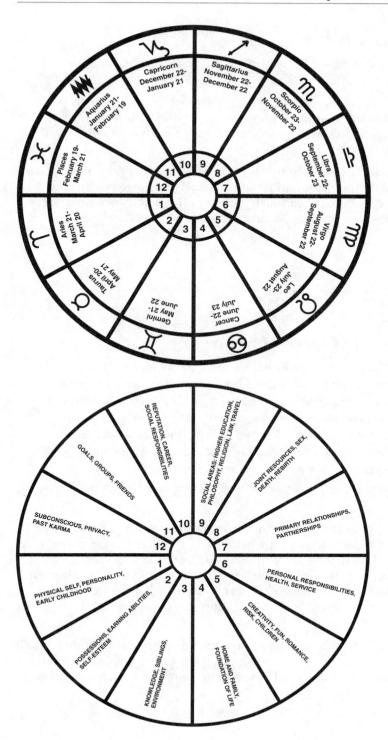

Look for your Sun sign on the Zodiac Wheel. The astrological houses reveal the energies of specific areas of life. You'll want to take note of where the planets appear in the houses of your astrological birthchart.

Knowing What to Believe

There are so many devices out there to help you tap into your psychic abilities—and so many possible meanings they can offer. Knowing what to believe can be confusing.

To keep yourself from getting too confused, or simply overwhelmed, try to keep a few things in mind. For one thing, be aware of why you are playing with these devices. Are you simply experimenting, or do you expect them to answer every question that life throws your way?

Try to approach these devices as tools for helping you experiment and learn. They can help you double check what your intuition is telling you. If you are using them to affirm your intuition, be certain to get in touch with your inner guidance first. Don't run to the tarot deck before you even feel clear about your own personal thoughts on any issue.

Unsolved Mystery

When the Tibetan lama Chogyam Trungpa Rinpoche, who later founded the Naropa Institute in Boulder, Colorado, was forced to flee Tibet for India, he faced an arduous journey. After weeks of difficult travel through the Himalayas, he came to a point where he had to choose which path he and his companions would take. Since food and energy levels were extremely low, this was a crucial decision. Trungpa consulted an ancient method of divination called prasena. After crossing the pass, he looked back and knew that no other path would have brought him across the mountains safely.

On the other hand, if you have issues that you are ambivalent about or that are not life-shattering, you might want to try seeing what these divination sources may say. As you look at their input, take a step back and watch your own first response. Seeing where you agree and disagree with the information you receive can offer you tremendous insight into your true feelings. Remember that you certainly needn't accept a reading at face value: You should follow the translation that comes from your own heart.

The most important point is that your ultimate source of information is inside you. All of the answers come from inside your own mind, not from a force outside yourself. By playing games or using tools, you are simply expanding your own awareness in a new way.

But what about those people who believe there are actually supernatural forces or perhaps superior beings? Is it possible that something beyond our wildest imaginings is actually calling the shots? We'll X-plore that question next!

The Least You Need to Know

➤ Devices to help with divination offer insight into the patterns of the inner and outer worlds.

➤ Each individual can find a specific method or two that works best for him or her.

➤ What you discover about the future isn't etched in an unchangeable stone tablet; it's a guidepost for where you can create change.

➤ Have fun! The key to that is: Don't take things too seriously!

Chapter 24

What's Out There: The Paranormal and Psi

In This Chapter

➤ Far-out psi: the paranormal

➤ Uninvited guests

➤ Unidentified visitors

➤ Science or science fiction?

"Paranormal" is a great catchall word for any experience that people can't explain with science. In a way, then, psi could be a subset of the blanket term "paranormal." But psi scientists strongly resist this idea because they don't want it grouped together with unusual—and perhaps spurious—phenomena such as Bigfoot or alien abductions.

However, despite the inherent strangeness of such sightings and experiences, the stories told by witnesses are surprisingly consistent—enough so that the U.S. government sends experts to research and record them.

One underlying theme that seems to surface fairly often is that paranormal sensitivity and psychic insight are linked in some way. This connection raises the question: Does psychic sensitivity open one up to having a paranormal experience, or does an experience with the paranormal increase one's psychic ability? Although there's no definitive answer to this question so far, the two types of awareness often seem to go hand-in-hand.

Whether there's any truth at all to reported paranormal experiences, one principle holds true: They are extremely popular in the media. From the magazine tabloid *The Star* to the television news tabloid *20/20*, the "weird and strange" attracts attention. In this chapter, we'll explore just how pervasive the paranormal is in our culture.

X-Files, Anyone?

The eerie music, the skewed camera angles, the pervasive sense of secrecy and doom—you all know it, or at least most of you do, because the television series *The X-Files* has made quite a splash. In its first season, *The X-Files* caught on as a cult hit and soon it was a hit series on a new network, winning a Golden Globe and earning an Emmy nomination for Best Television Drama in its second season. Its popularity continues after a 1998 summer movie hit enjoyed box office success.

From the ESP Files

A July 1998 Harris poll suggests that 59 percent of American adults believe intelligent life exists in outer space—that's a 6 percent increase over the previous poll, taken in 1996. But while more people believe in "aliens," fewer believe they've made their way to this solar system. Only 35 percent believe this alien intelligent life has reached this solar system, compared to 40 percent in 1996.

The X-Files' combination of quirky characters, featuring the leading pair Agents Fox Mulder and Dana Scully, with bizarre FBI investigations of anything from vampires to mutants to Loch Ness monsters, keeps everyone on their toes, wondering what will happen next from week to week. But the biggest boon to the show is its interspersed episodes involving aliens—and a governmental conspiracy to cover them up. The overwhelming fascination with this topic may reflect the public's rampant paranoia—or its obsession—with discovering the truth.

The X-Files isn't alone on a paranormal podium. The airwaves are exploding with popular perspectives on paranormal perils. Within the past few years, shows such as *Millennium* and *Buffy the Vampire Slayer* have won a loyal following. *Third Rock from the Sun* offers an absurdly silly look at life on Earth through the experiences of extraterrestrial guests. And then there's the perennial feel-good favorite, *Touched by an Angel*, which offers a comforting glimpse into the world of angels. No matter their tone or subject matter, these TV programs show how obsessed we are with all things "out there."

Ghostbusters

The mantra of *The X-Files* is "The truth is out there." But what about when the mysteries start closer to home? Is there any truth to the seemingly silly stories of ghosts and goblins haunting nearby locales? Indeed, these tales extend far back in time, beyond mere children's tales to some of the most basic beliefs in many cultures.

Ghosts certainly are not a new phenomenon. But trying to prove they exist is. Certain experts in the field have tried to categorize the various experiences people have reported in an attempt to understand what really is out there. The most commonly described categories include *apparitions*, *hauntings*, and *poltergeists* (which we'll discuss in the next section).

What most people think of as a ghost is called an apparition by those in the know. This spirit form can appear physically. It looks more like an image projected on a movie screen than a substantial body. (Remember: Spirits are a form of energy.) In addition to showing itself physically, an apparition usually communicates in some way with its observer. It may acknowledge your presence by looking at you or even speaking to you.

Apparitions are considered harmless by experts of the paranormal. The idea is that an apparition remains attached to the physical realm because of the psychological problems its human antecedent had. A person who died through trauma or who had a strong attachment to a certain place is more likely to come back as a ghost or apparition. He or she may need encouragement to help move on to another realm. As the famous ghostbuster Loyd Auerbach says, "The ghost can't hurt you. However, the ghost experience itself can hurt you psychologically, depending on the way you react to it." (If you have a ghost living in your home, you might need expert help to remove it.)

True apparitions are considered very rare. Slightly more common are "hauntings" (which is a noun). These repeated perceptions are thought to be imprints from past events, which do not involve spirits. The idea is that the vibrational frequency of a certain event was so intense that it left a strong imprint behind. This imprinted image appears like a film clip: It repeats the same brief image each time it appears, which is always in the same place.

Beyond Words

Webster's defines a **ghost** as the soul of a disembodied spirit, imagined to be wandering among the living. Actually, the word is used to describe various phenomena, some of which do not involve a soul or spirit at all. An **apparition** is probably closest to what people usually call a "ghost"—a spirit with an image that can be seen and can interact with its observer. A **haunting** is a repeated perception of an image, whether it's a sight, sound, or sense of movement. Experts suggest that it doesn't involve a spirit but an "energy imprint."

From the ESP Files

Do you ever get the sense that you're glimpsing something, or someone, other worldly from the corner of your eye? Well, you're not alone. Indeed, you're in excellent company.... In a recent interview on *60 Minutes*, best-selling author Stephen King talked about having a condition called macular degeneration; eventually he may be blind. The condition erases vision at the center of the field, but allows for peripheral vision. King says he's fine now, but he thinks the condition suits him because what he's really interested in is "what we can see from the corners of our eyes."

A classic example of a haunting involves the frequent sightings of Anne Boleyn in the Tower of London. Over the centuries, people have reported seeing her ghost near her place of execution there. The theory is that the intense emotions surrounding the event left their mark on time.

The most common category of ghost that people perceive actually comes from within—within their own homes and within their own minds. And yet, they're *not* imagining it!

Poltergeists: Uninvited House Guests

Poltergeists actually present a very good case for the power of PK (psychokinesis). The idea is that objects may move—shake or levitate, for instance—in response to intense mental energy coming from someone living in the house. This energy is not created consciously, which is why people suspect a ghost.

Beyond Words

A **poltergeist**, which means "noisy ghost" in German, isn't a ghost at all. It's a form of PK (psychokinesis) that is usually generated unconsciously.

Although the movie *Poltergeist* associated this phenomenon with ghosts, this isn't accurate. Also, the phenomenon is often pinned on young children, but the little guys really don't deserve the bad rap. Usually the source comes from adolescents, known for their intense emotions, or from adults, known for unconsciously burying some pretty heavy feelings of stress. Often, repressed feelings of anger are involved. The good news is that once the source is identified, the odd events quickly stop. By acknowledging that you have intense feelings, you can begin to deal with them. This opening up quickly clears the air.

Housecleaning: A Little Psychic Feng Shui

In recent years an ancient Chinese art has traveled westward to help do a little spiritual housecleaning. *Feng shui* (pronounced "fung shway") promotes the idea that the physical environment expresses—and affects—the people who live in it. It encourages people to become aware of their physical surroundings and to embrace them as part of themselves.

Feng shui combines a common-sense approach to arranging your home with transcendental techniques for balancing unseen life energies. If you want to balance your surroundings, they encourage you to imagine the ideal environment, filled with a nurturing sense of love and light. Then compare your ideal with your reality.

Beyond Words

Feng shui is an ancient Chinese philosophy of, and method for, creating harmonious environments.

In order to create your newly realized ideal, examine your internal world as well as your outer one. In a big way, they reflect each other. Is your home filled with clutter and possessions you aren't even sure why you own? Perhaps you are holding onto the past and preventing yourself from becoming part of the universal flow of giving and receiving. You can begin to clear the air by cleaning out your closets and clearing out your stuff. Don't be afraid to let go of old material attachments and personal beliefs.

According to feng shui, unnecessary feelings of attachment can create a less positive environment—whether they come from you, from the vibrations surrounding a traumatic event in the environment, or from a former occupant of a place. In clearing out these old energies, they suggest using sage, incense, candles, chimes, and singing and dancing throughout the environment with clear thoughts of love and light. They also recommend practicing mantras, mudras, and visualizations—some of our favorite tools for tapping into intuition! Fancy that!

Intuition Hotline

Practicing feng shui in its tangible terms involves many complex principles. For example, colors in your home should be balanced between all of the primary colors. Often, these are associated with the colors of the seven chakras: red, orange, yellow, green, blue, indigo, and purple. Since each color has its own vibrational frequency, creating this color harmony is one way of balancing energies in your home.

Feng shui acknowledges the important role that intuition plays in properly understanding and using this ancient philosophy. Your intuition can help you gain a sense of aspects in your environment that need to be assessed and improved. These lessons also offer insight into past habits, in thinking and feeling, that may create unnecessary burdens for you today.

Taking Possession

While feng shui focuses on how the "spirit" of material objects can interact with—and even dominate—their surroundings, this section talks more about a much different type of dominating spirits. Many people believe that certain not-so-nice spirits exist that can take over a human's body. Others suggest that just part of another spirit may become fragmented and attach itself to a human. Usually that human is someone who is depressed or feeling hopeless. Still others suggest that a person may lose a fragment of themselves, perhaps by remaining overly attached to a person who is no longer part of their lives.

Beyond Words

An **exorcism** is the act of expelling an unwanted spirit through religious or solemn ceremonies.

Mixed Messages

Don't face your fears alone. If you feel you or your home may be visited by an unwelcome guest, don't hesitate to contact an expert in this area. (You can find many of them on the Internet, some of whom are listed in Appendix C in the back of this book.) They may be able to clear up your own mistaken impressions that are unnecessarily frightening you. Or, if you're not mistaken, they can help you solve the problem—something you should *not* try to do alone.

The traditional view of spirit possession is that an evil, inhuman spirit attempts to take over a person's soul in order to bring the soul to the side of evil. People possessed may start to act in a bizarre fashion and report hearing voices, imagining seeing awful beings in mirrors, seeing strange lights or movements, and noticing a haunting phenomena in the home. Evidently, when caused by a malicious spirit, these occurrences quickly escalate in frequency and severity.

In such extreme cases, experts use *exorcism* to ask unwanted spirits to leave a person. Although this procedure has historically been practiced by religious authorities, such as the Catholic priest in the movie *The Exorcist*, a new breed of helper has come on the scene in recent years. These are specially trained therapists who use hypnosis and past-life regression to ascertain and aid a client in clearing any negative energy, as far as the spiritual realm is concerned.

Some of these specialists have found that a person with chronic depression or lingering feelings of guilt or despair may be helped by this treatment. Although they may not be overtaken by negative spiritual energy, they experience enough of it that it dampens their spirits. Of course, you should be careful when considering this theory. It's an interesting idea, but should be considered with some caution.

But if you find yourself falling into a familiar habit of fearing something you can't understand, affirmations offer a simple way of facing your fears. If you ever start to feel frightened when thinking about possibly unfriendly visitors, try repeating this affirmation, which comes from the Unity Church. (If the concept or word "God" isn't right for you, feel free to choose the word "universe," "spirit," or whatever feels comfortable for you.)

The Light of God surrounds me,
The Love of God enfolds me,
The Power of God protects me,
The Presence of God watches over me.
Wherever I am, God is.

As we've said before, it's up to you to choose what you believe and how you think. The ability and responsibility to decide for yourself is what makes you *you*. So now we're going to give you a chance to question your beliefs on a much larger—indeed, on a cosmic—scale.

Contact: UFOs and Extraterrestrials

Mixed Messages

Resist the temptation to blame bad spirits for your problems! For example, if you've been working all day on your computer and it suddenly starts acting up, take a break! It's not a malicious spirit, but it may a hint from your intuition that you're overdoing it.

At the opposite end of the uninvited guest spectrum are *aliens*. Technically, aliens span the gamut of any being that does not originate on planet Earth, whether it's as helpless as E.T. or as conniving as the extraterrestrials who abducted the Simpsons on the cartoon TV show *The Simpsons*.

Whenever the concept of aliens comes up, the term *UFO*, or unidentified flying object, is almost sure to follow. The idea is that aliens from faraway galaxies are flying to visit planet Earth in spaceships that are so sophisticated, or traveling so fast, that a witness can't explain exactly what it was that they saw. And yet thousands of people have felt sufficiently puzzled by what they saw to call the authorities and give a report.

Beyond Words

Webster's defines an **alien** simply as "a nonterrestrial," meaning a being that is not naturalized on Earth. A **UFO** is an unidentified flying object, which a witness cannot identify.

This puzzle is not new to the 20th century. Indeed, back in A.D. 810, the emperor Charlemagne was thrown to the ground after his horse was startled by a silver ball that came hurtling out of the sky. (Surely, Charlemagne was a good enough rider that he wouldn't need to save face by coming up with an excuse like that!)

Today science can explain many occurrences that once seemed phenomenal. (And until they can explain them, many scientists seem to prefer saying they don't exist, as is the case with psi. But we digress…) In recent history, one flying object appeared that seemed to stump authorities around the world. And it began the current surge of sightings that you continue to hear about today. This famous UFO is associated with the New Mexico town near where it landed: Roswell.

The story goes that a rancher named Mac Brazel heard a loud crash on the night of July 2, 1947. The next day he went to check it out and found bits of an unknown, paper-thin metal material spread over an area three quarters of a mile long and 300 feet wide. The metal was extremely light, but couldn't be burnt, cut, or broken. There was also an indentation in the ground, covering 500 feet in one direction and 10 feet in the other. Several days later, Brazel reported it to the authorities, who never adequately explained the crash and other unusual occurrences around the same time period.

In the study of UFOs, Roswell was the crash heard around the world. Since then, the study of UFOs has gained quite a following. These "UFOlogists" have developed specific systems for classifying sightings. These may include simply seeing a flying light, seeing an object that is also recorded on radar, or having an encounter of the third kind: seeing an occupant of a UFO. According to expert Dr. J. Allen Hynek, author of *The UFO Experience* (Aberlard-Schuman, 1972), third encounters are believed to occur in about 1 percent out of every 650 reports.

Unsolved Mystery

And you thought *Men in Black* was just a movie! Once again, truth may be stranger than fiction. According to certain witnesses, a group of odd men, always dressed in old-fashioned dark suits and driving cars from the 1950s, have shown up to frighten them out of talking about their reports. No one knows for sure who they work for, but suggestions include hoaxers, the government, or perhaps aliens themselves.

Some experts don't stop with identifying encounters of the third kind. The experience that people most commonly hear about—*alien abductions*—are close encounters of the fourth kind. Although people—and the media—love to speculate about abductions, actual occurrences are considered rare.

Believers in the alien phenomenon have different theories on the origins of UFOs. They seem to focus on four main ideas:

➤ UFOs reflect some form of advanced technology, perhaps extraterrestrial.

➤ UFOs may transport time travelers.

➤ UFOs may be a new form of natural phenomenon.

➤ UFOs may be a type of psychic phenomenon.

Whether or not this last idea is true, many people with strong psychic abilities have had experience with some form of UFO sighting—and claim that their psychic abilities either began, or greatly increased, after the experience. Some of these people suggest that they were able to perceive the alien presence because they were intuitive to begin with. They believe the alien presence actually comes from another dimension, perhaps similar to the realm that channelers perceive when contacting spirit guides.

Beyond Words

Alien abductions involve a kidnapping of a human individual by an alien being.

Yet there appear to be some souvenirs left behind by these unexpected guests. Material evidence includes burned grass and earth where UFOs have landed, UFOs on film and in photos, and UFOs shown on radar tapes. Abductees show evidence of scoop marks in their flesh, incisions, burns, apparent radiation exposure, bruises, and inflammation. And yet, according to most people and particularly scientists, these oddities still aren't considered proof.

A Rational Explanation: From the Supernatural to Science

Despite all the reports, careful investigation reveals that over 90 percent of UFO reports have reasonable explanations of manmade or natural phenomena. One theory about UFO sightings is called the Gibbs-Smith's rule in honor of the man who formulated it. Charles H. Gibbs-Smith was aviation historian to the Victoria and Albert Museum in London. He remarked that when studying UFO reports, "the strangeness of a case increases in proportion to the distance, in either time or geographical distance, between the investigator and the location of the report." The moral is: If you want to prove what you saw, you'd better spot your alien inside a governmental UFO research lab, with the investigators present.

From the ESP Files

Compiled reports by various researchers describe about 12 different types of alien. The most common is gray, about 4 feet tall, with large oval black eyes. Another popular type, said to be slightly taller with long blond hair, are called "Venusians" because the first person who reported seeing them, in the 1950s, claimed that they told him they came from Venus.

Leading skeptics have theories about where UFO sightings originate. According to one well-known skeptic, abductees who are hypnotized to recall their experiences are simply following the lead of the hypnotist's suggestions. Furthermore, they speculate that the media, including shows like *The X-Files*, fills people's heads with information about paranormal experiences. Then, if a person is hypnotized to report on her UFO experiences, she has a wealth of information—albeit from sci-fi sources—at her mental fingertips.

Both the abductees' and skeptics' perspectives may seem equally odd at times. But it's always wise to hear both sides of any story. The skeptics have logic and rational arguments on their side; the abductees have experience—and a transformed perception of reality—on theirs.

Keeping an Open Mind

If you find yourself thinking that abductee or other paranormal experiences sound too foreign to possibly be true, just think of your own experiences. Since you've begun to practice some intuition exercises, have you begun to notice some odd occurrences, unusual impressions, or astounding insights? Do you find yourself accepting some possibilities and believing some ideas that you would have shrugged off a few months ago?

From the ESP Files

In the 1998 movie *Contact*, Jodie Foster plays a skeptical scientist who sees extraterrestrial exploration in a whole new light. She—and the movie—explore the next dimension in perceiving the alien situation, which is just that: a dimension perspective This idea suggests that people witness unusual "life forms" that come from another dimension. (Interestingly, it sounds like something along the lines of spirit guides.)

The impressions and experiences you have had may seem simple. People start calling you more often when you're thinking about them, you suddenly know a bit of information that can help you out in a pinch, or perhaps you feel filled with a sense of peace or energy when you're meditating. Any or all these show that you are being more in touch with a greater awareness, your inner knowing. And how could you prove any of it to anyone? Your only proof is that you experienced it.

Beyond the scope of physical proof is the possibility of a different sort of time travel: looking forward to the future. In our upcoming—and final—chapters, you can learn how to give your own readings, check out upcoming trends in technology and intuition, and find out what the prophets of long ago saw on their forays into the future.

The Least You Need to Know

➤ The media encourages a popular belief in the presence of unseen beings.

➤ Ghosts may exist in various forms—most of which are much more benign than people expect.

➤ Many people accept aliens and UFOs as a truly believable and real phenomenon, although their purpose is unknown.

➤ When considering possible realities, remain open-minded and respectful—without obsessing!

Part 7

What the Future Holds: For You!

We believe in free will, so we're not going to tell you all about the future. But we do offer instructions for how to do your own readings—for yourself and others.

In addition to describing details for doing readings, Part 7 looks at predictions for the new millennium. We touch on how technology affects intuition—and how intuition can create its own incredible force for change. And it starts where? You guessed it: within you!

Chapter 25

Giving a Psychic Reading

In This Chapter

➤ Reading yourself

➤ Reading someone else

➤ Possible pitfalls

➤ Intuitive interpreting

So far, we've talked about the many different types of intuitive abilities that a person can have. We've talked about how to recognize them and how to develop them. We've even talked about various ways to access these abilities on different levels. But we haven't talked about how you can call up your intuitive powers to give a reading.

A reading is the forum where most people want to put their intuitive abilities to use. It sets aside a specific time and place to truly focus on what you want to learn about the bigger issues in life. It's what takes this amazing knowledge base you've tapped into out of some faraway realm and puts it right in front of you, with a specific sense of what it means in your life—and what your life means. A reading helps both the reader and the sitter (the person who's getting the reading) feel connected with the universe.

Giving a Reading: You Can Do It!

Why bother calling a psychic hotline when you're wired for psychic insight yourself? We've told you from the start that you have this ability, now here's your chance to test your wings.

In a way, a reading draws on any and all of the various skills you've developed. You never know ahead of time how information may come to you, so be prepared to take it as it comes—in whatever form it arrives. Because you'll be focusing all of your abilities on one person, the information is likely to come in a way best suited for his or her—or your own—understanding. That principle applies whether or not the person to whom you're giving the reading is a complete stranger, a close friend, and even yourself. In fact, when you first start to perform readings, you might want to start where you know you'll get the most feedback: yourself.

Reading Yourself

In Chapter 19, we talked about the Akashic records—the extrasensory information that exists in another dimension, kind of like the ultimate, cosmic library. The records contain information about your lives—past, and present (and perhaps, future). It also contains this information about everyone else, so it's basically a history of the world.

Unsolved Mystery

Although the image of books stored in the Akashic records has a symbolic more than a literary meaning, sometimes intuitive information is so accurate that it seems as though someone read it in a book. There's a perfect literary example of amazing foresight that relates to the world's most famous "unsinkable" ship. More than 10 years before the tragic maiden voyage of the real *Titanic*, Morgan Robertson wrote a novel about an ocean liner that hits an iceberg (also in April in the North Atlantic) and sinks on its maiden voyage. And what was the name of the novel—and the fictional ship? *The Titan.*

What's important for you is that the Akashic records contain information about your soul's growth and your present life's goals and purposes. The following meditation is a way to access the information about why you chose this lifetime and the people in it. Knowing this can help you understand what your life lessons may be and how you can better serve the world.

Meditation for a Journey to the Akashic Records

As with many of the meditations in this book, you may want to record this yourself or have a friend read it to you. Quiet music in the background is helpful when trying to focus your thoughts.

1. Get into a comfortable, relaxed position and close your eyes. Imagine that you are in your Inner Sanctuary. You and your sanctuary are surrounded and filled with a brilliant, white light. As you bathe in this light, imagine it becoming even more beautiful and radiant.

2. Imagine now that a bubble of light comes to you; you are able to step inside it. You feel safe, protected, and relaxed. The bubble of light carries you up and up, into a higher, finer dimension. Take a deep breath, exhale, and imagine you are moving into a higher, finer vibration.

3. The bubble sets down and releases you at a magnificent library. You stand in awe of its brilliance and light. You feel drawn to go in. As you enter the library, you see many rows of books lined up, from ceiling to floor. You understand that this is the Hall of Records. You are here to find the book that represents your soul's history.

4. A wise woman dressed in flowing white, a very high being, comes to greet you. She mentally asks you to sit for a moment and rest. She asks you to pause while she sends you light. You feel your heart, third eye, and crown chakras opening, and feel surrounded and filled by her love.

5. Mentally you tell this wise being that you would like to be shown your book from the Hall of Records. She has been awaiting your arrival and gestures to a table, which holds a thick book that shines with light. You look at it closely and find it has your name emblazoned on the front.

6. Your guide instructs you to think of a question that you would like the book to answer. Take a deep breath and exhale slowly. What would you like the book to reveal?

7. Open the book. It immediately falls open to the page that contains your answer.(pause)

    What does it say? (pause)

8. The next page contains information about the qualities, such as love, patience, and honesty, that you are to develop in this lifetime. Turn the page. You are able to read the answer. (pause)

    What does it say? (pause)

9. The next page contains information about your contribution to the world in this lifetime. Turn the page. You are able to read the answer. (pause)

    What does it say? (pause)

10. You can return to the Hall of Records at any time. Are there any last questions you would like to have answered? Turn the page. You are able to read the answer. (pause)

    What does it say? (pause)

11. When you are ready to leave, you walk outside the Hall. You see your light-filled bubble, like a chariot, is awaiting you. You step inside and are transported back to your Inner Sanctuary.

12. Rest here for a moment and reflect on all that you have seen, felt, and heard. If you have a guide that works with you in your sanctuary, ask him or her to be present to help you process the information or to sit quietly beside you and send you light.

13. When you feel ready, slowly open your eyes and come back to the room.

This journey to the Akashic records is a very personal meditation. It enables you to directly access information from your own higher mind. You can go there whenever you want to understand how specific issues in your life fit into the grander scheme of things. But when it comes to someone else, you may not be able to read the book with that person's name on it. You'll want to develop a separate set of skills for accessing someone else's information.

Reading Someone Else

We have mentioned several times that when you receive intuitive information you often feel that you are making it up. I have heard many of my students tell me the following—just before they have a brilliant, highly accurate psychic perception:

➤ "I don't know how to do this."

➤ "You can't just make it up and claim it's intuition."

➤ "This doesn't make sense."

➤ "This is really stupid, but…"

➤ "How can anyone know this?"

You may feel or believe any or all of the above, but try to have fun with these exercises. Play at them. Loosen up and give it a try. It's really the only way to learn.

Here are some steps to help you get started doing a reading for someone else. Beforehand, make sure you both feel comfortable enough around each other. Ask the person ahead of time what he is interested in learning. You'll do best when you have the right frame of mind: focused relaxation.

1. Quiet your mind. Take a few deep breaths. Let go of any worries. You may find it helpful to do one of the relaxation exercises we described earlier in the book. Some people do the exercise under the "Inner Sanctuary" section in Chapter 8 before giving a reading.

2. Focus your attention. Concentrate.

3. Ask your intuition a question about an issue or problem the person you are reading has presented. You may also simply ask your intuition, "Please give me information about this person that will assist him."

4. Allow information to come into your mind. Receive it. Don't push it. You may receive this information in words, images, symbols, dialog, physical sensations, feelings, and/or ideas. However you receive it is right for you.

5. Verbalize all of the information coming in to your mind. If you are not clear, you may ask your intuition for more information. Pay attention to all of your impressions. Your conscious mind may want to censor the information because it doesn't "make sense." State it anyway. Remember that you are learning a new skill. You will get better at this with practice and become more sure of your information and your accuracy. Later we'll address the issue of what to do if you receive bad news or negative information.

6. If information comes in too quickly, ask for it to slow down. If it comes too slowly, ask it to speed up.

7. If you are not receiving information about a specific question, there may be a reason. The answer may interfere with the lesson the person is learning around this issue. Ask the question in a more general way, such as "What can I say about this issue that would be helpful?"

8. Don't edit the information. It may make sense to the person you're reading. Check it out with him or her when you have finished receiving your impressions.

Intuition Hotline

When doing a reading for someone else, keep in mind that information often comes in images—symbolic or literal. If you receive an impression of an odd image, don't try to assign it a meaning. Often, the person you're reading can tell you that.

Remember that helping someone gain insight is the main purpose of giving that person a reading. You don't need to know his life story or predict his future. The important thing is to share the impressions you receive and try to help the person understand them. Here are a few more miscellaneous tips to keep in mind when you're first getting started:

➤ If you are just beginning to use your intuition, you may not be 100 percent accurate. Be gentle with yourself. Remember, every skill takes practice.

➤ You may find it helpful to close your eyes or look down in order to concentrate better.

➤ You may find it helps you to hold an object or a photograph belonging to the person you are tuning into. (In Chapter 7 we explained this as psychometry.)

When I first began developing my psychic abilities I practiced with friends and family a lot. But I began to realize that it can be difficult to read for people you already know, because you have too much information to be objective. So I asked my friend Sarah to help. She comes from a large family, but I hadn't met any of her family members. I asked for their names and the towns that they lived in. (The latter helps me focus.) I then described to Sarah what psychic impressions I received about her siblings and parents. She was able to confirm when I was accurate, or not, which helped me to practice and hone my skills.

Doing a Minireading

I call these unofficial readings "minireadings." As a way to practice, I ask friends for the names and locations of their friends and relatives. I can pick up information, but never need to share it with the person I'm reading. For example, my friend Sarah (whom I mentioned in the previous paragraph) could tell me whether my information about her Uncle Herbert was correct, but she never needed to let Uncle Herb know I'd done the reading. You can do this, too.

Here's an exercise that you can do to practice your own minireadings. As I explained, it's most useful when you can get psychic impressions about someone you don't know, so ask your friend to give you the name of someone he knows well, but whom you don't know at all. Clearly, the person you're reading doesn't need to be physically present for you to get information about them.

Try to have fun with this exercise for evoking intuitive impressions. I consistently find that people who feel okay about sounding a little silly and "making things up" get better results with this. Perhaps it's an aspect of that relaxed focus that keeps coming up.

Intuition Hotline

Some people are difficult to read. If someone is abusing drugs or alcohol, that person may be harder to read. I also find that someone who is testing me is difficult to read. Sometimes people are extremely anxious, which also makes receiving intuitive information about them difficult.

Exercise for Evoking Intuitive Impressions

The list that follows contains the general areas that I try to tune into and receive information about when I'm giving a reading to a client. When you're doing a reading, as you look at each word on the list, quickly write down your very first impression as it pertains to the other person's life. You don't have to write your responses in the exact order of the list. Information about a certain area, such as childhood, may pop into your mind first; then something about the person's relationships may come next. Follow your inner prompting.

➤ Relationships

➤ Career/Work

➤ Goals

➤ Talents

➤ Childhood

➤ Health/Physical Body

➤ Emotions

➤ Home

➤ Greatest Strength

➤ Greatest Obstacle

➤ Greatest Potential

➤ Other Spontaneous Impressions

Now evaluate the information you received:

1. Check this information with your friend to see how you did with your psychic impressions. Were you completely right? Was anything completely wrong?

2. How did you receive the information? Did you get it in words, images, feelings, a body sensation—or did you "just know?"

3. When you were wrong about a piece of information, do you remember how you felt when you received it? Did it feel fuzzy? Were you feeling blocked? Was an image or word unclear in some way? You can become a better psychic by understanding when you're not receiving clear information as well as when you are. If you're unclear, you might try asking the question in a different way. Instead of asking your intuition, "What does their home look like?" You might ask, "Do they live in a large house or a small one?" By varying the question, you may receive the information differently.

4. When you were accurate about some information, do you remember how you felt when you received it? Did you feel tingly, or simply certain you were right? Was there anything different that you felt when you had a correct answer versus a mistaken one?

Intuition Hotline

Remember to keep track of all the readings you do in your psychic journal, even if they are minireadings or self-readings. If you start to do a lot of them over time, you may want to start a separate notebook that includes just the date of the reading, who it was with, and any impressions that really stand out.

339

I do this exercise frequently in my classes on "Developing Your Intuition." I am constantly amazed at what beginners in the class come up with. One man's partner in the class was a lively, nicely dressed, older woman. He went through the exercise quickly, easily using his intuition to fill in the whole list—with one exception. The only category he couldn't figure out was "Career." He kept hearing the word "none," so he assumed she didn't work. When it came time for the partners to process the information, I heard a loud guffaw from the older woman. Then she exclaimed, "How could you possibly have known that I am a nun!"

Another student in the class was working with a partner and got stuck on the category of "Home." She found she kept getting impressions about the woman's kitchen. The student was concerned because the room kept changing from yellow, to light green, and then to peach. The woman laughed and explained that she was planning to have her kitchen painted. In fact, that morning before the class she had been going over color swatches with her husband. They were trying to decide between yellow, green, and peach!

Creating the Right Environment

Feeling comfortable with others—and with yourself—is essential to building the confidence that is necessary to gain trust and offer insight. When someone arrives at my office, I try to help that person feel as calm and relaxed as possible. This helps us work together as an intuitive team, making it easier for me to tune into her.

Another important part of getting a clear reading is to set aside as many of my own opinions, feelings, and judgments as possible. In this way, intuitive counselors are similar to psychotherapists. I have found that much of the judgment I used to hold about others has diminished over the years as I have given more readings.

People usually act out, hurt others, and do irrational things because they've been so emotionally injured themselves. I'm not saying that to condone their behavior. But if you are reading for people like this, you need to respect and honor their path. They are the only ones who are ultimately responsible for their direction in life and for the outcomes of the choices they make. You can only be there as a guide to help along the way.

When You're Stuck

Just as you strive to make doing a reading comfortable for others, you must do the same for yourself. Sometimes you may have such high expectations of yourself that you put far more pressure on yourself than anyone else could. Of course, this can't possibly help you achieve relaxed focus.

Your intuition rarely acts in a radical fashion, such as shutting down. So take that to heart and simply help yourself to relax. When you feel that your access to intuitive information is blocked, try taking a few small steps:

➤ Quiet the chatter of your conscious mind through meditation.

➤ Schedule a retreat for yourself.

➤ Engage in meditative activities, such as art, knitting, making bread, day dreaming, or even walking.

➤ Create a healthy balance between work and recreation.

➤ Try new things; break patterns.

➤ Take a nap.

➤ Do something to make yourself laugh.

➤ Try speaking your options out loud and seeing which one feels right in your gut.

➤ Go to your sanctuary and speak with your guide.

➤ Ask for a dream about your concerns.

➤ Pray to a Higher Power for guidance.

➤ Come up with a few of your own ideas:

_____

_____

_____

The main thing is to relax. Stop pressuring yourself and start trusting your intuition. Trusting your intuition is what a reading is all about: a confident sharing of information that comes to you as a gift. Remember to celebrate that!

Turning It Off

So, we've told you how to get up a good head of steam to really get in touch with your psychic side. But what happens if your brain feels like it's in overdrive? Can you decide that you want to take a break?

To generalize a little, some psychics do seem to be "on" or "open" all the time. They pick up information about people and situations around them at any time. I personally would find this very exhausting. It has happened to me only once, after I had done too many readings in one day. I couldn't seem to shut myself down.

I went to a mall after seeing my clients and found myself at the shopping center getting swamped with psychic information about other shoppers. I walked through the mall while being bombarded

Mixed Messages

Don't let yourself become overwhelmed by your psychic abilities. If you're ready for a break, stop making quite as much effort to open to your intuitive side. But if you do this, don't wait too long to get back on track, since you can see that consistent awareness and regular practice help a lot in bringing you closer to your intuition.

with impressions. Here's a sampling: The guy in the gray suit was having an affair and felt guilty about it; the short man coming out of the drug store was worrying about his sick mother; the teenage girl sitting on the bench was obsessed with a boy who wasn't interested in her...it went on and on. After only a few minutes of this, I fled the mall, fearing I had a sign on me that read "BEWARE PSYCHIC SNOOP!" I went home, fell asleep, and felt fine the next day.

When speaking with other intuitive counselors about preparing for readings, everyone I spoke with said they did some meditation or ritual to open up to more psychic awareness, but that shutting down just seemed normal and didn't require a ritual of any sort. When the reading is over, they simply return to a normal state. One woman said that what shuts her down is a shift in awareness away from her client as she ends the reading. Another woman said that as soon as she hung up after a phone session or after the door shut behind a client leaving her office, she felt she returned to a normal state.

Some intuitives practice a regular routine of closing down after they do readings. Some find it helpful to be outdoors near nature or to go for a short walk. Others have a set of words they repeat. Still others may do something creative with their hands, such as gardening or cooking. One woman holds a piece of green fluorite crystal at the end of her readings because she feels it helps keep her grounded. Turning off psychic input can be a challenge for some people, but it's not all that difficult to overcome.

Setting Boundaries

Boundaries are imaginary lines you establish around yourself to protect yourself from the unhealthy or damaging behavior of others. Boundaries are the proverbial "line in the sand." They establish what you will tolerate in another's behavior, and thereby establish what people can and cannot do to you.

Knowing how to establish boundaries for yourself is a valuable tool to have, whether you are giving readings or not. When you establish clear boundaries for yourself, your anxiety starts to lessen, people respect you, and you experience the world as a safe place. Generally you have more energy, as well as a deep inner peace. While most people have learned how to set boundaries of some sort between themselves and others, applying these principles to the psychic realm requires a different approach.

Psychic Protection

I don't perceive myself as being at risk for any bad energy or bad vibes when opening up psychically. But some people do, and many recommend establishing some habits to ensure psychic protection. These may include doing a "psychic protection" exercise before opening up to do readings.

My favorite exercise for this comes from author and psychic Belleruth Naparstek: "I imagine being surrounded and protected by a magical cushion of protective, intelligent, vibrating energy, which draws to it all the love and sweetness that has ever been sent my way—every prayer, smile, good wish, and gesture of gratitude drawn there as if by a powerful magnet, to surround and protect me."

I usually do a light meditation before I see clients and ask my guides, angels, and God to help me with my readings. I ask that I be a clear and open channel for any of their wisdom that my clients need to hear. I find that the best protection to my own energy is getting enough rest, paying attention to my intuition regarding my own life, eating a healthy, balanced diet, setting appropriate boundaries in my work, and making sure I have enough time for play and fun.

Intuition Hotline

For people who like to draw on their visual resources, indigo is often recommended as the color of psychic protection. (If you recall, this is the color associated with the third-eye chakra.) After a reading, you can imagine yourself wrapped in an indigo cloak. Another spiritual color that evokes purity is, of course, white.

I usually find my work energizing and I enjoy it. It's a privilege to watch people grow and change, and I feel honored to be included in that process. I also have learned to be clear in my boundaries while doing readings. I have learned that I can do only a certain number of readings in a day or a week. If I do more than that, I get exhausted. I've learned how to say "No" to requests that drain me.

Problem Clients

Of course, life would be less interesting—and certainly less challenging—if I didn't have the occasional really difficult client. A difficult client for me is someone who wants me to have all the answers. He hopes that I will have a revelation that will dramatically change his life, yet he does nothing to create any changes on his own.

I feel drained by people who don't take the initiative to help change themselves. If I reach a point where I feel I can't help them when they call for an appointment, I make an appropriate referral. I have a huge resource list of therapists, career counselors, mediums, holistic physicians, and personal coaches, to name a few. Many times people call me because they don't know whom else to call. (But, dear reader, I hope you don't do that. The resources we list in Appendix C can help you take the initiative to help yourself. These organizations can lead you to the specific information or person you need much quicker than I can!)

Sharing Psychic Information

Receiving intuitive information is one thing; sharing it is quite another. Knowing how to share intuitive information is an art in and of itself. The unwritten social rules of sitting down to do a reading can be as complex as dining at the Vanderbilts'.

Mixed Messages

Be careful how you handle the psychic information that comes to you. If information about someone comes to you outside of the context of a reading, then be even more careful about how you handle it. It may be news that's intended for your own growth—not for that of the innocent bystander the information concerns.

But don't let this intimidate you. For one thing, the "rules" certainly are not etched in stone. Because each reading is different and presents its own unique type of information, no simple rules can apply to every reading. Your actions definitely depend on your own intuitive assessment about how to handle each situation. Following are a few guidelines to keep in mind when broaching a few basic areas.

Bear in mind that receiving the information doesn't always mean that you have to share it. You can't always judge correctly what it means, and the more serious the news is, the more cautious you should be in passing it along. Belleruth Naparstek states this succinctly: "It would be arrogant and intrusive to assume we'd all been deputized by God to interfere with other people's lives, sometimes even if they ask us to."

If the News Seems Bad

I am often faced with the question of what to do when I receive difficult information, such as an impending death, illness, or accident. I am of two minds here, and my response depends on the situation and what I receive intuitively. My first impression is usually to say whatever it is that I've received. I may try to couch it in a way that softens the blow. Sometimes I receive the information as a warning, which I can offer someone in enough time for them to take effective action.

In very serious cases, I get quiet and ask my intuition to give me a way to talk to the person about the information. If I share it, I will talk to my client about possible courses of action to either support her in what may be inevitable or to sort through possible options to prevent the outcome that I'm perceiving.

What's the Answer? Yes or No (or Maybe)

I often have clients call me and ask if I can answer just one or two quick questions. I don't know if all intuitive counselors experience this type of request for quick answers. And I don't know how they respond. I find them difficult.

I usually ask them to make an appointment with me, so that I'm in the proper frame of mind to give accurate input. In general, I find that these clients make the assumption that I'm "on" all the time. There's also an assumption that I have the right answer as opposed to their own remarkable built-in intuition. I'll explain further by describing a client whose name I've changed to "Sally."

Sally called with a quick question: "Should I take this job that I've been offered?" To answer this question, I would need to psychically climb into Sally's life. Here are the questions that I would want to look at intuitively to answer the quick question:

What's going on with Sally? Is she in a life situation that supports a change? Does she feel confident? Would another job be better? Is there another job coming along soon? How does she feel about the job? Can I see her happy in her position?

What's the job about? Who's her boss? Will he or she be a good match for Sally? Will the company be successful? What are the political dynamics in the company? What would Sally's coworkers be like? Will they be a good team for Sally to work with? Is this generally a good career move for Sally? Is it a growing company? Would Sally's position change for the better or worse once she had the job? Will she still be there in a year?

Intuition Hotline

For some reason, newcomers to receiving psychic information tend to be bombarded with information of the negative variety. As tempting as it may be to share your insights, try to avoid being like the newscasters on the evening news: Don't make a show at someone else's expense.

Certainly you and I can get a general intuitive feeling about a "yes" or "no" decision. But, as you can see, a good many intricacies are involved in answering someone's quick question. I would want to look at all of those issues so that I could answer with honesty and integrity.

You Can't Predict Free Will

In my practice, I am often asked if I am 100 percent accurate. I'm the first to say, "No, I am not 100 percent accurate." I also don't believe that measuring percentages really means anything when it comes to readings. I think it's extremely difficult—in fact, practically impossible—to assess a percentage of accuracy when it comes to intuition.

I think even the most skilled psychic is wrong a fair percentage of the time. Remember all those scientific tests we have spoken about in past chapters? The highest scores on many of those tests are around 65 percent. And those scores are considered quite impressive.

I am also a firm believer in free will. Without pushing, I often try to steer clients away from what looks like a disastrous path. Am I inaccurate because my client took my advice and the disaster never happened? In that case, I'd be happy with a zero percent accuracy rate!

You can't predict free will. I believe the future is full of probabilities. If you go to a psychic who sees a future event for you, he or she is looking at one probable future for you. What happens to you is influenced by your thoughts, beliefs, and emotions. Whenever you change a belief, alter a thought, or release a strong emotion, you are changing your future.

From the ESP Files

In their recent research with quarks, thought to be the smallest particles of matter, modern physicists have noted an interesting catch-22. Whenever trying to observe and measure these tiny tidbits, physicists find that the particles' expected "behavior" suddenly changes: The theory is that the act of observing them actually changes them. A similar principle may apply to psi: Taking it out of its everyday context of being useful on a spiritual level to scrutinize it in a laboratory test may change the nature of its response.

As a psychic I see my role as helping you understand the path you're on and where it's heading at present. I try to use my psychic abilities to help you see where you're blocked and help you get unstuck. I'd rather teach you the tools to create a life you love rather than have you believe you're stuck with a life you don't want!

But some people believe that fate, or destiny, is inescapable. These beliefs have especially come to the fore in light of the millennium. So many prophets, from ages past to just days and decades ago, have foretold doom for the days surrounding the year 2000. For those, such as Nostradamus, who seem so right, is it now their fate to be proven wrong? You can take action to create that change. Find out how in the next chapter.

The Least You Need to Know

➤ You can do a reading for yourself or someone else.

➤ When doing a reading, your intuition helps guide your way of sharing information as well as receiving it.

➤ Accurate reading for others responds to your careful attention to your own condition.

➤ Information offered in a reading is not inevitable; rather, it presents possibilities for change.

Chapter 26

Reading the Trends: Where We're At

In This Chapter

➤ The instant information age

➤ In the skeptics' corner...

➤ Psi-fi or scientific fact?

➤ Relying on your own mind

We've talked about using readings as a way to see what your probable path is and what your options may be. But what about events on a larger scale? Don't things seem to "just happen," regardless of your input? Yes, outside changes can come along, but it is possible that your input *was* and *is* involved, whether you're aware of it or not.

Discoveries and trends that affect everyone at once usually develop and evolve parallel (and perhaps in response) to a thought or need. The larger the change, the more widespread the desire to have the change. The growing interest in psi, just like the widespread access to technology, parallels a fairly recent urge for information—and instantaneous information, at that. While psi enables you to access personal insight quickly, technology helps you connect with others. In this chapter, we'll show you what we think the trends in the psychic world may be in the near and distant future.

Life in the Fast Lane: The Information Age

Information is the name of the game these days. From inventors to sales executives, knowing what's out there, what's possible, and what's likely to be next, is the crux of survival and success.

Technology can provide new ways of doing things, as well as entirely new products. But to tap into technology and use it to its fullest, you need information. But people who want to be at the forefront of a new phenomenon need to know what's ahead from a source that exceeds anything a database can offer: the future. This desire for insight into the future has led to a high demand for accurate intuitives in the business and technological communities.

Technology and Intuition

Intuitives with expertise in various fields, such as computer science, business planning, stock investing, and social research, have been contacted to give private business forecasts or to speak at corporate planning seminars. Big business, along with other fields, seems to acknowledge the importance of intuition when making plans in this rapidly changing world.

The same principle that applies to organizations and large corporations also applies to you. Everyone wants to know where to invest their time and energy (as well as their savings). Via the Internet, you can now access all sorts of information that you couldn't get 10 years ago. But having all that information can just add more confusion, if you haven't developed some way of processing it.

Mixed Messages

The Internet offers a wonderful way to get in touch with others who are as curious as you about psychic phenomena. But use some judgement when jumping into experiments or groups, especially if someone asks you to contribute money or suggests you give them your credit card or bank account number.

The Wide World of the Internet

In addition to helping you access information for your financial, business, and social life, the Internet can help you learn a lot more about tapping into your own and others' intuition. For one thing, several sites offer opportunities for computer users to get involved in experiments from the comfort of home, via the Internet.

In an earlier chapter, we listed the Web site for remote viewing experiments. Other Web sites, including that of the American Society for Psychical Research, include surveys and even welcome write-ups of personal paranormal experiences. (See Appendix C for further information.) In addition to helping scientists do research, this newfound ability to share so openly has allowed many people, who may have previously been afraid to talk about their experiences, to get in touch with a support network.

Another way that people are using the Internet in a psychic way is to bring many minds together and direct their thoughts—all at the same time—toward accomplishing a certain goal. Recently, for instance, organizers used the Internet to establish a prayer event intended to promote world peace. On August 22, 1998, the World Peace Prayer Ceremony was broadcast between 3:30 and 4 p.m. Eastern time. It claimed to be the first peace rally of its kind.

If you're interested in making friends with folks much, *much* farther away, The Internet can help you contact them. Or rather, *you* can help the Internet contact them: There's now a new program that enables you to contribute your computer power to the Web for UFO sightings. It's billed as "a grand experiment that will harness the spare power of hundreds of thousands of Internet-connected computers in the Search for Extraterrestrial Intelligence (SETI). With a program called SETI@home, computer users from around the world will participate in a major scientific experiment. The program works like a screen saver: Whenever you're not using your computer, it starts to analyze data taken by the world's largest radio telescope—in hopes that some of the signals it picks up are from faraway civilizations.

From the silly to the sublime, the Internet has something for everyone. It enables anyone to express their views. In addition to learning more about peoples' personal experiences with psychic phenomena, you can tap into information on the truly esoteric side. And, of course, you can find a lot on information from psi's critics, as well, as we'll show you in the next section.

The Skeptics' View

Admittedly, some of the paranormal events that people describe seem a bit...shall we say, far-fetched? Just as the phenomenal world has its extremists, so does the purely physical world. These people who are committed to questioning everything call themselves *skeptics*.

Skeptics take their beliefs so seriously that they have formed several different organizations. The best-known is probably The Committee for the Scientific Investigation of Claims of the Paranormal, founded in 1980 by scientists, academics, and science writers, including Carl Sagan, Isaac Asimov, Ray Hyman, James Randi, and others. Its self-

Beyond Words

A **skeptic** is someone who questions the validity of something purporting to be factual or who maintains a doubting attitude.

described goal is to encourage "the critical investigation of paranormal and fringe-science claims from a responsible, scientific point of view and disseminate factual information about the results of such inquiries to the scientific community and the public. It also promotes science and scientific inquiry, critical thinking, science education, and the use of reason in examining important issues."

Despite its rational stance, the public may confuse these two types of extremists—fanatical followers of all things paranormal and ever-suspicious skeptics—at times. For example, many of Internet sites about psychic phenomena are actually created by skeptics. They express themselves with such vehemence that you can't tell whether you're reading about ideas of rational scientists or inane parodies of the skeptic viewpoint.

From the ESP Files

Carl Sagan, one of the great scientists and skeptics of the 20th century, claimed that one thing made him consider the possible existence of a certain psychic phenomena—reincarnation. And what caused him to think that? The stories of young children who described former lives in details that children couldn't ordinarily know.

At times, skeptics have done more research on a phenomenal event than someone who was present to experience it. But because the skeptics haven't experienced the phenomenal world themselves, they have no firsthand knowledge of an alternate reality. And because they are not open to experiencing it, they are very unlikely to do so. This creates a huge catch-22, which they are quick to point out.

Another catch-22 is that carefully monitored psi tests show that psi works best in a positive and receptive atmosphere, not a negative and suspicious one. Interestingly, while psi researchers are put in the position of proving psi does exist, the skeptics are finding they have a far more difficult task: proving that psi doesn't exist.

The Amazing Randi

One of the best-known popular skeptics regarding the paranormal is The Amazing Randi, a.k.a. James Randi. Trained as a magician, Randi is on a personal crusade to prove that psi effects are a hoax. He has written several books on the topic and has traveled extensively to lecture on the subjects of pseudoscience and supernatural claims.

In some instances, Randi has even taught people how to commit fraud, and then sent them into psi labs to fool scientists. The best-known case occurred in 1979 with two teenagers, Steve Shaw and Michael Edwards. Randi taught them how to fake having PK powers, and then sent them to McDonnell Laboratory at Washington University to demonstrate their abilities. Psi researcher Peter Phillips, publicized their feats, albeit cautiously—until Randi exposed his scheme.

Randi's current claim to fame involves his offer of $1 million to anyone who can prove they have psychic powers. Of course, Randi expects the psychic to be tested according to his standards and on his turf, which is likely to involve some pretty negative attitudes and auras. (If you want to contact him for details, his Web page is http://www.randi.org.)

Myth, Magic, or Miracle?

Randi, like other skeptics, argues that all psychic demonstrations are actually cleverly concealed tricks. This criticism isn't new. In fact, some of the first scientists to investigate psi were conscientious about inviting magicians to witness the experiments in order to rule out fraud.

In 1923, the independent founder of the National Laboratory of Psychical Research in London, Harry Price, performed a series of PK experiments with a young woman of seemingly astounding abilities named Stella Cranshaw. Her séances involved impressive displays, such as levitation of tables and severe drops in temperature, but she soon refused to continue the work. Although Price did much to further psychic research, including inventing machines to measure psi and detect fraud, records after his death suggest he may have engineered a little foul play at Stella Cranshaw's séances.

Unsolved Mystery

One of the world's most determined skeptics was also one of its best known magicians. Harry Houdini (1874–1926) always made it clear that his work was based on tricks. He had a strong dislike of those who used the art of trickery to cheat people, and exposed frauds whenever he could. Later in his life, when the Spiritualist movement became so popular, he went on a personal crusade to expose phony mediums and the ghostly apparitions, noises, and levitations they created. Although he was highly skeptical of all things mystical, he promised his wife that if he died before her, he would return to visit her in a séance, if such a feat were possible. As far as anyone knows, he never did.

In the mid 1950s, another amazing feat was the ability of a British physician, Dr. Rolf Alexander, to move cumulus clouds. Before beginning a demonstration, he would point out which parts of clouds would separate and rejoin in another formation. And, sure enough, as he concentrated during his four-minute demonstrations, the clouds would move—just as he predicted! What close observers later discovered, all cumulus cloud formations tend to follow the same pattern he described.

In recent decades, occasional attempts at fraud have been brought to the public's attention. In the case of metal bending, even young children have got into the conjuring act. In a series of tests at the University of Bath, six children claimed to have the spoon-bending ability of young Uri Geller (see Chapter 22)—until they were caught cheating. One child even stood up to bend a spoon underfoot, not realizing she was being observed through a one-way mirror.

From the ESP Files

For all those *Star Trek* fans out there, don't give up hope of ever seeing a true-to-life transporter. According to IBM, they already have the physics to show how an object can disintegrate in one location and reappear in another. Unfortunately, this type of travel is far from instantaneous. In fact, calculations suggest that transporting the entire subatomic makeup of a human being would take about 100 million centuries. Don't try this one as a way to speed up your commute!

The skeptics' commitment to doubt may appear the safest approach if you're afraid of looking like a fool. But what will they say when evidence finally arrives that proves psi exists as a natural force? Perhaps the truly safest approach to avoid appearing a fool is to keep an open mind. But even the most open-minded of us may have trouble believing that what happens to some people is actually based in external reality (as opposed to a dream, or simply a need for new glasses). Clearly, everyone needs to exercise a certain amount of judgment about what to explore and where to focus their energy.

Taking Charge of Your Future

Controlling your own future is a far cry from the conjuring tricks that Randi and others are obsessed with. Rather than focusing on what's *not* true, we recommend making your own choices about what will be. As authors Gail Straub and David Gershon write in *Empowerment: The Art of Creating Your Life As You Want It* (Ten Speed Press, 1991), "What you think and believe will manifest in your life. By becoming adept at intelligently directing your thoughts, you can become adept at creating the life that you want. You can take charge of your destiny."

Your intuition is constantly informing you of new directions you can take in order to experience more joy, peace, and happiness. You can only benefit by paying attention to these intuitive cues for change in your personal life. Many times people push aside the intuitive messages they receive and, like Scarlett O'Hara in *Gone With the Wind*, they decide to "think about it tomorrow."

Life is short. Why not do all you can to enjoy it? For instance, you probably spend most of your day working, but do you really love what you do? Do you feel a sense of purpose and fulfillment in what you're doing? Or does that sound like a dream worthy of the Wizard of Oz? Well, like the Wizard, you can find a way to get a (bigger) heart and find more courage. And you can even create a new brain—by changing the way you think.

Realizing Long-Term Goals

If you feel hopeless about changing your life, you continue to create a hopeless situation. If you decide to look at life differently and try something new, you're well on your way to making great changes.

The following exercise may help you access some of your deepest hopes and dreams for your future. The first question—"If you did not have to worry about making money, what would you spend your time doing?"—usually stops people in their tracks. I realize that's a big "If."

I have consistently observed that when I ask people what work they want to do, they usually respond with some variation of the theme, "I'd love to do _____, but there's no money in it." The subject usually ends right there, and they continue on disliking their jobs, regretting their lives, and dispassionately doing what they've always done until they retire.

Mixed Messages

Don't throw the baby out with the bath water when it comes to making changes. Take a little time to consider what you may be taking for granted. For example, you may not like your position at your current job, but that doesn't necessarily mean you have to leave there. Try looking around at other alternatives in the company. You may be able to train for a type of work you like better—and keep your perks and benefits too!

What if it didn't have to be that way? Remember the saying: "If you always do what you've always done, you'll always get what you've always gotten." Your intuition doesn't necessarily demand that you make a huge change in your life. Instead, it may suggest, through gentle nudging, that you pay attention to its wisdom and begin to take small steps toward creating a life you love.

I could give you example after example of clients, friends, and students who have taken the small steps that their intuitions suggested to them. Typically, they went from jobs they hated to careers and lives that were fun, meaningful, financially successful, and all-around rewarding. But I won't tell you that this happens overnight.

Intuition Hotline

When you examine your own thinking, don't let your ego get too involved. After all, would you rather be right (and stuck) or would you rather be happy (after facing some possibly painful changes)?

For more insight on the topic of careers, ask your intuition to lead you to the appropriate resources. You can start with the book *Do What You Love, the Money Will Follow* by Marsha Sinetar (Paulist Press, 1989). It's a terrific resource when you are struggling with the concept of finding your passion and being paid enough to do it. If you are having trouble figuring out what your true passion in life might be, check out *Doing Work You Love: Discovering Your Purpose and Realizing Your Dreams* by career coach Cheryl Gilman (Contemporary Books, 1997). This insightful book is full of exercises that help you respect your intuitive messages.

For now, here's an exercise to get you thinking about what your life's passion may be, and how you could possibly transform that into your life's work.

Life Purpose Worksheet

1. If I did not have to worry about making money, what would I spend my time doing?

   _____

   _____

2. I enjoy myself most when I am…(gardening, giving parties, decorating, reading, for example).

   _____

   _____

3. I most love to learn about:

   _____

   _____

4. If I had just found out that I have only one year to live, I would want to have these seven experiences before the end of that year:

   _____

   _____

   _____

   _____

   _____

   _____

5. In my free time, I like to...

_____

_____

_____

6. I believe I have the following seven qualities that help create success in my life (examples include: determined, easygoing, aggressive, empathetic):

_____

_____

_____

_____

_____

_____

_____

7. I believe my life purpose or life mission may be...

_____

_____

8. Quickly list ten ways you could make money by doing what you love to do in your free time. Suspend your judgment about whether these ideas are possible or whether you would make enough money.

_____

_____

_____

_____

_____

_____

_____

_____

_____

9. Of the ten items you just listed, pick the two or three that you feel most excited about and list them here:

_____

_____

_____

10. What action steps could you take that would move you closer to doing the two or three favorite things you listed? (For example, you can: Take a course in small business administration, talk to a friend who started a similar business, read more on the subject, go back to school, see a career counselor.)

_____

_____

_____

11. Are you willing to take the steps you just listed? If not, write about what is preventing you from taking these steps.

_____

_____

_____

Feeling afraid to try something new is…nothing new. In fact, it's human nature. Old, familiar habits, as unpleasant as they may be, provide some strange sort of comfort. So whenever your feel an urge to question your internal status quo, listen up! Whatever energy appears from outside your normal pattern of thought and action is probably a wake-up call, or more like a gentle whisper to awaken, that comes from your intuition.

Listening to Your Intuition

An important part of listening to, and learning from, your intuition is understanding how it speaks to you. Your urge to pick up this book and read it is one way that your intuition spoke to you. It said, "Hey, here's a possible path for you to pursue." And now this page is showing you how you can take what you've learned and put it into practice in your life, and specifically your work.

From the ESP Files

Have you ever noticed that when you're late in driving somewhere, traffic seems to be blocked wherever you turn? Here's an experiment to try when you're late: Simply slow down. As you approach each possible turn, your intuition will guide you whether to turn or not. But if you just rush through traffic without thinking, you may follow your routine patterns that actually lead to unnecessary delays.

Following are some more ways that you can learn to tap into information that your intuition makes available to you. By becoming more aware, you can begin to take charge of your life. Here's how to get started:

1. *Listen to what you tell yourself about your life.* Pay attention to your thoughts and beliefs. Do you believe you have a right to be happy? Do you trust yourself to make good decisions for your future? Do you believe that other people wish you well? Do you believe there is a loving universe that will support you in your decisions for change?

   Your thoughts, beliefs, and emotions have a huge impact on what you create around you in your life. If your thoughts tend to be negative or pessimistic, ask yourself, "What's another way of thinking about this?" or "What do I want to create in my life?" When you discover flawed thinking, apply the necessary turnaround in your thoughts.

2. *Practice positive statements and envision success.* Do your beliefs and dominant thoughts express the true expectations you have for your life? Soren Kierkegard said, "Our life always expresses the result of our dominant thoughts." Many successful people confess to me that they spend time daydreaming about their futures. They enjoy seeing positive outcomes.

   As these successful types visualize, they practice what we have come to know as affirmations. They tell themselves positive statements about their lives and their ability to achieve their goals. The power of your mind to imagine success is a key to creating a life you love. You might want to tape up written affirmations around your home or office. Many people find listening to uplifting motivational tapes helpful as they drive to work.

3. *Pay attention to what excites you.* Continue to think about what you would like to create in your life. Pay special attention to the interests in your life that bring you joy or make you feel excited. These are the ways that your intuition brings information to you through your emotions. Simply put: If it feels exciting and enjoyable, take some steps toward it and test it out. If you feel upset or drained by some situation, figure out a way to change it or let it go entirely.

4. *Ask your intuition questions and listen for the answer.* Pay attention to how your intuition communicates with you. Do you typically get answers in words, emotions, images, physical sensations, or simply knowing? Learn to seek out the wisdom of your intuition. Ask it questions throughout the day: "How should I handle this situation?" "Should I take this action or that action?" "Is this the best time for me to move ahead on this project?" These are all questions to which your intuition has a ready answer. Whenever something happens to make you think, "Wow! What a strange coincidence! This is bizarre," consider it a tip from your intuition.

5. *Pray and meditate.* Ask for guidance from your Higher Power. State your intentions and ask for help if you're having difficulties. Spend time each day listening for guidance, meditating, or simply imagining yourself in the flow of Spirit and Divine Wisdom.

6. *Take action.* Take action on at least three things each week that will move you closer to your goals, visions, and dreams. Making any change in your life often feels uncomfortable at first. Small steps count. Move the energy to create new things in your life out into the world. Your intuition will guide you as to what actions to take.

   Following are a few examples for putting thought into action:

   ➤ Call a career counselor and make an appointment to discuss your interests. Work with her to create an action plan to bring your dreams into reality.

   ➤ Talk to someone who made a successful career change about how he did it.

   ➤ Interview someone who has your dream job.

   ➤ Sign up for a class on something that is purely fun, or on a subject you may want to explore for a new career.

   ➤ Make an appointment with a financial planner to evaluate how you could make a career switch and maintain your financial security.

   ➤ Research your interests on the Internet or at the library. Remember: Small steps count. You are building a bridge to create the life you want!

7. *Expect ebbs and flows.* View all obstacles as lessons and challenges (and we mean challenge in the healthiest sense of the word). Obstacles are not indications of failure. Sometimes the biggest challenge is to practice patience and detachment from the outcome you want. When something appears to be an obstacle, do not simply assume you have made a mistake. Everything that shows up in your life is meant to be there: Even an obstacle is a gift.

Life doesn't always go in a straight line, even when you're doing everything "right." Just as nature has seasons, cycles, ebbs, and flows, so does your life. In fact, your life is integrally linked to the ebbs and flows of nature. As you gain greater insight into how intuition affects you, you also see how it interacts with all that surrounds you.

Our next, and final, chapter talks about intuition and its interaction with the larger events of life, the universe, and everything. We'll look at some intuitive messages sent to the world long ago, and what they may mean today, in light of the new millennium. Stay tuned…

The Least You Need to Know

➤ Information, from any source, offers a powerful starting point for creating change.

➤ Although people have better access to information than ever before, they need to know how to use it.

➤ Leaders and individuals alike seek intuition as a way of processing information.

➤ Skeptics insist that we question the source of any information we receive.

➤ Ultimately, you choose which information you accept and how to use it.

Chapter 27

Eye on the 21st Century

In This Chapter

➤ Who controls the future?

➤ Prophecies for the millennium

➤ Opportunities for change

➤ Spreading the vibes

Do you shape the future, or does it shape you? What, or who, is in control? These questions have befuddled even the greatest of philosophers since the beginning of mankind. In recent centuries especially, many great minds have proclaimed that existence is random. No god or divine power exists, and even attempts to gain control remain subject to simple chance.

And yet some of the greatest minds of humankind have agreed upon just the opposite: that some conscious force is aware of everything that happens. And yet they still can't answer the ultimate question: Does this force control all that happens or does it leave the choice to us? The answer is up to each individual. Do you choose free will? These are some of the questions we'll explore in our final chapter.

Our Gaia Mind, Revisited: Do We Shape the Future?

In the 1940s, James Lovelock, an English inventor and atmospheric chemist, proposed the "Gaia Hypothesis." This is the idea, which we first discussed in Chapter 5, that the earth is actually its own entity, an enormous biological system that embodies a single living organism. Lovelock describes it thus: "...the biosphere is a self-regulating entity with the capacity to keep our planet healthy by controlling the chemical and physical environment." According to the principles of evolution, this living organism does whatever is necessary to ensure its own survival.

From the ESP Files

Check out this timeline for understanding how long humans have been part of the planet Earth, which is 4.6 billion years old. To put that on a more conceivable level, let's scale it down to 46 years. In comparison, humans have been around for four hours—and the Industrial Revolution began about a minute ago.

In the big picture of life on Earth, humankind's time and role thus far has been pretty insignificant. Yes, humankind has managed to wipe out countless species of plants and animals, but in doing so has led to our own demise...perhaps. The loss of other species is a warning of things to come: People can heed it, or ignore it. Either way shows a choice. Life goes on—whether it includes humans or not. The question is: If humans are just a part of a larger living organism, do they want to be an annoying toe fungus or a fresh set of brain cells?

Ten years before Lovelock's idea surfaced, a visionary French Jesuit, who was also a paleontologist, biologist, and philosopher, put forth his ideas about humans interacting with the earth. Pierre Teilhard de Chardin (1881–1955) devoted his life to integrating Christian theology with scientific theories of evolution. In the process, he foresaw a convergence of the earth and humankind, which he called the "Omega point."

Teilhard de Chardin proposed that a unity in human consciousness, motivated by the sense of the earth having its own spiritual identity, would lead to a new era of peace. He stated, "The Age of Nations is past. The task before us now, if we would not perish, is to build the Earth." With the earth as the guiding force of the future, humankind will come together with a united concern for preserving and progressing consciousness. Teilhard de Chardin called this new level of consciousness the *noosphere.*

While predicting that a global information network would come into play, at the time of his death Teilhard de Chardin would have had no concept of the Internet or even that computers could even be small enough for practical use. Despite tipping his hat to technology, he insisted, "It is not our heads or our bodies which we must bring together, but our hearts—Humanity is building its composite brain beneath our eyes. May it not be that tomorrow, through the logical and biological deepening of the movement drawing it together, it will find its *heart*, without which the ultimate wholeness of its power of unification can never be achieved?"

While this visionary of the recent century had great hope for the new millennium, many prophets have not been quite so optimistic. In fact, the turning of 2000 offered a focal point to every sort of doomsayer for the past four millennia.

Beyond Words

The **noosphere** has been described as a "planetary thinking network." The word was used by Teilhard de Chardin to suggest a system of consciousness, wherein the earth and humankind evolved a global net of instantaneous awareness and communication.

The Millennium Predictions

If you're like most people, every time you think of the new millennium, you're filled with a sense of dread, however subtle it may be. Just consider the popularity of the TV show *Millennium*, which features psychic seer and detective Frank Black and his clairvoyant visions as he counts down the days until 2000. A recent episode of Millenium involved the computer glitches that may occur—and supposedly disrupt every institution from the Social Security Administration to banks and airlines—when the date rolls over to the year 2000.

But have you ever stopped to ask yourself what causes this near-panic whenever the new millennium comes to mind? What does a millennium change really mean? Basically, it's just watching the first two numbers of the year change on the calendar as the clock strikes midnight on January 1.

Well, that doesn't sound so scary after all. To us, that change sounds hopeful: It's a milestone in bringing all the nations together. It marks the first time in history that the entire world will share the changing of a millennium because the Gregorian calendar was not followed worldwide until after World War I. This time around, technology such as satellite television and the Internet shows that we can all share the changing times in tandem.

But what about all the bad press surrounding the millennium? Writers from a long way back have been spreading the news of negative prophecies. What's their source? And shouldn't you pay them some mind? We say: Yes, pay them some mind. Learn the lessons they offered by acting to create change. Don't just grovel in potential misery.

Earth Changes

So is there any truth to all the bad press? According to weather reports from different points on the globe, there is. And it doesn't take a weatherman to notice recent extremes in your own local weather patterns.

From the ESP Files

On April 23, 1998, millions of people prayed and meditated in an effort to use their collective power to change the world. "The Great Experiment" involved a plan to bring together the minds of people from at least 75 countries around the world to heal the planet. Actually measuring the impact was practically impossible, due to the current flux in the earth's own energy fields. Nevertheless, many participants described feeling a "profound shift"—within the world and within themselves.

Prophets from seemingly every culture have predicted an increase in the earth's changes leading up to and following the year 2000. The classics include earthquakes, volcanic activity, and just generally massive geophysical changes.

Other favorites, although not quite as frequent, include the earth shifting on its axis, chunks of continents dropping into the ocean, and icebergs drifting lose. Sounds like a global version of *Titanic*, just waiting to happen.

It also sounds like recent newspaper headlines. Some of these events certainly seem to be taking place. Global warming has caused icebergs the size of Rhode Island to break off from the Antarctic and set sail. A shortage of rain in some areas is causing severe drought, while an abundance elsewhere leads to flooding. Tornadoes are popping up just about everywhere, and hurricanes are more frequent than ever before.

Is the earth offering a glimpse of changes to come, or taking the first steps on an inevitable journey to doom? The prophets have offered fair warning, and the earth is now confirming: Take these signs as a wake-up call. Don't just roll over and go back to sleep!

The Prophecies

So, if some of the ancient prophecies seem to be coming true, what else do we have to look forward to? Let's start with a general consensus of what various prophets predict will happen. It goes something like this: The earth will undergo drastic changes in its weather patterns due to upsets in various geophysical phenomena. These changing weather patterns will diminish the world's food supply, which will be accompanied by epidemics and famine. The world will undergo an economic collapse and possibly a nuclear war or accident. And then the lucky survivors will get to pick up the pieces and start a brand new beautiful world of peace and cooperation. Sounds pretty wonderful, huh?

Not really? Well, it's certainly sensational. Which is why the media loves to talk about it. If newscasters were in the business of making everybody feel good, they'd probably be out of business. Similarly, prophets tend to be quoted and "kept around" because their messages offer warnings that are scary enough to catch your attention. Interestingly, many prophets from various cultures and locations—many of whom had no way of accessing each other's work—somehow came up with some of the same foresights. Let's look at a few.

Unsolved Mystery

The Great Pyramid of Giza in Egypt is a mystery in an of itself. No one is certain of how the huge structure was built, but scholars claim its numerous chambers are packed full of predictions. These prophecies are thought to contain information for events dating thousands of years before the appearance of Christ and yet they end on September 17, 2001. The reason? Perhaps the Egyptians picked this as the day the world would end.

Some of the most overlooked forward thinkers were the Mayan scholars. Their civilization produced astounding buildings and amazingly accurate calendar systems based on astrology. Their yearly calendar consisted of 365.24 days, which they believed was part of a greater cycle of 5,124.4 years. The current cycle is fated to end on December 21, 2012, when disasters of all sorts will increase. At that time, a new type of reality will transform life on Earth.

Other ancient prophets weren't quite so specific about forecasting their dates. In fact, none of the Biblical writers specifically refer to the year 2000. John, in *The Book of Revelation*, predicted "signs and wonders in the heavens" that can be interpreted as the changes in weather patterns and possibly other cosmic events that may occur. But more specific types of information predicting the future depend on the interpreter.

Many Christians today site certain events as pointing to the last days, including the formation of the nation of Israel. Some literal types associate the Biblical 10-horned beast with the European economic community. This and the coming of a world leader as an anti-Christ are part of the Apocalypse. From a literal perspective, they foresee rebuilding of the temple in Jerusalem as a step toward Armageddon, which includes World War III. This destruction will be followed by Christ's return, Rapture, Judgement Day, and a thousand years of peace on Earth, with Christ as king.

About 450 years ago, Nostradamus presented many predictions that have since rung true. In fact, for him the third millennium was a favorite focal point for declarations of doom. But, in a sense, one needs to be almost as psychic as Nostradamus was in order to interpret them. Since he recorded his foresights in four-line poems, they can be a bit vague.

Yet certain interpreters explain that Nostradamus predicted that a volcanic explosion occurring in the northern Rocky Mountains before the year 2000 will lead to lots of cold weather across the entire country for years to come. Supposedly, he specifies the last decade of the 20th century as the arrival date for the anti-Christ, as well as an apocalyptic war. A popular prophecy for getting specific is: "The year 1999, seventh month, a great king of terror will descend from the skies…" We can hardly wait!

Madame Blavatsy, the 19th-century founder of theosophy, had a more spiritual focus for her prophecies. She theorized that a group of spiritual leaders, who have lived in the Himalayas and guided humanity's evolution throughout time, would come forward and even start a new culture in America. The modern voice of the the osphists is Benjamin Creme in Great Britain. He has successfully predicted the release of Nelson Mandela, the 1988 earthquake in Armenia, and the cease-fire between Iran and Iraq. He now predicts that a world teacher for the new age will soon present himself, and gain immediate acceptance.

From the ESP Files

Ever wonder what "the dawning of the Age of Aquarius" means? (Probably so, if you were born after 1950.) It refers to astrological eras, when the current Age of Pisces, known for materialism and acquisition, gives way to the upcoming Age of Aquarius, known for intuition, peace, and cooperation. This change of eras occurs every 2,000 years (the previous one coincided with the arrival of Christ). Supposedly, more enlightened individuals are focusing on humanity, kindness, truth, and spirituality. In contrast, people who are less evolved are reacting to changes with negative behaviors, which contribute to current levels of chaos and negativity.

The "sleeping prophet," Edgar Cayce, was known as both a healer and a prophet. His Association of Research and Enlightenment was located in Virginia Beach, Virginia, because his followers believe the area is least likely to be affected by the drastic events that Cayce predicted for the years surrounding 2000.

Cayce's predictions include massive seismic disruptions, hurricanes, floods, and other climactic changes. He claimed that sections of New York City, as well as huge chunks of California, would simply drop into the ocean. He also described the planet's axis shifting wildly. Understandably, the world would be sent into a time of crisis and disarray, which would eventually transform into a "new age." During this era, he claimed that telepathy and other forms of psychic communication would become common ways of communicating.

Of course, there are more prophets who we haven't touched on here, but you get the picture. The bad news is: Terrible upheaval seems to be what's in store, according to just about all of these psychic seers. The good news is: A blissful new age will ensue. And there's more good news, too: Predictions aren't set in stone.

Exploring prophecies and practicing divination can easily become a favorite pastime. It's certainly fun to speculate, but beware of obsessing. For one thing, predictions don't have to come true if you take action. Rather than fearing what doom may come, make a plan for where to start making changes today. That's a much more productive use of your time and energy.

Mixed Messages

Remember how we talked about the vibrations that emanate from your thoughts and actions? If you think positive thoughts about the future, positive thoughts—and actions—will follow. If you focus on fear, you attract those situations to yourself. Think about what frightens you, and then take steps to remedy it.

Nurturing Psychic Ability

We recommend covering the odds. Whether drastic changes come or whether we can avoid them, the necessary survival skills are probably the same: flexibility, self-awareness, cooperation, and—the thing that aids and enhances all of these other abilities—intuition.

Certainly, these skills are necessary to creating the enormous social and personal changes that would forestall an environmental and economic disaster. And if such a terrible fate were to ensue, they could be equally important as survival mechanisms.

Imagine a world where suddenly no one knew what to do. Everybody was in the same boat, trying to discover lost knowledge, learn new methods for doing things, test their own limits, and understand each other well enough to work together efficiently. That could be the predicament some people face in the new millennium. But it's also the situation that everyone faces now.

From the ESP Files

Dr. Elaine de Beauport, the educator who founded the Mead School in 1969, recently published in her book *The Three Faces of Mind* (Quest Books, 1997) her theory that the mind has 10 types of intelligence. One of these types is—not surprisingly—intuitive intelligence. She even offers courses for both children and adults on how to incorporate this, and other right brain types of intelligence, into the educational process, as well as everyday life. This educational trend is likely to increase into the 21st century.

In any context, having knowledge about the self leads to a greater sense and understanding of the world. In any context, health and survival—whether planet's or your own—may depend on how that knowledge is put to use. Knowledge, whether it comes from a source within or without, is a great gift and responsibility. And it's available to you whenever you want—just ask.

Second Sight: A New You

We seem to have undergone a long journey, and ended up back where we started. So, we'll repeat what we said at the start: A new way of seeing begins with you. Seeing that your intuition exists must come from within yourself. Discovering how it speaks also comes from within. Understanding how it interacts with the worlds outside your physical self also comes from within. To gain greater insights, expand your internal viewpoint.

Try a new perspective for seeing yourself: Imagine yourself as a god sent to Earth in human form. If this were the case, you would need to change your focus. Rather than focusing on how powerless you feel and how you need to strive to gain more power and control, you would need to remind yourself constantly of how powerful you are. Consider yourself so powerful that you need to execute every action and thought with tremendous care and caution. Even the slightest movement or word could move out in all directions, affecting everything around you and even beyond you.

This empowered way of thinking certainly seems foreign to most people, but not to everyone. Certain spiritual leaders, such as the Dalai Lama, approach every aspect of their lives in this way. Where they direct their energy and thoughts has a profound effect and creates a lingering reverberation. They are constantly aware of their responsibility for careful and thoughtful action. And this awareness is what sets them apart.

Most people do not view themselves in this way, whether due to insecurity or humility. And yet this awareness of all being's interconnection with the divine, and the responsibility to share this fact, is what makes one divine. The more that one is aware of one's divine interconnectedness, the closer one comes to the divine.

One quality that we attribute to an all-powerful god is one that spiritual people tend to have: insight without a known source. To the extreme, this ability is called omniscience: all-knowing. Spiritual leaders often have several types of intuitive ability, which enable them to access information through a combination of clairsentience, clairvoyance, clairaudience, and empathy.

It's All About Compassion and Empathy

In his famous letter to the Corinthians, Paul said, "Now I will show you the way which surpasses all the others. If I speak with human tongues and angelic as well, but do not have love, I am a noisy gong, a clanging cymbal. If I have the gift of prophecy and, with full knowledge, comprehend all mysteries, if I have faith enough to move mountains, but have not love, I am nothing."

Intuition Hotline

If you're seeking some personal, hands-on instruction, you may have difficulty finding a personal teacher. However, most people who have published a book about psychic ability or intuition also teach it in workshops and conferences across the country. I have a monthly e-mail Intuition Newsletter that has lots of hot tips for developing your intuition as well as a seminar schedule. You can subscribe by e-mailing me at *Lynn@lynnrobinson.com* and putting "newsletter" in the subject line. Also, *Intuition Magazine*, as well as universities or centers for higher learning, are good sources for finding courses that cover this material.

Popular clichés, often truer than one realizes, say that love makes the world go round. Deepak Chopra, mind-body doctor and spiritual author, compares love to the forces that create the laws of nature. The Dalai Lama, who is considered the incarnation of the Buddha of Love, says that love is the natural state of the universe, which is why negative news stands out: Bad news goes against the norm.

What would be the purpose of all that happens, of eons of existence, of ages of awareness, if its overriding essence were negative? The ongoing urge to connect with others, to understand and empathize with them, continues to run through all that exists. To become more at one with this force, you can cultivate compassion and empathy.

As you move into the 21st century, the universe has many ways to help you learn the lessons presented in the classroom called "Earth." Your task as a spiritual being is no small challenge, and yet it's profoundly simple. Learn how to love and forgive. Open yourself to experiencing peace and sharing it with others. Offer service. Express compassion. And enjoy yourself!

The Least You Need to Know

➤ Humans share an integral interconnection with the earth.

➤ Prophecies focus on earth-shattering events occurring around the year 2000.

➤ Prophecies predict an era of peace for the next thousand years.

➤ Expressing love toward the earth and others extends ever outward as a positive force.

Glossary

affirmations   Statements that create a reality or truth through frequent repetition.

age regression   An application of hypnosis whereby the client regresses to a younger age (with the guidance of a hypnotherapist trained in this technique), often in order to explore unresolved emotional issues.

Akashic records   A "cosmic memory bank" containing information about everything that has occurred in the universe, including details of every soul and every life ever lived.

Alien abductions   A kidnapping of a human individual by an alien being.

aliens   Nonterrestrial beings, or nonhumans from another planet or star.

apparition   The closest thing to what people usually call a "ghost": a spirit with an image that can be seen and can interact with its observer.

archetypes   Common themes that arise from the collective unconscious and repeatedly appear as symbols in myths, symbol systems, and dreams.

astral body   A "second self" or energy body that consists of a subtle field of light that encases the physical body. It is thought that the astral body can separate from the physical body during sleep, which results in flying dreams.

astral projection   An awareness that the conscious mind has separated from the physical body, usually during a sleeplike state. It enables one to float above oneself and view one's own physical body.

astral travel   A step beyond astral projection that enables a "dreamer" to travel to a different locale while being conscious that he is not in his physical body.

astrology   A form of divination that studies the positions of heavenly bodies to determine their influence on human affairs.

aura   The field of electromagnetic energies that permeate and surround every living being. The word comes from the Greek "avra," which means breeze.

automatic writing   A form of creative expression that involves writing words. It occurs during an altered state of consciousness, when the rational mind is shut off and the intuitive mind takes a more active role.

bilocation   A phenomenon that occurs when a living person is witnessed at a second location, while continuing to function normally in her physical body at her original location.

brainwaves   Currents of electrical impulses that are constantly produced and given off by the brain.

chakras   Centers of energy that run throughout the body. The seven major chakras are situated between the base of the spinal column and the top of the head. In Western medicine, they are referred to as the nerve plexus.

channeler   A person who communicates with spirits who do not currently inhabit bodies. Sometimes called a medium.

channeling   The process of communicating with spirits who do not currently inhabit bodies.

chanting   The repetitive singing of a short simple melody or even a few monotonous notes. This repetition of the same words or sounds aids in attaining a deeper spiritual state.

chi   According to ancient Chinese medicine, the universal energy that flows through the body's vital organs, bones, bloodstream, and other parts. The Japanese call it ki.

clairaudience   The ability to hear sounds that aren't accessible to the physical ear.

clairsentience   The ability to perceive information out of the range of ordinary perception. Translated as "clear thinking" or "clear knowing."

clairvoyance   The ability to perceive things that cannot be seen with the physical eye. French for "clear seeing," it also refers to keen perception and insight.

coincidence   A striking occurrence of two or more events at the same time that seems to happen by mere chance.

collective unconscious   A level of the mind believed by Carl Jung to be inherited and to contain a reservoir of ideas, symbols, and archetypes that form the world's myths and belief systems.

contemplation   Deep thought or reflection as a type of meditation or prayer.

creative visualization   The idea that mentally creating a visual image promotes a desired outcome. This image is often called to mind during meditation or deep relaxation.

déjà vu   French for "already seen," an event that feels so familiar that it seems you have experienced it before.

discernment   In the telepathic sense, refers to the ability to discriminate between personal desires, such as wishful thinking, and intuitive information.

distant healing   The idea that healing can occur through directed thoughts, such as prayer, even when the patient is not present. Distant healing can be considered a form of telepathy.

divination   The practice of foretelling future events through supernatural means, prophecy, or intuition.

dowsing   A traditional method of detecting underground sources of water and other material by using divining rods.

ectoplasm   An emanation, through a channeler, of physical material from the spirit realm.

enteric nervous system   A primitive brain located in the layers of tissue lining a person's esophagus, stomach, small intestine, and colon. It connects directly through a vein to the main brain (in the head).

essential oils   Oils obtained from plants that retain the aroma and other characteristic properties of the plant. Their scents are used as perfumes, flavorings, and medicines.

exorcism   The act of expelling an unwanted spirit through religious or solemn ceremonies.

extrasensory perception (ESP)   Perception of thoughts, situations, or issues without using one of the five "ordinary" senses.

feng shui   An ancient Chinese philosophy for creating harmonious environments.

field consciousness   The idea that awareness exists on a plane that is interconnected and shared by all minds. This suggests that mental awareness comes from a source beyond the physical cells contained inside each individual's brain.

focus   A central point of attention that aids in concentration.

Gaia hypothesis   The idea that the earth is actually its own entity, an enormous biological system that embodies a single living organism.

ganzfeld   German for "whole field," refers to opening the inner mind by shutting out external data, such as light and sound. When these distractions are eliminated, the mind is more susceptible to picking up psychic signals.

373

ghost   A word used to describe various phenomena, the most common of which is the soul of a disembodied spirit, imagined to be wandering among the living. Actually, some phenomena that people calls "ghosts" do not involve a soul or spirit at all.

guardian angels   Loving spiritual beings who help guide you through life. In reincarnation theory, they prepare and help you through your current incarnation.

guided imagery   Directed daydreaming or meditation that uses the imagination in a focused, directed way to achieve goals and heal the mind and body.

haunting   A repeated perception of an image, whether a sight, sound, or sense of movement, of a past event. Experts suggest that it doesn't involve a spirit but an "energy imprint."

holotropic breathwork   A method of self-exploration and healing that combines consciousness research, psychology, Eastern spirituality, and mystical traditions. Originated by psychiatrist Stanislov Grof and transpersonal trainer Christina Grof.

hunch   An unexplained sense of a future event or outcome.

hypnosis   An altered mental state characterized by intense focus that results in heightened susceptibility to suggestion.

hypnotherapist   A hypnotist trained to help people explore deeply buried sources of their problems in order to understand and change their life patterns.

hypnotist   A trained expert who directs and leads a client through a hypnotic trance.

I Ching   An ancient Chinese book of divination based on creating pairs of eight basic symbols and their interpretations.

inference   The process of deriving logical conclusions from premises assumed to be true.

karma   The law of cause and effect. The idea is that whatever a person does affects the universe and also comes back to him eventually.

Kirlian photography   A type of photography, using a system of metal plates and electrodes, that shows a bright glowing energy field that emanates from living things.

levitation   A phenomenon whereby objects, people, and animals lift into the air without any physical means of support.

lucid dreaming   An awareness that occurs during dreaming wherein the dreamer consciously realizes she is dreaming and is able to continue. Novices may not be able to direct the dream, but they can eventually learn the skill of controlling the course of a dream.

mandala   A schematic drawing of the cosmos, characterized by a concentric arrangement of geometric shapes, each one showing an image or attribute of a deity. Sanskrit for "circle," it alludes to "the circle of life" on a cosmic scale.

mantra   A word or formula that is recited or sung repeatedly. The sound is intended to resonate in the body and evoke certain energies during meditation.

materialization   Making an object appear from seemingly nowhere.

medium   Someone who serves as an instrument though which another personality can manifest itself. Also called a channeler.

meliomancy   A form of fortune-telling based on reading moles.

meridians   According to ancient Chinese medicine, pathways that carry chi (the body's vital life force) throughout the body. Each of the 14 major meridians passes through many parts of the body.

meta-analysis   The analysis of analyses. This process combines the results of similar experiments performed by various researchers to get an overview of their outcomes.

metaphysics   A branch of philosophy that focuses on the basic philosophical principles of being and meaning.

metoscopy   A form of fortune-telling based on analyzing lines on the forehead.

mudra   Subtle hand gestures used during meditation to enhance focus on specific ideals or concepts. They are traditionally used in India's classical dances to represent specific feelings or concepts.

nadis   Passageways, thought to work like vibrating energy currents, for the psychospiritual energy called prana.

near-death experience (NDE)   An occurrence wherein a person who is considered dead experiences a vivid awareness of separating from his body. He eventually revives, and reveals his experiences. The traits of near-death experiences appear similar for all those who report them.

neocortex   The uppermost region of the brain, responsible for rational and higher thought.

nonlocal mind   In psi circles, refers to accessing a vast, eternal mind that transcends space and time. It suggests that individuals' minds are infinite and united in one whole.

nonlocal reality   The concept that events that are distant can, nevertheless, have a local effect.

nonlocality   The idea that a thing or a thought is not located in a specific region of space and time. This view suggests that the mind is not limited to given points in space or time, such as the body or the present moment.

noosphere   A "planetary thinking network." The word was used by Teilhard de Chardin to suggest a system of consciousness, wherein the earth and humankind evolved a global net of instantaneous awareness and communication.

Ouija board   A board with letters, numbers, and words printed on it that is paired with a planchette, a plate-like device designed to glide easily along the board's surface. People place their fingertips on the planchette as it moves across the board to spell out answers (supposedly from spirits) to specific questions.

out-of-body-experience (OBE)   An unusual and brief occasion when a person's consciousness seems to depart from her body, allowing her to observe the world from a point of view that transcends the physical body and bypasses the physical senses.

paganism   Loosely defined as any religion outside of the Judaic, Christian, or Muslim traditions. It typically involves *polytheism*, belief in many gods.

paranormal   Beyond the range of scientifically known phenomena. This implies that although causes of paranormal phenomena are not currently known by scientists, they someday may be.

parapsychology   The branch of psychology that studies psychic experiences. This refers to the types of behavior that allow us to perceive information beyond the boundaries of space, time, and our ordinary senses.

past-life regression therapy   Therapy that explores emotional and physical feelings in order to recognize past life problems that are deeply connected to present life issues.

pathological   A deviation from a healthy, normal mental state.

pendulum   An object suspended from a fixed point that moves in response to a natural force. In psychic terms, it responds to a mental inquiry.

phobia   A persistent, irrational fear.

physical medium   A channeler who can make ectoplasm materialize.

poltergeist   A form of PK (psychokinesis) that is generated unconsciously by a person with intense, but unacknowledged, emotions. Although it means "noisy ghost" in German, it doesn't involve a ghost at all.

prana   According to the Indian yogic tradition, a form of energy that animates all physical matter, including the human body.

prayer   A solemn and humble intention to communicate, in word or thought, with a divine force.

precognition   Foreknowledge or awareness of a future event before it occurs.

premonition   A precognitive sense of danger or forewarning of an unfortunate future event.

presentiment   A sensing of a future feeling.

projection   A psychological term that refers to attributing personal emotions or traits to someone else; this is usually done in order to avoid facing one's own feelings or traits.

prophecy   Foreknowledge that comes in the form of a vision or dream. Traditionally, its source is believed to be divine revelation.

prophetic dreams   Dreams that pertain to sensing or predicting the future.

psi   A letter of the Greek alphabet, and the first letter of the Greek word *psyche,* which literally means "breath" in Greek and refers to the human soul. In scientific study, it refers to the force that causes psychic phenomena.

psychic attack   An occasion when someone willfully and consciously directs negative energy toward another person. This energy usually does not come from someone who has developed psychic skills.

psychoanalysis   A systematic approach for investigating the unconscious as a means of mental and emotional healing.

psychokinesis (PK)   The ability to use the mind to move objects without touching them.

psychometry   The ability to touch an object and thereby tap into the past of it and its owner. This may occur when a person picks up the vibrations that accompany an object's past.

psychosomatic   A physical condition that is caused or influenced by the patient's emotional state.

reflexology   A form of hands-on healing based on the principal that every part of the body directly communicates with a reference point on the foot, hand, and ear. Massaging these points helps the corresponding body part to heal by improving circulation, eliminating toxins, and reducing stress.

reiki   A method of hands-on healing, wherein a trained practitioner places her hands, using specific positions, on six points of the body. Doing this enables vital life energy to flow freely throughout the body.

reincarnation   The belief that after death a person is reborn into another lifetime.

REM sleep   Rapid eye movement is a phase of sleep when the eyelids appear to twitch constantly. It is closely linked to vivid dreams.

remote perception   Similar to remote viewing, but refers to any type of sensory data (such as sound) perceived from a distance.

remote viewing   Using the mind to see a person, place, or object that's located some distance away and beyond the physical range of sight. This ability also enables one to witness events at a remote site without using the known senses.

retrocognition   A form of ESP wherein one has an intuitive knowledge of past events without having obtained information through the five physical senses.

schizophrenia   A mental disease marked by withdrawn, bizarre, and delusional behavior.

scrying   The practice of divination that induces clairvoyance when a reader stares into a reflective surface while deeply concentrating.

séance   A meeting, session, or sitting in which a channeler attempts to communicate with the spirits of the dead.

second sight   The ability to see future events. It can refer to a wide range of abilities, including being extremely wise, prophesying, or divining through the use of devices such as crystal balls.

skeptic   A person who questions the validity of something purporting to be factual and tends to maintain a doubting attitude.

spiritual regeneration   A spiritual rebirth or religious conversion. It suggests that a person who experiences this is made over, usually in a new and improved condition.

spontaneous drawing   A form of creative expression that produces visual images or pictures. It occurs during an altered state of consciousness, when the rational mind is shut off and the intuitive mind takes a more active role.

targeting   A technique, used during astral travel, for shifting consciousness by focusing on a person or place in ordinary reality in order to visit that person or place.

tarot   A special deck of 78 cards that are used as an approach to predicting the future.

telepathy   The communication of thoughts and/or feelings between minds, without the use of the ordinary senses.

thoughtography   A type of psychic photography wherein an individual with this particular skill projects an image in her mind onto a negative, as though the camera reads the person's mind.

trance   A half-conscious state, seemingly between waking and sleeping, which involves complete mental absorption.

UFO   An unidentified flying object that a witness cannot identify.

wishful thinking   An expression of personal inner desires that may distort the perception of reality in order to make the desires seem like external truth.

Suggested Reading

There's a world of wisdom right at your fingertips. All you have to do is check it out—at the library or your nearest bookseller. Here is just a small sampling of the tremendous resources that are available to you.

Abadie, M. J. *Your Psychic Potential*. Holbrook, Massachusetts: Adams Media Corporation, 1995.

Ban Breathnach, Sarah. *Simple Abundance: A Daybook of Comfort and Joy*. New York: Warner Books, 1995.

Brennan, Barbara. *Hands of Light:* A Guide to Healing Through the Human Energy Field. New York: Bantam, 1987.

Cappon, Daniel, Ph.D. *Intuition and Management*. Glenview, IL: Quorum Books, 1994.

Chopra, Deepak. *The Way of the Wizard: Twenty Spiritual Lessons for Creating the Life You Want*. New York: Harmony Books, 1995.

Choquette, Sonia. *The Psychic Pathway: A Workbook for Reawakening the Voice of Your Soul*. New York: Crown, 1994.

Connolly, Eileen, Ph.D. *Developing Your Psychic Powers*. North Hollywood, California: Newcastle Publishing, 1990.

Day, Laura. *Practical Intuition: How to Harness the Power of Your Instinct and Make it Work for You*. New York: Villard, 1996.

de Beauport, Elaine, Ph.D. *The Three Faces of Mind*. Wheaton, Illinois: Quest Books, 1997.

Gerwick-Brodeur, Madeline and Lisa Lenard. *The Complete Idiot's Guide to Astrology*. New York: Alpha Books, 1997.

Delaney, Gayle, Ph.D. *Breakthrough Dreaming: How to Tap the Power of Your 24-Hour Mind*. New York: Bantam Books, 1991.

Dossey, Larry, M.D. *Healing Words: The Power of Prayer and the Practice of Medicine*. San Francisco: HarperSanFrancisco, 1993.

Emery, Marcia, Ph.D. *Intuition Workbook: An Expert's Guide to Unlocking the Wisdom of Your Subconscious Mind*. Englewood Cliffs, New Jersey: Prentice Hall, 1994.

Gilman, Cheryl. *Doing Work You Love: Discovering Your Purpose and Realizing Your Dreams*. Chicago: Contemporary Books, 1997.

Hamilton-Parker, Craig. *The Psychic Workbook*. London: Vermilion, 1995.

Harwig, Kathryn J. *The Millennium Effect*. Saint Paul, Minnesota: Spring Press, 1996.

Hoffman, Enid. *Develop Your Psychic Skills*. Atglen, Pennsylvania: Whitford Press, 1981.

Hynek, J. Allen, Ph.D. *The UFO Experience*. Chicago: H. Regnery, 1972.

Jeffers, Susan. *Feel the Fear and Do It Anyway*. New York: Fawcett, 1993.

Klimo, Jon. *Channeling: Investigations on Receiving Information from Paranormal Sources*. Berkeley, California: North Atlantic Books, 1998.

LaBerge, Stephen, Ph.D. *Lucid Dreaming: The Power of Being Awake and Aware in Your Dreams*. New York: Jeremy P. Tarcher, 1985.

Lawson, David. *Your Psychic Potential*. London: Thorsons, 1997.

Maisel, Eric. *Fearless Creating*. New York: Putnam, 1995.

Monroe, Robert. *Far Journeys*. New York: Doubleday Dolphin, 1987.

_____. *Journeys Out of the Body*. New York: Anchor, 1977.

Moody, Raymond Jr., M.D. *Life After Life*. New York: Bantam Books, 1975.

Morehouse, David. *Psychic Warrior: Inside the CIA's Stargate Program*. New York: St. Martin's Press, 1996.

Moss, Robert. *Dreamgates: An Explorer's Guide to the World of Soul, Imagination, and Life Beyond Death*. New York: Three Rivers Press, 1998.

Naparstek, Belleruth. *Staying Well with Guided Imagery*. New York: Warner, 1994.

_____. *Your Sixth Sense: Activating Your Psychic Potential*. San Francisco: HarperSanFrancisco, 1997.

Pliskin, Marci, CSW, ACSU. *The Complete Idiot's Guide to Interpreting Your Dreams*. New York: Alpha Books, 1998.

Radin, Dean, Ph.D. *The Conscious Universe: The Scientific Truth of Psychic Phenomena*. San Francisco: HarperSanFrancisco, 1997.

Rand, William. *Reiki, The Healing Touch*. Southfield, Michigan: Vision Publications, 1992.

Richards, Douglas G., Ph.D. *The Psychic Quest: Understanding Your Psychic Potential*. New York: Signet Visions, 1998.

Roman, Sanaya. *Opening to Channel*. Tiburon, California: H.J. Kramer, 1987.

Rosanoff, Nancy. *Intuition Workout: A Practical Guide to Discovering and Developing Your Inner Knowing*. Boulder Creek, California: Aslan Publishing, 1991.

Schulz, Mona Lisa, M.D., Ph.D. *Awakening Intuition: Using Your Mind-Body Network for Insight and Healing*. New York: Harmony Books, 1998.

Sinetar, Marsha. *Developing a 21st-Century Mind*. New York: Ballantine, 1991.

_____. *Do What You Love, the Money Will Follow*. New York: Dell, 1989.

Stevenson, Ian, Ph.D. *Telepathic Impressions*. Charlottseville: University Press of Virginia, 1978.

Straub, Gail and David Gershon. *Empowerment: The Art of Creating Your Life As You Want It*. Berkeley, California: Ten Speed Press, 1991.

Targ, Russell and Jane Katra, Ph.D. *Miracles of Mind: Exploring Nonlocal Consciousness and Spiritual Healing*. Novato, California: New World Library, 1998.

Tognetti, Arlene and Lisa Lenard. *The Complete Idiot's Guide to Tarot and Fortune-Telling*. New York: Alpha Books, 1999.

Walsch, Neale Donald. *Conversations with God: An Uncommon Dialogue, Book 1*. New York: Putnam, 1995.

Wise, Anna. *The High-Performance Mind*. New York: Tarcher, 1995.

Resources for Increasing Insight

Getting in touch with your intuition is just a first step along a lifelong path of discovery. We encourage you to continue seeking new growth within this huge wide world of intuitive insight. Listed here are just a handful of resources to help you along. Let your intuition lead the way.

Organizations

American Society for Psychical Research
5 West 73rd Street
New York, NY 10023
(212) 799-5050
Web site: **http://www.aspr.com**

This membership organization publishes a journal and a newsletter. It also has an extensive library. The ASPR publishes a list of courses in parapsychology offered at colleges and universities around the world.

Association for Research and Enlightenment (A.R.E.)
P.O. Box 595
Virginia Beach, VA 23451-0595
(800) 333-4499 or (757) 428-3588
Web site: **http://www.are-cayce.com**
E-mail: *are@are-cayce.com*

This membership organization has the mission of promoting the study, application, and dissemination of the information in the psychic readings of Edgar Cayce. The A.R.E. publishes books and a magazine, and has a library of more than 60,000 volumes on parapsychology, spirituality, and related topics. It holds workshops and conferences, and sponsors the "A Search for God" study groups.

Association for the Study of Dreams
P.O. Box 1600
Vienna, VA 22183
(703) 242-0062
Web site: **http://www.ASDreams.org**
E-mail: *ASDreams@aol.com*

This membership organization publishes the newsletter *Dream Time*. It also holds conferences.

Association for Transpersonal Psychology
P.O. Box 3049
Stanford, CA 94305
(650) 327-2066
Web site: **http://www.igc.apc.org**
E-mail: *atp@igc.apc.org*

This membership organization publishes *The Journal of Transpersonal Psychology*. It also publishes a list of transpersonal schools and programs and holds conferences.

Atlantic University
Building 3300, Suite 100
397 Little Neck Road
Virginia Beach, VA 23452
(800) 428-1512
Web site: **http://www.atlanticuniv.edu**
E-mail: *info@atlanticuniv.edu*

Atlantic University was founded by the A.R.E. and offers a master's degree program in transpersonal studies. They have a degree concentration in Intuitive Studies. Courses can be taken by correspondence as well as in residence.

Barbara Brennan School of Healing
P.O. Box 2005
East Hampton, NY 11937
(516) 329-0951
Web site: **http://www.barbarabrennan.com**

Barbara Brennan is a leading expert on working with auras in the area of energy healing. Her school offers training programs for developing these healing techniques.

Exceptional Human Experience Network
Rhea White
414 Rockledge Road
New Bern, NC 28562
(919) 636-8734
Web site: **http://www.ehe.org**
E-mail: *ehen@ix.gen.com*

This organization publishes a journal of people's stories of their "exceptional" experiences, including psychic and mystical experiences.

Greenwich University
103 Kapiolani Street
Hilo, HI 96720
(808) 935-9934
E-mail: *grnichu@aloha.net*

This institute of learning offers an M.S. or Ph.D. in Integrated Health Care and Science of Intuition and Energy Medicine.

Institute for Parapsychology (Rhine Research Center)
402 North Buchanan Boulevard
Durham, NC 27701-1728
(919) 688-8241
Web site: **http://www.rhine.org**

This is the organization founded by J.B. and Louisa Rhine. It conducts laboratory and field research. It also hosts programs and publishes the *Journal of Parapsychology*. Of special interest is its annual Summer Study Program in parapsychology.

Institute of Noetic Sciences
475 Gate Five Road, Suite 300
Sausalito, CA 94965
(415) 331-5650
Web site: **www.noetic.org**

This membership organization sponsors research, conferences, and publications on psychic and transpersonal themes.

Intuition Network Study Groups
c/o INREACHING
1502 Tenth Street
Berkeley, CA 94710
(510) 526-5510
Web site: **http://www.intuition.org**
E-mail: *Inreaching@aol.com*

Join or create a local intuition study group sponsored by the Intuition Network. Training materials, audio- and videotapes, and study guides are available.

385

Mikel Institute and Center
Sunset Ridge Business Park
5821 Cedar Lake Road
St. Louis Park, MN 55416
(612) 546-7902

This organization offers a four-year course entitled The Program for Intuitive Living.

The National Guild of Hypnotists, Inc.
P.O. Box 308
Merrimack, NH 03054
(888) 617-6179
Web site: **http://www.ngh.net**

This organization provides seminars, workshops, and an annual convention, in addition to training for members and other professionals.

Parapsychology Foundation
228 East 71st Street
New York, NY 10021
(212) 628-1550
Web site: **http://www.parapsychology.org**

This organization, founded by Eileen Garret, maintains a speaker's bureau and offers grants for research and study in parapsychology. It has an excellent library.

Spiritual Emergence Network
930 Mission Street #7
Santa Cruz, CA 95060
(415)648-2610
sen@cruzio.com
Web site: **http://elfi.com/sen**

This organization was founded to help people who may be experiencing problems during the process of opening up psychically.

Touching Spirit Center
Elizabeth Stratton
P.O. Box 240
Litchfield, CT 06759
(860) 567-0600
Web site: **http://www.touchingspirit.org**

This center offers training in intuitive development and healing.

Intuition On-Line

Consciousness Research Laboratory
www.PsiResearch.org

This popular and informative Web site has several parapsychology experiments. It is home of the Parapsychology FAQ, an authoritative "frequently asked questions" list created by Dr. Dean Radin with the assistance of leading scientists in the field.

HOPE (The Hartford Office of Paranormal Experience)
http://www.haunt.net

This organization has a lot of info on how they deal with hauntings and possessions, including case histories, how to investigate a possible occurrence, and more.

Intuition Network
http://www.intuition.org

The purpose of Intuition Network is to help create a world in which people feel encouraged to cultivate and use their inner intuitive resources. The site contains transcripts of the *Thinking Allowed* television series. It also provides lists of intuition-related publications, study groups, and e-mail newsgroups.

Intuition Newsletter
Lynn@lynnrobinson.com

Sign up for Lynn Robinson's e-mail Intuition Newsletter. It offers tips on how to use your intuition, resources for further study, book reviews, and Lynn's national seminar schedule. To subscribe, send an e-mail with "newsletter" in the subject line.

Spirit Web
http://www.spiritweb.org

This site features an amazing assortment of articles on psychic topics and a search engine on paranormal occurrences.

UFO Mind
http://www.ufomind.com

One of the world's largest and best organized paranormal Web sites.

All of the following Web sites have a wealth of information on the various topics we covered in this book:

http://www.dreamgate.com

http://www.dreamtree.com

http://www.newage.com

http://www.spiritonline.org

Practical Periodicals

Common Boundary
5272 River Road, Suite 650
Bethesda, MD 20816
(301) 652-9495

This magazine is published through the organization called Common Boundary (referring to the common boundary of psychotherapy, creativity, and spirituality). It hosts annual conferences and also publishes a directory of transpersonal education programs throughout the country.

Intuition Magazine
275 Brannan Street
San Francisco, CA 94107
(415) 538-8171
Web site: **http://www.intuitionmagazine.com**
E-mail: *IntuitMag@aol.com*

This magazine is a fount of information on all things intuitive. It stays abreast of the leading edge in the field, and keeps readers informed of various organizations and upcoming events.

New Age Journal
P.O. Box 1949
Marion, OH 43305
(740) 375-2332

This magazine contains lots of terrific articles about mind-body healing, religion, ecological issues, activism, spiritual matters, music and book reviews, and nutrition.

Index

F

G

physical blocks, 170-171
physical feelings, analyzing, 168-170
receiving information, 71
clairaudience, 73-74
clairsentience, 74-75
clairvoyance, 72-73
exercises, 76-82
physical knowing, 75-76
tastes and smells, 76
recognizing, 10
sixth sense, 224-228
personal growth, 228
shaping the future,
225-226
values and beliefs,
226-228
staying in touch with,
235-236
taking your time, 128-130
affirmations, 129
creative visualization,
129
slowing down your
pace, 130
technology (World Wide
Web), 348-349
using the information
(intuitive thinking), 222
Intuition Magazine, 388
Intuition Network Web
site, 387
Intuition Network Study
Group Web site, 385
Intuition Newsletter Web
site, 387
intuitive messages exercise,
168-170

J

James, William, 129, 272
Jewish mysticism (Kabbalah),
21-22
Zohar, 22
Joan of Arc, 24
Journal of Parapsychology, 217

journals
dream, 205-206
interpretation, 188-190
exercise, 188-189
measuring your psychic
ability, 96-97
Jung, Carl, 58-59, 196

K

Kabbalah (Jewish mysticism),
21-22
Zohar, 22
Kamamaya Kosha, 280
karma, 249-252
reincarnation, 250-251,
256-258
déjà vu, 258
guidance from past
lives, 257
learning from past lives,
258-263
preparing for your
next life, 251-252
recalling past lives,
252-256
vibrations, 256-257
Kirlian, Semyon, 150
Kiyota, Masuaki, 297
Koestler Parapsychology
Unit, 49
Koshas (yogic Sheaths of
Existence), 279-280
Kulagina, Nina, 296
Kunz, Dora, 154

L

Layne, Al, 28
learning
channeling, 268-271
exercise, 269-270
from intuition, 10
LeBerge, Stephen, 205
Let Your Intuition Decide
exercise, 80-82

levitation, 295-296
Liester, Mitchell B., 66
life forces
auras, 144-149
colors, 146-147
drawing, 148-149
floaters and
after-images, 145
photographs, 150
reading, 147-148
seeing, 146
chi (Chinese medicine),
135
compassion and empathy,
155-156
healing touch, 149-155
aura photographs, 150
hands, 150-151
Reiki, 152-154
therapeutic touch,
154-155
mind-body connections,
135
natural forces, 141
prana (Indian medicine),
136-137
chakras (current), 137
nadis (pathways), 136
spiritual healing, 143-144
life purpose, 352-359
following your own
intuition, 356-359
long-term goals, 353-356
exercise, 354-356
light-trance channeling, 267
literal dreams, 198
logical thinking versus
intuitive thinking, 222
long-term goals, 353-356
exercise, 354-356
loved ones, channeling,
275-276
Lovelock, James, 362
lucid dreams, 204-205
astral projection, 284
luck (psychological
research), 66

M

S

401

SPECIAL OFFER FOR READERS OF THE COMPLETE IDIOT'S GUIDE TO Being Psychic!

Free: Call for Lynn Robinson's free psychic referral list: (800) 925-4002.

Free: Sign up for a free *e-mail* Intuition Newsletter. Order through Lynn's Web site: **www.lynnrobinson.com.**

AUDIO TAPES BY LYNN ROBINSON, M.Ed.

Prosperity! The Intuitive Path to Creating Abundance (ICC101) $10.00

Side 1 - *Prosperity Meditation*

Prosperity begins in your mind and imagination. Use this powerful guided meditation to attract the prosperity you desire.

Side 2 - *Affirmations for Prosperity*

Enlist the power of your subconscious mind to create prosperity by listening to affirmations of abundance and success.

Your Inner Sanctuary/Inner Guide* (ICC102) $10.00

Side 1 - *Your Inner Sanctuary Meditation*

Create a unique inner sanctuary in your mind where you can access wise intuitive guidance.

Side 2 - *Your Inner Guide Meditation*

Tap into your higher self to gain greater wisdom and spiritual growth. Learn to trust your intuition to enhance your decision-making.

Creating the Life You Want* (ICC103) $10.00

Side 1 - *Creating the Life You Want Meditation*

This tape will assist you in using your mind's ability to create reality from your hopes and dreams.

Side 2 - *Affirmations for Success*

Positive affirmations will fill you with confidence and enable you to create the life you want. Listen while driving to work!

How to Develop Your Intuition (ICC104) $5.00

You'll learn new skills to deepen your intuition in this lively half-hour interview with Lynn.

*These audio tapes contain the remarkable music of Thaddeus, created to assist you in expanding your consciousness and opening up to higher realms. Music by Thaddeus is available from LuminEssence Productions. Please call for details.

BOOKLET

Prosperity! The Intuitive Path to Creating Abundance (ICC105)

$5.00

This 20-page booklet includes simple, effective methods for creating more abundance.

3 WAYS TO ORDER

By phone:

Call Intuitive Consulting & Communication (IC&C) at (800) 925-4002. We accept MasterCard and Visa.

Via Internet:

Order through Lynn's Web site: www.lynnrobinson.com

By Mail:

Please include your name, address, phone number, and the title and order number for the tape or booklet you are ordering. Massachusetts residents add 5% sales tax. Send your check or money order to:

Intuitive Consulting & Communication (IC&C)
P.O. Box 81218
Wellesley Hills, MA 02481

Please add $3.50 to all orders for shipping & handling.

Allow 4 to 6 weeks for delivery. All payment to be made in U.S. funds. Prices and availability are subject to change without notice.